# THE ADOPTION PLAN

THE ADOPTION PLAN

# THE ADOPTION PLAN

## CHINA AND THE REMAKING
## OF GLOBAL HUMANITARIANISM

JACK NEUBAUER

Columbia University Press
*New York*

Columbia University Press
*Publishers Since 1893*
New York   Chichester, West Sussex
cup.columbia.edu
Copyright © 2025 Columbia University Press
All rights reserved

Library of Congress Cataloging-in-Publication Data

Names: Neubauer, Jack, author.
Title: The adoption plan : China and the remaking of global humanitarianism / Jack Neubauer.
Description: New York : Columbia University Press, [2025] | Includes bibliographical references and index.
Identifiers: LCCN 2024033964 (print) | LCCN 2024033965 (ebook) | ISBN 9780231218023 (hardback) | ISBN 9780231218030 (trade paperback) | ISBN 9780231562034 (ebook)
Subjects: LCSH: Humanitarian assistance—China. | Economic assistance—China—History—20th century. | Child welfare—China—International cooperation. | China—Economic conditions—1949-
Classification: LCC HV555.C5 N48 2025  (print) | LCC HV555.C5  (ebook) | DDC 361.2/60951—dc23/eng/20240816
LC record available at https://lccn.loc.gov/2024033964
LC ebook record available at https://lccn.loc.gov/2024033965

Printed and bound by CPI Group (UK) Ltd, Croydon, CR0 4YY

Cover design: Elliott S. Cairns
Cover image: Photograph from May-ling Soong Chiang, *A Letter from Madame Chiang Kai-shek to Boys and Girls Across the Ocean.*

# CONTENTS

*Acknowledgments*   *vii*

INTRODUCTION   1

1. CHINA AND THE BIRTH OF
GLOBAL HUMANITARIANISM   29

2. GLOBAL HUMANITARIANISM'S INTIMATE TURN   63

3. INSTITUTIONALIZING THE INTIMATE TURN   97

4. ADOPTING REVOLUTION   129

5. THE HUMANITARIAN CLOAK   161

6. COLD WAR HUMANITARIANISM   194

CONCLUSION   227

*Glossary of Chinese Names and Terms*   *243*
*Notes*   *249*
*Bibliography*   *295*
*Index*   *311*

# ACKNOWLEDGMENTS

After spending more than a decade working on this book, it is a pleasure to thank the many people who supported me along the way. Eugenia Lean has been a generous teacher, insightful critic, tireless advocate, and supportive friend. Mae Ngai has been a consistent source of guidance and support, even though it became clear early on that my research would veer far from my initial project. Madeleine Zelin asked probing questions that reshaped my thinking at important stages of my research. Nara Milanich introduced me to the history of childhood and youth and has always been extraordinarily generous with her encouragement and insight. Sam Moyn's insightful comments helped shape how I approached the writing and revising process. Adam McKeown introduced me to global history and shaped my thinking more than he ever knew.

I am deeply appreciative of the communities of scholars and teachers who helped me develop this project. In New York, I am grateful to Lydia Liu, Matt Connelly, Lisa Tiersten, Yuan-yuan Meng, and Rebecca Karl. I had the opportunity to share research-in-progress and receive feedback from colleagues at conferences and workshops and in other settings across the world. I am especially grateful to Susan Koshy, Na-Sil Heo, Leslie Wang, Janet Chen, Madeline Hsu, Violeta Ruiz Cuenca, Ute Frevert, Judd Kinzley, Zach Fredman, Lynn Hollen Lees, Young Sun Park, Kristen Roebuck, David Pomfret, Yuri Doolan, Isabella Jackson, Aaron Moore, Xu Xin, David Cheng Chang, Shi-chi Mike Lan, Ling-Wei Kung, Eno Chen,

VIII ACKNOWLEDGMENTS

Wendy Fu, Hsiao-ching Liao, Po-hsi Chen, and Johanna Ransmeier. Their comments and questions were significant in the shaping of this book.

Several colleagues and friends shared sources with me from their own research and personal collections. In the small world of the history of childhood in China, Margaret Tillman has been a generous mentor and friend, and she kindly pointed me to sources on China Child Welfare, Inc. Chunmei Du generously offered newspaper articles about "jeep babies" in post–World War II Chongqing. Wendy Lewis and Terry Halot, nieces of Gerald Tannebaum, kindly shared memories and stories about their uncle. They also provided me with copies of Tannebaum's correspondence while living in China, a treasure trove of materials that I plan to use in future research. I owe special thanks to Becky Powers for allowing me to consult her personal collection of materials pertaining to Laura Richards and the Canaan Children's Home.

I received generous funding for research, writing, and language study from two Social Science Research Council fellowships, the IIE Fulbright Fellowship, the Weatherhead East Asian Institute Daniel and Marianne Spiegel Fund Grant, the Foreign Languages and Area Studies Fellowship, the Columbia University History Department, and the Columbia University Graduate School of Arts and Sciences. This support in turn afforded me the opportunity to spend several transformative years researching, studying, and living in China and Taiwan. At the International Chinese Language Program in Taipei, Yang Ningyuan and Chen Yurong taught me to analyze Chinese texts across a wide range of genres and time periods and shared their deep knowledge of Chinese history and literature. At Fudan University in Shanghai, Zhang Zhongmin and Xu Mingjie provided an institutional home and facilitated my access to archival materials. The archival and library staff at institutions too numerous to list here provided expert help accessing sources; they are the unsung heroes of both this book and virtually all historical scholarship.

As an undergraduate at Northwestern University, I had the good fortune to receive my foundational education in Chinese history from two excellent teachers and scholars, Melissa Macauley and Peter J. Carroll. Michael Sherry taught me the mechanics of historical research, and Michael Allen patiently counseled me on applying to graduate school. At George C. Marshall High School, Tom Brannan, history teacher extraordinaire, cultivated in his students an interest in history as a professional discipline.

I am so thankful for the group of brilliant, generous, fun, and kind friends I met in graduate school: KumHee Cho, Owen Miller, Chris Chang, John Chen, Chien-Wen Kung, Dongxin Zou, Rachel Newman, John Alekna, Yiren Zheng, Susan Su, Ye Yuan, Yanjie Huang, Nataly Shahaf, Elizabeth Reynolds, John Thompson, Tristan Revells, Brianna Nofil, Nancy Ng Tam, Chengji Xing, Ivón Padilla-Rodríguez, Chloe Estep, Chris Peacock, Allison Bernard, and Zach Berge-Becker. I could not imagine my time in New York and Taiwan without the friendship of James Gerien-Chen. I still take visiting friends and colleagues to restaurants in Taipei that James first introduced me to a decade ago. My SSRC friends—Sarah Mellors Rodriguez, Sandy Chang, and Jeff Guarneri—have been a wonderful source of camaraderie and support throughout the ups and downs of academia and life. Gal Gvili, Uluğ Kuzuoğlu, and Peter Hamilton have been founts of wisdom, guidance, and good cheer at every stage of my academic career.

I am very thankful for the generous welcome I received from students and colleagues during brief but highly enjoyable stints teaching at Marymount Manhattan College and Miami University. At Marymount, I owe special thanks to Carrie-Ann Biondi and Lauren Brown for their mentorship. At Miami, I am especially grateful to Wietse de Boer for helping me develop into a better teacher. Although the outbreak of COVID-19 cut short my time as a teaching fellow at Schwarzman College, Tsinghua University, in Beijing, my experience there was greatly enriched by the friendship of Ariel Shangguan and Arn Howitt. During the challenging early days of the pandemic, the entire leadership team of the Schwarzman Scholars Program—especially Joan Kaufman—provided a model of how to be a responsible, generous, and empathetic employer.

The Department of History at National Chengchi University provided me with what is now a rare luxury in academia: a stable job. It took no small amount of luck to land this job, and I certainly would not have finished this book without it. Hsiu-fen Chen and Shih-Chi Chin supported me from the moment I arrived on campus. I could not ask for better colleagues and friends than Yi-lin Chiang, Ryan Holroyd, Hsin-fang Wu, Lev Nachman, and Jen-tzu Huang.

I am grateful to Caelyn Cobb and Emily Simon at Columbia University Press for believing in this project and for expertly guiding it through the publication process. Anonymous reviewers of the manuscript offered insightful criticisms and constructive suggestions.

An earlier version of chapter 4 was previously published as "Adopting Revolution: The Chinese Communist Revolution and the Politics of Global Humanitarianism" in *Modern China* 47, no. 5 (2021): 598–627.

This book is dedicated to my family. My sister, Rachel, and my brother-in-law, Ben, are the toughest, most inspiring, and most fun people I know. Thank you for bringing Noah into this world; he makes it brighter for all of us. Words could never express my love and gratitude to my parents, Ron and Ellen. They have been helping me with my homework since elementary school, and this book is no exception. They carefully edited the entire manuscript. Readers should also be grateful to them for making it a far better piece of writing than it otherwise would have been. Finally, to Sau-yi Fong: during the time I spent working on this project, we met, fell in love, got married, and built a life together. In part so that I could finish writing this book, we had to spend the past couple of years living on opposite sides of the world, one of us calling to say goodnight as the other was waking up. It's finally done. Here's to spending the rest of our years together.

# THE ADOPTION PLAN

THE ADOPTION PLAN

# INTRODUCTION

Feng-ming's path to the Yu Tsai School was as tortuous as it was tragic. She was born in Jiangsu Province, China, in October 1934. Both of her parents died during the War of Resistance Against Japan when she was only a small child, and several years later her older brother died of tuberculosis. Orphaned and alone, she was adopted by a cousin's friend, who forced her to perform hard labor and beat her daily. Feng-ming managed to escape to her cousin's home, where she hoped to earn her keep by helping with chores while studying at the local night school. But her cousin objected to her attending the school and even threw away her books. Finally, Feng-ming was "saved" when the school's headmaster arranged for her to study dance at the Yu Tsai School, a prestigious arts school in the northern suburbs of Shanghai. It was the fall of 1948. She was thirteen years old.[1]

Feng-ming's expenses at the Yu Tsai School were paid by the China Branch of an international child welfare organization called Foster Parents Plan for War Children (PLAN China Branch). Opened in 1947, the PLAN China Branch supported children through a humanitarian fundraising strategy known as the "adoption plan" for international child sponsorship. Under the adoption plan, foreign "foster parents" could "adopt" individual Chinese children by paying for them to live in child welfare institutions in China while exchanging photographs, gifts, and translated letters that used familial terms of address. The PLAN China Branch assigned an American woman named Joy as Feng-ming's foster mother, and for the next eight months Joy and Feng-ming corresponded regularly. Joy sent Feng-ming numerous gifts, including pictures, books, and a dress and skirt that turned out to be just her size. Then, on April 19, 1949, the PLAN China Branch sent Joy a letter informing her that Feng-ming had left the program: "We know that for Feng-ming's sake you will be pleased to learn that she has now left Plan care since she has found work which she believes will help her greatly; even more than her school work, and so she is very thankful to you for all that you have done in her behalf and now she will make it possible for another child to be taken into Plan in her place."[2]

Perhaps Joy was pleased, as the letter suggested she should be, to read that Feng-ming had found meaningful work. Or perhaps she was angry that Feng-ming had been permitted to drop out of school at the young age of fourteen. Almost certainly, Joy never expected that she would hear from Feng-ming again.

So it must have come as quite a surprise when in November 1949, six months since she had last heard word of Feng-ming, Joy received a long letter from Feng-ming herself. Full of shocking revelations, dramatic tales, and one piece of tragic, life-altering news, the letter explained where Feng-ming had actually been those past six months, why she could not write sooner, and why she desperately desired to get back in touch now.

> *Dear Joy:*
>
> *I have not been able to write to you for almost six months. I miss you a lot. I left here this February . . . for the [Communist] guerilla territory of the Chekiang Province. I went with many other schoolmates of mine. When we reached there, we organized a cultural workers' corps. . . . I was then responsible for the instruction of dancing and other performances. . . . When we left the school, Shanghai was still under the [Nationalist Party's] reactionary rule, and the people of Shanghai were all leading a most stifling life. . . . Countless numbers of youths were then massacred by the reactionaries, especially on the eve of the liberation of Shanghai. That was why we had to sneak away in secret. I hope this can serve to explain why I failed to inform you.[3]*

The Yu Tsai School had long maintained ties with the underground Communist Party in Shanghai, and in spring 1949 it sent several of its older students, including Feng-ming, to Communist-held territory in Zhejiang (Chekiang) to form a "cultural workers' corps" to travel with its guerilla fighters. Feng-ming's letter went on to describe the arduous but meaning-ful life she found among the Communist soldiers: "When I was engaged in guerilla warfare in the hills, I had to walk seventy to eighty 'li' of hill path all on foot, each day. Yet I never felt tired." It was only at this point of her letter that Feng-ming divulged the tragic reason why she was once again writing to Joy. Feng-ming had been diagnosed with severe heart disease and sent back to the Yu Tsai School for rest. She wanted to know if Joy would agree to sponsor her once again: "I wish that you could allow me to continue to be a friend of yours, and let me keep on writing to you. I won-der if you would consent. This is the only thing that I want of you."

Feng-ming's letter was one of thousands that Chinese children wrote to their American foster parents during the tumultuous period surrounding the Chinese Communist revolution of 1949. In that year, Mao Zedong's Communist Party defeated Chiang Kai-shek's Nationalist Party in what had been a protracted civil war. The United States had supported the Nationalists, and many regarded the Communists' victory as a dramatic defeat for the United States in the emerging Cold War.[4] Against this global political backdrop, Feng-ming and many other Chinese children wrote to their American foster parents with deeply personal stories of the Chinese Communist revolution—stories that were strikingly different from what their foster parents might have encountered in the American press.

Between the lines of the intimate revelations about her disease, despair, and desires, Feng-ming's letter narrated for Joy the story of the revolution as refracted through the experiences of a girl for whom Joy had already come to care deeply. In Feng-ming's account, the U.S.-supported Nation-alists had oppressed and massacred countless children—the very children Joy and Americans like her had "adopted." On the other hand, the Chi-nese Communist guerillas had provided her with refuge, purpose, and a chance to pursue her passion for dance. We do not know how, or even whether, Joy responded to Feng-ming's letter. But especially considering her emotional and monetary investment in Feng-ming, it is possible that the letter prompted Joy to reconsider what she knew—or thought she knew—about China and its revolution.

This book tells the story of how Chinese children like Feng-ming became a global cause célèbre—and how the recipients of humanitar-ian aid in China battled to control its symbolic and practical uses. When people today think about the humanitarian rescue of Chinese children, they likely think about the more than 150,000 Chinese girls who have been adopted internationally since the 1990s, when draconian enforcement of the one-child policy led many parents to relinquish baby girls to underfunded state-run orphanages, which in turn made them available for adoption by foreign families.[5] Yet humanitarian interest in China's children has a much longer history. Transnational humanitarian projects on behalf of children in China date back to the mid-nineteenth century, when the Qing empire's defeat in the Opium Wars led to China's violent incorporation into the uneven terrain of global capitalism. Protected by unequal treaties and foreign gunboats, Christian missionaries descended on China, where they perceived a litany of problems facing its children—from foot-binding and female infanticide to child trafficking and child hunger—which they saw as crying out for outside intervention.[6] The history of international child-saving projects in China is therefore inseparable from the larger context of Western and Japanese imperialism, which both made humanitarian work in China possible to begin with and also engendered the persistent skepticism with which many Chinese people have viewed the motives of would-be child savers from abroad. In this regard, international interest in China's children was part of a much larger history of philanthropic institutions in imperial metropoles that came to see it as their duty to launch charitable projects for children in their colonies.[7] However, China was never colonized by a single power but rather was exploited by many foreign powers at once. As a result, rather than the delimited ethic of colonial responsibility that informed child-saving projects in other colonial settings, efforts to save the children in China were supported by a geographically dispersed network of donors who conceptualized their concern for China's children in new global humanitarian terms. To uncover the history of long-distance advocacy on behalf of China's children is to help uncover the roots of global humanitarianism itself.

Within the long historical arc of humanitarian concern for China's children, the fifteen years from 1937 to 1951 are of particular importance. In global historical time, these years coincided with World War II and the early Cold War. In China, this was a period of near-constant violence, encompassing the War of Resistance Against Japan (1937–1945), the Chinese Civil War (1945–1949), and the beginning of the Korean War (1950–1953). These conflicts caused death and destruction on an unspeakable scale. During the course of World War II in China, as many as eighty million people became refugees, and it is likely that more than ten million of them were children under the age of fifteen.[8] The plight of Chinese refugee children circulated globally through the rise of wartime photojournalism, such as the "Bloody Saturday" photograph of a Chinese baby wailing alone amid the rubble of Shanghai's South Station, which was reportedly seen by 136 million people within a single month.[9] During these years of war and displacement, Chinese diasporic organizations around the world organized constant fundraisers to direct global attention to the suffering of children in China. And as illustrated by the case of Feng-ming, the Chinese Communist Party continued to welcome foreign aid on behalf of China's children after founding the People's Republic of China (PRC) in 1949. It was not until 1951, with China at war with the U.S.-led United Nations Command in Korea, that the Communists made the decision to cut off all humanitarian aid from abroad. Forced to leave China, international humanitarian organizations shifted their focus to Taiwan, Hong Kong, Japan, and South Korea, where they reconceptualized humanitarian aid as a tool for forging closer ties with U.S. Cold War allies in East Asia.

It was also during World War II and the early Cold War that the adoption plan for international child sponsorship emerged as one of the most effective strategies for attracting private humanitarian aid to China. Taking advantage of improved transportation and communication technologies, the relationships forged between Chinese children and foreign sponsors through the adoption plan constituted a new mode of affective and material exchange across national, racial, and cultural boundaries that I call "global intimacy." Crucially, this intimate turn in global humanitarian practice also transformed its political possibilities. In the past, the recipients of humanitarian aid had few opportunities to communicate with distant benefactors. However, by crafting narratives of children's lives, staging photographs, and coaching children on how to write letters, Chinese relief institutions funded by the adoption plan were newly empowered to shape the symbolic meanings attached to the transnational aid they received. Against the backdrop of World War II and the emerging Cold War, Chinese child welfare institutions associated with both the Chinese Nationalist and Communist parties mobilized the emotional bonds between children and their foster parents to secure international support for their competing political projects. At once emotional and economic, humanitarian and political, the adoption plan transformed the emotional loyalties of children into a key battleground on the affective terrain of these global conflicts.

A relatively new field of historical inquiry that has come to prominence alongside the rise of global history more generally over the past several decades, scholarship on the history of humanitarianism has been centrally concerned with analyzing the connections between humanitarianism and imperialism.[10] Written primarily by historians of Europe and the United States using the Western-language archives of major international humanitarian organizations, these studies necessarily focus on the motivations and actions of the Western organizations that set out to save suffering populations across Asia, Africa, and Latin America. Nevertheless, in their justifiable zeal to critique the complicity of humanitarian organizations in imperialist expansion, this scholarship risks overstating the extent to which Western aid agencies and their donors were able to determine what meanings their aid held for its recipients in faraway locations around the world. *The Adoption Plan* takes a different approach. Based on extensive research in Chinese archives, it offers a bottom-up account of the history of global humanitarianism that places the recipients, administrators, and critics of humanitarian aid in China at the center of the story. Challenging decades of scholarship that has focused on the political motives of Western humanitarian organizations, this book demonstrates that it was often the Chinese recipients of aid, rather than Western donors, who were best able to control its material and ideological uses.

## EVERYONE, EVERYWHERE, ALL AT ONCE: THE RISE OF GLOBAL HUMANITARIANISM

Many humanitarian organizations define humanitarian aid as "aid and action designed to save lives, alleviate suffering, and maintain and protect human dignity during and in the aftermath of emergencies."[11] Moreover, according to the International Committee of the Red Cross, aid must be provided in accordance with the principles of "impartiality, neutrality, and independence" in order to "qualify as fully humanitarian."[12] This definition, however, does not capture how humanitarianism has been practiced historically. As historians have amply demonstrated, humanitarian aid has been deeply intertwined with political, economic, religious, and social agendas from its inception. For this reason, I follow numerous other scholars in using the term "humanitarianism" to refer broadly to aid to distant strangers.[13] By identifying the recipients of humanitarian aid as "distant strangers," this definition also distinguishes humanitarianism from the many ancient traditions of charity found in cultures around the world. Predicated on the ability to know about and intervene in the suffering of people far away, humanitarianism is a distinctly modern ethical paradigm, inconceivable before the world was linked by the new communication and transportation technologies that developed alongside the rise of capitalism and imperialism. Tracing the roots of institutionalized humanitarianism to the British abolitionist movement in the late eighteenth and early nineteenth centuries, many historians have argued that the rise of capitalism was a necessary condition for the development of humanitarian sentiment. In outline, the rise of a new bourgeoisie with control over society's means of production had a class interest in measures that ensured the docility and productivity of the work force. Benevolent measures to abolish slavery and prevent the worst abuses of colonized peoples were therefore also self-interested policies promoted by imperialist powers to prevent any major disruptions to their own power and profits.[14]

While there is a considerable degree of consensus around the idea that institutionalized humanitarian action arose in the late eighteenth and early nineteenth centuries, there is much less agreement about when and why humanitarianism became "global." Many social scientists have treated global humanitarianism as a novel phenomenon of the post–World War II period, when the perceived threat of Communist expansion led the United States and its allies to attribute new significance to the suffering of people in far-flung locations around the globe to which they had previously paid little attention.[15] Historian Kevin O'Sullivan locates the "globalization of compassion" in the late 1960s to mid-1980s, when an explosion of new nongovernmental organizations (NGOs), inspired both by the legacies of empire and by the new possibilities of decolonization, came to see their mission as alleviating suffering anywhere on earth.[16] In contrast, sociologist Peter Stamatov has argued that global humanitarianism was institutionalized by religious actors concerned with the treatment of non-Europeans during the process of colonization between the sixteenth and eighteenth centuries.[17] Stamatov, however, does not specify what distinguishes "global" humanitarianism from other forms of humanitarianism. Who has the responsibility (or even the right) to succor which distant strangers? Whose suffering stands for the suffering of humanity writ large? The answers that humanitarians provided to these questions changed significantly between the rise of Enlightenment humanitarianism in the late eighteenth century and the emergence of Cold War humanitarianism in the late twentieth century. By focusing on transnational fundraising campaigns for children in China, I argue that during the first half of the twentieth century, a European-dominated "imperial" humanitarian order was challenged and displaced by a new, U.S.-led "global" humanitarian order.

As numerous scholars have pointed out, there is a close historical connection "between the extension of western concern for distant strangers and the expansion of western empires."[18] By the late nineteenth century, European empires had increasingly embraced an ideology of imperial benevolence that recognized the obligation of colonial governments to relieve the suffering of their subjects.[19] For example, the British Empire's embrace of humanitarian governance can be observed through the evolution of its approach to famine in India. Recurrent famines belied claims that colonial rule would bring prosperity to India and fueled sharp critiques of Britain's economic exploitation of India by both Indian Nationalists and British socialists.[20] Reversing its longstanding emphasis on "nonintervention," in 1880 the British colonial government introduced famine codes that "officially acknowledged its duty to mitigate famines in India."[21] On the other hand, colonial governments' loud proclamations of their own benevolence provided critics of empire with a powerful rhetoric to denounce imperialist powers when they almost invariably failed to honor their humanitarian ideals.[22]

While deploying the universalist rhetoric of "humanity," humanitarianism in the age of empires was often confined within imperial boundaries. The international activism of the Congo Reform Association, founded in 1904 by British journalist E. D. Morel to expose the horrific treatment of Africans in King Leopold II of Belgium's Congo Free State, is an exception that helps prove the rule. Despite extensive evidence of humanitarian violations, the British government was hesitant to get involved for fear of calling greater attention to its own treatment of colonial populations. Ultimately, the Congo Reform Association's successful international pressure campaign to end Leopold II's rule in the Congo was rooted less in universal principles of human sympathy than in a critique of King Leopold II's failure to fulfill his specific responsibility to his Congolese subjects under the principle of imperial benevolence.[23] Well into the twentieth century, colonial powers sometimes sought to reserve the *exclusive* right to take humanitarian action within their colonies. During the interwar period, international organizations such as the Geneva-based International Labour Organization (ILO) occasionally attempted to hold colonial powers to account for the suffering of their colonial subjects. But European powers resisted these efforts, insisting that "the governing of colonies was strictly a domestic political concern not open to international critique."[24] In arguing that colonies were off-limits to outside intervention, they revealed the limits of their humanitarian vision. Despite their use of universal rhetoric, European empires repeatedly reaffirmed the view that humanitarian responsibility did not extend beyond the borders of empires.

After World War I, British and American humanitarian organizations expanded beyond the imperial realm to embrace a new vision of "international" humanitarianism. In her work on the British Save the Children Fund, Emily Baughan traces the rise of a "new generation of humanitarians" that "styled their work as an internationalist attempt to create mutual peace and prosperity across Europe in the aftermath of war."[25] Around the turn of the twentieth century, American philanthropic organizations also emerged as major players in the world of international humanitarianism.[26] For example, during the Russian famine of 1921–1922, the American Relief Administration provided an astonishing 90 percent of all humanitarian aid from abroad.[27] Another key American humanitarian organization in the aftermath of World War I was Near East Relief. Founded in 1915 in response to reports of atrocities against Armenian Christians in the Ottoman Empire, Near East Relief distributed approximately $116 million in relief aid between 1918 and 1929.[28] Yet the "humanitarian internationalism" of the interwar era was largely limited to Europe and guided by particular conceptions of racial and religious affinity. In fact, much of this aid flowed to particular groups—Austrian, German, Russian, and Armenian—that donors viewed as especially deserving because they were white and/or Christian.[29]

At the same time, however, new humanitarian networks that stretched across imperial, racial, and religious divides were developing in China. During the nineteenth and early twentieth centuries, the Qing government was forced to sign unequal treaties with a large number of countries, including Britain, the United States, France, Sweden-Norway, Russia, Prussia, Portugal, Denmark, the Netherlands, Spain, Belgium, Italy, Austria, Japan, Brazil, and Mexico. These treaties granted foreign powers in China numerous special privileges, including fixed low tariffs, extraterritoriality, as well as international settlements and concessions that they governed and occupied.[30] With so many different imperialist nations present in China, no individual state claimed "colonial responsibility" for the welfare of Chinese people.[31] Yet this did not mean that citizens of foreign countries were indifferent to the problems of poverty, violence, and natural disaster in "semicolonial" China. On the contrary, humanitarian crises in China attracted interest from private organizations and donors throughout the many foreign powers with interests in China—as well as their colonial holdings in Asia, Africa, Latin America, and Oceania. Another key factor in attracting widespread attention to human suffering in China was the global Chinese diaspora. Recent scholarship has highlighted the important role of diasporic Chinese investment in modernization projects and charitable endeavors in China.[32] However, less attention has been paid to the role of diasporic Chinese as humanitarian fundraisers. During moments of crisis in China, diasporic groups around the world organized fundraisers to cultivate international sympathy for victims of war and disaster in China. Precisely because no colonial power claimed responsibility for the well-being of Chinese people, humanitarian causes in China were able to attract attention from private organizations and donors on a global scale.

In many ways, humanitarian aid to relieve suffering in China from the mid-nineteenth to the mid-twentieth centuries resembled the humanitarian fundraising campaigns typically associated with late-twentieth-century globalization. First, aid was provided primarily by transnational humanitarian organizations (what today would be called international NGOs) that attracted a large number of small donations from private citizens in many countries around the world. Moreover, humanitarian organizations and their donors did not claim any particularistic ties to the Chinese recipients of their aid. They did not count Chinese people as their colonial subjects, and they did not see themselves as having racial, religious, or cultural affinities to Chinese people. In other words, they contributed to Chinese causes not out of a sense of "imperial benevolence" but rather according to a global humanitarian logic in which the suffering of people anywhere was the concern of people everywhere. The flip side of this logic was that they did not see the provision of aid to China as their responsibility, but rather as something above and beyond the normal call of duty. While transnational humanitarian organizations provided significant quantities of life-saving aid to Chinese children suffering from war and famine, it was often only a drop in the bucket of overall need. Yet these organizations believed they should be congratulated for the thousands of children they helped, not criticized because there were millions more equally needy children whom their aid would never reach. In all these regards, humanitarian organizations working in China from the mid-nineteenth to the mid-twentieth century forged an inchoate model of global humanitarian aid—a model they took with them as they expanded their work across East Asia and much of the world during the latter half of the twentieth century.

## AMERICA'S FAVORITE CHARITY: CHINA AND THE U.S.-LED GLOBAL HUMANITARIAN ORDER

It was also in China during the first half of the twentieth century that the United States began to displace the European powers as the dominant player within the field of transnational philanthropy. Since the early nineteenth century, American Christians had supported the charitable work of missionaries around the world out of a belief that all humans were created by a single God and therefore shared a certain "oneness." This idea, which Hillary Kaell has called "Christian globalism," played an important role in motivating Americans' increasingly active role in humanitarian work during the early twentieth century.[33] According to Akira Iriye, the explosion of U.S.-based international humanitarian organizations in the twentieth century was also an extension of Americans' longstanding proclivity for forming civic associations.[34] China emerged as a focus of American humanitarianism in the early twentieth century in the context of U.S. fears that Europe and Japan would carve up China into spheres of influence, locking American businesses out of the China market.[35] Lacking its own territorial concessions in China, the United States promoted an "Open Door Policy" that called for maintaining China's territorial integrity and ensuring that all foreign nations had equal rights to trade in China. The Open Door Policy was self-interested and of limited benefit to China. Nevertheless, it helped convince many Americans and some Chinese that, in contrast to the "blatant territorial aggression" of Europe and Japan, the United States and China shared a "special relationship" defined by "American benevolence, Chinese gratitude, and mutual good will."[36] As part of this concerted push to cultivate an altruistic image in China, Chinese humanitarian causes quickly moved to the center of the American moral universe. In the words of famous journalist and political scientist Harold Isaacs: "An extraordinarily large number of Americans came to think of themselves as the benevolent guardians and benefactors of China and the Chinese. . . . It was an experience shared by all the millions who put pennies, dimes, and quarters on collection plates for generations [and] who contributed to relief funds for the Chinese."[37] Or, as the eminent American China scholar John Fairbank once put it, "China became our favorite charity."[38]

The outsized U.S. role in humanitarian work in China was spearheaded by the rapidly expanding number of American Protestant missionaries in China. By the 1920s, China was the most popular destination for American missionaries, and Americans constituted the largest group of foreign missionaries in China. American missionaries in China engaged in a wide range of philanthropic and social welfare work, particularly in the fields of education and health care.[39] Americans also played a leading role in international famine relief work in China.[40] The Peking United International Famine Relief Committee, which was formed to provide aid during the Chinese famine of 1920–1921, received approximately 40 percent of its funding from the American Advisory Committee and Protestant Episcopal Church of America, and nearly 60 percent of its foreign relief workers were American.[41] China also came to occupy a central place within the overseas philanthropy of major American philanthropic institutions, such as the Rockefeller Foundation and the American Red Cross. As of 1950, the Rockefeller Foundation had contributed $54 million to institutions and individuals in China—more than five times its expenditures in any other country.[42] By the end of the 1920s, the American Red Cross had spent approximately $2.5 million in China. As Karen Brewer put it, "In no other foreign country did the American Red Cross spend so much in so many operations."[43] While early humanitarian campaigns in China were global in scope, Americans carved out leading roles in both fundraising and the administration of aid on the ground in China—foreshadowing the rising significance of American humanitarian aid in East Asia and across the world in the post–World War II period.

By emphasizing the linkages between semicolonial China and the U.S.-led postwar world order, *The Adoption Plan* also intervenes in longstanding debates over the particularity of China's experience with imperialism. Informed by postcolonial theory, in recent decades scholars have sought to integrate China into the global history of empires. Highlighting the similarities between China and other colonial settings, scholars such as James Hevia have rejected terms like "semicolonialism" for implying that China was outside the history of "real" colonialism most often typified by British India.[44] Other scholars have deployed terms such as semicolonialism not to diminish the impact of imperialism in China but rather to highlight its distinctive nature. For example, Shu-mei Shih deploys the term to refer to "the specific effects of multiple imperialist presences in China and their fragmentary colonial geography."[45] Building off this scholarship, I argue that the overlapping presence of many imperialist powers in China created a unique situation in which no foreign power acknowledged a colonial responsibility to provide relief aid to China, and yet humanitarian crises in China attracted widespread support from a globally dispersed assemblage of private organizations and individual donors. However, I also move beyond the comparative framework of research that seeks to distinguish China from other colonial settings by showing how the humanitarian practices that took shape in semicolonial China traveled beyond the country's borders to become important features of a new global humanitarian order during the post–World War II period. More broadly, I argue for understanding China not as a unique case in the history of imperialism, but rather as a laboratory for developing new modes of informal empire that proved essential to the U.S.-led postwar order in East Asia and beyond.

14 INTRODUCTION

## GLOBAL HUMANITARIANISM FROM BELOW

During the post–World War II period, as decolonization disrupted older patterns of colonial benevolence, and as human suffering acquired new political significance in the context of the Cold War, the models of global humanitarian fundraising developed in semicolonial China were applied to an increasing number of humanitarian crises around the world. But were the politics behind this new global humanitarianism all that different from the politics of imperial humanitarianism? Based on most research on the postwar globalization of humanitarian aid, the answer would seem to be no. Referring to the period from 1945 to 1989 as the "age of neo-humanitarianism," Michael Barnett argues that the United States and Britain were increasingly willing "to underwrite a humanitarianism that they viewed as vehicles of influence."[46] In line with this broader narrative, historians have argued that the rise of international adoption and child sponsorship in Cold War East Asia served U.S. foreign policy goals. For instance, recent research has shown that the earliest large-scale programs for legal international adoption, which targeted the mixed-race children of local women and U.S. soldiers in Japan and South Korea in the 1950s, helped bolster U.S. alliances in East Asia by presenting the expansive U.S. presence in the region as benevolent in nature.[47] Likewise, scholars such as Christina Klein and Sara Fieldston have argued that Cold War–era child sponsorship programs were premised on the idea that "intimate relationships between Americans and children overseas would curtail the spread of communism, binding together the citizens of the free world with ties that supported the United States' political alliances."[48] In other words, just as colonial empires used humanitarianism as a justification for imperialism, in the post–World War II period humanitarian aid became a means to promote the moral authority of the U.S.-led liberal world order.

Historians have paid less attention, however, to how the people who received aid in the non-Western world reshaped humanitarian programs to suit their own social and political priorities.[49] In a recent conversation about the history of humanitarianism published in *Past & Present*, leading scholars in the field agreed that its most pressing problem was a lack of research that used non-Western languages and archives to "account for the agency of the populations who are recipients of this aid."[50] On one hand, scholars have justifiably criticized humanitarians past and present for failing "to ensure the 'victims' of the world can speak on their own behalf and define their own vision of progress."[51] On the other hand, an almost exclusive focus on the providers rather than the recipients of aid has ultimately reinforced the impression that only the perspectives of the would-be rescuers matter.

In contrast, this book asks how the global history of humanitarianism might appear differently by focusing on those who received help in addition to those who provided it. By the "recipients" of humanitarian aid, I refer broadly to the people and institutions that were its intended beneficiaries. In the case of the adoption plan, these include the China branch offices of transnational humanitarian organizations, the child welfare institutions they funded, individual "foster children," and the Chinese government agencies that had their social welfare burdens lightened by aid from abroad. Based on years of research in municipal and provincial archives across China, as well as in the records of transnational humanitarian organizations based outside of China, my analysis toggles across five distinct but overlapping levels:

1. The overseas headquarters of the transnational organizations that sent aid to China
2. The China branch offices of these organizations in cities like Shanghai, Guangzhou, and Chongqing
3. Chinese child welfare institutions that received aid from abroad
4. Individual "foster parents" and the children they sponsored
5. Local and national government agencies in China that regulated humanitarian aid

This multisite archival research reveals the disagreements, disjunctures, and communication delays that characterized global humanitarian work. It is worth noting that I found little evidence of fraud. Rather, people across all levels of the global humanitarian project generally appear to have been committed to the shared goal of providing food, shelter, and education for children in need. Nevertheless, if humanitarian programs like the adoption plan were first and foremost about caring for children, they were always also about something else—and the political significance attributed to the adoption plan varied widely among actors at different levels of humanitarian institutions. Often the Chinese recipients of aid were able to use the adoption plan to secure funding and build international support for their own interests. Challenging interpretations of humanitarianism as a vector of Western influence, I instead conceptualize humanitarianism as a global field in which a variety of actors collaborated and competed, albeit on unequal terms, for control over a vast pool of material and symbolic resources.

## FROM DISTANT STRANGERS TO FICTIVE KIN: GLOBAL HUMANITARIANISM'S INTIMATE TURN

The global rhetoric that humanitarian organizations used to fundraise on behalf of suffering children in China proved to be a double-edged sword. On the one hand, their message of human sympathy and global community helped convince private citizens around the world to donate to Chinese children with whom they shared no cultural, racial, or religious ties—and to whom they acknowledged no particular obligation of colonial benevolence. On the other hand, none of the reasons they offered to care about children in China were actually specific to children in China. They applied equally, for example, to children suffering during the Armenian Genocide of 1915–1917 or in the aftermath of the Great Kantō Earthquake of 1923 in Japan—both events that inspired large international relief efforts.[52] The rise of global humanitarianism greatly exacerbated the problem of the limited resources of potential donors. The amount of suffering in the world was too great, and it was impossible to aid everyone, everywhere, all at once. By the 1930s, as a proliferation of urgent crises around the world drew attention away from the long-suffering children of China, international fundraising for child welfare work in China began to dry up. Before full-scale war between China and Japan broke out in 1937, humanitarian interest in China's children may have been at its lowest point in decades. Faced with an acute child refugee crisis on a scale unprecedented in Chinese history, overwhelmed Chinese relief institutions needed new ways to make their cause stand out. It was at this moment that Chinese child welfare organizations began experimenting with the adoption plan as an attempt to rekindle international interest in China's children by forging specific ties of obligation between donors and children across the divides of nation, race, and culture. People around the world had long seen China's children as quintessential distant strangers. Through the adoption plan, Chinese relief institutions invited foreign donors to see them instead as fictive kin.

Chinese relief institutions did not invent international child sponsorship out of thin air amid the death and destruction of the Sino-Japanese War. Among the most successful humanitarian fundraising techniques in modern history, child sponsorship has roots in both Chinese and Western philanthropy. Within China, philanthropic fundraising practices resembling child sponsorship date to the 1870s, when infant protection societies throughout the Jiangnan region implemented a new fundraising strategy known as the "adoption system" (*renyu zhi*) in which local donors made monthly contributions to sustain the care of one or more babies.[53] In the Western context, American Protestant missionaries used sponsorship to support foreign children studying in residential missionary schools beginning in the early nineteenth century. However, early sponsorship programs did not emphasize personal relationships between individual donors and children. Most often, groups of donors "pooled their pennies" to support a child with whom they did not correspond directly.[54] After World War I, humanitarian organizations like Save the Children and Near East Relief also fundraised via child sponsorship. Despite their internationalist rhetoric, however, these interwar sponsorship programs primarily targeted white, male, Christian children of middle-class origin, who sponsors believed were better "investments" because they were more likely to grow up to become productive citizens.[55]

Moreover, during the interwar period sponsorship programs still found it difficult to facilitate the exchange of letters and photographs.[56] The struggles of China Child Welfare, Inc., the first transnational aid organization to attempt to use child sponsorship to fundraise for child welfare work in China, provide an illustrative example. Founded in New York in 1928, China Child Welfare raised money for a Chinese organization called the National Child Welfare Association (NCWA).[57] In its publicity materials, China Child Welfare advertised that "thirty dollars will provide adequate care for one child for a year."[58] Individual donors sometimes wrote to China Child Welfare hoping to establish personal contact with a Chinese child.[59] While China Child Welfare forwarded such requests to the NCWA in China, the NCWA does not appear to have responded to any of them.

When Peggy Dougherty of China Child Welfare traveled to China to meet with NCWA leaders, she explained the concept of child sponsorship and tried to secure their cooperation in providing photos of children. Nevertheless, Dougherty quickly realized the immense difficulties involved. She explained, "It is not possible to get pictures in these localities. The children run away from the camera and the adults drive the photographer off. For these reasons I had no success in getting pictures though I tried it many times."[60] Prior to World War II, child sponsorship programs generally could not offer a personal relationship with an individual child.

Early in World War II, Chinese relief organizations reinvented child sponsorship as a tool for forging intimate, fictive kinship ties between the givers and receivers of aid across racial and cultural boundaries. Founded in 1938, the National Association for Refugee Children (NARC), the largest child welfare organization in wartime China, made the adoption plan for international child sponsorship the centerpiece of its global fundraising efforts. A semiofficial institution led by the first lady of Nationalist China, Madame Chiang Kai-shek, the NARC attracted sponsors from across Oceania, North America, Europe, and Southeast Asia by promising a personal relationship with an "adopted" Chinese child through the exchange of photographs, gifts, and translated letters. Over the ensuing years of World War II and the Chinese Civil War, new transnational humanitarian organizations—such as China's Children Fund, PLAN, and the American-Oriental Friendship Association—made the adoption plan into one of the most effective fundraising strategies for child welfare work in China. During the 1950s the adoption plan exploded in popularity as a humanitarian fundraising tool to support children across East Asia, particularly in Japan and South Korea. At the same time, legal international adoption of children in Japan and South Korea, especially the "Amerasian" children of U.S. soldiers and Asian women, emerged as a popular form of humanitarian rescue and transnational family formation.[61]

The rise of international adoption and child sponsorship played a key role in transforming the emotional logic of humanitarianism for the post–World War II international order. The globalization of humanitarian causes during and after the war had rendered human sympathy insufficient as an impetus to humanitarian action. When countless tales of human suffering arrived simultaneously from different corners of the world, sympathy with the suffering of one's fellow humanity provided little guidance on where to direct limited resources. In part for this reason, U.S. private humanitarian giving decreased sharply in the immediate postwar period, an early example of the now-familiar phenomenon of "compassion fatigue." At this moment when overall humanitarian giving was in precipitous decline, the adoption plan flourished by appealing to intimacy in addition to sympathy as a driver of humanitarian engagement. From 1945 to 1949 the total revenue of American private voluntary organizations fell by approximately 70 percent.[62] Yet, during this same time period, the largest U.S.-based international child sponsorship organization, China's Children Fund, saw its total revenue more than double.[63] What explains the extraordinary fundraising success of the adoption plan? The adoption plan differed from other humanitarian fundraising strategies (including earlier versions of child sponsorship) by using improved transportation and communications technologies to foster personal relationships among the givers and receivers of humanitarian aid. The fictive kinship ties created by the exchange of photographs, gifts, and letters created a sense of personalized obligation—a reason to donate to one specific child despite the near-infinite number of worthy causes competing for donors' attention. The foster parent who wrote a check every month to support a Chinese war orphan did so not simply because the child was human, but because the child was *hers*.

This "intimate turn" in global humanitarian practice constitutes a crucial but overlooked transformation in the development of what Didier Fassin calls "humanitarian reason." According to Fassin, humanitarian reason posits "that all lives are equally sacred and that all sufferings deserved to be relieved."[64] Nevertheless, Fassin argues that, in practice, humanitarian projects prioritize certain lives over others according to implicit "hierarchies of humanity." For example, international organizations often prioritize assistance to children, seen as innocent and vulnerable, rather than adults, who are often blamed for their own suffering. Yet Fassin's concept of humanitarian reason does not explain how donors allocate limited resources among suffering populations on the same rung of the hierarchy of humanity. For example, why would an American donor choose to aid refugee children in China, as opposed to equally needy children in Spain or Ethiopia? For organizations like the NARC, the adoption plan was a way to cultivate feelings of personal obligation to a specific Chinese child across cultural, racial, religious, and linguistic divides. The adoption plan operated according to "humanitarian reason" in the sense that any suffering child—regardless of race or nationality—was a potential object of rescue. But its emotional power derived from the idea that it was the formation of a personal connection that provided the moral impetus to help. The personalization and globalization of humanitarianism were two sides of the same coin.

## INTIMATE RELATIONS AND INTERNATIONAL RELATIONS

The intimate turn in global humanitarianism created new possibilities for the recipients of aid to shape its symbolic meanings. In the context of World War II and the Cold War, different organizations sought to mobilize the economic and emotional bonds forged through the adoption plan in the service of diverse, often competing political and religious projects. During the early years of China's war with Japan, the Nationalist-affiliated NARC hoped that the adoption plan would help call international attention to China's heroic resistance against a barbaric Japanese invasion, and it encouraged children to write their sponsors with heartbreaking stories of how their families and homes had been destroyed by the Japanese. The transnational humanitarian organizations using the adoption plan to fundraise for child welfare work in China relied on their China branch offices, which employed almost exclusively Chinese staff, to determine which specific child welfare institutions to fund, guide children in writing their letters, and translate the correspondence going both ways. In this context, organizations such as the PLAN China Branch could systematically transfer PLAN funds to Communist-affiliated institutions such as the Yu Tsai School while encouraging children like Feng-ming to write letters describing in intimate detail how they had been persecuted by the Nationalists and rescued by the Communists. The adoption plan became a powerful tool deployed by local actors to secure funding and build international support for their own political and social projects.

The adoption plan's political potency depended on the maintenance of affectionate relationships between children and foster parents. Using the exchange of photographs and letters to mobilize what Sabine Frühstück has called the "emotional capital" of children, Chinese relief institutions hoped that the adoption plan would produce strong emotional bonds between children and sponsors, which in turn would lead to more concrete forms of economic support (in the form of continued donations) and political support (in the form of public advocacy).[65] For contemporary readers, it may strain credulity to imagine that many children felt a sense of intimacy with foreign strangers whom they almost never met in person. And, of course, the actual extent of intimacy developed through the adoption plan varied enormously. Nevertheless, a significant number of children wrote letters that went far beyond the generic requirements imposed on them in expressing their depth of feeling toward their foster parents. One letter from a boy named Cheng-ho to his foster father Gerald provides a window into the significance he attached to the adoption plan: "I miss you all very much. Every day when I have nothing to do I take out your picture and look at it, and I always wish that I could talk to you in person. Or I take out the letters you've sent and read through them again. . . . I hope that you will write me often. Will you do that?"[66]

The adoption plan could also leave children feeling jealous, lonely, and confused. A letter from a boy named Jin-chun to his foster father Marvin divulged the deep anxieties he felt regarding their relationship:

> Why haven't you written to me in so long? I really miss you very much, and I often feel frustrated because I don't get letters from you. Even if you sent a letter writing just one sentence or even one word it would make me so happy that I would jump for joy. Because it was written with your own hand. I would feel your love and care for me from the letter. I still remember how happy I was when I received the letter that you wrote me before and all the things you sent. . . . Sometimes I also feel afraid to write you letters, because I don't know what it is that I'm supposed to write to you. What do you want to know? What would make you happy to know?[67]

By investigating how these intimate expressions of love, longing, anxiety, and frustration intersected with the explicitly political goals of the adoption plan, this book explores how global politics shape intimate relationships, and how intimate relationships in turn reshape global politics.

Sociologist Viviana Zelizer has argued that intimate relationships are almost always inseparable from issues of power and money.[68] The global inequalities that underpinned the transfer of large quantities of monetary aid from foreign donors to Chinese children likewise structured the relationships they formed through sponsorship. While the adoption plan could be used as a form of soft power to influence international donors' views of China, Chinese children and the institutions that housed them ultimately remained economically dependent on the emotional satisfaction of their foreign sponsors. Participation in the adoption plan also made Chinese child welfare institutions complicit in constructing the Global North's relationship to China as paternal, benevolent, and humanitarian. These unequal power relations, rooted in racialized hierarchies and deep-seated Orientalist prejudices, proved a consistent challenge for those who sought to use the adoption plan in service of the anti-imperialist agendas of the War of Resistance Against Japan and the Chinese Communist revolution. Intimate ties between Chinese children and foreign adults could also be dangerous. During the Korean War, Chinese Communist authorities began to fear that children who participated in the adoption plan would grow up loyal to China's new mortal enemy—the United States. After the Chinese Communist government turned against global humanitarianism, having previously lived in a foreign-funded orphanage became a black mark that haunted the former recipients of humanitarian aid for decades, especially during the Cultural Revolution.

Due to the high stakes involved, children in the adoption plan were rarely free to write whatever they wanted to the sponsors on whose donations their livelihood depended. Rather, both the organizations that coordinated the adoption plan and the child welfare institutions they funded devoted considerable resources to ensuring that children wrote letters that furthered their philanthropic and political goals. By turning to the ways adults shaped, translated, and censored children's letters, we can unravel the specific roles played by children in the larger project of cultivating global intimacy to influence global politics.

## CAN THE CHINESE CHILD SPEAK?

In 2008 Peter Stearns wrote in the inaugural issue of the *Journal of the History of Childhood and Youth* that the "granddaddy issue" facing historians of childhood involves "the virtually unprecedented problems of getting information from children themselves as opposed to adult perceptions and recommendations."[69] This issue has been especially acute in the field of modern Chinese history. In recent years, a small body of scholarship has emerged to address the central place of children in the discourses and practices of Chinese modernity by examining topics such as child welfare institutions, childhood education, children's literature, child labor, and youth groups.[70] In writing this book, I have been particularly indebted to the pioneering research of scholars in China and Taiwan, including Zhang Chun's work on the National Association for Refugee Children, Xu Fenghua's research on the China Welfare Fund, and Huang Wende's scholarship on international famine relief committees.[71] Citing a lack of sources, however, research on the history of childhood in China has only rarely incorporated the voices and perspectives of children themselves.[72] Instead, historians have focused primarily on adult prescriptions for children—what Margaret Tillman terms "the discursive construction of modern childhood and the institutional mechanisms used to construct it."[73] While we have learned much about conceptions of *childhood* in modern China, we know less about actual *children*. Children are central characters in the story of modern Chinese history, but historians have yet to give them a speaking role.

*The Adoption Plan* uses a variety of previously overlooked source materials to incorporate the voices of Chinese refugee children into the story of the transnational humanitarian projects carried out on their behalf. At the heart of my analysis is a collection of 546 letters exchanged between Chinese children and their foreign foster parents. While the letters were not systematically copied or archived, many have nevertheless been preserved in ways both deliberate and accidental. I found caches of sponsorship letters in places ranging from Chinese state archives to a storage closet in the basement of a U.S.-based child sponsorship agency. Generally speaking, sponsorship letters were archived for one of several reasons. Some letters were donated to child welfare organizations by the descendants of foster parents after they passed away. Others appear to have been returned to aid organizations because they were unable to be delivered. In certain instances, letters were copied for administrative reasons or so that they might be reproduced in publicity materials. While 546 letters constitute only a small fraction of the many thousands sent and received through the adoption plan, it is nevertheless a sizable source base for analysis.

Like all historical records, sources purporting to represent children's words, thoughts, and emotions raise a fundamental methodological question: How do we interpret them? Of course, it would be naïve to assume that children's letters provide unmediated access to their experiences of the world-historical events unfolding around them.[74] Sarah Maza recently called on historians to abandon the elusive search for children's voices and instead pivot toward writing "history *through* children"—that is, using children as a novel vantage point onto larger issues so as to unsettle dominant historical narratives.[75] In precisely this vein, *The Adoption Plan* centers the child recipients of aid to challenge conventional wisdom on the politics of humanitarianism, Chinese soft power, and Cold War politics. At the same time, I do not abdicate the task of determining, as precisely as possible, what role real, flesh-and-blood children played in the humanitarian and political projects carried out in their names. The letters Chinese children wrote through the adoption plan provide a rare opportunity to treat the ways adults shaped and censored children's writing as an object of analysis rather than an obstacle to analysis. The Chinese-language archives of the organizations that were funded by the adoption plan contain voluminous discussion of how to guide children in their letter writing and many specific examples of adult intervention. Nevertheless, reading actual children's letters against agency regulations, it is apparent how difficult it was to enforce rigid rules on children writing from institutions dispersed across China under unstable conditions of war and revolution. Every one of the letters I have read is unique, and many diverged sharply from prescribed topics and forms. In the gaps between what transnational aid agencies wanted children to write and what they actually wrote, it is clear that these organizations required the active participation of children in order to achieve their charitable and ideological aims.

When aid agencies feared that the content or tone of a child's letter threatened their philanthropic or political goals, they used the necessity of translation as an opportunity to edit or even censor children's letters. When foster parents received their adoptees' letters, they typically received both the handwritten Chinese original as well as a typewritten translation. In the vast majority of cases, I have been able to locate both the Chinese originals and English-language translations of children's letters, usually still stapled together in the archives. Since the majority of sponsors could not read Chinese, if children's letters included content that their sponsoring organizations found problematic, the translators often removed the offending portion from the English translation. In some cases, translation was used to smooth over discrepancies in how Chinese children and their foster parents expressed familial intimacy. In other instances, letters were censored for overtly political reasons. By systematically comparing the translations of children's letters with the Chinese originals, I reverse engineer the logics of cultural communication and political censorship through which aid organizations mediated the interactions between children and their foster parents.

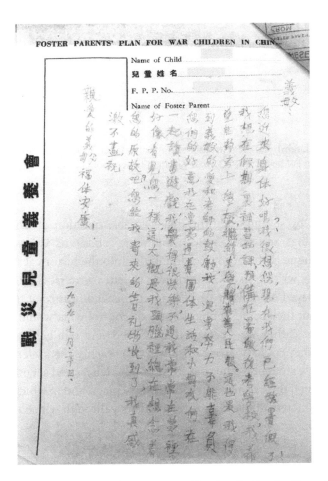

FIGURE I.1 Letter from Yu-dee, a fourteen-year-old girl in the Tianjin Chang-lu Foundling Home, to her American foster mother, Lindsay, July 20, 1949. Box 114, Folder 83, *FPP*. Courtesy of Plan International.

## 26 INTRODUCTION

| ...NESE | No. | | NAME | |
|---|---|---|---|---|
| FOSTER PARENT FROM | F | | | July 20, 1949 |
| FOSTER CHILD | C | | | Translated on August 2,1949 |

Dear Foster Mother,

How are you now? I have been thinking much of you all the time. We are now on our summer vacation. Planning to enter another school of a higher grade, I am using this vacation in making preparation and reviewing my lessons. I hope that I may enter that school to go on with my schooling so that I may serve my people in the future.

With the love and encouragement from you and my teachers, I have decided to work hard and I won't disappoint you. We have a very good group life in school. Playing and studying together with the little friends, I feel very happy. Sometimes in the dreams it seems to me that I see you. Perhaps that is because I think of you too much.

I have received your gift for my birthday, and I thank you very much.

With best wishes,                              Your foster child,

FIGURE I.2 English-language translation of letter from Yu-dee to Lindsay, August 2, 1949. Box 114, Folder 83, *FPP*. Courtesy of Plan International.

In sum, by setting aside the unanswerable question of whether children's writings accurately reflect "authentic" children's voices, I instead use this unique cache of sources to inquire into the historical significance of children's writing itself. In their role as letter writers, Chinese refugee children played an active role in shaping the significance of the aid they received, but they could neither know nor control what would become of their letters as they were censored, translated, and sent across the world. Certainly, they could not have imagined that seventy years later an American graduate student would find some of their letters and set out to write a book in which their own words took pride of place, and in which they were central characters in the extraordinary history through which they lived.

## CHAPTER OUTLINE

The remainder of this book is organized into six chapters and a conclusion. Chapter 1 traces how semicolonial China became a laboratory for the development of new global humanitarian ideas and practices. By exploring the emergence of some of the earliest global fundraising campaigns to save the children in China—as well as efforts by Chinese officials and intellectuals to renegotiate the terms on which China accepted aid from abroad—it shows how an inchoate system of global humanitarian aid took shape in China between the mid-nineteenth and mid-twentieth centuries. Chapter 2 analyzes the "intimate turn" in global humanitarianism from the perspective of World War II–era China. Focusing on the NARC's use of the adoption plan for international child sponsorship, it investigates the practices of writing, translation, photography, and gift exchange through which displaced Chinese children and foreign foster parents cultivated intimate ties across geographic and cultural boundaries under conditions of total war.

In the years after the war, new transnational humanitarian organizations such as China's Children Fund overcame the logistical obstacles that had plagued earlier incarnations of the adoption plan to make international child sponsorship into one of the most popular humanitarian programs in postwar Asia. Chapter 3 reconstructs the invisible labor of the Chinese welfare workers who made it possible to expand the adoption plan on a mass scale by systematizing the process of collecting children's personal histories, letters, and photographs for distribution to foreign donors. It shows that the personalization of humanitarian giving was paradoxically predicated on incorporating orphanages across China into a vast transnational bureaucracy that processed massive quantities of standardized paperwork according to rigid administrative procedures. When the Chinese Communist Party came to power in 1949, rather than dismiss the adoption plan as a tool of imperialism, it instead sought to transform it into the centerpiece of a new form of revolutionary humanitarianism. Chapter 4 uses the case study of the PLAN China Branch to examine how Chinese child welfare workers mobilized the ties between children and foster parents to meet the new ideological and material needs of the revolution.

In the context of the Korean War, however, the adoption plan appeared to have created a sizable cohort of children both emotionally and economically indebted to China's greatest ideological and military enemy— the United States. Tracing the efforts of the newly created People's Relief Administration of China to uproot all foreign humanitarian activity in China, chapter 5 analyzes how the bonds forged between children and their foster parents became explosive symbols of how humanitarianism functioned as a "cloak" for imperialist exploitation. The Communist Party's decision to cut off humanitarian aid to China in 1951 fundamentally reshaped the geopolitics of humanitarianism in East Asia, foreclosing the possibility of a humanitarianism of international solidarity and ushering in a new age of Cold War humanitarianism. Chapter 6 follows the former humanitarian aid workers who helped construct the Mao-era international propaganda industry while the humanitarian organizations for which they used to work shifted their focus to U.S. Cold War allies in East Asia. It reveals how the legacies of humanitarian aid to China's children shaped the global soft power competition between China and the United States during the Cold War. The conclusion brings the intertwined histories of international adoption and child sponsorship up to the present as a way to reflect on the mutually transformative encounter between China and the global humanitarian system.

# 1

## CHINA AND THE BIRTH OF
## GLOBAL HUMANITARIANISM

On February 3, 1924, Sun Yat-sen, the "father of modern China," delivered a lecture in which he argued that China should be viewed as a "hypo-colony" (*ci zhimindi*) rather than the more commonly used term "semicolony" (*ban zhimindi*). "Semicolony" typically denoted that, in contrast to "full colonies" such as French Indochina or Korea under Japanese rule, China had ceded only small portions of territory to foreign powers and retained formal sovereignty. Yet Sun claimed that semicolony was nothing more than a euphemism Chinese people used to delude themselves into thinking they were of higher status than other colonized peoples. In fact, he contended, China was worse off than formal colonies because it was simultaneously exploited by all the imperialist powers that had signed unequal treaties with China. Sun proposed the term "hypo-colony" to emphasize that "China is not just the colony of one country; it is the colony of many countries. We are not just the slaves one of country, but the slaves of many countries."[1]

Sun Yat-sen's notion of China as a hypo-colony is well known, but less attention has been paid to the only specific example he provided of why it was worse to be a hypo-colony than a full colony. According to Sun, when full colonies experienced "natural disasters like flood and drought," their colonial "masters" regarded the provision of relief aid as an integral part of their responsibilities to their subjects. In a hypo-colony, however, even this minimal sense of obligation did not exist. Sun continued: "But when

North China suffered drought several years ago, the foreign powers did not regard it as their responsibility to appropriate funds and distribute relief; only those foreigners resident in China raised funds for the drought victims, whereupon Chinese observers remarked on the great generosity of the foreign countries who bore no responsibility to help. . . . From this, we can see that . . . being the slave of one country represents a far higher status than being the slave of many, and is far more advantageous."[2]

In essence, Sun argued that China's hypo-colonial status rendered it dependent on the "great generosity" of international society to scrape together relief funds that amounted to less than what colonial governments were expected to provide as a matter of course. Put differently, China's particular plight as a hypo-colony was its overreliance on voluntary aid. To be sure, we need not accept Sun's highly questionable ranking of the relative evils of different forms of colonialism. Sun overstates the effectiveness of famine relief in formal colonies while downplaying the significant quantities of life-saving aid distributed by foreign humanitarian organizations in China. Nevertheless, his critique of hypo-colonialism suggests how the distinct nature of imperialism in China led to the development of a new form of global humanitarianism that transcended—and ultimately displaced—older modes of colonial benevolence.

This chapter analyzes the emergence of global humanitarian thought and practice in China from the mid-nineteenth century to the mid-twentieth century. Due to the overlapping presence of many imperialist powers in China, no foreign state acknowledged a colonial responsibility to provide relief aid to China, and yet humanitarian crises there attracted support from private organizations and individual donors across much of the world. At first, Chinese officials and intellectuals were deeply ambivalent about foreign humanitarian aid. On the one hand, they criticized foreign powers for exploiting China economically while leaving it to a patchwork of private aid organizations to mitigate the suffering exacerbated by imperialist exploitation. On the other hand, many feared that any attempt by foreign powers to expand their humanitarian responsibilities in China could be used as a Trojan horse to further erode China's sovereignty. In response to this dilemma, both the Qing and Nationalist governments turned to overseas Chinese communities as an alternative source of philanthropic contributions that could lessen China's dependence on "foreign" help. Ultimately, however, the existential crisis posed by the outbreak of full-scale war with Japan in 1937 led the Nationalist government to set aside its misgivings about foreign relief aid. During World War II, the Nationalist government helped mobilize a global network of Chinese diasporic organizations that used their multicultural skills and transnational social connections to rekindle humanitarian interest in China. In particular, the National Association for Refugee Children, the largest child welfare organization in wartime China, enlisted overseas Chinese groups to promote the adoption plan for international child sponsorship as a novel means to attract private humanitarian donations to China from far-flung locations around the world.

By tracing the rise of global fundraising campaigns to alleviate human suffering in China, this chapter uncovers an alternative genealogy of global humanitarianism. As explained in the introduction, during the nineteenth century imperial metropoles embraced an ideology of "colonial humanitarianism" in which they acknowledged responsibility for the well-being of their colonial subjects but only rarely attempted to alleviate the suffering of people beyond the boundaries of their own empires. In the early twentieth century, new British and American humanitarian organizations like Save the Children and Near East Relief expanded beyond the imperial realm to implement a new vision of "international humanitarianism." Yet their humanitarian work was primarily limited to Europe, and they often chose the recipients of their aid based on particularistic racial and religious affinities. As Michael Barnett and others have argued, it was not until after World War II that humanitarianism "went global."[3] But historians have yet to explain convincingly how new global conceptions of humanitarianism came to displace earlier forms of colonial and international humanitarianism. This chapter demonstrates that China was a crucial site for the development of a humanitarian ethic that transcended imperial, racial, and religious boundaries. In particular, I argue that two factors transformed China into a key node within emerging global networks of philanthropy: (1) the presence of multiple imperialist powers in China; and (2) the fundraising prowess of the global Chinese diaspora. I show how a wide range of Chinese actors—from Nationalist jurists to Communist labor organizers to diasporic elites—resisted and reshaped the inchoate system of global humanitarian aid that took shape in China between the mid-nineteenth and mid-twentieth centuries. Finally, I demonstrate that from anti-infanticide campaigns to famine relief work to wartime refugee relief efforts, early global humanitarian projects in China focused especially on children. By the outbreak of World War II, China's children had become the archetypal victims around which coalesced a new global humanitarian imagination.

From the perspective of foreign humanitarian organizations and their donors, providing succor to suffering Chinese children represented the triumphant global expansion of their moral responsibility. Yet to some Chinese observers, these purely voluntary private humanitarian campaigns seemed more like a *contraction* of the moral responsibility colonial powers had once acknowledged to the people they dominated and exploited. Global in scope, universal in framing, voluntary in character, and grossly inadequate in practice, efforts to save the children in hypocolonial China foreshadowed the global humanitarian campaigns that have been ubiquitous in response to humanitarian crises in postcolonial states since the late twentieth century.

## GOOD NEIGHBORS: THE LANDSCAPE OF PHILANTHROPY IN CHINA

As Christian missionaries and other foreign philanthropists descended on China in the nineteenth and early twentieth centuries, they spun self-congratulatory tales of how their humanitarian activities injected a new charitable spirit into Chinese society—which they caricatured as callously indifferent to human suffering. In the process, they erased the long history and impressive achievements of native Chinese philanthropy.[4] An opinion piece published in the *New York Times* in 1989 claimed, "The restraining philosophy of humanitarianism is absent or nearly absent in Chinese tradition. . . . China developed no great philosophy of charity, aid to the downtrodden or an obligation to help the less fortunate."[5] In recent years, however, the long-neglected history of Chinese charitable traditions has received overdue scholarly attention.[6] The history of Chinese philanthropy is not the primary subject of this book. Nevertheless, to analyze the significance of international humanitarianism in Chinese history, it is important to understand the vibrant world of Chinese charity that foreign institutions entered uninvited during the nineteenth and twentieth centuries. New global humanitarian networks coalesced around the cause of saving the children in China, but they were only part of a multilayered landscape of relief work in which local charities and compassionate neighbors often provided the bulk of life-saving aid.

In the centuries prior to the arrival of foreign humanitarians, private philanthropic institutions funded by wealthy merchants emerged as the key providers of social welfare services and emergency relief aid in Chinese society. During the late Ming and early Qing periods (1580–1750), new voluntary institutions dedicated specifically to charity emerged in localities across much of China, including benevolent halls (*shantang*), orphanages, and societies for aiding young widows.[7] These charitable institutions were initially dominated by traditional scholarly elites. With increased commercialization, however, merchants began participating in philanthropy as a means to improve their social standing by showing that the accumulation of money could serve moral ends. As Joanna Handlin Smith has shown, by the mid-nineteenth century, major urban centers contained large-scale charitable institutions that were endorsed by the imperial government but primarily funded by merchants.[8] Yang Jianli argues that by the late nineteenth century, private charity (*yi zhen*) had replaced government aid (*huang zheng*) as the primary source of disaster relief and social welfare in China.[9] These merchant-led philanthropies operated primarily on a local scale until the mid-nineteenth century. However, in the context of mass refugee flight during the Taiping Civil War (1850–1864) and mass starvation during the North China Famine of 1876–1879, wealthy philanthropists from the Jiangnan region led nationwide relief efforts through which they sought to cultivate moral responsibility for providing aid beyond the local community.[10]

While organized efforts to relieve human suffering in China long predated the arrival of concerned foreigners, the influx of foreign charities in the late nineteenth century added urgency to Chinese philanthropists' efforts to expand native charitable institutions so as to render foreign help unnecessary—a phenomenon Michelle King has called "orphanage competition."[11] In response to conflicts surrounding foreign orphanages in China (more on that later), the prominent modernizing official Li Hongzhang wrote, "Recently I have been informed that there are many unfortunate incidents involving foreigners' churches. Most of these stem from the foreigners' establishment of orphanages. If our local officials would set up more orphanages to care for our children, then ugly occurrences such as these could be avoided."[12] In this context, Chinese charitable institutions increasingly adopted modern tactics such as circulating philanthropic appeals through newspapers and providing vocational training within orphanages to transform the recipients of charity into modern citizens capable of participating in an industrializing economy.[13] Nevertheless, merchant-funded charity continued to be promoted through the traditional registers of Confucianism and Buddhism. Vivienne Shue has shown that even as benevolent halls embraced modern tactics in the early twentieth century, they continued to promote Confucian values such as protecting widow chastity, cultivating propriety, and cherishing the written word. Likewise, competition from Christian missionary philanthropies inspired a commensurate rise in Buddhist charitable activities in the late nineteenth century, which Andrea Janku argues played a role in the larger "Buddhist revival" of this period.[14]

Despite international humanitarian organizations' repeated criticisms of China for not taking responsibility for the welfare of its own people, the majority of relief aid provided to Chinese disaster victims during the early twentieth century came from their fellow Chinese. Founded in 1904 and officially recognized by the International Committee of the Red Cross in 1912, the Chinese Red Cross Society quickly developed into an effective national-scale relief organization. By the 1920s more than three hundred chapters were providing aid to victims of natural disasters and military conflicts across China.[15] Chinese religious charities also flourished during the early twentieth century. The most prominent of these was the World Red Swastika Society, which was associated with the *daoyuan* religious movement. Founded in North China in 1922, by the mid-1930s the society had grown into an enormous, nationwide organization that mobilized hundreds of thousands of volunteers to provide relief aid to millions of victims of warfare and natural disaster.[16] As Xia Shi has shown, Chinese culture had long sanctioned women's charitable activities, and married nonprofessional women played leading roles in Chinese philanthropic institutions during this period.[17] Yet the largest quantities of aid were often provided by less heralded groups and individuals. During the North China Famine of 1920–1921, the Beijing-based Buddhist Relief Society contributed more than 14 million kilograms of relief grain by fundraising at temples across the country and distributing grain through far-flung monastic networks. And as Pierre Fuller has argued, neighbor-to-neighbor mutual help—the majority of which was not recorded by formal institutions—played a key role in limiting mortality from famine in early twentieth-century China.[18]

The new foreign humanitarian institutions that swept across China during the nineteenth and twentieth centuries transformed both China and the practice of humanitarianism itself. Nevertheless, the unheralded work of Chinese good Samaritans to help neighbors in need continued to play a crucial role in mitigating the human toll of war and famine during the tumultuous decades following China's violent incorporation in the modern world order.

## HUMANITARIANISM IN HYPO-COLONIAL CHINA

Humanitarian interest in China's children followed quickly upon the Opium Wars that violently incorporated China into an unequal world system of commerce, migration, cultural exchange—and philanthropy. After its defeat by Britain in the first Opium War, in 1842 the Qing government was forced to sign the Treaty of Nanjing, the first of the infamous "unequal treaties" that ceded Hong Kong to the British, granted extraterritoriality to British citizens, and opened five treaty ports to foreign trade. In short order, the United States, France, and other Western countries concluded similar treaties, all of which included "most favored nation" clauses ensuring that concessions granted to one imperial power would be enjoyed by all.[19] This system of unequal treaties enabled increasing numbers of Christian missionaries to go to China, and among the many reports they sent home were tales of rampant female infanticide driven by poverty and the Confucian preference for sons over daughters. These stories were often exaggerated, and infanticide and infant abandonment were also widespread problems in contemporary Western societies. Nevertheless, it was this perception of infanticide as a particularly Chinese problem that first made the Chinese child into an object of global pity.[20]

Among the earliest large-scale transnational aid organizations, the Holy Childhood Association (l'Oeuvre de la Sainte Enfance) played an important role in popularizing the cause of saving Chinese babies from infanticide. Founded in 1843 by the French bishop Charles-Auguste-Marie-Joseph de Forbin Janson, the Holy Childhood Association encouraged Western children to donate small monthly sums to rescue and baptize infants in China. The association's most popular fundraising technique were lotteries in which the winner would become the "godparent" of a Chinese baby with the privilege of choosing its baptismal name. The Holy Childhood Association achieved extraordinary fundraising success, reaching an annual income of two million francs by 1869.[21] While the majority of its funds came from Europe (especially France, Germany, Belgium, Italy, the Netherlands, and Austria-Hungry), the association also received donations from the Americas, Africa, Asia, and Oceania.[22] Yet despite its global profile and fundraising prowess, the Holy Child Association's child welfare work on the ground in China left much to be desired. The association often prioritized saving children's souls over saving their lives, and a startlingly high percentage of children taken in by its orphanages died shortly after their baptisms.[23] In part for this reason, the Holy Child Association's work became highly controversial in China. The most explosive of these conflicts erupted in Tianjin in the summer of 1870, when rumors spread that a Holy Childhood Association orphanage was kidnapping children to gouge out their eyes and hearts for use in medicine. After a heated confrontation with local officials, the French consul shot and killed a servant of the local magistrate, setting off a riot known as the Tianjin Massacre in which twenty foreigners and an unknown number of Chinese Christians were killed.[24]

The Holy Childhood Association's transnational campaigns on behalf of China's infant girls diverged from prevailing patterns of colonial humanitarianism and pioneered new methods of humanitarian fundraising that would gain traction over the ensuing decades of hypo-colonial rule in China. At the same time as the association was raising alarms about female infanticide in China, Christian missionaries and colonial administrators were doing the same in India. In India, however, infanticide was viewed as a problem to be solved by the colonial government. In 1870 the British colonial government passed the Act for the Prevention of Female Infanticide, endowing colonial authorities with vast powers to expose and punish perpetrators of infanticide in India.[25] No foreign power in China claimed such responsibility. Rather, it fell to a private organization, the Holy Childhood Association, to mobilize individual donors to tackle the problem of infanticide one child at a time. Highlighting the plight of Chinese children through vast transnational fundraising campaigns, the association attracted large numbers of small contributions from across Europe, North America, and much of the world. The global fundraising strategies it helped pioneer—and the practical and political problems it encountered in China—would continue to characterize humanitarian efforts on behalf of China's children for decades to come.

Infanticide and child abandonment were the issues that first trained global humanitarian attention on the figure of the Chinese child, but it was the problem of recurrent famine that sparked the expansion and systematization of humanitarian relief to China. The North China Famine of 1876–1879, among the worst famines in recorded human history, with an estimated death toll of nine to thirteen million people, attracted considerable international attention.[26] To help fundraise for relief work, foreign missionaries responding to the crisis frequently deployed images of starving children in the publicity materials they sent back home. For example, the China Inland Mission's London-based publication, *China's Millions*, published a letter entitled "For the Young: A Letter from Shan-Si" that sought to cultivate sympathy among British children for their Chinese peers:

> I am sure all of you would pity the poor little boys and girls of this great country if you could but see all that I have seen. They have no homes like most of you have, but live in houses built with mud and reeds; they live on rice, and wheat, and bread, and such things as many of you dislike, and do not get meat and nice cakes as you do; so whenever you hear boy or girl complaining of what they get to eat, just remind them of the poor children in China.[27]

By the end of the nineteenth century, "the poor children in China" had emerged as highly sympathetic figures drawing ever-greater humanitarian attention to the persistent problem of famine in China.

It was not until the early twentieth century, however, that international famine relief to China was systematized through the formation of a new humanitarian institution—the international famine relief committee.[28] The first of these committees, the Central China Famine Relief Fund, was founded in Shanghai during the Chinese Famine of 1906–1907. Under the

## 38 CHINA AND THE BIRTH OF GLOBAL HUMANITARIANISM

leadership of British businessman Edward Selby Little, the fund's goal was to enlist "the charitably disposed all over the earth" to contribute to "the humanitarian work of attempting to save life, and bringing succour and comfort to those suffering from the famine" in China.[29] During the 1910–1911 famine a new Central China Famine Relief Committee was created to coordinate and distribute relief aid. This was followed by the founding of the Peking United International Famine Relief Committee during the North China Famine of 1920–1921, which was finally replaced by a permanent organization called the China International Famine Relief Commission (CIFRC). Tasked with fundraising as well as coordinating and distributing relief aid, these committees were led by a combination of prominent foreigners living in China and Chinese elites, many of whom had been educated abroad. The evolving, often contentious work of the international famine relief committees provides a useful illustration of how key features of global humanitarian thought and practice took shape in the context of hypo-colonial China.

Much like the Holy Childhood Association, international famine relief committees were supported by a large number of small donations from virtually all the countries that had significant interests in China. From 1911 to 1912, the Central China Famine Relief Committee wrote to 650 newspaper editors and 3,800 other prominent individuals around the world as part of its publicity campaign. The committee ultimately reported donations from the United States, Canada, Britain, Germany, Scandinavia, Russia, Japan, Korea, Australia, and Africa.[30] The Peking United International Famine Relief Committee was led by an international executive committee with representatives from eleven countries, all of which had signed unequal treaties with China. In addition to receiving donations from Europe and North America, the Peking Committee also received significant donations from European colonies such as Malaya, Singapore, Hong Kong, Macao, and Indochina.[31] In contrast to disaster relief efforts in other colonial settings, which were typically led by colonial governments and supported by fundraising from within individual empires, international famine relief work in China provided a forum for the development of interimperial networks of humanitarian aid that appealed to a global base of donors. While colonial famine relief was framed as a way to enhance the legitimacy of empire, international famine relief committees in China instead emphasized how their work would benefit international business interests. In one pamphlet published in 1923, the CIFRC included a section titled "Benefits to Be Expected" that explained how its humanitarian work would increase "the ability of Chinese merchants, artizans [sic], and residents of the cities and towns generally to buy foreign goods." The pamphlet added, "In one district in the province of Hupeh where some important dyke work was carried out, we were informed by two large foreign corporations that their sales had doubled during the past year as a result of the improvement in the buying power of the people through prevention of the usual annual floods."[32] As early as the 1920s, international famine relief committees in China were making explicit arguments for how the global expansion of humanitarian work would facilitate the development of global capitalism.

Unlike the Holy Childhood Association, international famine relief committees did not focus directly on children. Nevertheless, children continued to occupy an outsized role in both humanitarian fundraising materials and the distribution of relief aid. The starving child was the quintessential symbol of famine in China. In its 1912 report, the Central China Famine Relief Committee wrote, "There is perhaps no more heart-rending sight in this world than to see a woman, who loves her child and sees it starving before her eyes, forced to make the decision as to whether she shall keep her child and see it die a lingering death in her arms, or sell it to some stranger, perhaps to a life of misery or even of vice." By presenting maternal love as a universal value, the committee underscored the common humanity of Chinese famine victims and international donors. It claimed, "No one who can imagine himself in a similar position but must have the deepest sympathy for a mother who must make such a decision."[33] In addition to textual description, international relief committees used copious numbers of photographs in their publicity materials, and images of starving children were the most powerful tool in their visual rhetoric of humanitarianism. For example, graphic photographs of starving children—their stomachs distended and their faces forlorn—feature throughout a report from 1921 on famine relief work in China by the American Red Cross.[34] The Peking United International Famine Relief Committee included no fewer than twenty-one photographs of children in its report in 1922. Beyond using the image of the starving child as a fundraising tool, the Peking Committee also prioritized children in its relief work. During the North China Famine of 1921–1922, the committee opened 672 schools that cared for 45,787 pupils, providing each child with $1.40 per month so that they became "an economic asset instead of a liability to the family." In addition, the committee founded 166 "hairnet schools" that taught some 31,165 girls to make hairnets for export to Europe and the United States so that they could contribute economically to their families. The committee even created a Committee on the Prevention of the Sale of Children to help families "buy back" children whom they had sold during the famine.[35] Humanitarian aid campaigns around the world have often highlighted the sympathetic figure of the helpless child. However, the international relief committees' focus on the child victims of famine in China was particularly significant as a strategy for cultivating humanitarian feeling for a Chinese population for which foreign powers admitted no special responsibility.

Nevertheless, international relief aid was not nearly sufficient to avert mass starvation and suffering. Unquestionably, international relief committees contributed considerable sums of life-saving aid that helped mitigate the effects of famine in early twentieth-century China. The Peking United International Famine Relief Committee reported that international committees raised more than 17 million yuan during the North China Famine of 1920–1921, and it estimated that 40 percent of all relief funds came from foreign sources.[36] However, as Pierre Fuller has shown, foreign contributions to famine relief in China were widely exaggerated.[37] According to Fuller, a more plausible estimate would be that foreign sources accounted for approximately 20 percent of total relief funds during the 1920–1921 famine.[38] In the aftermath of the 1910–1911 famine, the Central China Famine Relief Committee reflected critically on the inadequacy of its own work. Its summary report admitted: "The funds available for famine relief in this as in previous years were far too small to relieve the distress . . . and famine relief that does not at least save the lives of a large portion of the needy population must be looked upon as most inadequate."[39] In addition to insufficient funds, another problem faced by the committee was the lack of a professionally trained staff fully committed to the task of famine relief. Its report noted that "many volunteers were recent arrivals in China and had but slight knowledge of the language and the people. Fully half of them had no previous famine experience." Moreover, many missionaries "volunteered for only a few weeks," leading to constant turnover that exacerbated logistical problems. They concluded,

"No Committee dependent upon benevolent contributions and upon volunteers to act as overseers of its relief can deal in a satisfactory manner with problems such as these."[40]

But while international relief committees could not provide sufficient aid to avert mass suffering, they consistently maintained that it was not their responsibility to do so. Among the most common refrains within committee reports was that ultimate responsibility for famine relief belonged with the Chinese government. In 1912 the Central China Famine Relief Committee accused the recently overthrown Qing government of "almost criminal indifference to human suffering" and suggested that "in the future all who are deeply interested in the people in the famine region can best serve them by throwing the full responsibility for their care upon the Government."[41] The Peking United International Famine Relief Committee recognized "the primary responsibility of the government" for relief work and limited its own aid to suffering that resulted from "natural causes" rather than "civil strife," contending that providing aid to those whose suffering could be attributed to political causes "would only encourage those who were responsible for the disorder." It also noted that publicizing domestic famine relief efforts within China would help to "stimulate large contributions from foreign nations." The Peking Committee described its own work as "a living testimony of humanitarian motives" and "an investment in international brotherhood unparalleled in the history of relief movements."[42] But it also made clear that it was not obligated to provide aid and would not do so unconditionally. Rather, to be worthy of humanitarian help in the committee's eyes, Chinese people could not be deemed responsible for their own suffering, and they had to be seen to be doing all they could to help themselves.

In both theory and practice, humanitarian aid to hypo-colonial China differed from earlier forms of colonial benevolence and anticipated the global humanitarianism of the post–World War II period. By the early twentieth century, China's suffering masses—particularly the children among them—had become the object of humanitarian fundraising campaigns that were global, universalist, voluntary, and utterly insufficient. The private citizens around the world who responded to appeals on behalf of China's children acknowledged no special responsibility for their welfare, nor did they claim any particular ties to the young Chinese beneficiaries of their aid except for their shared humanity. It was for this reason that they viewed their aid to China as "a living testimony of humanitarian motives . . . unparalleled in the history of relief movements," or, in Sun Yat-sen's sardonic phrasing, as "the great generosity of foreign countries who bore no responsibility to help." China's children emerged as a powerful symbol of humanity qua humanity precisely because China's hypo-colonial status absolved the many imperialist powers with interests in China of any responsibility for protecting their livelihood—in their own and Chinese eyes. But the rise of global humanitarianism in late-nineteenth- and early twentieth-century China was not a smooth or inevitable process. Chinese officials, intellectuals, and activists criticized and resisted what many viewed as the troubling trend of China's increasing reliance on aid from abroad.

## DEBATING GLOBAL HUMANITARIANISM IN CHINA

The influx of humanitarian aid to China during the late nineteenth and early twentieth centuries provoked a range of complex, often contradictory responses among Chinese leaders. Sun Yat-sen criticized foreign powers for exploiting China economically while denying any official responsibility for the welfare of Chinese people, leaving the fate of Chinese disaster victims to the whims of private donors. Other leading Nationalist figures, however, worried that foreign powers could appeal to a humanitarian responsibility to relieve suffering in China as a pretext for even greater infringements of China's sovereignty. In 1919, Zhu Zhixin, a longtime ally of Sun Yat-sen who had been among the first intellectuals to introduce *The Communist Manifesto* to Chinese readers, penned an essay titled "The Violation of Sovereignty and Humanitarianism" in which he argued that European countries often used humanitarianism as a justification for colonialism. Zhu wrote, "So-called humanitarians claim to speak on behalf of all humanity. If the actions of one nation violate the interests of all humanity, then from the perspective of humanitarianism sometimes we cannot give free reign to the principle of national self-determination. Herein lies the pretext for violating sovereignty." Noting that "invaders never admit that they are invaders," Zhu went on to explain that "this kind of argument has often been promoted and implemented by Europeans" to justify their colonial conquests.[43] Zhu's concerns were echoed by Wang Chonghui, an important Chinese jurist who went on to become the first president of the Judicial Yuan, the Republic of China's highest judicial organ. In an April 1928 speech, Wang noted that the notion of "economic uplift" had become fashionable in international circles. "But," he added, "so-called uplift should be mutual. Lifting others up while binding their hands and feet cannot be called uplift."[44] While Sun Yat-sen castigated the imperialist powers for not doing more to alleviate suffering in China, Zhu and Wang cautioned that China should be careful what it wished for. Well-versed in the history of imperialism, they warned that humanitarian projects promising to uplift the Chinese people could also be a means of deepening colonial control.

China's dilemma with regard to foreign humanitarian aid was reflected in a series of high-profile controversies involving the work of the Japanese and American Red Cross societies in China during World War I. After the outbreak of World War I, Japan declared war on Germany and seized its colonial holdings in Shandong Province with the clear goal of expanding its own territorial possessions in China. The fighting on the Shandong Peninsula coincided with widespread flooding in the region to create a severe humanitarian crisis. In December 1916 the Chinese Red Cross reported that a Japanese Red Cross branch and a Japanese Red Cross hospital had begun operating in the port city of Longkou.[45] As Caroline Reeves noted in her account of the ensuing controversy, "The principle of one country, one Red Cross was an established and fundamental tenet of the ICRC." Therefore, Reeves argues, Japan's decision to open a Red Cross branch in Shandong was a deliberate attempt to assert sovereignty over the contested territory, "just as if they were raising a Japanese national flag."[46] In response, China's Foreign Ministry dispatched the Yantai commissioner of foreign affairs to the Japanese Consulate to "strictly prohibit" the operation of the Japanese Red Cross in Chinese territory. Ultimately, however, the commissioner decided that because the "temporary" Japanese Red Cross branch had already been dissolved, and the hospital was located in a treaty port, there was no threat to China's sovereignty, and no further action needed to be taken.[47] Nevertheless, the case established the principle that any attempt to found a foreign Red Cross society in

China would be treated as a violation of Chinese sovereignty. Sun Yat-sen claimed that colonial rule created a mutually acknowledged responsibility to provide relief aid to colonial subjects. The controversy surrounding the Japanese Red Cross branch in Longkou suggested that the converse was also true: assuming responsibility for relief work was a means of staking a claim to sovereignty.

Only two years later, an even bigger controversy broke out concerning the fundraising activities of the American Red Cross in China. During World War I, the American Red Cross established chapters throughout China that were initially intended to promote wartime philanthropy among expatriate Americans. In the spring of 1918, however, Julean Arnold, the field representative of the American Red Cross in China, launched a large-scale campaign to enlist Chinese citizens as paying members of American Red Cross chapters. Many within Chinese government and philanthropic circles viewed Arnold's recruitment drive as a flagrant violation of Chinese sovereignty that severely damaged the credibility of the Chinese Red Cross.[48] Citing the Longkou incident as precedent, the Ministry of the Army issued instructions prohibiting the formation of new American Red Cross branches in China.[49] Shen Dunhe, the founder of the Chinese Red Cross Society, wrote directly both to Arnold and to U.S. president William Howard Taft to protest the American Red Cross's infringement of Chinese sovereignty in violation of international Red Cross principles.[50] But far from acceding to Shen's request, Arnold and the American Red Cross pressured the Chinese government into removing Shen from his position as director of the Chinese Red Cross. Painfully aware of their dependence on American Red Cross aid and friendly relations with the United States more generally, the Chinese government dismissed Shen and replaced him with the more American-friendly Admiral Cai Tinggan.[51] As one representative of the American Red Cross in China remarked in a moment of candor, "China is unique in many ways and this is one of them, for what other country will you find agreeable to allow a foreign Red Cross to step in and take command of its relief situations to the extent we have done."[52] Chinese officials were well aware that foreign powers like Japan and the United States were using humanitarian institutions to wrest greater control over Chinese politics and society. Nevertheless, due to China's weak international position and pressing need for foreign relief aid, they were often left with little choice but to accede to these countries' demands.

By the late 1920s the Communist-affiliated Chinese labor movement had also begun to challenge the terms of international humanitarian aid. While Nationalist intellectuals critiqued humanitarianism from the perspective of national sovereignty, left-wing labor activists sought to expose humanitarian work as another form of economic exploitation. The tensions between the Chinese labor movement and international humanitarian organizations are well-illustrated by conflicts surrounding the work of the CIFRC in Wuhan, the capital of Hubei Province in Central China. In the midst of its Northern Expedition to reunify China, in late 1926 the Nationalist government relocated its capital from Guangzhou to Wuhan and formed the short-lived Wuhan Nationalist government under the leadership of the party's left-wing faction. In this environment, a Communist-led labor movement quickly began to flourish in Wuhan and throughout Hubei. The Hubei Federation of Trade Unions was established in October 1926, and high-level Communist leaders, including Liu Shaoqi and Li Lisan, arrived in Wuhan to lead the labor movement. Over the ensuing months, they launched a highly militant labor campaign, organizing dozens of strikes as well as anti-imperialist protests that ultimately led Britain to abandon its foreign concession in the city in 1927.[53] The CIFRC did not escape the attention of the labor movement. In 1927 the CIFRC Committee for Hupeh (Hubei) allocated $46,000 to repair the Chang-kung Dike that protected Hankow from flooding. However, the committee found it very difficult to carry out this work under what it described as "the most impossible conditions of the incessantly changing whims of labour—individuals and unions, and threats by them under the slightest pretext to kill not only the Secretaries and resident engineers, but even Dr. O.R. Wold of the Lutheran Theological Seminary . . . who had kindly agreed to assist in the complicated task of recruiting labour." The committee's 1927 annual report added that "it was pretty clear that failure of the dike due to poor or slow work would more likely than not result first of all in the engineers' being mobbed or buried alive for 'counter revolutionary activities.'"[54] While the CIFRC was clearly chagrined that anyone would doubt its altruism, militant Chinese labor activists insisted that foreign humanitarian institutions should offer fair treatment to the local workers who performed the actual labor of global humanitarianism.

As it turned out, labor unrest was only the beginning of the CIFRC's troubles with the Communists in Hubei. One of the CIFRC's core "principles of famine relief" stated that "except in emergencies, appropriations for famine relief work will be considered in the nature of a loan."[55] Since 1922 the CIFRC Committee for Hupeh had made loans for dike repair at an annual interest rate of 12 percent.[56] By 1928, however, the Hupeh Committee found that localities were no longer willing to pay back loans they had received over the previous years—a phenomenon it attributed to "a notion which had been inculcated by communist propaganda that nothing should be repaid on the loans." The committee went on to excoriate the area's "Bolshevik experiment" for uprooting "the whole web of social relations and common traditions that make for organized social life."[57] By 1929, still unable to secure repayment on its previous loans, the Hupeh Committee announced that it would "do no more work and advance no more money until the local people re-pay the loans."[58] Whereas past annual reports detailed the humanitarian work accomplished over the previous year, the Hupeh Committee's annual report in 1929 was entirely devoted to a detailed description of its frustrated efforts to force repayment on its loans. Founded to provide humanitarian assistance, the CIFRC Committee for Hupeh had been reduced to little more than a debt collection agency.

Long-simmering debates over the proper role for foreign humanitarian organizations in China reached a climax in 1929 when the American Red Cross made the bombshell announcement that it would no longer provide relief aid to China. After decades of fundraising for Chinese famine relief, some within the American Red Cross began to voice concerns that aid from overseas was enabling the Chinese government to avoid making the fundamental changes needed to prevent famines from occurring in the first place. During the summer of 1929, the American Red Cross sent a commission to China to study famine conditions and the effects of relief aid. On the basis of the commission's report, the central committee of the American Red Cross argued that "Chinese leaders would no doubt give more thought to the removal of the causes which impoverish their people and bring on such tragedies if they realized the necessity of assuming full responsibility for resulting relief needs; any acceptance of that responsibility by foreign agencies cannot but retard this all important result." Therefore, the central committee concluded, conditions in China "do not warrant an appeal by the Red Cross to the generosity of the American people."[59]

In response to the American Red Cross's sudden disavowal of aid to China, the CIFRC issued a rejoinder in which it reiterated the global logic underlying its humanitarian work. In a statement published on November 6, 1929, the CIFRC executive committee argued that "the question of relief for severe destitution should be considered without reference to distinctions of race or nationality." The statement concluded that the CIFRC "felt entirely justified in appealing to the American people for money for famine relief work in China . . . because those who are starving are human beings."[60] The CIFRC did not claim that American people had any specific obligation to Chinese people. Rather, they argued that it was the responsibility of the global community to aid their fellow human beings whenever there was both severe need and the means to provide effective relief. Nevertheless, the American Red Cross report in 1929 anticipated a problem that would increasingly plague organizations that sought to use *global* humanitarian logic to justify aid to China *in particular*. For decades, global humanitarian thinking had supported the idea that foreign citizens should expend significant humanitarian resources in China despite not claiming any special responsibility for its welfare needs. But once China became entrenched as a large recipient of aid from abroad, humanitarian organizations and their donors began to turn this logic on its head. If all suffering human beings were equally worthy of relief aid, how could groups like the American Red Cross justify continuing to devote such a large share of their limited resources to China specifically?

Within China, the American Red Cross's decision to stop supporting Chinese causes prompted both outrage and critical reflection about China's reliance on humanitarian aid. In November 1929 the Foreign Ministry instructed China's minister to the United States, Wu Chaoshu, to express its grave concerns about the American Red Cross report.[61] Xu Shiying, head of the National Government's Disaster Relief Commission, stated that he would never "beg" for American relief and instead criticized the arbitrary nature of humanitarian aid decisions and the untenable status quo of relying on foreign organizations to provide relief services.[62] On the editorial pages of major Chinese newspapers, some commentators essentially agreed with the American Red Cross that cutting off aid could provide impetus to necessary reforms in China. An editorial published in *Da gong bao* began by acknowledging that "accepting international relief aid is a common occurrence around the world and is nothing to be ashamed of." "But," it hastened to add, "there has never been a great nation that truly relies on others to rescue it." The editorial concluded that if the American Red Cross report could shame China's leaders into "conducting emergency relief and abandoning oppressive policies . . . then its effect will be greater than vast sums of donations."[63] Other Chinese commentators placed more weight on the immediate human consequences of the American Red Cross's decision. An editorial in the *Republic of China Daily* conceded that ultimate responsibility for famine relief rested with the Chinese government but argued that encouraging American people to aid China during a moment of crisis would be in keeping with the Red Cross's fundamental principles of "human sympathy" and "universal love."[64] Chinese officials and major newspapers were critical of the American Red Cross's decision and dismayed by the additional lives that would certainly be lost to famine. But they also saw the report as an opportunity to reimagine China's relationship with global humanitarianism—and to seek out alternative ways of funding social welfare and relief work.

The many conflicts surrounding the work of foreign humanitarian organizations in early twentieth-century China laid bare the hypo-colonial quandary that Chinese leaders faced as they attempted to navigate their increasing reliance on aid from abroad. On the one hand, Chinese officials and intellectuals reasonably feared that international organizations were using humanitarian need as a pretext to wrest control over China's social infrastructure—often out of self-interested motives and on exploitative terms. On the other hand, Chinese leaders also recognized that any sudden withdrawal of foreign humanitarian resources would lead to increased suffering and death, at least in the short term. Yet while virtually all international humanitarian organizations and Chinese commentators agreed that the Chinese state should bear ultimate responsibility for the well-being of its people, the fledgling Nationalist government did not have the capacity to construct a viable social safety net on a national scale. In this context, the Nationalist government instead sought to mobilize an alternative source of funding for social welfare and relief work—the global Chinese diaspora.

## THE CHINESE DIASPORA AND
## GLOBAL HUMANITARIANISM IN CHINA

From the mid-nineteenth century to the mid-twentieth century, overseas Chinese communities constructed global networks of diasporic philanthropy that rivaled foreign humanitarian institutions in their contributions to disaster relief and social welfare work in China. Between 1840 and 1940, tens of millions of Chinese people migrated overseas to destinations across Southeast Asia, the Americas, and Oceania. In the 1920s, the rate of overseas migration from South China reached levels comparable to the better-known transatlantic migrations from Europe to the Americas.[65] By the turn of the twentieth century, leading reformist intellectuals such as Kang Youwei and Liang Qichao had begun to view China's global diaspora as crucial to its economic development. For instance, in 1902 Liang's highly influential journal, *Xinmin congbao*, published a two-part essay titled "On the Grand Trend of World Economic Competition," which argued that remittances from Chinese overseas constituted China's best hope for increasing its economic competitiveness in the face of imperialist exploitation.[66] As Chinese officials and intellectuals courted greater economic investment from Chinese abroad, they also came to view overseas Chinese as an alternative source of philanthropic donations that could reduce the need for foreign charity.

Initially, diasporic Chinese made charitable contributions primarily on a local scale by instructing that a portion of the remittances they sent their families be used to support causes such as orphanages, schools, and famine relief.[67] But in response to repeated controversies surrounding foreign humanitarian work in China, Chinese officials attempted to lessen the need for foreign help by persuading overseas Chinese to expand the scope of their philanthropic giving to include national causes. As early as the self-strengthening movement of the 1860s–1870s, reformers such as Li Hongzhang and Zhang Zhidong had begun appealing to the patriotism of Chinese communities in Southeast Asia to solicit contributions for disaster relief efforts and modernization projects in China—even conferring honorary imperial titles on overseas Chinese in Singapore and Malaya who donated large sums during the North China famine.[68] Numerous case studies from across the diaspora point toward a dramatic increase in the role of nationalism in directing overseas Chinese philanthropy toward national-level causes in the early twentieth century. John Fitzgerald and Mei-fun Kuo have argued that the high-profile philanthropic activities of Chinese Australian merchant William Yinson Lee were motivated in large part by a patriotic desire to recover "welfare sovereignty" from foreign charities.[69] Although most Chinese in California hailed from South China, in 1907 they raised nearly US$20,000 for famine relief in Central China.[70] For diasporic Chinese, making "patriotic" contributions to China's development as an independent, strong, and internationally respected nation offered the prospect of better business opportunities, enhanced political status in China, and greater respect as ethnic Chinese abroad.[71] For the Chinese state, donations from diasporic Chinese provided a more politically palatable alternative to foreign humanitarianism in its pursuit of modernization and economic independence.

State-sponsored efforts to extract ever-greater levels of financial support from Chinese diasporic communities reached their zenith after the outbreak of full-scale war between China and Japan in 1937. During the war, the Nationalist government promoted a "monthly donation quota" (*chang yue juan*) system that required overseas Chinese to make minimum monthly contributions to wartime causes typically calculated as a percentage of their income. The system was implemented throughout the diaspora by local overseas Chinese associations that relied on public shaming, a quasi-judicial authority to punish members, and vigilante violence to ensure compliance. Akin to an informal system of extraterritorial taxation, the monthly donation quota system was hugely successful as a fundraising mechanism. According to Ren Guixiang, from 1937 to 1942 overseas Chinese donated an estimated 700 million yuan to the war effort, equivalent to approximately 25 percent of the Nationalist government's military expenditures during this period.[72] Nevertheless, the monthly donation quota system devastated transnational Chinese families by hindering the ability of overseas men to send remittances to family members in China, pushing many families to the brink of starvation even before the outbreak of the Pacific War in December 1941 partially cut off the flow of remittances from abroad.[73] Already stretching the limits of diasporic communities' ability to contribute to wartime causes, and increasingly in need of funds to meet the cascade of humanitarian crises brought on by total war, Nationalist authorities began to rethink the role that its global diaspora could play in helping to fund war relief work in China.

The outbreak of World War II ushered in a fundamental reversal in the relationship between Chinese diasporic philanthropy and global humanitarianism in China. Prior to the war, the Chinese state viewed diasporic philanthropy as an *alternative* to foreign philanthropy, a way to fundraise for disaster relief and social welfare projects without further compromising China's sovereignty or igniting social unrest. Full-scale war, however, had created an urgent, virtually unlimited need for emergency aid that far exceeded what diasporic Chinese communities could provide on their own. In the face of the existential crisis posed by war with Japan, China's longstanding ambivalence about foreign humanitarianism quickly gave way to frenetic efforts to attract as much international aid as possible. Ironically, it was the same Chinese diasporic organizations that were supposed to obviate the need for foreign charity that were best positioned to solicit and coordinate foreign donations for wartime humanitarian work in China. Less than a decade after the American Red Cross's decision to discontinue aid to China had prompted widespread soul-searching about China's reliance on foreign charity, Chinese diasporic organizations would play a leading role in the wartime effort to make China into a focal point of global humanitarian activity once again.

Chinese diasporic organizations throughout Asia, Oceania, Europe, and North America launched a variety of grassroots campaigns to solicit contributions from the wider societies in which they lived. One of the most popular strategies for fundraising among non-Chinese populations was the organization of cultural performances to benefit relief efforts in China. For example, in November 1937 the Chinese and Foreign Goods Association in Singapore sponsored a dramatic performance in support of the China Relief Fund that sold 5,000 Straits dollars worth of tickets primarily to members of the European firms that were their customers.[74] Similar fundraising efforts were organized by overseas Chinese communities in Europe and Oceania. In London, the Chinese ambassador, Quo Tai-Chi, organized a Chinese art exhibition to fundraise for medical aid to China.[75] The Chinese Women's Relief Association in Wellington, New

Zealand, appealed constantly to the general public to donate to Chinese relief work through fundraising schemes that included benefit concerts and knitting blankets to be sent to China.[76] In Australia, it was often Chinese youth groups that took the lead in organizing grassroots fundraisers targeting the wider Australian population. In Sydney, the Young Chinese Relief Movement organized fundraising events that included a concert at the Tivoli Theatre, numerous picnics, and a ball headlined by visiting Chinese American Hollywood star Anna May Wong.[77] Cumulatively, these small-scale fundraisers organized by local Chinese organizations helped transform war relief work in China into a prominent humanitarian cause in Europe, among European colonists in Southeast Asia, and in the settler societies of Oceania.

Chinese Americans campaigned especially vigorously to solicit donations for wartime relief work in China. For example, the Chinese Hand Laundry Alliance placed five thousand collection boxes in Chinese laundries across New York City for donations on behalf of "wounded soldiers and refugees" in China.[78] In one of the most elaborately coordinated efforts by diasporic communities to focus humanitarian attention on the war in China, on June 17, 1938, at least 1,561 American cities and towns held "Bowl of Rice" parties to fundraise for relief efforts in China.[79] The United Council for Civilian Relief in China estimated that as many as one million people attended Bowl of Rice parties nationwide—including 200,000 in San Francisco, 85,000 in New York City, 10,000 in Birmingham, and sizable crowds in cities such as Louisville, Pittsburgh, Richmond, St. Louis, Boston, and Baltimore.[80] At the Bowl of Rice party in New York City's Chinatown, donors paid US$6 per ticket for a program called "A Night in Old China," which "entitle[d] the bearer to view an elaborate entertainment program, eat a seven-course Chinese dinner and dance to music by Milt Britton's band."[81] In San Francisco the crowds were reportedly so large that many tourists missed their outbound ships due to the traffic in Chinatown.[82] Through an extraordinary number of locally organized fundraisers in cities and towns across much of the world, diasporic Chinese groups transformed China's wartime suffering into a humanitarian cause célèbre on a global scale. Originally conceptualized as a politically acceptable alternative to foreign charity, by the outbreak of the Pacific War the Chinese diaspora had instead become China's most effective conduit for attracting foreign charity.

## CHINESE DIASPORIC NETWORKS AND THE "ADOPTION OF WARPHANS BY FOREIGN NATIONALS"

The adoption plan for international child sponsorship proved to be one of the most effective tools deployed by Chinese diasporic organizations to attract global humanitarian interest in the child victims of China's war with Japan. The adoption plan was first popularized as a humanitarian fundraising strategy in China by the National Association for Refugee Children, the largest child welfare organization in World War II–era China. Founded on March 10, 1938, the NARC funded a total of sixty-one orphanage-schools that provided food, shelter, and education to more than thirty thousand children during the course of the war.[83] While the NARC was a united front organization that included Nationalists, Communists, and those affiliated with neither party among its leadership, it was deeply enmeshed within a network of Nationalist-led women's relief organizations headquartered in the wartime capital of Chongqing.[84] Soong Mei-ling (more popularly known as Madame Chiang Kai-shek, the first lady of Nationalist China) served as the organization's president. The Wellesley-educated daughter of a prominent Chinese Methodist family, Madame Chiang was among the most famous women in the world, and she used her work with war orphans to cultivate her own global cult of personality as well as to bolster the international reputation of the Nationalist Party.

Despite its semiofficial status, the NARC relied primarily on private donations from overseas to shelter, clothe, feed, and educate the tens of thousands of children under its care. While the Nationalist government was sincerely committed to wartime relief work, it had limited resources with which to fund the ambitious relief programs of organizations like the NARC. The Nationalists' wartime retreat from eastern China into the interior had cut off many crucial sources of state income, including duties collected by the Chinese Maritime Customs Service. Between 1937 and 1939, annual government revenues fell by 63 percent while expenditures increased by 33 percent.[85] As a result, from its founding in March 1938 through June 1943, the NARC received only approximately 26.3 percent of its funding from government sources, primarily via the newly created National Relief Commission, the highest government body coordinating

## 54 CHINA AND THE BIRTH OF GLOBAL HUMANITARIANISM

and funding wartime relief work. The rest of the NARC's funding—approximately 73.7 percent—came from private donations.[86] Especially during the early years of the war, the NARC attracted a meaningful number of donations from within China through its own domestic child sponsorship program.[87] As of 1939 at least 3,240 people in China were sponsoring one or more children at the rate of 60 yuan per year.[88] Nevertheless, donations from abroad constituted the NARC's single largest revenue source. As Zhang Aizhen, head of the NARC secretariat, wrote in 1944, "flipping through the donation books, about seven or eight out of ten are sent from abroad (including overseas Chinese)."[89] Underscoring the global scope of NARC fundraising, its records show donations in thirteen different foreign currencies.[90]

At the heart of the NARC's global fundraising efforts was a child sponsorship program it termed "the adoption of warphans by foreign nationals." The NARC's adoption plan sought to attract donors from across the world by offering them the opportunity to receive photographs, progress reports, and personal letters from the children they "adopted."[91] After the founding of the NARC, Madame Chiang Kai-shek personally promoted the adoption plan through cables and letters to prominent diasporic Chinese organizations abroad. For example, in June 1938 she cabled a message to be read out loud at the "Bowl of Rice Party" hosted in New York City's Chinatown by the United Council for Civilian Relief in China. Her message urged Americans to "vicariously adopt little Chinese children and thus acquire merit upon earth and Grace of Heaven."[92] Interestingly, it was in New Zealand where the NARC's adoption plan was implemented earliest and most enthusiastically. On June 4, 1938, the *Press* in Christchurch ran an article that described the New Zealand people's sympathy for the "many thousand Chinese children" orphaned by the war with Japan and noted that "a movement is now afoot to raise funds to 'adopt' a certain number of children by paying for their upkeep, the amount being computed at £4 a year for each child." The article acknowledged that the idea of "adopting" Chinese children had reached New Zealand through a letter that Madame Chiang Kai-shek had sent to the New Zealand Branch of the Chinese Women's Relief Association:

> There are tens of thousands of war orphans who are destitute, homeless, and uncared-for. Our women here have undertaken, as a first step, to

arrange to care for 20,000 of these little ones. I am wondering whether it would be possible for women in New Zealand and their colleagues to raise funds for this project. They might try to interest various towns and cities to 'adopt' a certain number of orphans by paying for their upkeep, and if such a plan could be carried out we shall be glad to send a group of photographs of the children "adopted."[93]

Three weeks later, on the evening of June 24, a collection of prominent New Zealand citizens gathered in Wellington to form the New Zealand Council for the Adoption of Chinese Refugee Children, tasked with "the organisation on a Dominion-wide scale of an appeal for funds to 'adopt' Chinese refugee children by providing £4 a year for their upkeep." The Honorable W. E. Barnard, speaker of the New Zealand House of Representatives, was appointed chairman, and other executive officers were selected among prominent business, philanthropic, academic, and religious leaders.[94] The council was extraordinarily successful, raising more than £13,000 through the adoption plan during the course of the war.[95]

Among New Zealand's most prominent Chinese citizens, the Chinese consul to New Zealand, Wang Feng, and his wife, Wu Aizhuang (known in New Zealand as "Madame Feng Wang"), the president of the Wellington Branch of the Chinese Women's War Relief Association, played important roles in promoting the NARC's adoption plan across New Zealand. On June 4, 1938, the *Press* published an interview with Wang Feng in which he expressed enthusiastic support for the adoption plan:

> The Association for War Refugee Children in China, which was sponsored by Madame Chiang Kai-shek, is now making a drive for funds. They estimate that it will cost 60 Chinese dollars, which is approximately £4 in New Zealand currency, to house, feed, clothe, and educate in a simple way one child for a year. . . . The people of New Zealand, with their intense love of children and their strong sense of humanity, will naturally not fail to give a response to Madame Chiang's appeal.[96]

Madame Feng Wang was appointed an ex officio member of the New Zealand Council for the Adoption of Chinese Refugee Children, and over the next two years she worked tirelessly on its behalf—promoting the adoption plan via radio broadcasts and on a speaking tour across New

Zealand.[97] In a speech delivered on August 5, 1938, Madame Feng Wang implored:

> I am sure that, with the splendid efforts of the council and with the kind support of the people of this Dominion, New Zealand will play a leading part in the accomplishment of this great humanitarian work. I am also sure that those who give towards the fund will be making a real contribution to the building up of a new generation in China, and, on the other hand, those little ones who have been "adopted" will not forget the great kindness that has been extended to them by their foster-parents in this fair Dominion.[98]

On November 22, 1939, a Wellington *Evening Post* article offered an appraisal of the impact of her efforts: "Madame Feng Wang's lectures on behalf of the 'adoption fund' aroused enthusiasm throughout New Zealand, and were responsible for raising a good part of the £9000 donated in little over a year."[99] Madame Feng Wang also worked to forge connections between the NARC and fundraising groups in New Zealand. She remitted funds on behalf of the Wellington Chinese Women's Relief Association and wrote personally to Madame Chiang Kai-shek requesting signed photographs for the committee members of the New Zealand Council.[100] She was one of many overseas Chinese leaders across the world who played a crucial role in promoting and coordinating the adoption plan.

The NARC relied on elite overseas Chinese like Madame Feng Wang to quickly build a global base of donors through the adoption plan. Between March 1938 and March 1940, the organization attracted at least 3,500 sponsors from across the United States, Europe, Southeast Asia, and Oceania. As of March 1940, New Zealand was the adoption plan's leading source of donors (1,094), followed by Indonesia (879), the United States (436), British Malaya (421), France (376), the Netherlands (100), Australia (90), and England (54).[101] In each of these locations, prominent Chinese community members took the lead in forming "cooperating organizations" to publicize and coordinate the adoption plan. The NARC sent photographs of warphans to each cooperating organization, which in turn found local adopters to sponsor the children and reported back to the NARC with the details of all new or discontinued adoptions on a quarterly basis.[102]

One such cooperating organization was the Comité de Secours aux Réfugiés et Blessés Chinois in Paris. The committee was founded by a group of some of the most prominent Chinese women in Europe, including Oei Hui-lan (the Chinese Indonesian fashion icon and wife of China's ambassador to France, Wellington Koo), Liao Tsuifeng (wife of renowned author Lin Yutang), and Chen Suk-ying (wife of the president of the Legislative Yuan, Sun Fo).[103] Much like the New Zealand Council for the Adoption of Chinese Refugee Children and the New York–based United Council for Civilian Relief in China, the Comité de Secours first implemented the adoption plan upon the personal suggestion of Madame Chiang Kai-shek. Oei Hui-lan wrote to Madame Chiang on June 8, 1938: "As regards your admirable suggestion about the adoption of orphans, I am striving to interest my friends in it and solicit their help. I am glad to be able to report to you that already three persons whom I approached have already indicated their willingness to adopt two orphans by paying for their upkeep."[104] Relying on the prestige and personal networks of its founders, the Comité de Secours quickly built the adoption plan into its primary fundraising method. Liao Tsuifeng reported in October 1938, "We were very happy to receive the 55 photographs of war orphans sent to this Committee. Half of them were taken up immediately, and we have already sent you seventeen thousand francs (17,000fr.) on this account. We are, however, only beginning to push this work ahead by circularizing an appeal to all our known friends and expect a great response."[105] By November the Comité was signing up new adopters faster than the NARC could send photos. Liao wrote again in November concerning a delayed shipment of three hundred photographs: "We shall be very happy if we can have the orphans' photographs soon as there are many people waiting anxiously to see the pictures of their adopted children. Please ask the person who is in charge of this work to send the 300 photos to this Committee at once by Air-Mail."[106]

Chinese diasporic networks also facilitated the exchange of materials and information about the adoption plan among individuals and coordinating organizations in far-flung locations across the world. For example, the president of the Chinese Women's Relief Organization of New York was Mrs. C. H. Wang, a friend and former classmate of Madame Chiang Kai-shek at Wellesley.[107] She received 360 children's photographs from the

Comité de Secours in Paris, after which her organization began using the adoption plan for its own fundraising work.[108] Wang Sheng Chih of the Oversea-Chinese Banking Corporation in Singapore learned of the adoption plan from publicity materials sent to him by his former high school classmate, C. T. Tseng, who was then working for the Hong Kong office of the Central Bank of China. Wang published the NARC's regulations for "the adoption of warphans by foreign nationals" in the Singapore-based *Malaya Tribune* and took it on himself to remit funds donated through the adoption plan to the NARC.[109] In Launceston, Tasmania, Ann Chung organized the city's only two Chinese families to create an organization called the Chinese Relief Fund to Aid Victims of Japanese Aggression, which managed to facilitate at least ten adoptions through the NARC.[110] By the outbreak of the Pacific War, Chinese diasporic communities across much of the world had created cooperating organizations to publicize and facilitate the NARC's adoption plan.

Not only were Chinese diasporic networks crucial to coordinating the adoption plan on a global scale, some overseas Chinese also sponsored children through the NARC's adoption plan. Across Southeast Asia, diasporic Chinese associations that had long contributed to charitable and political causes in China enthusiastically sponsored children. In May 1938 the Malacca Overseas Chinese Refugee Relief Committee Women's Fundraising Group resolved that its members would sponsor children through the NARC according to their means and encourage their relatives and friends to do the same.[111] In July 1939 the Kampar Chinese Merchants Association Club donated 1,200 yuan to adopt twenty warphans through the NARC and similarly vowed to solicit contributions from the overseas Chinese community.[112] Perhaps the most enthusiastic of all overseas Chinese participants in the adoption plan was Kuo-ching ("K. C.") Li, the founder of the Wah Chang Trading Corporation in New York, who was dubbed "the richest Chinese in America."[113] In 1940 Li requested that the NARC identify twenty children "who appear to be endowed with unusual possibilities" whom he would pledge to support until they reached eighteen years of age. Complying with his request, the NARC selected "twenty worthy warphans" who had "been tested and found to be comparatively higher in I.Q." as the recipients of Li's aid.[114] In addition to the standard sponsorship costs, Li donated US$1,600 annually to be held in trust on their behalf, "so that in the event things should turn out so that I cannot see them through some year, they would nevertheless be provided for."[115] Of course, few people had the resources to participate in the adoption plan on such a grand scale. Nevertheless, K. C. Li's case provides one extraordinary example of the overseas Chinese donors who sought to build personal ties with Chinese children through the NARC's adoption plan.

Overseas Chinese philanthropists also used their multicultural knowledge to package the adoption plan for a global audience by articulating its significance in the languages of humanitarianism and Christian love. For example, one report by the Hong Kong Branch of NARC suggested that there was a universal moral imperative to aid suffering children common to both Confucianism and Christianity: "Mencius has vividly described how any person, upon seeing an infant in danger of falling into a well, would instinctively become sympathetic and endeavor to do all he could to save it. . . . Jesus also said: 'Suffer little children to come unto me, for theirs is the Kingdom of Heaven.'"[116] Upon learning that some New Zealanders were hesitant to contribute to the NARC because many of the children were not exposed to Christianity, Madame Chiang Kai-shek replied by expressing her belief that "often people who are not professed Christians, and there are many such in China who have never heard of the teachings of Christ, put into practice the desire and spirit to serve mankind which characterize Christ's teachings." She added, "I wonder whether it would do any good for you to point out to the small number of people who have refused to subscribe because not all of our children are receiving Christian training, the fact that the Good Samaritan never inquired what religion, if any, the wayfarer, who fell in the hands of the robbers, professed."[117] Another New Zealand fundraising appeal circulated by Madame Feng Wang implicitly addressed such concerns by declaring the universality of humanitarian sentiment: "Nationality, politics, creed, these make no barrier to such a call for sympathy and help."[118] By skillfully crafting appeals to adopt Chinese children in terms of humanitarianism and Christian love, elite diasporic Chinese helped the NARC attract global interest in the adoption plan.

---

Perhaps it is not surprising that China became a key site in the development of global humanitarianism. After all, as Kenneth Pomeranz pointed out, "It is China, more than any other place, that has served as the 'other' for the modern West's stories about itself."[119] During the late eighteenth and nineteenth centuries, a number of prominent European thinkers wrote different versions of an ethical parable—sometimes known as the "Mandarin Paradox"—that probed one's feelings toward the death of anonymous Chinese people as a litmus test for humanitarian sentiment.[120] The famous Scottish economist and philosopher Adam Smith once posited that the death of one hundred million Chinese people in a great earthquake would not disturb a typical European as much as losing his own little finger.[121] Shortly thereafter, in his book *The Genius of Christianity* (1802), the French writer François-René de Chateaubriand asked readers: "If thou couldst by a mere wish kill a fellow-creature in China, and inherit his fortune in Europe, with the supernatural conviction that the fact would never be known wouldst thou consent to form such a wish?"[122] In the Mandarin Paradox, a "fellow-creature in China" represents someone who—due to geographical, cultural, and social distance—bears no conceivable relationship to the European subject of the parable. If Europeans could muster concern *even* for Chinese lives, the parable implies, then they must care about *all* human lives. Even before foreign gunboats descended on China in the mid-nineteenth century, Chinese people already served as a powerful symbol of humanity qua humanity.

After the Opium Wars and ensuing unequal treaties, the question of the relative value of Chinese lives was transposed from the realm of armchair theorizing into a set of material choices about whether and how to intervene in humanitarian crises in China. As if to prove Adam Smith wrong about their indifference to Chinese victims of disaster, missionaries and other humanitarians founded large-scale organizations that devoted significant resources to the alleviation of Chinese suffering in the name of humanity writ large. In the process, they helped develop the ideas and fundraising practices that would come to characterize global humanitarianism. To be sure, institutionalized efforts to relieve the suffering of distant strangers had existed for decades. Yet these were typically rooted in particularistic obligations associated with colonial rule or racial or religious affinity. In contrast, in hypo-colonial China, foreign humanitarian organizations launched transimperial fundraising campaigns that appealed to a globally dispersed base of private donors who acknowledged no specific ties to the Chinese beneficiaries of their charity besides their shared humanity. By giving to China, they signaled that, at least theoretically, they would give to suffering humanity anywhere on earth.

But unlike the earthquake victims of Adam Smith's imagination, the Chinese recipients of foreign largesse in the nineteenth and twentieth centuries were neither hypothetical nor silent. Both Nationalist officials and Communist-affiliated labor leaders critiqued the motives of international humanitarian organizations and expressed concern that overreliance on aid from abroad eroded China's sovereignty and exacerbated the exploitation of Chinese workers. Instead, China turned to its diaspora as an alternative source of disaster relief aid that could mitigate China's dependence on "foreign" help. And when the eruption of full-scale war with Japan in 1937 led the Chinese state to set aside its qualms about accepting foreign aid, Chinese diasporic communities mobilized to bring global attention to the mass-scale civilian suffering caused by the Japanese invasion. In the years after the American Red Cross report of 1929 had dulled foreign interest in Chinese causes, it was Chinese diasporic groups fundraising for Chinese relief institutions that returned China to the center of global humanitarian activity.

Yet the dispute surrounding the American Red Cross report laid bare a fundamental tension in the universal rhetoric deployed by humanitarian organizations to fundraise for Chinese causes: *global* humanitarian logic offered no compelling means by which to navigate a situation in which many humanitarian crises contended for the limited resources of organizations and donors. During the early decades of the twentieth century, a string of crises in different regions around the world—including the Armenian Genocide of 1915–1917, the Great Kantō Earthquake of 1923 in Japan, and the outbreak of the Spanish Civil War in 1936—also inspired global fundraising campaigns that competed with Chinese causes for resources and attention. Moreover, after the outbreak of World War II, would-be donors in the United States, in Europe, and across much of the world had urgent crises closer to home vying for their contributions. The problem facing relief institutions like the NARC was how to make humanitarian aid to China into a global priority within an altered humanitarian landscape in which numerous worthy and urgent causes competed for attention on the world stage. The NARC's adoption plan—which promised to forge intimate bonds between the givers and recipients of aid across national, racial, and cultural boundaries—quickly proved to be a highly effective fundraising strategy for this newly globalized humanitarian landscape. But could the NARC live up to its promise to forge meaningful adoptive relationships between foreign adults and Chinese children across geographic and linguistic divides under conditions of global war?

# 2

## GLOBAL HUMANITARIANISM'S
## INTIMATE TURN

On December 1, 1939, a woman named Gladys from the dairy farming district of Matamata, New Zealand, wrote a letter to a Chinese boy named Chi-ming, whom she referred to as her "foster son," although they had never met in person. Gladys's letter begins like this:

> It will be strange to you to receive a letter from New Zealand and you will wonder about the people who are writing to you. Perhaps you know that friends in New Zealand are trying to help China and especially its boys and girls. We are told that we can help you. Your photograph has recently been sent to us so we know what you look like. We do not know what part of China you come from or even where you are living. . . . This, our first letter to you, is to welcome you into our family.[1]

Gladys had donated £4 to "adopt" Chi-ming through the National Association for Refugee Children. As discussed in the previous chapter, the NARC was the largest child welfare organization in World War II–era China, founded by an elite group of Chinese women—including the first lady of Nationalist China, Madame Chiang Kai-shek—to provide succor to children displaced by the war. The NARC funded its child welfare work in large part through an international child sponsorship program called "the adoption of warphans by foreign nationals." Under the NARC's adoption plan, foreign "adopters" were invited to build personal relationships with their Chinese "adoptees" through the exchange of photographs, gifts, and translated letters that used familial terms of address. Gladys was one of thousands of individuals across the world, the majority of them women, who sponsored a Chinese child through the NARC.

Gladys's rather self-aware and sensitive letter makes explicit an aspect of the adoption plan that often went unspoken: the utter strangeness of a Chinese child receiving a letter from a foreigner who knew little about him and yet claimed to be his foster mother. And much as Gladys imagined, children at first often did find it befuddling—alarming, even—to receive such letters. One boy named Kuo-hwa recounted his initial confusion upon receiving his sponsor's first letter: "When I was playing most happily, a child suddenly came in from outside carrying the letter and the lovely picture you gave me. After I looked at them, at first I simply could not understand what was really going on."[2] Nevertheless, in many cases both children and their sponsors overcame this initial unfamiliarity to build meaningful adoptive relationships. By the end of her lengthy letter, Gladys had already come to feel deeply for Chi-ming. She concludes, "Now we think of you as our foster-son and send you our love as we would if you were our son indeed and hope you are well. We want you to try and forget the sadness of the past and to look forward with hope. We shall be thinking much about you, and eagerly await news of you." Likewise, Kuo-hwa's confusion upon receiving his foster mother's letter was soon replaced with sheer joy: "After listening to many friends' explanations, my mood eventually started to improve, slowly. It turns out that you have already adopted me as your foster son. This made me very delighted! My dear foster mother! I am so happy!"

Focusing on the NARC's adoption plan, this chapter explores how foreign foster parents and Chinese refugee children cultivated intimate ties across geographic and cultural boundaries under conditions of global war. I explore the practices of writing, translation, and gift exchange that facilitated meaningful communication between Chinese children and foreign adults who came from societies with radically different (and rapidly changing) notions of charity, family, and intimacy. This chapter also explores how the NARC's adoption plan became intertwined with the development of new forms of child welfare work in wartime China. In particular, the adoption plan funded efforts to study and ameliorate the emotional trauma of refugee children, creating an ironic situation in which children known to be suffering from severe psychological pain were required to do the "emotion work" of performing happiness in photographs and letters to sponsors. While the NARC's adoption plan was effective at attracting donors, facilitating the exchange of letters and gifts between Chinese children and foreign sponsors in the midst of a war was difficult and costly work. Nevertheless, the NARC tolerated the program's high overhead costs due to its political value as a kind of "intimate diplomacy" that could attract international support for China's war with Japan.

The NARC's adoption plan was at the forefront of what I call the "intimate turn" in global humanitarian practice. As it took shape in World War II–era China, global humanitarianism's intimate turn consisted of two interrelated transformations. First, the expansion of modern banking and postal systems made it possible to personalize the provision of humanitarian aid by facilitating direct relationships between its givers and recipients across vast geographic distances. Unlike most donors to far-away causes in earlier eras, Gladys from Matamata could put a name and a face to the young recipient of her £4 donation. Moreover, she could exchange letters with Chi-ming, whom she addressed as the newest member of her own family. Second, the transnational circulation of child psychology as a field of scientific knowledge transformed the intimate details of children's emotional well-being into an important subject of humanitarian concern. In his letter to his foster mother quoted earlier, Kuo-hwa focuses not on the material benefits provided by her donation (food, shelter, and education) but rather on the "delight" he derived from her letter. These two distinct aspects of global humanitarianism's intimate turn were closely intertwined. Revenue from the adoption plan funded the expansion of psychological testing on refugee children, and NARC publicity materials emphasized that foreign sponsors could contribute to the emotional healing of their adoptee by assuming the role of surrogate parents. Yet a detailed examination of the inner workings of the NARC's adoption plan reveals that the intimate turn in global humanitarianism was neither smooth nor inevitable. Rather, it was a fraught and contingent process marked by logistical problems, cultural miscommunications, and ethical dilemmas regarding fundraising practices and the best use of limited resources. These problems became so severe that the NARC was forced to discontinue its adoption plan in 1942, but during its brief existence the program helped pave the way for international adoption and child sponsorship to become highly popular humanitarian programs in post–World War II Asia.

To be sure, the NARC's adoption plan offered only a very limited form of intimacy—one exchange of translated letters per year plus the occasional exchange of photographs or gifts. Yet the mediated form of long-distance intimacy on offer through the adoption plan was part of its appeal. The intimate turn in humanitarian practice was conditioned by the long history of what Ann Stoler calls "colonial intimacy," a descriptor for the fraught transracial intimate relationships formed between colonizers and colonized. As Stoler notes, colonial officials were especially concerned that colonization might muddle racial hierarchies by leading to the birth of large numbers of mixed-race children as well as to the "cultural defection" of white children exposed to native culture.[3] For example, in French Indochina, paternity law limited the ability of the *métis* children of French men and Asian women to claim French citizenship.[4] In early twentieth-century China, American missionaries fretted about their children's closeness to their Chinese domestic servants, describing with disapprobation how their children spoke Chinese better than English, preferred Chinese to Western food, and liked to play with Chinese rather than American dolls.[5] In short, it was the prospect of eliminating racial hierarchy that made transracial intimacies so threatening.

The adoption plan flourished in part because it offered a circumscribed form of transnational intimacy that reinforced, rather than threatened, racialized hierarchies. The adoption plan created fictive transracial families without transracial sex or transracial children. Rather, by casting foreign donors as "foster parents," the adoption plan positively associated fictive kinship ties with a paternalistic humanitarianism that promised to rescue China and uplift it into the community of civilized nations. Ensuring that adoptees remained "over there" in China, the NARC's adoption plan promoted a form of global intimacy that was consistent with exclusionary immigration laws, taboos against interracial sex, and the stigmatization of mixed-race children. Yet the NARC's adoption plan also set into motion larger changes to prevailing norms of transnational and transracial intimacy. By encouraging foreign adults and Asian children to imagine themselves as part of transnational adoptive families, the adoption plan planted the seed of an idea that would come to fruition with the large-scale legal adoption of Asian children into families across the Global North in the post–World War II period.

## WRITING GLOBAL INTIMACY

The NARC's regulations governing the adoption plan specified that the NARC "shall ask all Adoptees to write to their respective Adopters once a year and these Chinese letters shall be translated and forwarded to the Adopters respectively."[6] These annual letters were at the core of the adoption plan. The NARC's international fundraising efforts—its ability to provide food, shelter, and education for the children under its care—depended in part on the success of children's letters in eliciting and sustaining the interest of donors. But who were the children who corresponded with foreign sponsors through the NARC's adoption plan? And how did they approach the task of composing these all-important letters?

In English-language publicity materials, the NARC referred to the children under its care as "warphans," a snappy shortening of the term "war orphans" that was meant to invoke an image of children utterly alone in the world, presumably because their parents had perished in the war.[7] The orphanage-schools in which the NARC housed these children were likewise referred to as "warphanages." In some international publicity materials, the NARC directly claimed that "all of the children" in its warphanages were "orphans."[8] As internal NARC records make clear, however, the majority of "warphans" were not literally orphans. According to records from an NARC warphanage in Chengdu in 1939, only 12 percent of the children in the warphanage had lost both of their parents, while 71 percent had two living parents. In the majority of cases the NARC admitted children not because they were orphans, but rather because their living relatives were too poor to feed them or unable to flee from advancing Japanese troops. Yet due to the enormous death toll of the war, many children who entered NARC warphanages with living parents eventually left as orphans. When the NARC concluded its work in 1946, about 40 percent of the remaining children had no living adult relatives to whom to return.[9] Despite the fact that the majority of children in NARC warphanages had at least one living parent, the NARC depicted them as unattached orphans to heighten the

*Remnants of Japanese destruction*
*—left alone in the world—*

**FIGURE 2.1** NARC publicity materials often conveyed the impression that all children under the organization's care were orphans entirely alone in the world. May-ling Soong Chiang, *A Letter from Madame Chiang Kai-shek to Boys and Girls Across the Ocean* (Chungking: China Information Pub. Co., 1940), 13.

sense that foreign sponsors were taking on the role of surrogate parents by "adopting" them.

NARC warphans hailed from all parts of China—from the southern province of Guangdong to Hubei in central China to the far northeastern province of Jilin. As a matter of policy, the NARC accepted children ranging from eighteen months to fifteen years of age. In practice, most children who made it into NARC warphanages were over nine years old. According to a survey conducted at NARC warphanages in 1940, 80 percent of the children were between the ages of nine and fourteen. NARC statistics also show that about 70 percent of the children who entered its warphanages over the course of the war were boys.[10] Guo Xiuyi, one of the NARC founders, explained that under conditions of wartime scarcity, desperate parents were more likely to leave a daughter behind in order to help a son reach safety in the interior. As Guo put it, "This is because for thousands of years our traditional patriarchal society's custom of valuing men more than women has still been preserved."[11] Among the millions of displaced children in wartime China, those who made it into NARC warphanages counted among the lucky ones—and they were much more likely to be boys.

The ways that these children comprehended and carried out the unfamiliar task of writing letters to foreign strangers who addressed them in familial terms was shaped by recent transformations of Chinese epistolary culture. By the time the NARC implemented its adoption plan in 1938, children's letters had already become a well-established genre of writing within educated Chinese families. As Danni Cai has shown, for the increasing number of children studying away from home in new-style schools during the early twentieth century, writing letters to family members and teachers was an important part of daily life. As a result, letter-writing manuals for students proliferated during this period, many of which achieved great commercial success and underwent dozens of printings.[12] Early twentieth-century letter-writing manuals inculcated schoolchildren with the idea that letter writing was an important medium through which to demonstrate love and filial piety for parents and family members during times of physical separation. In terms of content, the model "letters home" (*jia shu*) contained in these manuals typically consisted of straightforward academic progress updates. The purpose of such letters, however, was not simply to communicate information but also "to show familial love and concern for one's family members and relatives"— what was often described in letter manuals as "the sentiment of familial admiration" (*ru mu zhi qing*).[13] Nevertheless, familial intimacy was not communicated through direct emotional expression. Rather, children demonstrated sincere sentiment through the time and effort required to learn and follow formal epistolary conventions.

In some regards, the letters that children wrote to their foreign foster parents through the NARC's adoption plan resemble the model "letters home" contained in the letter-writing manuals for children popular at the time. For example, the vernacular version of a model letter to one's parents in the *New Letter Writing Manual for Students* reads:

> The conditions at school are not very different from last year, only the name of our "national literature" (*guo wen*) class has been changed to "national language" (*guo yu*). I study very hard for national language. After my classwork is finished, I play all sorts of beneficial games, like soccer, boxing, and "hop the iron bar," all of which can help develop the body and invigorate the spirit. After I started practicing, my body has felt well, and I am eating more than before. These are all benefits of exercise.[14]

Compare that to the letter a girl named Chia-chin wrote to her foster mother Helen in New Zealand in May 1941: "Now I will tell you about the situation at the orphanage. Every day we have four classes, three classes in the morning and one in the afternoon. There are three meals per day. We eat rice for two meals and porridge for the other. Our lives are very good. On Sundays we can go out and play. Now the orphanage is also giving us cotton-padded clothes. I am currently in second grade. My grades are very good."[15]

Often written as life updates that focused on their academic curriculum and the material conditions of their daily lives, the letters that children sent their foster parents through the adoption plan were in these respects not so different from the letters written by countless other Chinese students to their families back home. Despite these similarities, the letters children wrote for the adoption plan were sometimes characterized by an emotional exuberance that is decidedly absent from the model letters contained in instructional manuals. For example, a boy named Hew-wei wrote to his foster mother Bethea, "I was so happy when I received your picture and letter. I held your photograph in my two hands and stared at your happy face, and I could not stop myself from pressing it to my face over and over. Although we are separated by rivers and mountains, at that moment it was as if I had fallen into your embrace!"[16]

How did children in NARC warphanages learn to write in such a highly sentimental style? It is possible that the NARC explicitly instructed children to write with such unrestrained emotion to please their foreign sponsors, but I have not come across any instructions to this effect in the archives. The NARC's instructions regarding children's letters that are available in the archives are brief and matter-of-fact. For example, after receiving Bethea's letter to Hew-wei, the NARC office translated it into Chinese and forwarded it to the superintendent of the Guizhou Branch No. 4 Warphanage, where Hew-wei resided, along with the following directions: "Instruct [Hew-wei] to write a letter expressing gratitude as well as reporting on his personal experiences and the conditions of his life in the orphanage. Send it back to this office (ensuring that it is written neatly) so that it can be translated and forwarded."[17] In internal communications, however, the NARC often stressed the importance of creating sentimental bonds between children and their sponsors through correspondence. In one instance, the NARC headquarters wrote to the Sichuan Branch No. 5 Warphanage requesting that a child named I-cha write a letter to his foster mother in order to "strengthen the emotional connection between the two sides."[18] Perhaps most significantly, the cosmopolitan women who operated the NARC and its affiliated warphanages—many of whom had spent significant time abroad—would have been familiar with Western notions of familial intimacy and the types of "loving" letters most likely to please their foreign foster parents.

In letters to their Chinese adoptees, sponsors can also be seen groping for an appropriate language through which to express love and familial intimacy to children in a different cultural context about which they knew little. In some cases foster parents explicitly acknowledged their uncertainty about what to write. One woman from Auckland, New Zealand, began by admitting her ignorance of Chinese epistolary customs: "Please forgive me if I have not begun my letter to you in the way to which you are accustomed—the peoples of different countries do many things differently, but can be very good friends in spite of that!"[19] A woman named Joan from Paeroa, New Zealand, frankly acknowledged that so much time had passed between letters that she was unsure what to write: "I was very pleased to receive your letter with its translation this week. It took a long while to reach N.Z. but I am sure we are very lucky to receive letters at present. It is such a long time ago since I first wrote to you that I am not quite sure what to write about."[20] How then did sponsors write letters to foster the sense of a meaningful adoptive relationship with children about whom they knew little, and who knew little about them?

FIGURE 2.2 A child receiving a letter from and writing one to his American sponsor. *Asia Calling* 1, no. 5 (1947): 3.

While sponsors' letters vary in both tone and content, distinct patterns nevertheless emerge, suggesting a loosely coherent set of writing practices characteristic of global intimacy. One of the most common strategies that foster parents used to create a sense of familial intimacy with their adopted Chinese children was writing in extraordinary detail about their families and hometowns—almost as if offering a correspondence course in all the information a child in their family *would* know. While children's letters were typically one or two pages in length, sponsors' letters often stretched on for five, six, or even seven handwritten pages. After confessing that she was "not quite sure what to write about," Joan went on to write at length about everything from the history of New Zealand ("exactly 100 years ago N.Z. became part of the British Empire") to indigenous culinary tastes ("the Maoris eat humaras [sweet potato] and they are very fond of fish") to native bird species ("the most famous of N.Z.

birds is perhaps the <u>Kiwi</u>").[21] A woman named Alice described her seven children (six daughters and one adult son) in considerable detail before adding, "I am so glad that my adopted child is a boy—because I always wanted another boy."[22] Her description of their idyllic family life in New Zealand appears to have struck a chord with her foster son, who, after all, had been separated from his own family amid the horrors of war. He replied: "After I read your letter, I felt so many interesting things, like having such an admirable brother and six dear little sisters living in one family, playing together every day with all those lively animals in the pasture. I wish I could grow wings and fly over to also enjoy such amazing good fortune."[23] In another poignant example, a woman named Dorothy from Wanganui, New Zealand, wrote to her adopted son Chia Cheng, "I have no little boy or girl of my own, but have often wished I had, so I am getting the next best thing by adopting some."[24] For both sponsors and their adopted children, reading and writing about home and family helped make their adoptive relationship meaningful despite cultural, linguistic, and geographic barriers.

## FOUND IN TRANSLATION

The NARC relied on the necessity of translation as a means to smooth over discrepancies in how Chinese children and their foster parents expressed familial intimacy. By carefully comparing original letters with the translations prepared by the NARC staff in Chongqing, it is possible to reverse engineer the logic of the translational practices undergirding the adoption plan. For the NARC, translation was not an impediment to intimate communication but rather a technology of translingual intimacy through which their cosmopolitan staff members provided not only linguistic but also cultural mediation for children and their sponsors.

Many small discrepancies between the original and translated versions of letters were likely innocent translation errors on the part of NARC staff who were proficient but nonnative English speakers. However, most significant translation discrepancies appear to be deliberate attempts to remove or alter statements that would seem inappropriate outside of their original cultural and linguistic context. For instance, in his February 1941 letter Hsio-djen wrote, "In the morning we have four hours of classes, and in the afternoon we have four hours of sewing. I only regret that I am slow-witted by nature and that my progress in both my studies and work lags far behind." While such comments could perhaps be construed as appropriately humble in a Chinese context, in English they are at best awkward and at worst might cause his foster parents to wonder why their funds were being used on a child with so little natural aptitude. As a result, the offending sentence is simply omitted from the corresponding section of the English-language translation: "We have classes all morning and we learn sewing in the afternoon. I hope you will pray for our progress."[25] The letters that foreign sponsors wrote to their Chinese adoptees were similarly massaged in translation. For instance, in her first letter to her adopted child, a woman named Leska from Sherman, Texas, concluded with the line, "I like your picture <u>very</u> much—I keep it on my desk because I <u>love</u> you." In an American context, this statement can be read as warmly reassuring a war orphan that there is someone in the world who cares about him. However, the translator may have feared that such a bold declaration of love (the word "love" is thickly underlined in the original letter) from a foreign stranger in her first communication might make the child uncomfortable. Instead, the translator softened the sentiment by subtly altering it to read, "I like you and your picture, so I put your picture on top of my writing desk."[26] On one level, the necessity of translation limited the extent of intimacy possible through the adoption plan. After all, children and their sponsors could not communicate with each other in their own words. On another level, however, the NARC's translational practices made the letters they exchanged both linguistically comprehensible *and* culturally legible. In their roles as translators, NARC staff performed necessary work for facilitating the adoption plan across conflicting regimes of family and intimacy.

## THE INTIMACY OF OBJECTS

While the adoption plan sought to build sentimental ties between Chinese warphans and their foreign adopters, its success depended on the transnational exchange of physical objects—letters, photographs, and gifts—in a time of war. In the absence of physical contact between sponsors and their adoptees, these objects could take on immense significance as the only physical traces of a correspondent across the ocean. The adoptive relationship was officially initiated when sponsors received a photograph of their adoptee, and for many sponsors simply possessing a child's photograph was enough to foster a sense of personal connection. After receiving the photograph of her adoptee, Dung Ngao, a woman named Lillias wrote to the NARC, "I like the look of him very much indeed and very likely if I saw all your little boys and girls he would be the one I would choose to have for my little boy."[27] Sponsors often treasured such photographs and displayed them prominently within their homes and communities. A woman named Maria from Tauranga, New Zealand, wrote to her foster son Ren, "Your photograph looks so nice in a little round silver frame, on my bedroom changing piece."[28] Others exhibited their photographs in public. A woman from New Zealand named Esther wrote, "We, in Niho-tupu, are so glad to have your photograph—we are going to put it in a frame and keep it in our church and every day we will be asking the dear Lord Jesus to have you safe in his keeping."[29]

In addition to photographs, the letters that sponsors received from their adoptees were significant not only for their written content but also as physical objects produced by the children themselves. When children wrote letters to their foster parents, the NARC would send sponsors both the handwritten Chinese original as well as a typewritten translation. Although most sponsors could not read the handwritten Chinese original letters sent along with the translations, they attached profound significance to them as material testaments to their relationships with their Chinese adoptees. Bethea from North Otago, New Zealand, wrote to her adoptee Hew-wei, "You have made me so happy and satisfied, having your photo, and now a letter written by your own hand. I am feeling rich indeed."[30] Upon receiving another letter from him a year later, she was so moved that she physically embraced the letter as a totem of the child she would never hold in person: "I am ever so glad to get your dear loving letter. I just held it close to me in sheer delight." Bethea kept Hew-wei's photograph with her when she knelt for her twice-daily prayers, and the physical presence of his photograph enabled her to sense his spiritual presence. She wrote, "Every morning and night when I kneel down to pray you are there and oh so near."[31]

Some foster parents went beyond the exchange of photographs and letters that was standard in the adoption plan by sending handmade gifts to their adopted children. In a letter to her adoptee, Gladys described her four-year-old daughter Sally's penchant for arts and crafts: "We gave her a small pair of blunt-end scissors and she cuts out amazingly well for a small child. Here is a tiny shoe she has cut out!" She included both the paper cutout shoe as well as a photograph of Sally with the letter.[32] Other foster parents made clothes for their adopted children. On March 2, 1940, Dorothy wrote to her foster daughter, Tao-chuan, to tell her that she was making her a dress and asked, "Would you let me know whether the dress fits + whether it is the right length?"[33] On June 30 Tao-chuan replied, "I feel so grateful that Auntie made clothes for me. It made me feel an indescribable joy. Although I have not received it yet, I am sure that it will suit me."[34] On one hand, Tao-chuan's letter poignantly expressed her gratitude for her sponsor's personal efforts on her behalf. On the other hand, the fact that Tao-chuan had not yet received the dress nearly four months later suggests how the difficulties of wartime international transport constrained the possibilities for material exchange through the adoption plan.

In fact, some of the gifts that sponsors sent their adoptees never arrived at all. The prolonged saga that ensued when Bethea attempted to send Hew-wei a scrapbook provides an illustrative example. On May 24, 1940, Bethea sent the NARC a scrapbook with instructions to forward it to him.[35] On July 1, 1940, she wrote to Hew-wei himself to inform him that she had sent a parcel so that he might look out for it.[36] She received no reply until May 8, 1941, when the NARC wrote to Bethea to tell her that the package "never arrived and so we presume it has met with misfortune en route—perhaps by bombing either in your country or ours."[37] By this time, however, the package had already been returned to Bethea in New Zealand, "the reason given being the closing of the Burma Road." Finally, on May 21, 1941, almost one year after she first mailed the scrapbook, Bethea posted it once again, writing to Hew-wei: "I sincerely hope it reaches you this time. . . . I'll be thinking of you, and trying to imagine I see you getting the parcel."[38] Here the archival records of Bethea and Hew-wei's relationship trail off, and it is unclear whether he ever received the scrapbook. To avoid such costly and demoralizing affairs, the NARC began discouraging sponsors from sending packages, asking them instead to send extra money that could be used to buy gifts for children locally. As the NARC put it bluntly to one sponsor, "Packages, however, are very difficult to get through these days of war. Money, therefore, would be much better."[39]

## MISSING CHILDREN AND WHITE LIES

Even when postal services functioned relatively smoothly, there were typically monthslong gaps between when a letter was written, translated, and read. And in the chaos of wartime China, a lot could happen in a few months. The rapidly shifting lines of Japanese occupation and the omnipresent threat of air raids in the interior made keeping track of children who were part of a highly mobile refugee population spread out across dozens of warphanages a difficult and sometimes impossible task. The persistent logistical problems of coordinating the adoption plan on the ground in wartime China can be gleaned by returning to the story of Gladys from Matamata, whose December 1939 letter to her adoptee, Chi-ming, is quoted at the beginning of this chapter. As it turns out, Chi-ming never received her letter. On April 13, 1940, the NARC sent the following message to Gladys:

> Your lovely letter written to Chi-ming has been safely received (also illustrated paper) and translated into Chinese. However, Chi-ming, you will be glad to know, has already been able to be reunited with his family. We are always glad when members of a family succeed in finding each other and are able to live together. Consequently, we are holding your letter and if you and your husband are willing, we shall substitute for Chi-ming, little Chen-shih now thirteen years of age.[40]

The NARC's letter, however, was not true. Gladys's letter had in fact been received by the NARC headquarters in Chongqing, translated into Chinese, and forwarded to the Sichuan Branch No. 6 Warphanage where Chi-ming resided. But on March 14, 1940, the warphanage superintendent wrote to NARC headquarters with the following reply: "As that child fled the orphanage on October 13, 1939, and we remain unaware of his whereabouts, we are unable to deliver the translated letter and photograph to him. Therefore, we are returning the original documents to your office along with this letter."[41] Rather than deliver the uncomfortable truth that Chi-ming had run away from the warphanage, the NARC instead chose to tell Gladys that he had been reunited with his family. If their goal in telling such a falsehood was to ensure they would not lose Gladys as a sponsor, the gambit worked. On June 30, 1940, she wrote back to the NARC: "My husband and I were so glad to get your letter of April 13th and are very happy to know that Chi-ming has found his family—that is indeed wonderful news. . . . Yes, we shall be only too glad to 'adopt' little Chen-shih in Chi-ming's place."[42]

The quick turnover rates at NARC warphanages, in combination with the unreliability of wartime communications, made it extraordinarily difficult to build and sustain transnational intimate relationships through the NARC's adoption plan. Runaway children were an especially severe problem. In 1940 Du Junhui, one of the founders of the NARC, acknowledged that more than a hundred children had run away from NARC warphanages within the past six months.[43] The NARC archives document numerous similar cases in which sponsors were asked to accept a different child because their original adoptee had left the orphanage. Whenever a child left under tragic or embarrassing circumstances, the NARC simply invented a happy ending rather than risk losing the confidence (and annual contributions) of their overseas donors.[44] Nevertheless, the NARC persisted in its efforts to make the adoption plan work for its sponsors. On May 27, 1941, almost eighteen months after she had first written to Chi-ming, the NARC forwarded Gladys a letter from her new adoptee, Chen-shih.[45] While the NARC appears to have always asked for sponsors' permission before substituting children, the practice itself implied that Chinese children were interchangeable as objects of their foster parents' affection. A stark symbol of this interchangeability can be found on the Chinese translation of the letter sent by Alice to Kwang Foo, who it turned out had also already left his warphanage. The name "Kwang Foo" has simply been crossed out at the beginning of the letter, and the name of the substituted child, "Hsio-djen," squeezed into the margin beside it.[46]

## THE ADOPTION PLAN, *QIAOPI*, AND THE LIMITS OF GLOBAL INTIMACY

It may be tempting to see the geographic distance between foreign sponsors and Chinese adoptees, their reliance on translated letters and unreliable postal services, and the transparently monetary nature of their relationships as ways that the adoption plan failed to emulate genuine familial intimacy. In certain regards, however, the relationships between foreign sponsors and their Chinese adoptees bore striking similarities to how overseas Chinese migrants maintained ties with their children back in China. Many Chinese men who ventured abroad in search of work had to endure years or decades of continuous physical separation from wives and children who remained in China.[47] In the absence of physical contact, Chinese migrants preserved bonds with their families in China by sending them *qiaopi*—letters sent together with monetary remittances.[48] Through the frequent exchange of *qiaopi*, overseas fathers provided for their children's food, clothing, and education; stayed informed about their growth and maturation; and dispensed parental advice and guidance.[49] In addition to regular remittances, transnational Chinese families also used *qiaopi* to exchange gifts and photographs. According to Gregor Benton and Hong Liu, *qiaopi* assumed an enormous emotional significance for migrant families. As they put it, "The arrival of a *qiaopi* in the village was the equivalent for most recipients of a visit from a loved one, a form of intense psychological consolation."[50]

A *qiaopi* sent by Tan Yici in the Philippines to his family back in China in September 1939 illustrates how the exchange of letters, money, gifts, and photographs helped sustain affective bonds within transnational Chinese families. On September 19 Tan sent a *qiaopi* addressed to his wife, Peihua, along with a remittance of 100 yuan for regular family expenses. Tan also folded a Philippine two-peso note inside the letter and instructed his wife: "This is to be used only to buy candies, cakes, and snacks for our two little sons, Yehua and Kunhua, and should not be used for anything else." Tan also noted, "The two photographs of our two little sons that you sent last month along with the letters from you and Big Aunt have all been well-received. Please don't worry."[51] For Tan, sending letters, gifts, and money were ways to fulfill his familial duties while living abroad—and receiving photographs of his children enabled him to feel close to them and observe their growth, even though he could not be with them in person.

While the fictive kinship ties forged through the adoption plan were mediated by the teachers and staff who helped write and translate letters, most Chinese migrant families also required the assistance of third-party intermediaries to communicate in writing. Many overseas Chinese laborers were illiterate or semiliterate, and they often hired professional scribes to help compose their letters. Just as the difficulties of translation could inhibit precise communication between sponsors and adoptees, the scribes hired by migrants sometimes had to resort to guesswork when rendering names and places in unfamiliar local dialects into Chinese characters. And since the women and children who received *qiaopi* were also unlikely to be fully literate, couriers and postmen were often enlisted to read letters out loud and assist in preparing a response.[52] Heavily mediated epistolary communication and financial sponsorship were also the primary means through which "real" Chinese transnational families maintained close ties during long periods of physical separation.

Of course, the emotional and financial investment of migrant fathers in their children back in China far exceeded anything that was expected of "foster parents" in child sponsorship programs. Moreover, unlike foreign sponsors, transnational Chinese families held out hope that they would be reunited when circumstances permitted. Yet in terms of their material form, the relationships between sponsors and Chinese children in the adoption plan were not so different from those between overseas fathers and their children in China. They provided for children financially while sending letters and occasional gifts—and they eagerly waited to receive letters and photographs in return. By reading the letters sent through the adoption plan alongside the *qiaopi* exchanged within migrant families, we can glean the possibilities and limits of global intimacy in an era when the expansion of modern postal and banking services made it possible to maintain dense economic and emotional ties across national boundaries.

## "A SHOCK MUCH TOO GREAT FOR THEIR IMMATURE MINDS TO COMPREHEND"

The NARC's effort to build fictive kinship ties between the givers and receivers of aid was not the only novel aspect of its wartime humanitarian work. While earlier humanitarian programs sought to nourish children's bodies, save their souls, and educate their minds, during World War II humanitarian organizations like the NARC expanded their mission to include promoting children's mental health. On the one hand, the NARC used money raised through the adoption plan to fund programs to measure and mitigate the psychological toll of the war on children. On the other hand, the organization also advertised its sponsorship program in part by stressing its emotional benefits for children. Taken together, the NARC's adoption plan and its commitment to addressing children's emotional trauma transformed the intimate details of children's emotional lives into an issue of global humanitarian concern.

The NARC's focus on the emotional needs of children was shaped by the global circulation of child psychology as a field of scientific inquiry during the first half of the twentieth century. Among the key figures in bringing experimental child psychology to China was Xiao Xiaorong. Xiao had studied in both Germany and the United States, receiving his MA degree in psychology from Columbia University in 1926 and his PhD degree from the University of California, Berkeley, in 1930 before returning to China to serve as chair of the Psychology Department at National Central University in Nanjing.[53] Xiao was particularly interested in the concept of "mental hygiene."[54] First promoted by psychiatrists and mental health advocates in the United States in the early twentieth century, the goal of mental hygiene (translated into Chinese as *xinli weisheng*) was to prevent the emergence of mental illness primarily through education and early intervention in the case of children who exhibited "abnormal" tendencies. Xiao's research on mental hygiene would prove crucial to making Chinese children's emotional well-being a focus of humanitarian attention during World War II.

After returning to China, Xiao Xiaorong set out to develop a Chinese adaptation of the Woodworth Personal Data Sheet (the world's "first personality test") that could be used to measure the emotional stability of Chinese children. During World War I, the U.S. National Research Council created a Committee on Emotional Fitness for Warfare, chaired by Columbia University psychologist Robert Woodworth, which was tasked with developing a standardized test to evaluate the emotional stability of military recruits.[55] After the war, Ellen Mathews of Los Angeles City Schools adapted Woodworth's survey for the purpose of measuring the emotional stability of children.[56] It was this "Woodworth-Mathews Personal Data Sheet" that Xiao took as the basis for his effort to develop a test of emotional stability suitable for Chinese children. After several rounds of experimentation, in 1941 Xiao published the final version of his Chinese adaptation of the Woodworth-Mathews exam, a survey consisting of fifty-six yes-or-no questions that could be completed within thirty minutes.[57] Each question had a "normal" and "abnormal" response. Questions included: "Do you make friends easily?" (Normal answer: yes); "Are you afraid of the dark?" (Normal answer: no); and "In addition to the world you see, is there another world within your innermost being?" (Normal answer: no). One point was awarded for each "normal" answer. The higher a child's score, the higher their "emotional stability" was rated.[58] Touting its apparent 92 percent accuracy in predicting whether children displayed abnormal tendencies, Xiao promoted his version of the Woodworth-Mathews survey as an accurate, efficient means of identifying children with emotional problems.[59]

China's war with Japan brought unprecedented attention to children's mental health and imbued Xiao's research with added significance and urgency. As children's emotional well-being emerged as an important wartime issue, it was one of Xiao's protégés, Ding Zan, who successfully deployed Xiao's personal data sheet as part of an attempt to redirect international humanitarian funds to the goal of improving the emotional stability of China's children. Ding had studied mental hygiene at National Central University before training under acclaimed American psychiatrist Richard S. Lyman at Peking Union Medical College. In May 1942 he was selected as the director of the newly founded National Institute of Health Mental Hygiene Laboratory—the first government institution in China devoted to issues of mental health.[60] Ding believed that the immense emotional harm that war was inflicting on China's children threatened to impede the development of Chinese society.[61] As a result, under Ding's leadership the Mental Hygiene Laboratory's clinical work focused almost exclusively on children and youth.[62] Surveying the landscape of child welfare work in wartime Chongqing, Ding thought that more focus should be placed on children's psychological trauma. While praising the outpouring of international aid for Chinese refugee children, he argued that groups like the NARC should also make children's emotional well-being central to humanitarian work. Ding wrote, "With respect to the psychological condition of these refugee children, almost all of them have suffered the effects of intense emotional blows and abnormal social change, which can easily damage their psychological health and balance." "Therefore," he concluded, "when we now talk about the issue of welfare for our country's refugee children, we cannot overlook the work of examining, treating, and protecting their mental hygiene."[63] But how to convince perpetually cash-strapped organizations like the NARC to devote precious resources to children's emotional health?

In the spring of 1943 Ding's Mental Hygiene Laboratory undertook a large-scale investigation of the emotional stability of children in NARC warphanages with the explicit goal of inspiring the NARC to "place importance on mental hygiene work." In the first phase of the study, Xiao Xiaorong's revised personal data sheet was administered to ninety-nine children at the No. 1 Warphanage and NARC Sanatorium in Chongqing. Perhaps unsurprisingly, the results of the survey revealed that NARC children suffered from severe emotional problems. In Xiao's earlier studies, the median emotional stability score for Chinese children was usually about 40, and any child whose score was more than one standard deviation below the median (typically around 33) was considered very likely to be emotionally unstable. The Mental Hygiene Laboratory found that the median score for NARC children was about 30. In other words, they found that a significant majority of NARC children were emotionally unstable—many of them severely so. The Mental Hygiene Laboratory's report concluded, "The pain in their hearts is much greater than ordinary children, and therefore it is easy for their emotions to become unstable." Based on its findings, the Mental Hygiene Laboratory made several suggestions to the NARC regarding the emotional well-being of the children under its care. Its recommendations included conducting long-term observation and providing "mental hygiene guidance" to children, offering mental hygiene training to warphanage staff, and fostering friendly relationships among the children.[64]

In essence, the Mental Hygiene Laboratory transformed the commonsense observation that many children who had been separated from their families in a horrific war experienced emotional problems into a statistical fact—ascertained through scientific experiments designed by the credentialed experts of a central government institution. Moreover, these experts framed the war's quantifiable emotional toll on Chinese children as a crucial problem threatening China's ability to survive a protracted war with Japan and emerge as a modern nation-state. In doing so, the government-affiliated child psychologists of the Mental Hygiene Laboratory sought to promote the redistribution of international humanitarian resources toward the project of measuring and transforming the "emotional life" (*qingxu shenghuo*) of Chinese children.

In fact, the NARC had already begun emphasizing the emotional health of children even before the Mental Hygiene Laboratory's report. In 1942 the NARC began conducting in-depth interviews with newly admitted children and compiling detailed records about their psychological development. Between October 1942 and January 1944 it put together case files on the psychological condition of 2,277 children to be used as reference for their education and guidance.[65] Nevertheless, the Mental Hygiene Laboratory's report persuaded the NARC to devote even greater resources to mental health issues. Shortly after the report was released, the NARC approved a ten-million-yuan budget for a project to conduct mental health investigations into the children at ten warphanages in Sichuan. The budget included funding to hire Xiao Xiaorong himself to train ten staff members in psychological theory as well as the practice of conducting psychological tests on children.[66] To put that figure in context, ten million yuan was approximately 6 percent of the NARC's total budget for 1944—and considerably more than its annual distribution to each individual warphanage.[67]

The No. 3 Warphanage in Chongqing, under the leadership of Superintendent Zhao Juntao, provides an illustrative example of the NARC's increasing focus on children's emotional stability during the later years of the war. Noting that the horrors of war had caused serious harm to the children's "fragile psyches," Zhao instructed orphanage staff to pay close attention to their "emotional lives, attitudes toward their studies, and social behavior." All teachers at the No. 3 Warphanage were encouraged to study a list of books on children's mental health that included titles such as *Child Psychology*, *Educational Psychology*, and *Mental Hygiene of Mischievous Children* (*Wanlie ertong xinli weisheng*). Following the recommendations of the Mental Hygiene Laboratory, Zhao also compiled detailed case studies describing the diagnosis and treatment of children deemed emotionally unwell.[68] While this focus on children's mental health may seem uncontroversial, it is important to remember that NARC warphanages were perpetually underfunded and understaffed. Kuo-chih Lee, who later became an important scholar of modern Chinese history in Taiwan, lived at the No. 1 Warphanage in Chongqing during World War II. He remembered the warphanage's poor sanitary conditions, insufficient food, lack of medical supplies, and lax management. NARC staff were stretched so thin, Lee recalled, that when his parents came to collect him, staff members could not figure out to which warphanage he had been assigned.[69] Moreover, NARC warphanages were able to admit only a small fraction of children displaced by the war. All financial and human resources devoted to tracking the emotional life of warphanage children were resources not used on other urgently needed tasks—including feeding, housing, and clothing additional children.

Chinese child psychologists' and social welfare workers' concern with the emotional toll of war on children was part of a broader global pattern. As Tara Zahra shows in her study of post–World War II Europe, new theories of child psychology emphasizing the long-term consequences of childhood emotional trauma inspired "a gradual shift from material to psychological forms of relief among international organizations." Based on their wartime observations, psychoanalysts Anna Freud and Dorothy Burlingham concluded that the long-term psychological consequences of family separation were even more devastating to children than direct experiences of war. As a result, European and American child welfare workers grew increasingly skeptical of any child welfare scheme that separated children from their parents.[70] These ideas were popularized by bestselling books like Benjamin Spock's *The Common Sense Book of Baby and Child Care*, which emphasized the importance of a loving family environment for children's healthy emotional development. Since children were viewed as the future of the nation, ensuring that they grew up in nurturing family homes was considered essential to the construction of healthy, democratic societies in the aftermath of the war.[71]

However, there were key differences between how Chinese and Western psychologists conceptualized the "psychological best interests" of the child. While Chinese psychologists agreed with their Euro-American counterparts that the fate of nations depended on children's healthy emotional development, some were less convinced that the family home was the best environment for promoting children's mental health. Ding Zan was well-versed in the emerging consensus in Euro-American psychology that the inability of institutionalized life to "satisfy children's emotional needs" could have a negative influence on their moral and intellectual development. And yet, based on his own experience practicing psychology in China, he believed that growing up in a Chinese family was *itself* a frequent cause of emotional problems. Ding wrote, "With regard to its psychological aspects, so-called family life is not as healthy as would be ideal. Many mentally ill parents unknowingly induce psychological problems in their children."[72] Ding's comments reflected the widely held view among Chinese intellectuals at the time that the traditional family was "the root of all evil" (*wan'e zhi yuan*) in Chinese society. Since the early twentieth century, Chinese reformers and revolutionaries had argued that the Chinese family was a hotbed of outmoded cultural values in which the desires of children were suppressed by conservative elders unschooled in the needs of a modern society.[73] Against this backdrop, it is unsurprising that Chinese psychologists were more pessimistic than their Western counterparts about the benefits of family life for children's emotional development. At the same time, they were generally more optimistic than Western psychologists about the benefits of collective living in child welfare institutions. Ding Zan argued that as long as they "emphasized the principles and methods of mental hygiene," collective living arrangements like NARC warphanages could actually help facilitate displaced children's psychological adaptation to society.[74] But how to ensure that children's emotional needs were met within the warphanage?

The NARC's adoption plan promised to infuse some of the emotional benefits of family life into child welfare institutions without subjecting children to the corrupting influence of traditional Chinese families. The NARC often emphasized its commitment to children's emotional needs in its international publicity campaigns promoting the adoption plan. In a fundraising letter to the Victorian Chinese Women's Relief Committee in Australia, Madame Chiang Kai-shek emphasized the emotional support that the NARC provided to children: "We hope, by tender care and kind treatment to erase the horrors of this most fearful aggression from their young and impressionable minds. Some of the children need years of care as the effect of seeing their parents, relatives, and homes destroyed and desolated has been a shock much too great for their immature minds to comprehend."[75] Publicity materials distributed in the United States likewise highlighted the NARC's emphasis on emotional healing. One booklet promoting the adoption plan noted that due to "all of the horrible cruelty" they had witnessed, many warphans "sob and are frightened in the dark of the night." Therefore, the booklet went on to explain, the goal of the NARC was to "help them to forget the sad things they have seen, as well as to make up for the loss of their parents."[76] In line with these publicity materials, the letters that children sent their foster parents often stated that they had found happiness and a new sense of belonging after entering an NARC warphanage. For instance, a letter by Chen-shih begins by describing the horror of losing his family early in the war but quickly moves on to describe how much fun he has playing with his new friends at the warphanage. His letter concludes, "The days pass very happily."[77] Through publicity materials and children's letters, the NARC highlighted

"Listen, boys. Don't worry.
Boys and girls across the ocean understand and love us."

"I'm happy now. I've just been adopted!"

FIGURE 2.3 NARC publicity materials emphasized the emotional comfort that sponsors could provide to Chinese refugee children through the adoption plan. May-ling Soong Chiang, *A Letter from Madame Chiang Kai-shek to Boys and Girls Across the Ocean*, 1.

its focus on children's emotional health while implying that sponsors could help participate in fulfilling their adoptees' emotional needs.

Ironically, to make children's emotional well-being a focal point of its humanitarian fundraising, the NARC demanded that children do the emotion work of performing happiness in photographs and letters to their sponsors. Sociologist Arlie Hochschild coined the term "emotion work" to describe the effort required to manage one's own emotional expression out of deference to the feelings of others.[78] As Kristine Alexander has argued, emotion work can be a helpful concept for studying the affective labor often demanded of children to make adults feel happy by properly displaying emotions such as love and gratitude.[79] Emotion work is likewise a useful analytical tool for understanding how children helped secure their own livelihoods through participation in the adoption plan. Children's letters almost universally emphasized their contentment and gratitude, portraying warphanages as idyllic spaces in which they lived together with their classmates and teachers like "one big family of brothers and sisters, ready to help each other."[80] But the records of children's psychological examinations tell a different, darker story. The Mental Hygiene Laboratory also conducted in-depth interviews with seventy-eight children in NARC institutions identified by their initial survey as having abnormal emotional tendencies. These interviews offer a raw portrait of warphanages rife with suspicion, fighting, and bitter interpersonal conflict. An eleven-year-old girl named Le-hua, who was blind in her left eye, described how the older female students would humiliate her by forcing her to kneel on a bamboo rod and shoving her head into a chamber pot. A ten-year-old boy named Yanqing told investigators that his teacher often called him stupid. He suffered from anxiety, had trouble sleeping, was afraid of the dark, and frequently got into fights with his classmates. Summarizing the results of its interviews, the Mental Hygiene Laboratory concluded that nearly half of the children suffered from depression and had interpersonal problems with classmates, while other widespread psychological issues included insomnia, frequent nightmares, and delusions.[81] The disturbing findings of the Mental Hygiene Laboratory investigation into the emotional health of children at NARC warphanages provide sobering context to the sunnily optimistic letters they wrote to their foster parents abroad. Recently separated from their families and living through the routinized terror of regular air raids, children in NARC warphanages suffered from extreme emotional distress and exhibited a litany of troubling behavioral issues. Nevertheless, to ensure the emotional satisfaction of the sponsors on whose donations they depended, the children selected for the adoption plan had to do the emotion work of performing gratitude and optimism while suppressing any grievances or self-doubts.

## "EVERY CENT MUST BE SPENT ON THE CHILDREN THEMSELVES"

The NARC's adoption plan and its promise to emphasize children's emotional healing were highly successful in attracting global humanitarian interest in China's children. In the United States, the plan had immediately infused energy into fledgling efforts to raise money for wartime relief in China. After the outbreak of war between China and Japan, Emma DeLong Mills, a close friend of Madame Chiang Kai-shek dating back to their time as classmates at Wellesley, immediately devoted herself to fundraising for civilian relief in China. Yet as of the spring of 1938, she was disappointed by the tepid response to her fundraising appeals, which she blamed on competition from other humanitarian campaigns ("Spanish, German, and Austrian refugees, etc.") and the lack of "human interest" stories from China that "appeal directly to our imaginations."[82] As a result, Mills was thrilled to learn of the NARC's new child sponsorship program. She wrote to Madame Chiang that "'$20 an orphan' will get much better results than 'money for civilian refugees.'"[83] Sure enough, within months, requests to "adopt" Chinese orphans were coming in from across the country.[84] The chairman of the New Zealand Council for the Adoption of Chinese Refugee Children, W. E. Barnard, likewise attributed its fundraising success to the emotional power of the adoption plan. He wrote Madame Chiang, "The establishment of personal contact between the New Zealand person helping, and the child helped, is in my opinion— which is shared by the members of the Executive—of very great importance to the success of our endeavors."[85]

For the NARC, however, enthusiasm for its adoption plan proved a double-edged sword. The plan was highly popular, but it was also very expensive. As requests to adopt Chinese warphans poured in from around the world, the NARC's overhead expenses skyrocketed. Replying to Barnard on May 3, 1939, Madame Chiang sought to illustrate the enormous costs that would be involved if the adoption plan were to be carried out on an even larger scale:

> The money which would have to be spent on a staff to keep control of the registering, the photographing, and the answering of letters would use up a large sum of money which could be employed for the upkeep of many orphans. For instance, if only one letter from each of the 4,000 children was written and posted at ordinary mailing rates the postage cost would be Ch.$1,000.00. A lot of orphans can be kept for Ch.$1,000.00. Then would come the cost of overhead, and what is more frightening is the fact that when one year is up if "adopters" did not continue, the whole of that registration would have to be scrapped.

The necessity of translation was yet another labor-intensive task for the NARC's overworked staff: "You probably know that none of these little children can read or write English. . . . So, you can understand the difficulties that would be entailed in an endeavor to translate letters from these little ones."[86]

To rein in the rapidly ballooning overhead costs of the adoption plan, in 1940 the NARC began informing new donors that they could only provide photographs of "adopted" children and could no longer facilitate the exchange of letters. For example, on March 5, 1940, the organization wrote to the Central Committee for Relief of the Civilian Population of China in Amsterdam: "We are very sorry but only the photo can be given; no exchange of letters. This is because of the enormous staff necessitated to carry such on, and the expense of postage, etc. involved. Instead, every cent must be spent on the children themselves."[87] A month later the NARC wrote similarly to Wang Sheng-chih of the Oversea-Chinese Banking Corporation, who was helping to coordinate the adoption plan in Singapore: "It has been found quite impossible with our many scattered warphanages and frequently disrupted communications due to the war, and without a special staff to attend to all the translations—to say nothing of postal costs—to carry on correspondence between adopters and children, and to send reports of school grades."[88] The costs of carrying out the adoption plan were beginning to outweigh its benefits, and the

NARC hoped that people would continue to make annual contributions even without the opportunity to correspond with their adoptees.

However, having previously dangled the promise of personal connection with an adopted Chinese child, the NARC found it difficult to continue to attract sponsors without facilitating at least some correspondence. W. E. Barnard replied to Madame Chiang's concerns proposing a compromise in which the New Zealand Council would not encourage correspondence with Chinese warphans, but if people took the initiative to write their adoptees, the NARC would ensure they received a response. Perhaps reluctantly, the NARC agreed to make a "special exception" and ensure that sponsors in New Zealand who wrote their adopted children would continue to receive replies.[89] The persistence of correspondence between New Zealanders and Chinese warphans, dutifully translated by the NARC, shows that they generally honored this agreement. Just two days after the NARC had informed a group in Amsterdam that there could be no correspondence with adopted children, it wrote to a New Zealand woman to assure her that "the annual letter from the 'adopter' and the child will gladly be translated at Headquarters."[90] In fact, archival records show that the agreement reached between the NARC and the New Zealand Council was not such a "special" exception after all. Letters exchanged between Chinese warphans and sponsors in the United States can also be found from well after the NARC announced it would no longer facilitate correspondence as part of its adoption plan. The NARC's inability to sustain international donations without providing for the exchange of letters suggests the power of forging personal connections between the givers and receivers of humanitarian aid as a fundraising tool. However, Madame Chiang Kai-shek and the NARC had additional reasons for continuing to facilitate correspondence between Chinese children and their foreign foster parents in places like New Zealand and the United States.

## INTIMATE DIPLOMACY

During the nearly four and a half years that elapsed between the outbreak of full-scale war between China and Japan in July 1937 and the Japanese attack on Pearl Harbor in December 1941, China fought the powerful

Japanese military virtually alone. In this context, attracting international support for the war effort was the Nationalist government's most pressing foreign policy objective. While Japanese atrocities received significant coverage in the international press, the adoption plan made the Japanese occupation personal for foreign sponsors who received letters from their "own" adopted children describing how they had suffered at the hands of the Japanese. It offered an opportunity to circulate intimate narratives of Japanese cruelty to private citizens across the world—who, the NARC hoped, might in turn pressure their governments to provide greater aid to China in its struggle against Japan.

Children's letters to their sponsors often narrated their personal experiences of violence and dislocation at the hands of the Japanese. On May 27, 1941, a girl named Han at the Sichuan Branch No. 7 Warphanage wrote to her foster mother Karen in New Zealand:

> Ah! I think about my home, which is still being trampled by the enemy in a city in the occupied area. The scent of the fields and gardens in my lovely hometown has now been replaced by the stench of the smoke and fire of war, suffocating the innocent people. I think even more about my dear mother and my younger brothers and sisters, who must bow their heads and endure the life of a slave, living amongst those who don't treat people as people. Every day they see the ferocious faces and vicious eyes of those animals and hear their murderous screams. Their lives have no freedom. How painful! Such unreasonable oppression . . . I hate the Japanese bandits.[91]

Other letters contributed to the international prestige of Madame Chiang and the Nationalist Party by emphasizing her personal role in rescuing children from the Japanese invaders. A boy named Cheng Zur wrote to his foster mother Katherine: "Because the enemy occupied our native home, I had to leave my family. But friend, my luck is not so bad! Do you know that in China we have a great mother, Madame Chiang? She established many warphanages to take in child refugees. I was sent to the No. 2 Warphanage where I have the opportunity to attend school."[92] In fact, many sponsors appear to have been inspired to participate in the adoption plan by the heroic image of Madame Chiang Kai-shek as the great "mother" of all China's warphans. A woman named Kate from Wellington, New

Zealand, wrote to her foster son that she was adopting him through "that wonderful scheme where you are now cared for through the kindness + generosity of those great + noble people the Generalissimo Chiang Kai Shek + Madame."[93] Children's letters offered a unique opportunity for the NARC to simultaneously expose Japanese atrocities and bolster the reputation of Nationalist leaders before an international audience.

While many children's letters employed a simple narrative structure of tragedy at the hands of the Japanese and redemption through the NARC, others adopted a more explicitly political tone in denouncing Japanese brutality. For example, in December 1939 students at the Kemper Hall Boarding School for Girls in Kenosha, Wisconsin, raised funds to adopt seven children through the NARC.[94] The letters they received from their sponsored children—most of whom were about twelve years old and in the more advanced grades at NARC warphanages—are striking for the highly polemical tone with which they describe China's war with Japan.[95] A sixth-grade boy named Chung-ya wrote: "Rather than suffer oppression under the iron hoof of the Japanese bandits, we children would rather roam about the interior, enduring untold hardships. Fortunately, through the great benevolence of Madame Chiang Kai-shek, we were rescued from our hopeless plight and brought to the interior where we live a fine life and receive a good education. It can truly be said that we have been resurrected from death and given new life."[96] Such letters reframed the adoption plan not simply as humanitarian aid to needy children but as a political statement in support of Nationalist China in its War of Resistance Against Japan.

While letters that children sent through the adoption plan often reached only their individual sponsors, the NARC also used other types of publicity materials to cultivate political support for China's war effort on a broader scale. For example, the NARC asked one warphan to write a message to the "children of America" for a United China Relief radio program to be aired in New York on June 6, 1941. Much like the individual letters children sent to their foster parents, this message to the children of America combined harrowing accounts of child suffering with gratefulness for the work of Madame Chiang and the NARC:

> Although we have met with the cruel tragedies of broken homes, dead family members, and wandering about as refugees, now we have made it to the interior, where we rely on Father Chiang (Generalissimo Chiang

Kai-shek), Mother Chiang (Madame Chiang Soong Mei-ling), the NARC leaders, and all the warphanage superintendents and teachers, to take us in and provide us with a good education. Because of this, we are still able to grow up healthy and strong beneath the bombings of enemy planes. This is so lucky![97]

In the letters she wrote to promote the adoption plan to prominent individuals and charitable organizations abroad, Madame Chiang also took the opportunity to recount examples of Japanese barbarism that she felt received insufficient international attention. In letters to the New Zealand Council for the Adoption of Chinese Refugee Children, Madame Chiang wrote as if providing them with talking points to criticize neutrality in the Sino-Japanese War: "We are fighting not only for our own salvation but also for all those principles which the democratic governments espouse. Sad it is to say, however, that the democratic governments show no disposition to help China materially, not even to uphold the principles of the League of Nations which the democracies profess to maintain."[98] These materials were often effective in convincing both powerful politicians and ordinary citizens of the need to provide greater assistance to China. W. E. Barnard, who was also the Speaker of the New Zealand House of Representatives, responded to one of Madame Chiang's letters to admit:

In reference to the latter parts of your letter, I wish to say (unofficially) that I appreciate the painful truth of your observations. China is indeed fighting a battle not merely for her own preservation but for the democracies of the world. I sincerely trust that your nation will not be left to struggle on without the aid which you so badly need and to which you are justly entitled. One generous New Zealand contributor wrote, somewhat crudely but with truth, that "China is saving our skins."[99]

In a letter to the NARC enclosing money for the adoption of one warphan, the organizing secretary of the Texas State Committee of the Church Committee for China Relief wrote, "I hope and pray I may be of more and more help to you and China. We feel very proud and hopeful of dear China. We must win grandly. We shall."[100]

By fostering intimate relationships between the Chinese children who received aid and the foreign sponsors who provided it, the NARC's adoption plan transformed the political possibilities of global humanitarianism. The letters that children wrote to their foreign foster parents offered intimate narratives of Japanese brutality and Chinese heroism. For the NARC and the Nationalist Party, the adoption plan was not only a means of securing humanitarian aid but also a new form of intimate diplomacy through which it could build international support for its war effort. The Nationalist-affiliated NARC was among the first organizations to fully appreciate how global humanitarianism's intimate turn enabled the recipients of humanitarian aid to shape its political uses. They would not be the last.

⤝⤞

Through the NARC's program for the "adoption of warphans by foreign nationals," thousands of people across much of the world "adopted" Chinese children with whom they built personal relationships through the exchange of photographs, gifts, and translated letters. The NARC's adoption plan enabled sponsors to envision transnational adoptive families consisting primarily of white, middle-class parents and Chinese refugee children. Nearly two decades before systematic legal international adoption began in South Korea, the NARC's adoption plan had already popularized the idea of adopting Asian children as a form of humanitarian rescue. Anticipating these developments, donors sometimes wrote to the NARC hoping to legally adopt the children they sponsored. In 1938 a woman named Sophie in London, who was already sponsoring twelve children through the NARC, offered to adopt four children ("two boys and two girls, under the age of five"), whom she promised to support and educate at her own expense if their transport to England could be arranged.[101] Such offers were common enough that the NARC felt compelled to specify in its regulations for the adoption plan: "The Adopters are to be thanked for their financial support only. Adoptees cannot be taken away from the Society and shall remain in the charge of the Society."[102]

Japan's attack on Pearl Harbor and the outbreak of the Pacific War on December 7, 1941, only exacerbated the logistical difficulties and high overhead costs of the adoption plan, finally rendering it unsustainable. In an April 1943 letter to a donor in California, the NARC explained the litany of factors that had forced it to discontinue its adoption plan in 1942:

> Films for picture taking are now unobtainable, war prices for the support of the warphans so high, and office staff already so overworked that our "adoption" system has since last year been forced to cease. . . . When we started our warphan work, US$20 was sufficient to support a child for a year; now over US$200 is necessary!—to say nothing of other difficulties. Hence I must reply that we could not do as before; we could not send photos or assign individual children.[103]

Yet while the NARC's adoption plan was forced to close prematurely, the intimate turn in global humanitarian practice that it helped set into motion was just beginning. Coincidentally, around the same time that the NARC decided to halt its adoption plan, an American organization named China's Children Fund decided to start fundraising for orphanages in China via its own version of the adoption model of international child sponsorship. China's Children Fund would dramatically expand the use of child sponsorship—first in China and eventually across Asia and much of the world. In doing so, it would transform the practices of global intimacy that took shape in World War II–era China into central features of the postwar global humanitarian order.

# 3

## INSTITUTIONALIZING THE INTIMATE TURN

The Reverend Dr. J. Calvitt Clarke had a secret. By day, Clarke was the founder and executive chairman of the China's Children Fund (CCF). Founded in Richmond, Virginia, in 1938 to provide emergency relief to Chinese children displaced by the Sino-Japanese War, the CCF quickly became one of the most significant humanitarian organizations working in China.[1] It fundraised for orphanage-schools throughout China via its own version of the "adoption plan" for international child sponsorship. By 1949 the CCF's adoption plan supported approximately 5,113 children in forty-two institutions across China.[2] During the 1950s the CCF expanded the plan across East Asia and much of the world, and by 1961 it supported 36,000 children in fifty different countries.[3] Now called ChildFund International, the organization Clarke founded remains one of the largest child sponsorship agencies in the world today—making Clarke, in the judgment of one biographer, "one of the twentieth century's foremost and beloved figures in philanthropy."[4] But unbeknownst to all but a few of his closest confidants, Clarke also moonlighted as a prolific author of racy romance novels under the secret pen name Richard Grant. His many books included titles such as *Office Wife* ("Her boss believed in taking liberties!"), *Man Bait* ("She bartered love for vengeance!"), and *Eurasian Girl* ("Her blood ran hot with mingled fires!").[5] While Clarke's novels were primarily intended to sell copies by titillating readers, they also provide insight into the particular mixture of humanitarianism, Christianity, and Orientalism animating his career in transnational philanthropy.

From the perspective of his work with CCF, the most revealing of Clarke's novels was his book *Eurasian Girl* (1935). The titular character, Selene Ramsey ("She combined the exotic lure of an oriental geisha girl with the lovely, long-limbed appeal of an American debutante!"), had been raised in Singapore by white American parents before her family moved back to their home on Long Island. When Selene is made to believe that she is the illegitimate daughter of a Chinese prostitute, she becomes deeply depressed and loses her self-respect. While Selene had always rebuffed her many male suitors to save herself for marriage, upon learning that she is "Eurasian," she comes to believe that submitting to the sexual advances of unserious men is the closest thing to love to which she has a right. "I am only a Eurasian girl," Selene thinks to herself. "I'll take the crumbs that are left for me in love."[6] The novel's happy ending comes when Selene finds out that in fact she had been adopted by her uncle when her biological father (a white American) and his Chinese wife tragically passed away. Secure in the knowledge that her Chinese mother was a "most cultured" Christian woman, Selene eventually marries a white American man who had also grown up in Singapore as the child of missionaries.[7]

*Eurasian Girl* encapsulates the contradictory mixture of racial, sexual, and political ideologies animating Americans' views on Asia at the time. On its surface, the novel offers an antiracist message that reaffirms the possibility of love across racial boundaries. "You listen to me," Selene's adoptive father says in the novel's climactic scene. "Yellow, red, white, black—or green, for that matter—these hues make no difference. They are skin deep. The blood underneath is always red!" The novel even endorses a eugenic argument in favor of racial mixing: "Every scientist knows that the hybrid is the stronger breed."[8] Nevertheless, *Eurasian Girl* exhibits a profound uneasiness about the presence of sexualized Asian bodies in white American society. The entire plot depends on the hypersexualization of Asian women, and Selene's very existence poses a threat to social order. As one male suitor tells her, "You could make any man unfaithful to his spouse I believe."[9] At the same time, the novel also expresses an American moral responsibility to Asia—and to Asian children in particular. It is the American couple that adopts Selene, an orphaned Chinese girl, and raises her as their own that serves as the novel's moral compass.

The tension in *Eurasian Girl* between the sexually tinged fear of Asian migration and American moral responsibility toward Asia highlights a paradox of U.S.-East Asia relations during the first half of the twentieth century. When Clarke published *Eurasian Girl* in 1935, exclusion laws still prohibited the vast majority of Asian migration to the United States. Although the Chinese exclusion laws were formally repealed in 1943 as a gesture of wartime solidarity with China, it was largely a symbolic act, and Chinese immigration to the United States remained limited to a tiny annual quota. Moreover, as of 1950, fifteen U.S. states still enforced antimiscegenation laws prohibiting marriage between whites and Asians.[10] Nevertheless, many Americans felt a strong moral responsibility toward China rooted in the two nations' supposed "special relationship."[11] Granted extraterritorial privileges and the right to proselytize throughout China by the unequal treaties signed in the aftermath of the Opium Wars, thousands of American missionaries had traveled to China to build orphanages, schools, and hospitals. Although almost always discussed separately by historians—exclusion falling under the purview of American history and extraterritoriality under the purview of Chinese history—exclusion and extraterritoriality worked as a single regime to structure the field of possible relationships between Chinese and Americans. Allowing American money, missionaries, and military personnel into China while excluding most Chinese people from the United States, the regime of exclusion and extraterritoriality functioned as the legal architecture enabling Americans to "help" China while keeping actual Chinese people at bay.

The CCF's adoption plan—which enabled Americans to form personal bonds with Chinese children *without* bringing them to the United States—was a form of humanitarian rescue tailor-made for this era of U.S.-China relations. Like Selene's parents in *Eurasian Girl*, ordinary Americans could save Chinese orphans through "adoption." But unlike in the novel, they could do so without provoking the racial and sexual anxieties raised by the prospect of Asian bodies on American soil. Yet as World War II came to a close and the enormous task of postwar reconstruction in China began, it was by no means obvious that the CCF would be successful in using the adoption plan to fund an expansion of its child welfare work in China. In the United States, the jubilation of victory was accompanied by a profound sense of donor fatigue, and private American giving to humanitarian causes plummeted in the years after the war. Would it be possible to rekindle Americans' paternalistic desire to save China's children now that the war was won? Moreover, the NARC had discontinued its wartime version of the adoption plan due to logistical difficulties and high overhead costs (chapter 2). Could the CCF implement the adoption plan in a way that was cost effective, sustainable, and satisfying to donors? Ultimately, the CCF's attempt to revive the adoption plan in post–World War II China would serve as a test case for the viability of global humanitarianism's intimate turn. Could fostering intimate relationships between the givers and receivers of aid across geographic and cultural boundaries actually be made into a sustainable humanitarian fundraising strategy?

This chapter tells the story of how the CCF transformed the adoption plan for international child sponsorship into one of the most successful fundraising strategies for humanitarian work in postwar China. The CCF made the promise of a personal relationship with a Chinese child into a viable fundraising strategy by translating the adoption plan into a set of standardized documents and routinized administrative procedures—a phenomenon I call the "institutionalization of global intimacy." To facilitate fundraising on a large scale, the CCF developed a bilingual corpus of publicity materials that appealed to Americans' deep-seated sense of paternalistic responsibility for China by repackaging the adoption plan as a way for ordinary Americans to participate in the postwar reconstruction of China as a Christian, U.S.-allied, and democratic modern nation-state. At the same time, the CCF's fundraising success was made possible only by the ability of its China office in Guangzhou to deliver on the promise of meaningful adoptive relationships with Chinese children through the mass production of high-quality photographs, detailed case files, and substantive letters. As the case of the CCF's adoption plan shows, the intimate turn in humanitarian giving was paradoxically predicated on incorporating orphanages across China into a vast transnational bureaucracy that processed massive quantities of standardized paperwork according to rigid administrative procedures.

## CHINA'S CHILDREN AND THE POSTWAR WORLD

To jumpstart the global recovery from World War II, in November 1943 representatives of forty-four Allied nations met in Washington, D.C., to form the United Nations Relief and Rehabilitation Administration (UNRRA), an international organization that would pool resources to aid nations that had been decimated by the war.[12] Active in more than a dozen countries in Europe and East Asia from 1943 to 1947, the UNRRA distributed food, clothing, and medical supplies while also assisting with the postwar revival of agriculture and industry.[13] Devastated by eight years of total war, China was the largest recipient of UNRRA aid. In 1944 China's Nationalist government established the Chinese National Relief and Rehabilitation Administration (CNRRA) to administer aid received from the UNRRA.[14] Among the CNRRA's first tasks was surveying China's humanitarian needs. A CNRRA report issued in 1946 offered a sobering account of the scale of human suffering and physical destruction wrought by the war. It estimated that seven million people were "on the brink of famine" and thirty-three million more were "living on a diet barely above starvation." Tens of millions of Chinese people had fled their homes during the war, and yet many found that they had no home to which to return. At least 233 counties that had been occupied by Japan reported that anywhere from 50 to 90 percent of homes had been destroyed. In September 1944 the Nationalist government had estimated that US$3.5 billion would be needed for relief and rehabilitation in China.[15] Ultimately, the UNRRA allocated approximately US$518 million to China, a considerable sum, but far short of the overall need.[16] Moreover, as an UNRRA official explained shortly after Japan's surrender, the organization's role in China was to do the "temporary and short-term job of helping to meet only immediate basic needs."[17] The UNRRA concluded its assistance to China in 1947, long before postwar reconstruction was complete, and just as the escalating Chinese Civil War was beginning to plunge Chinese society into a new cycle of death and destruction.

Yet despite the ongoing need for humanitarian aid in China and elsewhere, due to donor fatigue and a sense of mission accomplished, private humanitarian giving dropped precipitously in the years after World War II. The total revenue of U.S. private voluntary organizations fell every year between 1945 and 1950—from a wartime peak of US$2.81 billion in 1945 down to US$843 million in 1950.[18] As wartime humanitarian programs quickly shut down, many Chinese child welfare institutions were left without funds to provide for the children under their care—let alone take in new children left homeless by the civil war. The NARC, the largest child welfare organization in World War II China, shut down in 1946. While the NARC went to great lengths to reunite children with parents or relatives, it estimated that nearly 40 percent of children could not be reunited with their families, either because they were orphans or because their living relatives did not have the means to care for them. Ultimately, the NARC turned many children over to underfunded state-run child welfare institutions, adding to the ballooning social welfare burdens of the Nationalist government.[19] Unexpectedly, the *end* of World War II precipitated another acute humanitarian crisis for China's children.

Although it could meet only a small fraction of China's child welfare needs, the CCF proved to be one of the most successful humanitarian organizations working in postwar China. Despite the sharp overall decline in American humanitarian giving, the CCF's adoption plan exploded in popularity during the postwar years. In the first year after the end of the war, the CCF's fundraising revenue increased by approximately 27 percent, from US$263,291 (1944–1945) to $334,265 (1945–1946). By 1949, annual contributions to the CCF had reached $525,119—an approximately 100 percent increase over wartime levels.[20] The CCF expanded its presence in postwar China by using the adoption plan to offer long-term financial support for orphanages that had lost their funding when other foreign humanitarian groups stopped fundraising for China after the Allied victory.[21] For example, in 1944 a Canadian missionary named Verent Mills had established six orphanages in the Siyi area of Guangdong with support from the Kwantung International Relief Committee, which in turn received funding from a number of foreign humanitarian groups, including United China Relief, the American Church Group for China Relief, the Canadian and British Red Cross societies, and British United Aid to China.[22] After Japan's surrender, all these funding sources dried up. Mills reunited as many children as possible with family members, but as of February 1946 he was left with 250 orphans and only enough money to feed them for one month. Fortunately, the CCF agreed to provide sponsors for the remaining children shortly thereafter. For dozens of orphanages throughout China, the CCF's adoption plan provided a means to survive the postwar evaporation of other funding sources and continue their work through the civil war years. Before leaving China in 1947, even the UNRRA often brought homeless children to CCF orphanages.[23]

How did the CCF sustain interest in China's children at a time when Americans were otherwise pulling back from their wartime support of far-away humanitarian causes? It did so, in large part, through a series of publicity campaigns that systematically reframed the adoption plan as a way for ordinary Americans to help spread Christianity and American moral influence in China while shoring up traditional family values at home.

## "THE MOST ECONOMICAL AND EFFICIENT INVESTMENT A CHRISTIAN CAN MAKE"

To grow the popularity of the adoption plan in the postwar period, the CCF produced voluminous publicity materials that ranged from its own quarterly newsletter, *China News*, to articles and advertisements in many mass circulation publications. Somewhat ironically, the CCF's standard-ized, boilerplate advertisements for the adoption plan promised a sub-stantive, deeply personal relationship with a Chinese child that approx-imated the intimacy of the parent-child bond. For example, one typical appeal in *China News* emphasized foster parents' role in providing "guid-ance" for their adopted children: "Even more than a child's dependence upon an adult for food and shelter, is his dependence upon him for ideals and visions. A child is but plastic clay in an adult's hand—to be moulded into evil or good. The homeless, hungry children of the Orient need more than food or shelter. They need guidance by those who are true friends of children."[24]

CCF advertisements often included rows of pictures of children avail-able for adoption, detailing the different available payment plans and recommending that prospective sponsors indicate a backup choice in case their preferred child had already been adopted.[25] The CCF explicitly embraced the commodification of children implicit in such fundraising strategies. In the 1944 issue of *China News*, Clarke relayed the follow-ing story: "Once a stranger on a train asked me what I sold. He looked surprised when I answered—'Children.' After I had explained to him he said thoughtfully, 'I think you sell the finest article in the world.'"[26] Another CCF publicity article bluntly stated, "Put a child on your shopping list."[27] In an era in which consumer choice increasingly defined the ideal family life, a "real son or daughter" could be placed on a shopping list without apparent contradiction.[28] To "sell" Chinese children, CCF fundraising appeals argued that the adoption plan was about much more than rescuing individual children—it was a way for ordinary Americans to help remake China in the image of an idealized American society, first and foremost by spreading Christianity.

In this regard, the rise of the adoption plan as one of the most popular forms of humanitarian fundraising in the post–World War II period was rooted in deeper changes within the project of global Christianity. As Christian missionaries expanded their global reach during the early twentieth century, China emerged as one of their most significant destinations. During the 1920s there were approximately eight thousand Protestant missionaries working in China, making it the largest Protestant missionary

FIGURE 3.1 An advertisement for the CCF's adoption plan. *China News* 4, no. 3 (Spring 1946): 3. Courtesy of ChildFund International.

field in the world.[29] Although the number of missionaries in China dwindled over the ensuing decades, about four thousand Protestant missionaries remained in China on the eve of the Chinese Communist revolution in the late 1940s.[30] Influenced by the social gospel movement, which argued that Christian missionaries should place greater emphasis on alleviating social problems, China missionaries expanded the scope of their activities to include social welfare and philanthropic work. Among the most famous missionaries in the world, the China-born Pearl Buck strongly articulated the social gospel critique of traditional proselytizing in a well-publicized speech in 1932 titled "Is There a Case for Foreign Missions?" Buck concluded her controversial speech:

> Above all, then, let the spirit of Christ be manifested by mode of life rather than by preaching. I am wearied unto death with this preaching. It deadens all thought, it confuses all issues, it is producing, in China at least, a horde of hypocrites, and in the theological seminaries a body of Chinese ministers which makes one despair for the future, because they are learning how to preach about Christianity rather than how to live the Christian life. Let us cease our talk for a time and cut off our talkers, and let us try to express our religion in terms of life.[31]

Buck's criticism of missionaries who arrogantly preached the gospel of Jesus Christ but failed to embody the Christian value of selfless service exemplified the increasingly liberal, modernist outlook of ecumenical Protestantism during this period.[32]

Founded by a Presbyterian minister, featuring Western missionaries and Chinese Christians as the superintendents of many of its orphanages, and yet dedicated to the secular task of child welfare, the CCF was emblematic of the missionary movement's broader turn from proselytizing to social welfare work. At the same time, its adoption plan offered a new vision of global Christianity rooted in direct, personal bonds between ordinary American Christians and the children of the non-Christian world. Rather than evangelize through traditional missionary work, the adoption plan incorporated everyday Americans into the project of Christianizing China by allowing them to serve as foster parents to individual Chinese children who would feel themselves a part of Christian families. In its fundraising materials, the CCF explicitly promoted the adoption plan as a new means of spreading Christianity. As one typical CCF advertisement stated, "As the contributor receives school reports, letters and perhaps occasionally an example of the child's school work, he gets to know the child and through exchange of letters can assist the child in Christian living."[33] CCF publicity materials frequently noted that it required all the orphanage-schools it supported to offer Christian instruction to the children.[34] Therefore, the CCF argued, its adoption plan was *the* most effective way to spread Christianity in China: "The future pillars of the native Christian churches of China are securing their instruction and inspiration in CCF orphanages. The most effective evangelism of China is the nurture of her children in the Christian faith. Dollar for dollar the investment in a child's life is the most economical and efficient investment a Christian can make."[35] By sponsoring Chinese children through the adoption plan, CCF publicity materials implied, any American Christian could become a China missionary from the comfort of her own home.

Due to the challenge it posed to traditional models of missionary work, the CCF encountered significant resistance from conservative missionary circles. The Foreign Mission Board of the Southern Baptist Convention was among the CCF's harshest critics. Especially because the CCF operated out of the Southern Baptist stronghold of Richmond, Virginia, the Foreign Mission Board feared that its fundraising would "drain" money and resources away from its fundamental task of proselytizing. On February 20, 1939, Charles E. Maddry, the executive secretary of the Foreign Mission Board, wrote to J. R. Saunders, a Southern Baptist missionary and the superintendent of the CCF-supported Pu Kong Orphanage: "I fear that this gentleman [Clarke] working in Richmond in the Child Relief Work for China is going to stir up trouble throughout the South. . . . I do wish so much that everybody would stick to their knitting and that all Baptists would stick to our plan of work and send the money through our regular channels."[36] Several months later, Maddry wrote to Saunders again to reproach him directly for his involvement with CCF: "If our missionaries, supported by this Board through all the years, would give themselves wholeheartedly to the program of Southern Baptists, without setting up these independent organizations that drain off the funds that ought to go through our regular channels, I think we would get a great deal further with our missionary program in China."[37] By the 1940s, Maddry had gone public with his crusade against the CCF. For example, in April 1944 he published an article in the *Baptist Record* noting that the CCF did not have "the consent or the approval" of the Foreign Mission Board.[38]

In response, Saunders and the CCF developed explicitly religious justifications for the adoption plan. Responding to Maddry, Saunders focused on the opportunity to convert and baptize children, noting that "about half" of the baptisms he had recently performed were of children at the CCF's Pu Kong Orphanage. Saunders further argued that raising children at CCF orphanages provided an opportunity to train future leaders of the native church: "I think in this great family of little children whose tender lives are wholly in our hands year by year we have the greatest opportunity to do a great work for Jesus Christ than we have in any other kind of work that we are doing at Shiu Chow."[39] At least tactically conceding the Foreign Mission Board's argument that conversion was the ultimate end of Christian work in China, Saunders contended that CCF's adoption plan was more effective than traditional proselytizing in achieving this goal. He also frequently deployed biblical passages that he interpreted as proving "the fundamental emphasis God's word places on children."[40] Among his favorites was Matthew 25:45: "Inasmuch as ye did it not to one of the least of these, ye did it not to me." For Saunders and the CCF, Chinese orphans stood in for "the least of these"—the most pitiful and helpless members of world society. Therefore, the best measure of the progress of world Christianity was the extent to which Christians extended material and spiritual help to these "least" members of the global community. In many regards, Saunders' arguments for the adoption plan as a form of missionary work prefigured American evangelicals' enthusiastic embrace of "orphan theology" to promote the cause of adopting children in the twenty-first century.[41]

## "UN-UGLY AMERICANS"

For the CCF, the mission of spreading Christianity was so closely related to the goal of promoting American influence in China that the two projects were often indistinguishable. In CCF publicity materials, the terms "Christianity," "democracy," and "America" were all inextricably linked.

For example, one article in *China News* explained, "No one can visit China today without being forcibly impressed with the number of leaders in that country who are *Christians*. If that were not true, there would be far less hope of China's survival on the side of *democracy*. The churches of America have poured many millions into China. . . . Even if we look at it from a purely selfish point of view, they have still been the best investment *America* has made in China."[42] In this regard, the CCF's religious-political appeals for the adoption plan constituted an early example of what Arissa Oh calls "Christian Americanism." Defined as "a fusion of vaguely Christian principles with values identified as exceptionally 'American' . . . Christian Americanism encapsulated the prevailing attitude that equated being a good Christian with being a good American."[43] To promote Christianity was also to promote democracy, and a Christian, democratic China was presumed to be in the "selfish" interest of the United States.

During World War II, the NARC had used the adoption plan as part of an explicitly political program to attract international support for China's war effort and enhance the prestige of the Nationalist Party abroad. After the war, the CCF began to consider how the adoption plan could be used to promote American influence in China. It staunchly supported the Nationalist Party and believed that the leadership of Chiang Kai-shek, who had been baptized as a Methodist in 1930, constituted the best hope for a Christian, democratic, and U.S.-friendly China. But while the NARC had emphasized how the adoption plan could influence foreigners' views of China, the CCF placed much more emphasis on how American foster parents could influence their adopted Chinese children's views of the United States. In later decades it would begin referring to foster parents as "un-ugly Americans" engaged in a form of personal diplomacy to bolster the image of the United States abroad.[44] The CCF believed that these un-ugly Americans, by participating in the adoption plan, not only would demonstrate American benevolence and moral authority but would also transform the United States into a place more worthy of emulation.

The CCF's publicity materials emphasized how its adoption plan fostered feelings of gratitude toward American sponsors, thereby helping to create a positive image of the United States as China's liberator and benefactor. In the fall of 1943 *China News* quoted T. S. Chen of China's National Child Welfare Association—which supported more than two thousand children through the CCF's adoption plan—as saying, "The influence of these 'adoptions' is deeply felt among our people. They tackle Sino-American friendly relations at the core—namely, in the very hearts of friends far away, unseen but so real."[45] In the summer of 1945 *China News* published a lengthy article written by F. C. Liu, also of the National Child Welfare Association, in which he explained how the exchange of gifts and letters through the adoption plan had "warmed the hearts of China's children toward America."[46] The CCF circulated examples of children's letters as evidence of how the plan helped spread American influence in China. For example, in 1944 it published a letter from a boy named Min Kei to his foster mother Maggie in which he wrote, "My teacher told me that you wrote your letter to me on George Washington's Birthday. I know who he is. I have heard stories about him. In China, we also have a General Washington. He is our Generalissimo! He is also as brave as your Washington."[47] Taking George Washington as a model against which to compare Chinese leaders, Min Kei's letter suggested how the adoption plan encouraged Chinese children to see the United States as a model for China's future. The cumulative effect of all the personal relationships forged through the plan, the CCF argued, would be a generation of Chinese children deeply grateful to the United States. The CCF circulated one story about a Communist cadre who visited a CCF orphanage in Guangzhou to lecture the children about Russia's help to the Chinese people. But when the cadre asked the children which country had helped China the most, they nevertheless responded, "America!"[48]

The CCF also tailored its publicity materials to appeal to more specific constituencies within American society. Among the groups the CCF targeted in particular were childless women. As Elaine Tyler May has argued, the cultural ascendancy of the nuclear family in the post–World War II period constituted a form of "domestic containment" in which the "traditional" family was imagined as a safe haven from anxieties about nuclear war and subversive social forces. In this context, "procreation took on almost mythic proportions," and childlessness came to be viewed as "deviant, selfish, and pitiable." For women in particular, "motherhood was the ultimate fulfillment of female sexuality and the primary source of a woman's identity."[49] However, this idealized version of family life was not attainable for all segments of society.[50] As the postwar baby boom enhanced the social stigma of childlessness, infertile couples increasingly turned to adoption as a means of attaining the child-centered family ideal.

But the demand for healthy adoptable babies quickly overwhelmed the "supply." In 1955 Senator Estes Kefauver testified, "There has been a tremendous increase over the last 10 years in the demand for children for adoption. As a result, the demand has far exceeded the number of babies available."[51] For the CCF, the pressure on women to perform the social role of motherhood constituted a distinct marketing opportunity.

The CCF often advertised its adoption plan as a way for childless women to experience the joys of motherhood. In the fall of 1947 *China News* published a testimonial from a female doctor who praised the adoption plan for enabling "old maids" like herself to experience the joys of motherhood: "I am surprised at the thrill I had when I said to my mother and my friends, 'I have a son in China.' All the frustrated motherhood suddenly released, did surprise even me—in spite of the hundreds of babies I have delivered. It was so different to say 'My son!' I recommend the experience for all the 'old maid' school teachers, editors, saleswomen, etc., that you can reach."[52] The author focused not on the experience of sponsoring a Chinese child but rather on the experience of *telling* her mother and friends about her "adopted" Chinese son. She promoted the adoption plan not so much as an alternative form of motherhood but rather as a way to relieve the social pressure to have children. Other CCF advertisements made emotional appeals for the adoption plan as a last chance for the childless to leave their mark on posterity:

> Some of us, for one reason or another, have never had a child of our own. Others of us have had and lost them. Some of these adopted children will be brought to America eventually by their foster parents but if your closest contact to "your" child is only by letter, the child still will feel he belongs. You will be the only parent that child has. And you may find that you belong, too, and that in your child you are building up something that will live on after you are gone.[53]

On one level, such advertisements testify to the normative power of the nuclear family ideal in postwar America. On another level, the CCF's advertisements appropriated the symbolism of the nuclear family to legitimize a very different type of "adoptive" relationship that crossed national and racial lines, overflowed the boundaries of the domestic home, and was rooted in intimacy rather than biology. The extraordinary popularity of the adoption plan in postwar America suggests that even during the apex of the nuclear family ideal, alternative conceptions of family making were beginning to acquire widespread legitimacy.

The CCF's framing of the adoption plan as a means to spread Christianity and American influence in China anticipated the political uses of international adoption and child sponsorship at the height of the Cold War. As scholars such as Eleana Kim, Catherine Ceniza Choy, and Arissa Oh have argued, the Cold War imperative to win Asian hearts and minds influenced the first large-scale programs for legal international adoption targeting the mixed-race children of U.S. soldiers and local women in Japan and Korea during the 1950s.[54] Likewise, Christina Klein and Sara Fieldston have shown that child sponsorship programs helped legitimize U.S. Cold War foreign policy in East Asia by inculcating a sense of moral responsibility to U.S. East Asian allies among ordinary Americans.[55] The CCF's postwar publicity materials show that what Klein calls "Cold War Orientalism" actually predates the Cold War. That potent mix of humanitarianism, Christianity, Orientalism, and American exceptionalism can be gleaned in novels such as *Eurasian Girl* as early as the 1930s—and it took full form in the CCF's promotional appeals for the adoption plan in wartime and postwar China.

Moreover, legitimizing the U.S. role in China to American audiences was only part of the CCF's ideological mission. In the postwar period, its arguably more urgent political task was to help justify the U.S. presence in China to *Chinese* audiences. To achieve that goal, it also produced Chinese-language publicity materials that aimed to convince Chinese readers that its adoption plan—and, by extension, the American people— could help facilitate China's reconstruction as a modern nation-state.

## THE ADOPTION PLAN AS *BO'AI*

The CCF's strategies for promoting its Christian humanitarian mission to Chinese audiences were informed by a decades-long trend of missionaries attempting to localize Christianity in China and other locations. In the aftermath of World War I, Christian missionaries around the world entered a period of profound self-reflection in which they questioned their connections to imperialism and began advocating for adapting Christianity to local cultural practices.[56] In China this position was forcefully argued by prominent American Protestant missionary Frank Rawlinson, whose book, *The Naturalization of Christianity in China* (1925), called for "synthesizing" Christianity and Chinese religious practices.[57] Although the extent to which Christian missionaries actually implemented such changes was uneven at best, the idea of indigenization gained widespread currency as the best path toward building Christianity in China and elsewhere.[58] The CCF strongly emphasized indigenization to promote its work in China. Among the many dedications published in the CCF's Chinese-language magazine, *Blessed Children*, were classical Confucian phrases such as "benevolence toward children" (*ci you*), "treat all children as one's own" (*bu du zi qi zi*), and "the young have the means to grow" (*you you suo zhang*). By interspersing such phrases among the magazine's many articles on Christianity, the CCF linked its Christian humanitarian program to traditional Confucian ideas about societal obligations to children. The CCF's commitment to indigenization was also reflected in the incorporation of elements of traditional Chinese familial practice into life at CCF-supported orphanages. For example, the Morning Star Orphanage in Guangzhou published its own "family precepts," a traditional genre of Chinese literature in which the patriarch of a family wrote moral exhortations for younger generations.[59] As Clarke told the assembled children during a speech at Morning Star in 1946, "The reason China's Children Fund is now helping you is not at all so that you will learn to become Americans, but rather so that you will learn to become good Chinese people."[60]

The CCF often appealed to the traditional concept of Christian love, translated into Chinese using the classical phrase *bo'ai* (literally, "universal love"), to explain the very untraditional practice of forging familial ties across national boundaries to Chinese audiences. In official government documents, CCF-supported orphanages often defined their institutional mission as "spreading Jesus's spirit of *bo'ai* among children."[61] Articles in *Blessed Children* likewise emphasized *bo'ai* as the core principle of Christianity.[62] In May 1948 the Pu Kong Orphanage held a speech competition in which the first-prize winner, a middle-school student named Haoxin, spoke on the topic of "Jesus Christ's Spirit of *Bo'ai*."[63] For Haoxin, *bo'ai* referred to humanitarian love that crossed national boundaries. He told the story of Jesus helping "the Samaritan woman from a different country" as evidence that the spirit of Christian love meant providing aid across national borders.[64] Haoxin's speech suggests the extent to which the CCF trained children to understand the help provided to them by foreign sponsors as an expression of universal Christian love.

Reflecting the Christian education provided at CCF orphanages, the language of Christian love also infused the letters that children wrote to their foster parents. For instance, Ting Sun wrote to his sponsor: "Though we are far away from each other, I feel we meet each other when your letter come. I always think of you because you are loving me. How can I repay you? I must pray that God will help me do. . . . Over 60 of our Home-mates have been baptized. I am one of them. I am very happy to be a Christian. Your supporting me is the special kindness of God."[65] Ting Sun's letter explicitly connects his sponsor's love to his own conversion to Christianity. Quoted in CCF publicity materials, it served as evidence that by building close relationships with Chinese children through the adoption plan, American foster parents were helping to build a Christian China. Likewise, in February 1949 a girl named Chau Ho at the Kiu Kong Orphanage wrote to her sponsor:

> I remember two weeks before Christmas a classmate received from her foster mother a very loveable doll. I thought to myself, how nice it would be if I were to have one like it. But who would have thought that I should receive one from you so very similar. I also received your letter, and the other things with the doll—a lovely pair of sleeping pyjamas, several small dresses. Thanks to God for His love which has given to me your loving heart and let me have these lovely things.[66]

Chau Ho's letter frames her sponsor's love as a manifestation of God's love. Nevertheless, recalling the negative stereotype of "rice Christians" who professed to believe in Christianity to obtain material benefits, she ultimately sees both God's and her sponsor's love as manifest in the "lovely" gifts she has received.

The CCF did not introduce the notion of *bo'ai* as Christian love into China. In fact, the idea of Christian love—long translated as *bo'ai*—had emerged in the early twentieth century as one of the most broadly resonating aspects of Christian doctrine in China. As unlikely a figure as

Chen Duxiu, one of the founders of the Chinese Communist Party, had strongly endorsed the concept of *bo'ai* as one of the most important ideas Chinese people could learn from Christianity. In his essay "Christianity and the Chinese People" (1920), Chen wrote, "The root teachings of Christianity are only faith and love; the others are just leaves and twigs." Crucially, Chen believed that equality was key to the idea of Christian love, which he sometimes referred to as "the equal spirit of *bo'ai*." If Christ loved all of humanity, then all of humanity was equal under Christ's love. Or as Chen put it, paraphrasing Genesis, "All humanity are brothers."[67] In light of Chen Duxiu's emphasis on *bo'ai* as a relationship of equality, the hierarchal dimensions of the CCF's reinvention of *bo'ai* through the adoption plan are all the clearer. For Chen Duxiu, the proper familial metaphor for Christian love was brotherhood. For the CCF, Christian love was expressed through the paternalistic relationship of "adoption"—in which American Christians were the "parents" and the Chinese people their adopted children. It was through this deeply paternalistic recasting of universal love that the CCF's goal of spreading Christianity melded with its aim of projecting American moral influence in China.

The CCF's efforts to promote its humanitarian and Christian mission in post–World War II China were complicated by its status as an American institution in a political climate marked by rising anti-American sentiment. While China and the United States were allies during World War II, the United States never treated China as an equal partner, and pervasive misconduct by American troops in China had embittered many Chinese by the end of the conflict.[68] Sino-American tensions only increased as the number of American GIs in China briefly swelled to a peak of 113,000 in the months after the war's end.[69] Reports of U.S. soldiers assaulting Chinese women provoked widespread outrage, and Chiang Kai-shek's efforts to censor news of American crimes only fueled accusations that he was an "American lackey."[70] In December 1946 the rape of a nineteen-year-old student named Shen Chong by an American Marine touched off a wave of mass protests and was frequently cited by the Communists in their calls for the U.S. military to withdraw from China.[71] U.S. support for the Nationalists in the Chinese Civil War was also a hotly contested issue. The United States supplied Chiang Kai-shek's government with approximately US$1 billion worth of military aid between 1945 and 1949.[72] While this aid was not enough to help the Nationalists defeat the Communists, it helped fuel Communist attacks that the United States was trying to "turn China into an American colony."[73] Large-scale public opinion surveys conducted by Chinese newspapers early in 1947 found that more than 90 percent of respondents opposed the U.S. military presence in China.[74]

Against this backdrop, the CCF aimed to improve the U.S. image in China by shifting attention to the efforts of private American citizens to rescue and nurture Chinese children. Launched in July 1946 by the CCF's South China District Orphanages Association, the monthly magazine *Blessed Children* offers a window into the CCF's Chinese-language publicity strategies.[75] As an indication of how much emphasis CCF placed on enhancing its image in China, it hired Xie Enqi, who had previously worked as an editor for the highly popular Shanghai-based magazine *Young Companion* (*Liang you*), as editor-in-chief of *Blessed Children*.[76] The first several issues were largely devoted to reassuring Chinese readers about the moral foundations of American interest in China. The introduction to the inaugural issue bluntly stated: "Americans care about Chinese children."[77] Acknowledging Chinese skepticism of American motives, another article stated, "There are still people who doubt the intentions of China's Children Fund. We can use the clearest of facts to tell them . . . China's Children Fund wants nothing other than to foster helpless children in postwar China so that they can be brought up as good Chinese compatriots."[78] While *Blessed Children* rarely discussed politics explicitly, the CCF's support for the Nationalist government was clear. Celebratory articles about the childhoods of Chiang Kai-shek and Sun Yat-sen both highlighted the importance of childhood for shaping China's future leaders and signaled the CCF's support for the Nationalist government under Chiang's leadership.[79] In *Blessed Children* and other Chinese-language publicity materials, the CCF clearly linked its humanitarian work on behalf of China's children to U.S. support for China's Nationalist government.

Through its English- and Chinese-language publicity materials, the CCF systematically linked its adoption plan to a set of intertwined political and religious projects. In the United States, the CCF framed the adoption plan as a way for ordinary Americans to help spread Christianity and American influence in China. In China, the CCF sought to rehabilitate the reputation of the United States by promoting its Christian child welfare work as representative of Americans' desire to help China develop as a modern nation. But the CCF's transpacific publicity campaigns would all be for naught if it could not deliver on its promise to facilitate meaningful relationships between American sponsors and Chinese children while providing stable, long-term funding to Chinese orphanages. After all, it had been logistical difficulties and skyrocketing overhead expenses—not a lack of interest—that had ultimately doomed the NARC's wartime child sponsorship program. Attempting to succeed where the NARC had failed, the CCF set out to establish standardized administrative procedures and a vast transnational bureaucracy capable of carrying out the adoption plan at scale.

## THE PAPERWORK OF GLOBAL INTIMACY

Reading through the CCF's internal correspondence, one thing that emerges clearly is the depth of Calvitt Clarke's personal commitment to making the adoption plan live up to its promise of fostering meaningful adoptive relationships. As Clarke wrote to Verent Mills in September 1946, "We want our adoption plan to be real and not just a sort of fake scheme for raising funds."[80] Clarke was tireless in his attempts to impress upon CCF orphanage staff the stakes of making the adoption plan as satisfying as possible for sponsors. He concluded one memo with the all-caps declaration:

> THE INVESTMENT IN TIME AND EFFORT, BOTH ON THE PART OF ORPHANAGE STAFFS IN CHINA AND OF THE CCF OFFICE STAFF IN AMERICA, IN KEEPING THESE "MOTHERS" AND "FATHERS" INFORMED ABOUT THEIR CHILDREN, WILL BE SUPREMELY WORTHWHILE— BOTH IN POINT OF THE PRACTICAL HELP THEY ARE ANXIOUS AND WILLING TO RENDER IF WE MEET THEM HALF-WAY, AND IN VIEW OF AN INIMITABLE SERVICE IN THE FIELD OF INTERNATIONAL RELATIONS WHICH THE ADOPTION PLAN INVOLVES.[81]

Yet Clarke often complained that the almost exclusively Chinese staffs of CCF orphanages did not put sufficient effort into the adoption plan. He confided to Mills, "We have great difficulty in getting reports from some of our workers. I know they are busy and that they do not realize the job it is to finance our program." Even when Clarke did receive the materials he requested from CCF-funded orphanages, he was not always pleased with their contents:

> Some of our workers, in making reports on the children, state that the boy or girl is lazy, or that the parents threw the child out, or that the child is not very bright, etc. We certainly do not want our workers to be untruthful but wish they could tell the better things about the child. You would be surprised how often, especially the Chinese, our workers send information about the child that would have a tendency to discourage the child's sponsor from continuing the child's support.[82]

The CCF's solution to the problem of how to create deep, personal relationships between children and their sponsors was to standardize procedures for carrying out the adoption plan and build a well-oiled bureaucracy to implement them. There was an unspoken irony at the heart of the adoption plan: the unique, personal relationships forged between American sponsors and Chinese children were based on formulaic documents and routine procedures that were both rigidly enforced and meticulously hidden from view.

After responding to one of the CCF's advertisements with a commitment to adopt a child for at least one year, sponsors received what the CCF referred to internally as an "assignment report"—including the adopted child's name, photograph, and personal history as well as information about the orphanage where the child lived.[83] The CCF's China office in Guangzhou provided detailed instructions to affiliated orphanages on how to prepare every element of the assignment report. Building on the strategies of American missionaries who had long used photography to promote their evangelical and humanitarian work in China, the CCF placed particular emphasis on the photographs.[84] Most sponsors would have first encountered pictures of Chinese children available for adoption in CCF newsletters or in the many advertisements it placed in major American newspapers and magazines. CCF advertisements featured heartbreaking images of children who appeared starving, desperate, and alone; their bodies emaciated, their clothes in tatters. These were classic humanitarian images. As Karen Halttunen has argued, "graphic representations of the spectacle of suffering" have been central to the visual rhetoric of humanitarianism since the eighteenth century.[85] By the early twentieth century, photography had become the dominant medium for producing humanitarian images that made human suffering "comprehensible, urgent, and actionable for European and American audiences."[86] The pictures of Chinese children in CCF advertisements were prototypical examples of this genre: photographs intended to inspire shock, pity, and, ultimately, action to ameliorate the suffering they depicted. They were, in the words of Susan Sontag, "an invitation to pay attention."[87]

But in contrast to the pitiful images of Chinese children found in CCF advertisements, the individual photographs sent to sponsors after they signed up for the adoption plan were in an entirely different visual register. For each new child, the CCF required orphanages to provide two half-body photographs measuring one *cun* (approximately 3.3 centimeters) in length.[88] The CCF provided orphanages with the following instructions regarding these photographs: "Individual pictures should present each child to best advantage and should be as clear and flawless as possible in order to lend themselves to reproduction and enlargement. All children receive the greatest sympathy but it is only a human trait expressing itself when sponsors evince particular gratification in helping bright, neat, attractive, promising looking children."[89] CCF orphanages generally appear to have been able to meet these standards. In the assignment report photographs I have been able to locate, children appear healthy, well-groomed, and nicely dressed. The stark juxtaposition between the miserable children sponsors saw in CCF advertisements and the good-looking child—"their" child—whose photograph they received in the mail offered a powerful visual narrative of humanitarian rescue—a before-and-after tale of personal transformation made possible by the foster parent's adoption. The CCF had good reason to view meticulous attention to the quality of photographs as crucial to the success of the adoption plan. One foster mother wrote to the CCF after receiving her adopted child's photograph, "I think you chose the right boy for me. I like his looks and, from my method of diagnosis, he seems to have the appearance and personal qualities for success and leadership."[90]

Besides the photograph, the other essential aspect of the assignment report was a "personal history" that provided sponsors with information about their adopted child's biography and personality. The CCF provided orphanages with standard forms listing various categories of information to be included, such as family background, progress in school, interests, and a personal message for the child's sponsor. In practice, however, the level of detail provided in these forms varied considerably across different CCF-sponsored orphanages. The Canaan Home in Beijing provided especially detailed information. For example, the sponsor of a boy named "Asaph" received a wealth of information about his family background, personality, and life at school:

> Asaph's father and mother are dead. His father was a rickshaw puller. He had two uncles, two younger sisters, and an older brother. This boy likes to study and he is preparing to take the examination for entrance into Yenching Industrial School. This is a fine opportunity and will enable him to learn useful trades. . . . The boys also learn to cook, and are taught to keep the rooms and the yard very clean. In the summertime they go swimming and fishing in the clear stream from the Jade Fountain which is nearby. . . . Asaph, in milking and caring for the goats, was found to do his work faithfully and well.[91]

On the other hand, the sponsors of a boy named Dai Gang at the Foochow City Orphanage may have been disappointed to read that he had "no particular message for sponsor."[92] Despite its best efforts to control the initial portrait of children presented in the assignment reports, the CCF remained dependent on the orphanages it funded to furnish information about the children.

In some cases, children's personal histories concealed more information than they revealed. In December 1947 the CCF agreed to sponsor 102 children at the Peh Chuan Orphanage in Chongqing and requested that the orphanage provide photographs and personal histories for each child.[93] The personal history of a thirteen-year-old girl named Yu Cheng stated that she liked to make clothes and play ping-pong and hoped to have the opportunity to travel.[94] What Yu Cheng's personal history did not mention were her severe psychological problems. When the Ministry of Social Affairs Beibei Experimental Child Welfare Center sent researchers to examine the emotional stability of children at Peh Chuan using Xiao Xiaorong's Personal Data Sheet, the results of Yu Cheng's survey showed that she was "extremely emotionally unstable." In fact, her responses were so disturbing—she scored an 18/56 on the exam, "far below the vast majority of children"—that the Child Welfare Center sent an alarmed follow-up letter urging the orphanage to pay special attention to her mental health.[95] Perhaps concerned that evidence of severe mental health problems would cause the CCF to reconsider its funding, the Peh Chuan Orphanage never shared this information with the CCF China office in Guangzhou, let alone CCF headquarters in Richmond or Yu Cheng's foster parents. As Yu Cheng's case reveals, despite the detailed documentation generated for each child in the adoption plan, the CCF and its sponsors ultimately knew only what the staffs at geographically dispersed orphanages told them.

After receipt of the initial assignment report, the core of the adoptive relationship was the exchange of letters. Children were required to send their foster parents two letters per year as well as additional thank-you letters whenever they received a gift from their foster parents. Of paramount importance to the CCF was ensuring that these letters were (or at least appeared to be) the authentic work of the individual adopted child. In an official letter to all CCF-sponsored orphanages, the CCF office in Guangzhou emphasized that it was "absolutely not permitted for one child to write out letters for several children." The CCF explained that some sponsors had adopted multiple children in the same orphanage, and although they generally could not read Chinese, they would be able to recognize if letters purporting to be from different children were written in the same hand.[96] For similar reasons, the CCF also insisted, "Every time the children write letters, each must write according to his or her own ideas. It is absolutely not permitted for several children's letters to use the same ideas or language." Beyond requiring that children wrote with their own hand and in their own words, the CCF also established meticulous requirements regarding the appearance of each letter. One set of instructions from the CCF office in Guangzhou specified that "for the sake of standardization," "from now on when any child writes a letter, regardless of whether it is an ordinary letter or a thank-you letter, they should use the letter paper prepared by this organization for each orphanage."[97] To avoid the jarring experience of foster parents receiving a letter from a name they did not recognize, CCF guidelines further stipulated that the letters must spell children's names exactly in accordance with the romanizations provided to each orphanage by the CCF. The CCF even codified such minute details as the requirement that children use the same ink they used to write the original Chinese letter when signing their romanized name.[98]

To be sure, the CCF's ever-expanding list of rules and regulations pertaining to children's letters is evidence of their perception that there was a widespread problem of children and orphanage staff not taking the letters seriously enough. On the other hand, it also reveals the CCF's sincere commitment to soliciting meaningful personal letters from each child who participated in the adoption plan—even if doing so paradoxically required the increasing standardization of the letter-writing process.

## THE ART OF LETTER WRITING

Beyond regulations designed to ensure that children's letters appeared authentic, the CCF also maintained an ever-expanding list of items children were prohibited from writing in their letters. Some of these rules aimed to prevent children from writing anything that implied the lack of a meaningful relationship with their foster parents. For instance, children were not allowed to write that they did not recognize their sponsor's name and address. They were also prohibited from writing anything that might suggest they were exploiting their foster parents for money. For example, children were not allowed to complain ("like a beggar") about things they lacked in the orphanage.[99] They were further forbidden from asking for additional money or material goods unless their sponsors specifically asked them for gift ideas. More surprisingly, children were instructed not to date their letters.[100] There were often long delays between when children wrote their letters and when their sponsors received them—to the extent that some orphanages had children write Christmas cards in August to ensure they reached their foster parents in time.[101] To avoid calling attention to these lengthy temporal gaps, the CCF simply asked children not to date their letters.

To facilitate meaningful correspondence between children and foster parents, the CCF not only instructed children on what *not* to write, it also had to teach them what *to* write. To this effect, *Blessed Children* included articles designed to provide children with guidelines for epistolary communication with their American foster parents. For instance, in the March 1948 issue, Calvin Lee, director of the CCF's South China District Orphanages Association, published an article titled "The Art of Letter Writing" that sought to teach children to effectively communicate their gratitude to their foster parents. Lee's article begins by expressing his appreciation for what a difficult task it was for Chinese children to write letters to American adults: "It's not easy for adults to cultivate the habit of letter writing, let alone for ordinary children! . . . It's not easy to pick up our pens and write letters to friends and family in China, let alone to find the words to say to foreign friends!" According to Lee, the fundamental difference between American and Chinese epistolary style was that while Chinese letters relied on a vast store of conventional expressions, American letters were frank in tone and specific in substance: "In their letters, Americans always describe things in great detail. For example, if they know that a friend has headaches, then they will go ahead and ask after the friend's headaches—which is not at all like the conventional phrase we would be accustomed to use: 'I have heard recently that your honorable body is indisposed.'" Lee instructed CCF children to adopt the American way of letter writing, which he summarized as "call a spade a spade—and sprinkle in a little humor." As an example, he described thank-you notes written by children at one CCF orphanage to a sponsor who had sent bags of sweets:

> Recently there was a sponsor who sent each child a bag of sweets. In our thank-you letters, we especially brought up that among all the countries on earth China gets to enjoy candy the least. On average Australians enjoy the most candy, about 100 pounds per year. But Chinese people only have about two pounds per year. Writing in this way not only demonstrates how much we appreciate the sweets that we received, it also lets the giver know how precious his gift was![102]

Echoing New Culture Movement intellectuals who argued that China must replace the "dead" language of classical Chinese with a modern, vernacular writing style in order to engage with the twentieth-century world, Lee argued that Chinese children would have to learn to express themselves in frank, direct prose in order to build personal relationships across national and cultural boundaries.

INSTITUTIONALIZING THE INTIMATE TURN 123

FIGURE 3.2 Articles in the CCF's Chinese-language periodical, *Blessed Children*, provided children with guidance on how to write letters to foreign sponsors. Li Qirong, "Xie xin de yishu" [The art of letter writing], *Fu er* 2, no. 7 (1948): 5. Courtesy of ChildFund International.

In a translingual twist on the popular letter-writing manuals for students consisting of exemplary letters for children to imitate, *Blessed Children* also published Chinese translations of American children's letters for use as models. A January 1949 article titled "What Kind of Letter to Write?" included a Chinese translation of a letter an American boy wrote to the Chinese child his family sponsored through the adoption plan.

Praising the letter for its clarity and detail, the article offered it as a model for CCF children to imitate when writing back to their foster families:

> I am in seventh grade in school, and now I am 12 years old. I have been studying in this school since I was five years old. I have a little brother who is nine years old. Right now it is summer vacation. My brother goes to the recreation center and I go to the YMCA. We have all kinds of different activities there. On Wednesdays and Fridays we go on field trips, and on Tuesdays and Thursdays we have day camp. At 9 a.m. we leave home with our lunches packed and go to the camp. We stay there all afternoon, and in the evening do exercises and swimming. This is my fourth year coming to this camp. I plan to do many different things while I'm in the camp.[103]

Beyond simply providing children with guidelines and templates for their own letters, the CCF's efforts to cultivate global standards for epistolary communication suggest how it conceptualized the relationship between global intimacy and literary modernity in China.[104] Only by replacing inherited habits of thought and speech with those favored in the modern West could Chinese children learn to cultivate meaningful relationships with people abroad. At the same time, the very process of participating in transnational and translingual epistolary exchanges would expose a generation of Chinese children to new ways of writing and feeling that would prepare them to participate in the modern world.

## THE BUREAUCRACY OF GLOBAL INTIMACY

To ensure compliance with its standards for children's letters, the CCF built a multilayered transnational bureaucracy dedicated to regulating, reviewing, tracking, and—if necessary—censoring children's letters. The first task of the CCF bureaucracy was to ensure that children wrote their letters at the appointed times. An August 21, 1946, message from the Guangzhou office to orphanage directors reminded them, "Whenever any sponsored child receives a letter from their foster parents, you must immediately have them write a response. When the child has written a reply, it should be translated by someone at the orphanage and sent along with the original to our office."[105] On May 25, 1947, the office sent a follow-up letter admonishing those orphanages with children who still had not written to their sponsors.[106] By 1948 the CCF was threatening to suspend funding to orphanages that did not send children's letters on time. In January the Guangzhou office wrote to orphanage directors, "Every orphanage must send Chinese and English sponsor letters by the end of February. Those whose letters are delinquent will not receive funds for the month of March."[107]

Each one of the thousands of letters sponsored children wrote each year then traveled a tortuous itinerary through the various levels of the CCF bureaucracy before finally reaching their foster parents in the United States. At the CCF-supported Lingnan Industrial School, the head teacher of each grade was responsible for collecting children's letters by the appointed date.[108] Once the letters were collected, it was the responsibility of each orphanage to provide English translations directly below the original Chinese on special letter paper provided by the CCF's Guangzhou office.[109] For tracking purposes, the orphanage was also required to mark each child's letter with three separate identifiers: the child's English name (following romanizations provided by the Guangzhou office), an orphanage number, and an adoption number.[110] Each orphanage then sent the children's letters to the CCF office in Guangzhou, which forwarded the letters to CCF headquarters in Richmond, which in turn forwarded them to their foster parents. Children were prohibited from sending any correspondence directly to their sponsors, and orphanages would stop receiving CCF funds for any child found to have done so.[111] Clarke explained the reason for this rule in a detailed set of instructions to CCF orphanages:

> It is <u>very important</u> that letters from children be handled carefully. We have no wish to put a censorship on the children's letters but, because several rather disgustingly begging letters (apparently inspired by adults outside the orphanage) have been received by Sponsors, we are now asking that all letters be supervised by the Superintendent of the orphanage and that they be sent to this office for forwarding—never direct to Sponsor. We are sorry to be arbitrary about this but we do not want unscrupulous

persons to destroy the fine relationships we are trying to build up. Please impress on the children that they must not have an outsider write letters directly to Sponsors for them and that begging letters are apt to make them "lose face" with Sponsors.[112]

By the time a child's letter reached his or her foster parents, it had been reviewed by the head teacher of his or her grade, the orphanage staff member tasked with translation, the orphanage director, the CCF office in Guangzhou, and CCF headquarters in Richmond.

Letters found to have violated the rules could be censored at any level of the CCF bureaucracy. For example, early in 1949 a young woman named Rui-tang, who had recently reached the age of eighteen and "graduated" from the Pu Kong Orphanage, wrote to her foster parents with a special request: she planned to go to Guangzhou to continue her studies, and she asked that her foster parents send money to cover her travel. Rui-tang had followed the CCF's standard procedures in writing the letter: first writing out her letter in Chinese, having it translated into English by a teacher at Pu Kong, and then sending it to the CCF office in Guangzhou to be forwarded to the United States. The office, however, refused to send the letter. Responding to Rui-tang to explain their reasoning, they wrote, "This kind of letter of request does not conform to the rules of our organization's American headquarters, as sponsored children are not permitted to write letters requesting any money or material goods from their foster parents." Therefore, they concluded, "We cannot forward the English letter for you."[113] Letters were also occasionally censored once they reached CCF headquarters in Richmond. For example, in February 1951 the Richmond office flagged two especially political letters from children at the Pu Kong Orphanage: "The children seem to be working for the government according to Chai Cheung with his story of being a tax collector. Luk Sing Cheung's letter sounds as if they may be getting some military training—with its 'practice in shooting.' Of course, this may only refer to darts, slings or other toys. But anyone would question it now." Received just as the CCF was evacuating from Communist-controlled China and refocusing on other parts of East Asia (chapter 6), the letters were not sent to the children's sponsors.[114] As the CCF broadened its geographic reach, it would need to refine the bureaucratic procedures it developed in China in order to coordinate transnational intimate relationships on an ever-expanding scale.

While it may seem paradoxical that the "intimate turn" in global humanitarianism was facilitated by its institutionalization, a similar process can again be observed with regard to the *qiaopi* sent by overseas Chinese to their families in China. Prior to the late nineteenth century, the letters and remittances that migrants sent back to their families were handled mostly by individual couriers who earned the trust of remitters through kinship and native place ties. Yet these couriers were unable to deal with the enormous expansion of overseas remittances that accompanied the rise of mass Chinese migration in the late nineteenth and early twentieth centuries.[115] To handle such large numbers of *qiaopi*, new specialized remittance offices began to institutionalize the process of sending letters and money home. Taking advantage of the expansion of modern banking and postal services throughout South China, remittance offices mailed letters to local agents in China and converted remittances into money orders that could be exchanged in Hong Kong or sold to a local bank in the interior. The increased frequency of steamship routes reduced transit time from months to weeks, and telegraphic transfers, while comparatively expensive, could deliver remittances almost instantly.[116] By the early to mid-twentieth century, these highly routinized and impersonal processes allowed overseas Chinese to keep in much closer contact with family members in China than previous generations of migrants. Likewise, the intimate turn in humanitarian giving was made possible by the bureaucratization of humanitarian organizations—and the improved communication and transportation infrastructures on which they relied.

In the short span of a few years, from 1945 to 1949, the CCF transformed the adoption plan into one of the most successful fundraising tools for humanitarian work in China. By constructing a transnational administrative apparatus capable of facilitating the adoption plan on a mass scale, the CCF made it possible for large numbers of Americans to "adopt" Chinese children without running afoul of U.S. immigration law or provoking the racialized and sexualized anxieties long associated with Asian migration to the United States. While the CCF could not meet all the enormous child welfare needs stemming from the Chinese Civil War, it helped support dozens of large-scale orphanages that otherwise would have closed due to the evaporation of World War II–era funding sources. Most tellingly, CCF fundraising through the adoption plan skyrocketed during the immediate postwar years—a time when private American giving to humanitarian causes was otherwise in free fall. The CCF accomplished this remarkable feat by institutionalizing intimacy as a form of global humanitarian fundraising. If the NARC's wartime sponsorship program proved that the promise of an intimate relationship with an individual Chinese child was a powerful fundraising tool, the CCF's postwar adoption plan showed that the intimate form of humanitarianism pioneered by the NARC could be carried out on a large scale. The CCF's fundraising success did not go unnoticed within the wider world of humanitarian aid. Over the ensuing decades, how to forge personal connections between the givers and receivers of aid across national, racial, and cultural boundaries would become a central concern of humanitarian organizations around the world.

Like the NARC, which viewed the adoption plan as a form of intimate diplomacy that could help build international support for China's War of Resistance Against Japan, the CCF also saw the adoption plan as a means to advance political and religious goals. In particular, it thought that the adoption plan could help raise a new generation of Chinese citizens capable of building a Christian, democratic, and U.S.-friendly China out of the ashes of war. The moment in which the adoption plan could be advertised unabashedly as a tool of American influence in China, however, was short-lived. Only four years after the end of World War II, the Chinese Communist revolution of 1949 called the entire global humanitarian project in China into question. But rather than dismiss the adoption plan as a tool of the American imperialists and Chinese Nationalist reactionaries, Chinese Communist authorities instead sought to transform it into a new form of "people's diplomacy" that could secure ideological and material support for the Chinese Communist revolution abroad. In the new People's Republic of China, the practices of global intimacy developed by the NARC and the CCF would be put to use in the service of a very different ideological project. How would the adoption plan need to change in order to serve the needs of the revolution?

# 4

## ADOPTING REVOLUTION

On July 1, 1949, a Chinese girl named Yin-ho, who lived and studied at the Yu Tsai School in the northern suburbs of Shanghai, wrote a letter to her American foster mother, Esther, a high school teacher in Worcester County, Massachusetts. Yin-ho's letter begins:

> *Dear Foster Mother:*
>
> *It is too bad that we cannot open our mouths and speak to each other directly but can only use this piece of white paper to say all that is in our hearts. But this piece of paper is too small for me to say everything. Would you like to hear more? Let me tell you!*[1]

Esther paid all of Yin-ho's expenses at the Yu Tsai School through the China Branch of an international child welfare organization called Foster Parents Plan for War Children (PLAN China Branch). Opened in 1947, the PLAN China Branch followed the example of other humanitarian organizations, including the National Association for Refugee Children and China's Children Fund, in using the adoption plan for international child sponsorship to fundraise for child welfare work in China. Under PLAN's version of the adoption program, foreign foster parents adopted individual Chinese children by paying their expenses at PLAN-supported institutions in China while exchanging photographs, gifts, and monthly letters. However, while the PLAN China Branch's fundraising strategy was similar to these other transnational child welfare organizations, its political orientation was radically different.

As it turns out, what Yin-ho wanted to share with her foster mother that day were all the positive changes she had observed since the Communists' People's Liberation Army (PLA) had liberated Shanghai one month earlier. Her letter continues: "It has been one month since the liberation of Shanghai and we can see that things have changed. For example, in the past nothing was ever given to the people in the villages, but now they are given fertilizer and the poorer farmers also get rice. Also, the soldiers are never seen bullying the people." Her letter is also full of anger at the American-allied Chinese Nationalist Party, whose bombing of Shanghai had recently destroyed her classmate's home:

> There is something else I want to tell you. It's that the day before yesterday the Nationalists sent planes to come and drop bombs. They came in the morning as soon as it was light and dropped 16 bombs in one place until the whole area was a tragic sight. We have a classmate whose home was bombed. Luckily no one in the family was killed, but everything was destroyed. The planes did not leave until the afternoon. It was truly terrible!

Yin-ho's letter was one of many that Chinese children sent to their American foster parents through the PLAN China Branch's adoption plan in the years surrounding the Chinese Communist revolution of 1949. Unlike almost any other source of information available to the American public, the monthly letters that Chinese children like Yin-ho wrote to their foster parents offered a child's-eye view of the revolution as it unfolded in real time. For Yin-ho, the revolution meant the arrival of kind Communist soldiers who gave fertilizer and extra rice to farmers in her neighborhood. It also meant that she and her classmates lived in constant fear of Nationalist air raids that were laying waste to large residential areas of Shanghai with planes supplied by the United States. In many regards, her letter was strikingly similar to those that children had written to foreign sponsors through Nationalist-affiliated child sponsorship programs during World War II, describing their harrowing experiences of Japanese bombing campaigns and praising the Nationalist government for rescuing them. In the summer of 1949, however, the Nationalists were the ones conducting the air raids, and the liberators whom Yin-ho described in such a favorable light were the Chinese Communists.

This chapter traces how the PLAN China Branch's adoption plan became a centerpiece of efforts to transform humanitarian practices inherited from the era of Nationalist rule to meet the new ideological and material needs of the Chinese Communist revolution. Under the rubric of "people's diplomacy," the PLAN China Branch channeled funding to "progressive" child welfare institutions while encouraging children to write their foster parents about how they had suffered under the American-allied Nationalist regime and were now thriving under the Communists. The organization coordinated with the highest rungs of Chinese Communist leadership, but responsibility for carrying out its experiment in revolutionary humanitarianism ultimately lay in the hands of the Chinese foster children and their local caretakers, who were suddenly thrust into the role of "people's diplomats." The Korean War forced the PLAN China Branch to shutter its adoption plan at the end of 1950, but the humanitarian networks and strategies it developed persisted to play important roles in mediating China's relationship with the world throughout the Mao era.

The story of the PLAN China Branch's adoption plan sheds new light on the politics of global humanitarianism in the post–World War II period. Previous scholarship has emphasized how the global proliferation of humanitarian programs after the war served the geopolitical and economic interests of the United States and Western Europe in the emerging Cold War.[2] In contrast, this chapter uses the case of the PLAN China Branch to illustrate how the recipients of humanitarian aid in Communist China were able to shape its symbolic and practical uses to align with their own domestic and international political agendas. Specifically, it shows how the PLAN China Branch mobilized the intimate ties forged between Chinese children and foreign foster parents to attract support for the Chinese Communist revolution abroad. More broadly, it uncovers the forgotten history of how the Chinese Communist Party briefly embraced an alternative politics of humanitarianism rooted in international solidarity and people-to-people diplomacy—a history that was suppressed after the Korean War led the party to disavow its experiment with revolutionary humanitarianism in favor of a more rigid Marxist interpretation of humanitarianism as inherently imperialist.

## 132 ADOPTING REVOLUTION

## BETWEEN TWO WORLDS:
## THE FOUNDING OF THE PLAN CHINA BRANCH

The PLAN China Branch was founded in September 1947 as a unique partnership between two humanitarian organizations—the U.S.-based Foster Parents Plan for War Children (PLAN) and the China-based China Welfare Fund (CWF). While PLAN and the CWF had very different histories, they shared the view that officially nonpolitical humanitarian work could help advance leftist political causes. This shared approach to managing the combustible mixture of humanitarianism and politics laid the foundation for the two organizations to collaborate on a bold experiment to reshape the politics of humanitarianism in the context of the Chinese Communist revolution.

Founded by English journalist John Langdon-Davies in April 1937 as the Foster Parents Scheme for Children in Spain, PLAN initially worked to support hostels for refugee children fleeing the fighting of the Spanish Civil War. Its founders strongly supported the Republicans against General Franco and the Nationalists, and they intended their work to bolster the Republican cause. Nevertheless, they believed that framing PLAN appeals in strictly humanitarian terms would best serve its political aims. The PLAN Board of Directors frankly acknowledged as much in its first official meeting on March 24, 1938: "although this Committee is created to aid the Loyalists . . . appeals to the public will be humanitarian, exclusively concerned with refugee children." PLAN was chartered as an independent corporation in New York on July 13, 1939, and during the course of World War II it gradually expanded its activities to support refugee children across Europe. After the conclusion of the war, it further expanded to open programs in Austria, Belgium, Czechoslovakia, Greece, the Netherlands, Switzerland, and China.[3] When called on to justify its continued work in China after the Chinese Communist revolution of 1949, PLAN explained to donors that its "purely humanitarian" character required that it not discriminate against children in Communist countries for political reasons.[4]

In much the same way that PLAN deployed humanitarian aid to support the Republicans during the Spanish Civil War, the CWF used its public commitment to politically neutral humanitarianism to justify providing aid to the Chinese Communist Party during World War II and the Chinese Civil War. Soong Ching-ling (also known as Madame Sun Yat-sen, widow of the Chinese revolutionary hero and older sister to Madame Chiang Kai-shek) founded the CWF as the China Defense League in Hong Kong in June 1938 to raise money and medical supplies abroad for wartime relief work in China.[5] While the CWF was officially neutral regarding conflicts between the Communists and Nationalists—who were then engaged in an uneasy alliance against Japan—it focused on directing aid to Communist-controlled guerilla areas. Since most aid provided to China during World War II was given to the Nationalists, the CWF argued that the principle of humanitarian neutrality demanded that it rebalance the scales by focusing its own work on Communist-controlled areas. As Soong put it, "We do not demand that they be given preferential treatment, but we demand that they be given equal treatment."[6] It was not until the liberation of Shanghai in May 1949 that the CWF abandoned its commitment to political neutrality and threw its support openly behind the Chinese Communist Party.[7]

The improbable partnership between these two geographically disparate humanitarian organizations was facilitated by an American named Gerald Tannebaum. Born in Baltimore in 1916, Tannebaum moved to Shanghai in the fall of 1945 to serve as the deputy director of an Armed Forces Radio station.[8] He quickly befriended Soong Ching-ling, and it was during a dinner at Soong's home with future premier of China Zhou Enlai that the two Chinese leaders persuaded Tannebaum to remain in China to work for the CWF. Tannebaum agreed, and on July 1, 1946, he began work as the CWF's general secretary.[9] On a brief visit to New York in 1947, he met PLAN's executive chairman, Edna Blue, who hired him to help PLAN expand into China.[10] Tannebaum opened the PLAN China Branch in Shanghai in September 1947 as a department within the CWF.[11] He would personally serve as its director while also continuing his duties as the CWF's general secretary. In addition to Tannebaum, the PLAN China Branch hired nine more staff members, all of whom were Chinese.[12]

This partnership between Tannebaum and Soong was briefly the subject of gossip that scandalized readers across the world. On December 8, 1947, Drew Pearson's infamous syndicated column, "Washington Merry-Go-Round," claimed that Tannebaum and Soong were engaged in a secret romantic relationship—what Pearson called "the greatest love story since King Edward VIII of England gave up the throne of England to marry Wally Simpson." The idea that Sun Yat-sen's widow—"the Martha Washington of modern China"—had fallen in love with an American soldier twenty-three years her junior was so appalling, Pearson claimed, that their relationship had been "fearfully hushed up by the Chinese government." Nevertheless, when Tannebaum was discharged from the army, Soong Ching-ling took the "daring step" of hiring him at the CWF so that he could remain with her in Shanghai.[13] Covered breathlessly in newspapers from Los Angeles to Shanghai to Mumbai, the story was lambasted by Tannebaum's family and by Soong Ching-ling herself as a baseless rumor.[14] Reports of Soong Ching-ling's romance with Tannebaum were but the latest in a long string of blatantly sexist attempts to undermine her moral stature in light of her persistent criticism of the Nationalist Party.[15] But regardless of their personal relationship, Gerald Tannebaum and Soong Ching-ling's shared humanitarian and political commitments would underpin a highly productive professional partnership that lasted for decades.

By the time of the Chinese Communist revolution in 1949, the PLAN China Branch had become a critical humanitarian organization relied on by dozens of child welfare institutions and thousands of children across China. PLAN advertisements in major American newspapers invited readers to become "foster parents" for US$180 per year, payable in $15 monthly installments.[16] As of 1949, PLAN foster parents had "adopted" 617 Chinese foster children who resided in twenty-seven child welfare institutions throughout China.[17] The PLAN China Branch did not provide cash grants directly to children but rather allocated money to each institution on a monthly basis.[18] As PLAN-supported child welfare institutions used the funds for general expenses like food, clothing, and medicine that benefited all children at the institution and not only those in the adoption plan, the PLAN China Branch estimated that approximately six thousand children benefited from its support.[19] In 1949 alone the PLAN China Branch received donations totaling US$65,516.25 as well as relief supplies valued at $5,813.21.[20]

Only two years after the founding of the PLAN China Branch, the Chinese Communist revolution rendered the future of all humanitarian activity in China uncertain. In this period of flux and instability, the organization's status as part of two larger humanitarian groups—one American, one Chinese—would provide both opportunities and liabilities as it sought to navigate the seismic shifts in local and global politics wrought by the revolution.

FIGURE 4.1 Advertisement for Foster Parents Plan for War Children quoting a letter from a Chinese boy to his American foster parent, in the *New York Herald Tribune*, October 24, 1948. Courtesy of Plan International.

## REVOLUTIONARY HUMANITARIANISM

After weeks of fierce fighting, on May 27, 1949, the People's Liberation Army pronounced the city of Shanghai liberated. For the PLAN China Branch—as for the rest of China's largest, wealthiest, and most cosmopolitan city—the revolution had arrived. In the ensuing months, the PLAN China Branch sought and received approval of its work from the highest ranks of the Chinese Communist Party. In July 1949 Tannebaum traveled to Beijing to meet with high-level Communist officials about the future of both the CWF in general and the PLAN China Branch in particular. While in Beijing, he managed to secure a meeting with Dong Biwu, who would soon become vice premier of the People's Republic of China (PRC), and his old acquaintance Zhou Enlai. While Zhou and Dong informed Tannebaum that it was too early to determine the long-term future of the CWF, they instructed him that it should continue all its current work and even "increase its work if not limited by manpower and financial resources."[21] Tannebaum also met with personnel from the foreign affairs office to discuss "the overall situation of organizations from different countries conducting relief work in China."[22] As of the summer of 1949, the PLAN China Branch had secured explicit but temporary approval from the highest echelons of the Chinese Communist Party to continue its humanitarian work.

The Chinese Communist government allowed humanitarian organizations like the PLAN China Branch to continue operating without a determination on their long-term futures until April 1950, when it convened the Chinese People's Relief Congress in Beijing to establish official policy toward social welfare and relief work.[23] A standing committee highlighted by Vice Premier Dong Biwu, Minister of Health Li Dequan, and Soong Ching-ling presided over the meeting.[24] Tannebaum also attended in his capacity as general secretary of the CWF and director of the PLAN China Branch.[25] The congress established the People's Relief Administration of China (PRAC) to coordinate and supervise social welfare and philanthropic activities nationwide.[26] Among the meeting's most passionately debated topics was whether to continue accepting humanitarian aid from countries like the United States, then considered among China's foremost enemies.

Speaking on the congress's second day, Soong Ching-ling forcefully articulated her vision for a new model of humanitarianism as "people's diplomacy" that could secure much-needed material aid while also forging people-to-people links with "progressive" forces abroad. Later published in the *People's Daily*, Soong's speech stands out as among the most influential public testimonials for how global humanitarian aid could serve the Chinese Communist revolution.[27] She singled out the PLAN China Branch for particular praise: "Before liberation, the recipients of PLAN aid were progressive or potentially progressive organizations. At that time, these schools and children's institutions had very few other sources of funding. Through PLAN's help, they were able to survive this extremely difficult time." While Soong acknowledged and echoed the congress's widespread criticism of "imperialist" humanitarian organizations that "use the issue of relief aid as an artifice for attacking new China," she did not call for ending all Western philanthropy in China. Rather, she called for using the transnational connections forged through humanitarianism to "transform foreign people's opinions" of China. In contrast to "formal government and news reports," global humanitarianism could better accomplish this goal by building "people-to-people relationships," which Soong argued were "more easily embraced by the people of imperialist countries." The PLAN China Branch's adoption plan, which sought to foster intimate ties between Americans and Chinese children, was the ideal vehicle for this new model of humanitarian aid. Arguing for the continued material and ideological value of its work, Soong trained a national spotlight on the PLAN China Branch as a model humanitarian organization for the Communist era.[28] Her address to the Chinese People's Relief Congress was well received, and her selection as the first chairman of the PRAC affirmed her vision for China's continued cooperation with foreign humanitarian organizations like PLAN.[29] In effect, her performance at the People's Relief Congress had green-lighted a bold experiment in revolutionary humanitarianism—an experiment to be spearheaded by the PLAN China Branch and the children under its care.

But, as would quickly become clear, maintaining a clear line of demarcation between "revolutionary" and "imperialist" humanitarianism was far from easy. While the congress was still in session, Soong received news that PLAN headquarters in New York intended to work with other, more conservative relief agencies, including United Service to China and Church World Service, to secure U.S. government aid for famine areas in China.[30] Blindsided, she immediately cabled executive chair Edna Blue to demand that she cut off all relations with those other relief groups. On April 26, 1950, only one day after her speech to the Chinese People's Relief Congress, Soong wrote to the PLAN China Branch's deputy secretary-general, Zhang Zong'an, to express her hope that "Mrs. Blue did not understand the political significance of her agreement." "If this is not the case," she added ominously, "then I feel the time has come to tell Foster Parents Plan for War Children that we do not want their help anymore."[31] The episode quickly blew over, and the PLAN China Branch continued its work uninterrupted. Nevertheless, the wide gulf between Soong's public assurances and private doubts foreshadowed the delicate tightrope act that she and the organization would have to maintain to continue accepting global humanitarian aid amid surging Chinese nationalism and the quickly descending Cold War.

## THE ADOPTION PLAN AS PEOPLE'S DIPLOMACY

The sheer volume of correspondence between Chinese children and their foreign foster parents marks the adoption plan as a highly significant avenue of communication between ordinary Chinese and Americans at a moment when the two nations were fast becoming enemies on opposite sides of a global Cold War. As stated in the PLAN China Branch bylaws, all children in the adoption plan were required to write one letter to their foster parents every month. If a child failed to write for two or more consecutive months without a valid excuse, the PLAN China Branch would consider terminating the child's financial assistance through the program.[32] In the year and a half between January 1949 and July 1950—the crucial period surrounding the Chinese Communist revolution—Chinese children wrote 6,385 letters to their foster parents as part of the PLAN China Branch's adoption plan. During that same period, American foster parents sent 1,437 letters to their Chinese foster children. These numbers would have been even greater if not for disruptions to China's domestic and international postal services due to the civil war.[33] In July 1948 a major Chinese newspaper, *Da gong bao*, had reported that some American foster mothers would send their Chinese children four or five letters in a single month.[34]

The PLAN China Branch sought to use this voluminous correspondence as a form of "people's diplomacy" that could help build support for the Chinese Communist revolution abroad. In its 1949 annual report, the PLAN China Branch argued that by providing an intimate view into how children's lives had improved under Communist rule, children's letters were winning friends for the Chinese revolution within American society:

> Before liberation, the content of the children's letters reflected the bleakness and corruption of the reactionary Nationalist regime and their collusion with the American government. On the other hand, since liberation the children's letters have instead reflected the excellent discipline of the People's Liberation Army and the new People's Government as well as the children's own progress. Their letters have made some PLAN donors believe that China is a country with a bright future and that the Chinese Communist Party is not what the American media makes it out to be.[35]

To be sure, the PLAN China Branch did not claim that it could turn large swaths of American society in favor of the Communist Party. Instead, the report deployed anecdotal examples of children's letters influencing their foster parents to suggest the effect such programs might have if carried out on a large scale: "There is one donor who has adopted a student at the Yu Tsai School who works for an American radio station. He read a letter written to him by the student he sponsors out loud over American airwaves. This is exactly what we're hoping for."[36] One letter at a time, children could reveal to their sponsors a different side of the Chinese Communist revolution from what they read in the newspapers.

In order for children's letters to function effectively as people's diplomacy, the PLAN China Branch issued prescriptions regarding both the content and structure of their letters. In November 1949 the organization published a Chinese-language booklet, *Work for the Suffering Children*, that posed the issue succinctly: "How can we take the exchange of ordinary pleasantries and dull greetings and transform them into people's diplomacy and international propaganda?" To achieve this goal, the book suggested potential topics for children's letters: "the construction of new China, the glorious achievements of the People's Liberation Army, the contrast between the People's Government and the government of the Nationalist reactionaries—all of these can serve as subjects for the children to report on." The PLAN China Branch even suggested specific narrative strategies suited to the particularities of the American psyche: "The majority of Americans' political level is low, but they are relatively inclined to seek out facts. For this reason, they will not easily accept empty sayings and slogans and on the contrary will feel an aversion to them. On the other hand, they are willing to accept narrative stories and specific facts and examples.... We think that the people who lead children in writing letters should grasp hold of this type of propaganda and reporting."[37] Through both personal stories and concrete details, children's letters could influence Americans' perception of China better than the dogmatic slogans of government propaganda.

FIGURE 4.2 Booklet published in 1949 to explain the PLAN China Branch's work to domestic audiences. *Wei kunan ertong er gongzuo: Zhanzai Ertong Yiyanghui Zhongguo Fenhui gongzuo baogao* [Work for the suffering children: Foster Parents' Plan for War Children China Branch work report] (Shanghai: Zhanzai Ertong Yiyanghui Zhongguo Fenhui, 1949). Courtesy of Plan International.

During the early months following the revolution, the PLAN China Branch repeatedly reassured PLAN headquarters in New York that its humanitarian mission could continue to thrive in Communist China. One report back to headquarters explained that the revolution had actually benefited their child welfare work by enabling them to operate safely in all areas of the country.[38] In addition to sending general work reports and translated excerpts from the inspection department's reviews of PLAN-supported orphanages back to New York, Gerald Tannebaum kept in close personal correspondence with Executive Chair Edna Blue.[39] In one letter he assured her that children's letters accurately reflected their experiences of the Chinese Communist revolution. "It was no propaganda that the PLA soldiers would not touch a needle or a thread which belonged to the people, and which many of the children wrote to their foster parents," Tannebaum insisted. "It was actual fact."[40] Such private reassurances that the Communist revolution had benefited PLAN's work in China complemented children's letters to their foster parents as a crucial aspect of the PLAN China Branch's strategy of people's diplomacy.

## "USE THE HEART TO INFLUENCE THE MIND"

The PLAN China Branch recognized that children's letters could be politically effective only if the children maintained close, affectionate relationships with their American foster parents. To this effect, the organization sought to use children's letters to foster what it called "sentiment across national boundaries" (*guoji jian de qinggan*)—its particular phrasing of the concept I call "global intimacy."[41] To be sure, the PLAN China Branch maintained that building sentimental ties between Chinese children and American donors was a valuable end in itself. Thanks to each foster parent, it wrote in *Work for the Suffering Children*, "a lonely and suffering child will feel that on the other side of the Atlantic Ocean there truly is a friend who cares about him. . . . As a result, not only can funding continue to be maintained, but more importantly a type of international sympathy and humanitarian love can also be created."[42] At the same time, in internal documents the PLAN China Branch acknowledged that maintaining these emotional attachments served both its fundraising and its political goals.[43] Through the exchange of translated letters, it set out to cultivate intimate ties between Chinese children and their American foster parents that were both emotional and economic, humanitarian and political.

The intimate disclosures contained in children's letters were not spontaneous outpourings of emotion but rather the result of the PLAN China Branch's concerted efforts to facilitate the formation of affective bonds between American foster parents and Chinese children by providing what was in effect an education in epistolary intimacy. To balance the twin imperatives of teaching foster parents about the Chinese revolution and sustaining their emotional investment in their foster children, its 1949 annual report instructed that children's letters "must be soft in tone but firm in substance" (*wai ruan nei ying*). The report went on to acknowledge, "Of course, this requires a comparatively high level of epistolary skill. Therefore, our education department must ensure that they clearly understand this point."[44] By 1950 the organization had refined its prescriptions on children's letters into a concise formulation: "Use the heart to influence the mind" (*cong ganqing dao lixing*).[45] Preserving affectionate ties with American foster parents would help ensure that children's stories of revolution were read with sympathy and open-mindedness.

The PLAN China Branch also sought to apply a veneer of equality to the adoption plan by replacing the familial terms of address children had long used for their sponsors with the language of friendship. At the PLAN-funded Shanghai Home for Destitute Children, this change was implemented in August 1949. In his July 1949 letter, a boy named Ping-wei addressed his monthly letter to his sponsor, a woman named Ruth, "Dear foster mother." He signed the letter, "Your foster son."[46] Just a month later, Ping-wei addressed his letter "Dear foster friend" and signed it using the identical term, "foster friend."[47] However, this new practice of avoiding overtly hierarchal language was unevenly enforced, and as long as the basic structure of foreign adults providing money to Chinese children remained unchanged, it seems unlikely that this shift in terminology would have caused either party to view their relationship as one between equals.

The imprint of the PLAN China Branch's prescriptions is visible in the generic quality of many of the children's letters. For example, on July 8, 1950, a fourteen-year-old boy named Cheng-chung at Shanghai Boystown

Orphanage wrote a letter that skillfully applied the PLAN China Branch's recommendations.[48] His letter begins: "Whenever I write letters to you a feeling of warmth and intimacy often rises up inside of me. This is because of the correspondence we have been exchanging back and forth." Only after this affectionate opening does the letter turn to politics: "I love peace. I hate those warmongers who go about starting wars. . . . I think that you also must support peace. Have you signed your name on the peace petition yet? I have already signed my name."[49] Written shortly after the United States had intervened in the Korean War, the letter (and the peace petition to which it referred) was clearly critical of the United States. However, by writing in broad terms against "war" and in favor of "peace," Cheng-chung's letter "used the heart to influence mind" by being "soft in tone but firm in substance."

In some cases, children's letters went well beyond these generic requirements to express a deep sense of family intimacy with their sponsors. On February 17, 1949, a boy named Pao at the Bailie School in Gansu Province wrote to his foster mother, Phyllis: "Your words are just those like those of my own mother ringing in my heart. You said that you love me so much. Now, we are mother and son. If the mother loves the child, the son no doubt also loves her. From the bottom of my heart I love you."[50] For some children, it was the exchange of photographs with their foster parents that contributed to a strong sense of familial love. A boy named Chi-hai wrote, "When I hold up my pen to write the letter to you, I first looked at your photograph for some time. . . . Although it is only a picture, it is as though I am talking to you face to face. Really my little soul is always with you. It is as if my lonely heart has found my mother's arms."[51] In an interview with the *New York Herald Tribune*, PLAN advisor Julia Chen relayed (perhaps hyperbolic) reports of children who spoke of their American foster parents in their dying breaths: "In nearly every case where a child in the plan has perished in the course of the war, she said, the workers in charge have reported that he died speaking of his American foster parent. Often the sick child's last act has been to write a letter thanking his foster mother and asking her not to grieve."[52] While not all relationships between Chinese children and their American foster parents reached such levels of emotional intensity, these letters and many others like them testify to the emotional significance that at least some children and foster parents invested in their "adoptive" relationships.

## TRANSLATION, CENSORSHIP, AND THE PROBLEM OF OFF-SCRIPT LETTERS

Imposing rigid discipline on children writing from twenty-seven institutions in fourteen cities across China was easier said than done. Every one of the letters written by children through the PLAN China Branch's adoption program that I have read is unique. With the exception of children who were too young to write, the organization's bylaws required that all children write out their letters in their own hand.[53] The variety of handwriting seen across these letters—sometimes precociously elegant, sometimes clumsy and juvenile, sometimes all but illegible—confirms that this rule was at least generally observed. Often the letters deviated dramatically from the recommendations. The PLAN China Branch readily admitted as much in an internal report from 1950: "We do not have enough control over the children's letters. Since liberation, the children's political level has become very high, but their propaganda skills remain poor. This has started to have some effect on the sentiments of the foster parents, causing the number of people who discontinue their adoptions to increase." For example, the report continued, some children "decry American imperialism and lecture to their sponsors, displaying the erroneous tendencies of excessively harsh language or excessively leftist ideology."[54]

Yet if the PLAN China Branch worried that children might alienate their sponsors with naked political propaganda, an analysis of their letters reveals that more often children deviated from their prescriptions by neglecting to promote the Chinese revolution altogether. On June 15, 1949, a girl named Hsiu-yun at the Hsiang Shan Orphanage near Beijing wrote a letter that eschewed politics and instead shared a poem she composed on a fan she made herself out of cardboard:

> The wind blows into the fan
> I grasp it inside of my hand
> If someone wants to borrow it
> They'll have to wait till winter hits.[55]

As this letter and many more like it demonstrate, children were not required to take up the explicitly political topics suggested by the PLAN China Branch.

Although I have not come across any letters that overtly criticize the Chinese Communist Party, some letters painted a bleak portrait of life after liberation. On July 12, 1949, nearly half a year after the liberation of Beijing, a boy named Chih-sun wrote to his foster mother to describe what he saw on a fieldtrip they took to the outskirts of the city. His letter reads like a chronicle of misery. He describes sweat-drenched workers emerging from a coal mine "like ants swarming out of a hole" and farmers "working with knitted brows" because drought had led to a poor wheat harvest. Finally, he describes returning to the city to see people who were once landlords, rich peasants, and Nationalist soldiers peddling their old possessions to eke out a living. "Before they enjoyed wealth," he wrote. "Now they are suffering."[56] By dramatically deviating from the script, letters such as this one reveal that the PLAN China Branch required the active participation of children for its adoption plan to function as "people's diplomacy."

When the PLAN China Branch felt that the content or tone of a child's letter threatened its philanthropic or political goals, it turned to the process of translation as a tool of censorship. Its booklet *Work for the Suffering Children* noted that the necessity of translating correspondence allowed them to mediate the relationships between children and their foster parents: "What needs to be explained here is that they do not communicate directly but instead through our organization. Therefore, we can pay close attention to and carefully translate their letters."[57] In internal reports, the PLAN China Branch more strongly hinted at the censorial function of translation. The 1949 annual report stated that until the education department had successfully trained children in the delicate art of writing letters "soft in tone but firm in substance," "all that we can do is to pay extra attention during the process of translation."[58] If these statements are perhaps deliberately vague, careful comparison of the original Chinese-language letters with their English translations reveals many examples in which translation was clearly used as a tool for political censorship. For instance, on August 8, 1950, a boy named Chih-kao at the Shanghai Home for Destitute Children wrote a letter praising Stalin's Soviet Union as a model for China.[59] A literal translation of an excerpt from his letter would read: "The people in the Soviet Union are very happy. It is only under Stalin's leadership that they are able to live in happiness, so China must try to emulate them, and the people must work proactively. Wouldn't you agree?" In contrast, the corresponding section of the PLAN

China Branch's English-language translation reads: "It is our belief that only when the government is in the hands of the people, the people are able to enjoy their happiness and peaceful living."[60] In the English translation, all references to Stalin and the Soviet Union have been excised, and Chih-kao's words have been edited to read as a bland statement about the importance of democratic governance in the abstract. Clearly, the PLAN China Branch feared that asking foster parents whether they thought it was a good idea to emulate Stalinism risked jeopardizing their support for the program.

The practice of censorship through translation benefits the historian by rendering the logic of censorship legible. The PLAN China Branch used its role as translator to omit the "excessively leftist" content they found counterproductive, but I have encountered no evidence that they fabricated the contents of letters. They could suggest potential topics for children's letters, coach them on style and tone, and even censor problematic passages, but the PLAN China Branch ultimately relied on the children themselves to provide the unique content of people's diplomacy through their inimitable stories of life during the Chinese Communist revolution.

The corpus of Chinese children's letters sent to the United States through the adoption plan raised several questions, as relevant to the PLAN China Branch at the time as they are to the historian today. Who were the Americans receiving these letters? What did they make of what their foster children told them about the Chinese revolution? In short, was the PLAN China Branch's attempt at people's diplomacy working? To answer these questions, the organization collected information about American donors through which it could analyze their class backgrounds and political leanings—and adjust its program accordingly.

## MEET THE FOSTER PARENTS

The PLAN China Branch's fundraising in the United States is best understood in the context of a decade-long history of humanitarian fundraising for vulnerable children abroad on the part of the American left. As Laura Briggs has written, Americans' concern with rescuing children overseas emerged in the 1930s out of a "left anti-Fascist internationalist front" arrayed against German Nazism, Franco's war against the Spanish Republic, and the Japanese invasion of China. Briggs argues that heart-rending photographic images of mothers and children affected by these conflicts were "leftist images that demanded attention for working-class lives" abroad. By portraying their subjects as "hardworking but down on their luck," these photographs simultaneously stirred sympathies for vulnerable children across national, racial, and cultural boundaries and "built support for popular organizations and socialist movements."[61] Originally focused on helping the Republicans in the Spanish Civil War, PLAN had been born out of this 1930s popular front movement. A decade later, PLAN fundraising campaigns built on this tradition by seeking to train the sympathies of its progressive, internationalist donor base on the figure of the Chinese child.

The advertisements that PLAN used to attract donors in the United States provide insight into the types of Americans it sought to recruit as foster parents. Unlike other humanitarian organizations that deployed Christian and anti-Communist rhetoric, PLAN avoided overtly religious or political appeals and instead focused directly on child suffering.[62] In some cases, however, its advertisements highlighted issues like social inequality more likely to appeal to the American left. An October 1948 advertisement quoted a letter from a thirteen-year-old boy named Tsen-yuan that observed the vast disparities between China's rich and poor: "In the cold winter it is not much surprise to hear that 40 to 50 children with not enough clothes died in one day of coldness . . . of course the rich people wear as much as they can carry."[63] PLAN advertisements also highlighted prominent progressive figures who served as foster parents, including First Ladies Eleanor Roosevelt and Bess Truman, writers Helen Keller and Thomas Mann, and Congressman Will Rogers Jr.[64] Moreover, Executive Chair Edna Blue strongly denounced those who would "use relief as a political weapon" by refusing to support children in Communist countries. She was quoted in the *New York Times* as saying, "They must learn the true meaning of relief work. I have never met a child who was a republican, Fascist or Communist."[65] As a result, conservatives sometimes criticized PLAN as a "Red front organization."[66] While PLAN was officially nonpolitical, it courted progressive Americans as foster parents and publicly criticized the use of humanitarian aid as a tool of U.S. Cold War foreign policy. In both these regards, it was an ideal partner for the CWF's experiment in revolutionary humanitarianism.

As the PLAN China Branch did not receive biographical information about American foster parents, it relied on information foster parents shared in their letters to gain an understanding of the donors who were the targets of people's diplomacy. According to their analysis, the categories of people most likely to serve as foster parents included students, religious people, teachers, community organizations, workers, capitalists, and public figures.[67] In addition to creating a demographic portrait of American donors, the PLAN China Branch also analyzed their letters to gauge how their participation in the adoption plan affected their views on China. While it found most foster parents ill-informed about Chinese politics, the organization concluded that children's letters were providing them with a favorable impression of the new China:

> From the foster parents' letters, we can see clearly that the majority of Americans do not have a good understanding of the surrounding political situation. Their letters generally discuss things like family affairs and religion. Although these kinds of people have an indifferent attitude toward China, their reaction to the People's Republic of China has actually been fairly good. Of course, there is also a minority of foster parents' letters that are indeed very reactionary.[68]

While some sponsors remained "indifferent" to the People's Republic of China, and a small number were apparently downright hostile, the PLAN China Branch initially remained optimistic that children's letters were gradually improving their American foster parents' views of the Chinese Communist revolution.

Unfortunately, I have not been able to locate any original letters that American foster parents wrote to Chinese children through the PLAN China Branch's adoption plan. However, *Work for the Suffering Children* included two examples of letters from American foster parents in Chinese translation. While these letters should not be read as representative of sponsors' letters in general, they modeled the type of responses the PLAN China Branch sought—and at least occasionally received—from American donors. The first letter, from an American identified as "E. H." to his foster child Ping on April 7, 1949, expresses approval of Ping's commitment to work for social equality: "I am extremely interested in your determination to dedicate yourself to improving the lives of working people. . . . From the perspective of morality, there are some people who have too much, and then there are others who have nothing at all and have even been deprived of life's basic necessities. This is wrong indeed. Therefore, we really must struggle to improve the lives of such people." The second letter, from Byron to Zhenru on November 12, 1948, asked after Zhenru's safety in the midst of China's civil war: "I read with great attention the news about your war. I pray that you and your compatriots will not endure even more suffering."[69] Expressing concern for the plight of working people and condemning the suffering wrought by the civil war, these letters meshed well with Chinese Communist rhetoric at the time. By publishing them as examples, the PLAN China Branch sought to show a domestic audience that American foster parents were not "imperialists" but ordinary people who shared their desires for China's future.

Privately, however, the organization's initial optimism that children's letters were improving Americans' views of Communist China gave way to the realization that most foster parents were unwilling to engage in protracted political exchanges. A mid-1950 report summarized the changes that foster parents' letters had undergone in the ten months that had elapsed since the founding of the PRC: "They go from not understanding Chinese affairs to having a favorable impression, but in the end they ultimately go silent. The majority of sponsors' letters do not say a single word about China's domestic situation. Those that do are a very small minority, and they often distort the facts."[70]

As of mid-1950 the results of people's diplomacy were decidedly mixed. PLAN had attracted a large and diverse group of left-leaning Americans by appealing to themes like combating poverty and inequality while publicly criticizing the denial of humanitarian aid to people in Communist states. Moreover, the PLAN China Branch's analysis of foster parents' letters suggested that many had gained a positive impression of the Chinese revolution from their foster children. Nevertheless, as time stretched on, foster parents became increasingly unwilling to engage with their foster children about the political situation in China, and some stopped writing altogether. Internally, the PLAN China Branch complained that "the American imperialists' actions to oppose our people have hindered donations and interfered with the affection between donors and their adopted children."[71] With the United States and China on the brink of war in Korea, its adoption plan, already on shaky ground, would face its most difficult challenge yet.

## FOLLOW THE MONEY

In the spring of 1949 the American sponsors of an eleven-year-old boy named Chin-chuen learned that he had been admitted to the Chun Yun School in Suzhou under the care of "Miss Sze Chien-chiao."[72] Almost certainly, this name was unfamiliar to Chin-chuen's foster parents. Yet the woman in charge of the Chun Yun School was none other than Shi Jianqiao, the famous female assassin who had murdered the warlord Sun Chuanfang in 1935 to avenge her father's death—only to be pardoned by the Supreme Court in Nanjing because she had been motivated by righteous passion. After her release from prison Shi Jianqiao met Soong Ching-ling and other progressive figures through her participation in patriotic fundraising campaigns during World War II. After the war, Shi founded the Chun Yun School for underprivileged children in Suzhou, which also served as an important base for underground Communist activities.[73] The PLAN China Branch provided funding for the school and assigned foster parents to sixteen of its students.[74] Moreover, the PLAN China Branch openly celebrated its connection to Shi Jianqiao. In March 1950 its Chinese-language newsletter, *FPP Correspondent*, published a poem about her titled "Learn from Big Sister Shi."[75] While the Chun Yun School was unique in being the only PLAN-funded institution founded by a famous assassin, it was otherwise typical of the institutions to which the PLAN China Branch channeled humanitarian aid—child welfare institutions run by progressive individuals with close ties to the underground Communist Party.

By accepting global humanitarian aid through the adoption plan, Soong Ching-ling and the PLAN China Branch aimed to serve not only the ideological but also the material needs of the Chinese Communist revolution. Therefore, an analysis of the politics of the adoption plan must also attend to a basic question: Where did the money go? The dislocations of World War II and the Chinese Civil War had left the new Communist government in desperate need of funds to meet basic social welfare needs. Against this backdrop, the PLAN China Branch channeled its precious humanitarian resources to "progressive" child welfare institutions that could simultaneously provide for impoverished children and train them to participate actively in the revolution.

The China Welfare Fund Children's Theatre makes a particularly good case study to examine how PLAN funds were spent on the ground in

China. Founded in Shanghai in the spring of 1947, the Children's Theatre was a children's theatrical troupe consisting of orphans and other impoverished children. Equal parts child welfare institution and performing arts ensemble, it provided shelter, education, and vocational training to its members while also offering cultural programming for a mass audience of children. As the only PLAN-supported institution directly operated by the CWF, it served as a model of the type of institution to which the CWF sought to direct global humanitarian aid. Moreover, the PLAN China Branch closely monitored and explicitly endorsed the Children's Theatre's work. Its 1949 annual report counted the Children's Theatre among several institutions that "maintain complete and friendly cooperation with PLAN."[76]

Despite its status as an educational and humanitarian institution, the Children's Theatre was deeply committed to furthering the revolution by inculcating socialist values among China's children and youth. During the Chinese Civil War the Children's Theatre quietly collaborated with schools and teachers affiliated with the underground Chinese Communist Party to stage clandestine performances of plays with pro-Communist themes.[77] After the liberation of Shanghai in May 1949, the Children's Theatre quickly emerged as one of the city's most influential cultural institutions. In the first two years of the PRC, it staged 217 performances that reached an estimated audience of 300,000 people.[78] Children's Theatre members also performed in at least sixteen parades and mass demonstrations during this period, for occasions ranging from the founding of the PRC to International Children's Day to the Movement to Oppose Currency Speculation.[79] As Children's Theatre reports would have it, the children enthusiastically embraced their heavy workload in the name of revolution: "They did not know fatigue. They did not know hardship. They had but one conviction: to work—for the fatherland, for the great working people who were sick and tired of pain and exploitation!"[80] Children's letters to their foster parents, however, sometimes told a different story. Thirteen-year-old Yu-li wrote to his foster parents: "Recently my health has not been good. I get sick often. I get sick more than once a week. This asthma is very difficult. But in this kind of organization, there's nothing that can be done."[81]

It was the Children's Theatre's June 1950 production of *Little Snowflake* that announced its arrival as a major cultural force in postrevolution Shanghai. An adaptation of a Russian children's play from 1948 about "how the American imperialists treat the Black children within their own country," *Little Snowflake* was performed thirty times during the summer of 1950 at Shanghai's Lanxin Theater, reaching a total estimated audience of 58,000 people, the vast majority of whom were children.[82] A highly polemical play that achieved wild popularity, *Little Snowflake* offers a vivid illustration of how the Children's Theatre channeled humanitarian funds into a potent mixture of social welfare, youth mobilization, and political propaganda. Set at a school somewhere in the U.S. South, the play follows the tribulations of a Black boy named Dick (nicknamed "Little Snowflake") who is abused by a white girl named Angel and her father, Big Capitalist Bill.[83] The child actors filled their letters to their American sponsors with their own interpretations of the play's educational value. As fifteen-year-old actor Su-ping wrote, "This play is mainly to teach children not to have close-minded racist thinking."[84] However, beneath the surface of its heavy-handed critique of American racism, the plot of *Little Snowflake* subtly reflected the CWF's efforts to justify accepting American humanitarian aid in the context of surging anti-American sentiment. The play is full of progressive American characters who ultimately succeed in defending Little Snowflake Dick against the likes of Big Capitalist Bill. Fervent advocates for downtrodden children, these Americans symbolized the international progressive forces through which the CWF sought to build "revolutionary humanitarianism."

Did *Little Snowflake* achieve its didactic goals? Contemporary accounts suggest that the play was very well received. In some cases, audience reactions were downright raucous. One vivid account from October 1950 describes (perhaps with some embellishment) the visceral responses of an audience of children:

> When the Black child was arrested by American agents—how they shouted! How they yelled! "Dick, look out! There's someone behind you who wants to arrest you!" And when the Black child escaped from jail with his clothes ripped and his body bloody from beatings, the actors cried and the audience cried with them. They cried with passion and some even sobbed out loud. However, when that capitalist again appeared on the stage, the children's tear-stained faces turned angry. "Scoundrel! Hey! Get out of here! Get!" They stomped the floor with their little legs and

stood up from their seats so that the theatre fell into chaos and the play was almost unable to continue.[85]

However, it was not until after the performances concluded that audiences truly got out of hand. In his July 4, 1950, letter to his foster parents, Yu-li wrote that "the little audience members" would sometimes charge backstage after the show hoping to beat up the young actor who had the misfortunate of playing Big Capitalist Bill.[86] The written reflections of the children and adults who watched *Little Snowflake* provide further evidence of the play's profound impact. After attending a performance, a fourteen-year-old girl named Chung-lan wrote to her American foster parents to describe how she was moved to tears by the play's depiction of violent American racism. Her letter concluded by pointedly asking her foster parents, "Why can white people bully Black people like that? It really is not right."[87] Chung-lan was not alone in being deeply affected by the play. After one performance of *Little Snowflake*, a middle school teacher wrote a letter to the Children's Theatre declaring, "There is not a single advanced teacher who could within one hundred minutes produce even one percent of the effectiveness of this work!"[88]

To be sure, the money that the PLAN China Branch sent to the Children's Theatre was used to provide food, shelter, education, and vocational training to the poor and orphaned children who were its members. At the same time, the Children's Theatre used PLAN funding to participate actively in the Chinese Communist revolution—sometimes to an extent that risked the health and safety of the children under its care. By using PLAN funds for its potent mixture of social welfare, youth mobilization, and propaganda, the Children's Theatre offered a new model for how to deploy global humanitarian aid in support of the Chinese Communist revolution.

In addition to the Children's Theatre, another of the most prominent institutions to receive PLAN China Branch support was a home for troubled youth called Shanghai Boystown (Shaonian Cun). Shanghai Boystown was originally founded by the Buddhist Jingye Society in June 1940 as a wartime shelter for "street urchins" called the Jingye Foundling.[89] After the conclusion of World War II, the Jingye Foundling was moved to Dachang in the northern outskirts of Shanghai and

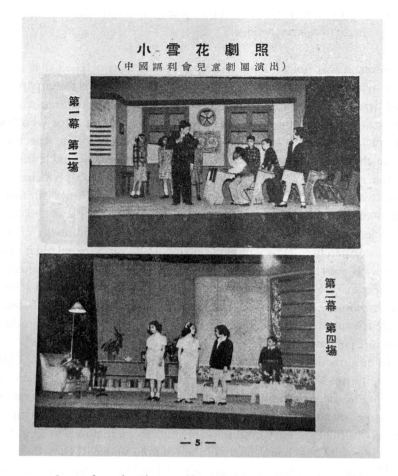

FIGURE 4.3 Scenes from the China Welfare Fund Children's Theatre's production of *Little Snowflake*. Vera Liubimova, *Xiao xuehua* [Little snowflake], trans. Liu Binyan (Beijing: Qingnian chubanshe, 1952), 5.

rechristened Shanghai Boystown after Irish Priest Edward Flanagan's famous "Boys Town" orphanage in Nebraska.[90] The important Buddhist writer and philanthropist Zhao Puchu was chosen to serve as its superintendent.[91] Shanghai Boystown began accepting PLAN funding in September 1947, and it quickly became almost entirely dependent on the adoption plan to meet its basic expenses. The PLAN China Branch's educational and inspection departments visited Boystown regularly, and, like the Children's Theatre, it was listed among the institutions with which the PLAN China Branch maintained "complete and friendly cooperation."[92]

Shanghai Boystown closely collaborated with the underground Communist Party in Shanghai, hiring numerous underground party members as teachers, their salaries paid with PLAN funds. The head instructor at Shanghai Boystown was an underground party member named Wang Juan, who worked under the alias Wang Danren. She later remembered, "We primarily used our work at Boystown as cover to penetrate deeply into the city and carry out some other activities. However, we also had a responsibility to educate the children and youth of Boystown. We also looked for opportunities to impart some revolutionary principles and to train and bring up some activists."[93] In September 1948 Wang Juan and two other Boystown teachers were convicted of conducting organizational and propaganda work for the Communist "bandits" and given multiyear prison sentences.[94] However, their arrests appear to have been treated as isolated cases and did not significantly disrupt life at Shanghai Boystown.[95]

What lessons did these teachers impart to the children under their care? Letters from the children at Shanghai Boystown to their American foster parents suggest the strong ideological bent of the education they received. On June 26, 1949, a boy named Zonghong wrote, "Since I have also suffered the pain of exploitation and oppression, now that I have freed myself, why would I not use my strength to work for the people?"[96] Two months later Lien-shoo wrote, "We still must study hard so that we can reconstruct new China, overthrow the dictatorial reactionary forces, and revive democracy, freedom, and equality. These are the thoughts that are in our minds."[97] Clearly, the underground Communist Party members who taught at Shanghai Boystown infused their political ideals into the education they provided their students, who in turn communicated them to their American foster parents. In addition to learning revolutionary principles in the classroom, children at Shanghai Boystown were sometimes enlisted to carry out dangerous tasks on behalf of the Chinese Communist Party. It was a fourteen-year-old boy named Zhang Weizhong who undertook perhaps the most daring mission of any

Boystown student. To avoid being caught in the fighting of the civil war, in April 1949 Shanghai Boystown evacuated to the original location of the Jingye Foundling in central Shanghai, where they shared a courtyard with a group of Nationalist soldiers recuperating from injuries. As Zhang was young and would not attract suspicion, the Jing'an District underground Communist Party instructed him to attempt to locate where the soldiers had hidden their weapons and ammunition. Zhang frequently went to play with the Nationalist soldiers while furtively searching out where they kept their weapons. Eventually he discovered that they had thrown their weapons and ammunition into a fishpond behind the courtyard. He informed his teachers, and the People's Liberation Army was able to salvage the material from the water.[98]

In the summer of 1949 many of the older boys left Boystown to join the People's Liberation Army. Shortly after the liberation of Shanghai, a contingent of PLA soldiers moved in beneath Shanghai Boystown in the former courtyard of the Jingye Foundling. At the encouragement of Boystown's head administrator, Zhou Wengeng, many boys enthusiastically signed up to join the army, and twenty-three ultimately met the requirements and enlisted. Most were assigned to serve in the cultural working corps (*wen gong dui*) that staged performances to encourage troops on their way into battle.[99] A boy named Teh-san wrote to his foster father explaining his decision to join the army: "Although I have left my beloved home Boystown, I will not forget your kindness in providing for me.... Although our life in the cultural working corps is difficult, I still get a lot of joy and comfort from the good impressions we make on the audiences in our performances every day."[100] The zeal with which the youth of Shanghai Boystown volunteered for the PLA is perhaps best revealed in the letters of those boys who were turned away because they were too young or did not meet the physical requirements. Chai-po wrote, "Originally I also joined, but I had to come back because I did not pass the physical requirements. I feel very depressed because I know that joining the army to serve the people is the most honorable thing."[101] As for those boys who succeeded in joining the PLA, little could they have expected that they would soon be deployed to Korea to fight against the United States, the country of their former foster parents—and that not all would make it back alive.

## UNHAPPY ENDINGS: THE KOREAN WAR AND THE CLOSING OF THE PLAN CHINA BRANCH

Gun-chun was one of the twenty-three Shanghai Boystown students who joined the People's Liberation Army in June 1949.[102] Later that month he wrote a letter to his foster parents, the Macauleys, explaining his decision. Although he asked them to continue writing, it was in effect his goodbye letter: "I am very thankful to you my foster parents for raising us. Although we have entered society on the path to serve humanity, I still hope that you will write to us, and finally I hope that you will send me pictures of my foster brothers."[103] In October 1950, approximately fourteen months after he wrote that letter, China intervened in the Korean War and Gun-chun was deployed to the Korean Peninsula, where he found himself at war with the country of the people he called his foster parents.

As a member of the cultural working corps, Gun-chun's job was to make costumes and props for a dance troupe that performed to encourage the troops. He was remembered as someone who talked little but was painstaking and meticulous in his work. During the summer of 1951, as the Chinese Army retreated north toward the 38th parallel, Gun-chun suffered severe burns on his face and hands from napalm bombs dropped by UN forces. He was rushed to a field hospital for treatment, but shortly thereafter the hospital was caught in an attack and he was never heard from again.[104] It was not until many years later that one of Gun-chun's former classmates and comrades, Wang Wenxiang, looked him up in the military archives and found the coordinates of his burial site just south of the 38th parallel.[105]

Gun-chun's tragic fate illustrates how the PLAN China Branch's strategy of cultivating global intimacy to ameliorate global politics eventually crumbled against the hard realities of war. At the time he left Shanghai Boystown, Gun-chun was, by all appearances, an adoption plan success story. He had received food, shelter, and an education through the support of his American foster parents, with whom he had built a mutually affectionate relationship. And he left Boystown ready to become a self-sufficient young man through a career in military service. Nevertheless, within two years of leaving the adoption plan, he was engaged in a vicious battle with the compatriots of his former foster parents that would leave him dead, laid to rest in an unmarked gravesite in an unfamiliar land. To the Macauleys, Gun-chun was a "foster son," but to the pilots of American warplanes dropping napalm bombs over Korea, he was simply "the enemy."

By the time Gun-chun met his fate in Korea, the PLAN China Branch had already been shuttered. The officially stated reason for closing in December 1950 stemmed from a dispute regarding whether PLAN funds could be subject to the approval of the People's Relief Administration of China. As part of a broader reorganization of the CWF in 1950, the organization's new regulations stated that "all money and goods donated by international friends must receive the approval of the PRAC before they can be accepted and used."[106] On October 11, 1950, Tannebaum wrote to Edna Blue in New York to explain this new policy: "The reason for this . . . is that a national plan on relief and welfare is being developed and it is their intention to muster all possible aid to effecting this plan." Tannebaum added that he had met with PRAC vice secretary Dong Biwu, and he assured Blue that there was "no question" that the PRAC "clearly understand our operation in China, and are in agreement with allowing us to function."[107] Nevertheless, on November 2, 1950, the PLAN General Committee decided that requiring funds to be cleared by the PRAC violated the PLAN charter's insistence that it "should be free from any connection with, or allegiance to any group having any political or propagandistic interest of any kind." A motion to immediately terminate PLAN's work in China passed unanimously.[108]

The PLAN China Branch, the CWF, and the PRAC were outraged by PLAN's decision to terminate the China program, which they viewed as PLAN succumbing to domestic pressure not to do anything that might help the Chinese people under the leadership of the Communist Party. Tannebaum wrote to Blue, "The American government is making the breach between the Chinese people and the American people wider and wider. . . . If there is anything you can do to correct it, the American people will be ever appreciative to you."[109] Nevertheless, PLAN headquarters explained in a series of telegrams and letters that it had become "difficult for one to believe that the relief funds can directly benefit the children." In response, the PLAN China Branch reluctantly informed the PRAC that it had no choice but to shutter its operations at the end of the year: "We unanimously felt that this was the inevitable result of the American imperialists' longstanding opposition to the Chinese people."[110] In their capacities as chair and vice-chair of the PRAC, Soong Ching-ling and Dong Biwu excoriated the termination of PLAN aid to China as politically motivated: "We were extremely indignant to hear of this measure, which is obviously searching for a pretext to treat the Chinese people as an enemy." However, in a separate letter to the CWF, Soong Ching-ling struck a somewhat softer tone, noting that PLAN "always helped the Chinese people in the past."[111]

Soong Ching-ling, Dong Biwu, and the PLAN China Branch were probably justified in viewing PLAN's stated reason for terminating its China program as a "pretext." While subjecting PLAN funds to PRAC approval could be read as violating the letter of the PLAN charter, PLAN frequently coordinated with politicians and government bodies in other contexts. In fact, its founding mission in 1937 was to provide funding for an effort by the Duchess of Atholl, a prominent Conservative member of the British Parliament who strongly supported the Republicans, to establish hostels for refugee children in Spain. Shortly after closing its China Branch, PLAN began operating in Korea, where "institutions were supported only upon the recommendation of the Korean Ministry of Social Affairs."[112]

Ultimately, the PLAN China Branch's experiment in revolutionary humanitarianism ended because PLAN's New York headquarters would no longer fund what it correctly perceived as a humanitarian program that served the interests of the Chinese Communist revolution. At the same time, other humanitarian organizations that had continued operating child sponsorship programs in China after the Communist revolution, including China's Children Fund and the American-Oriental Friendship Association, were also coming under increasing pressure to leave China, albeit for very different reasons.

On July 3, 1950, a boy named Da-Chwen at the World Red Swastika Society's Orphanage for Homeless Children in Tianjin wrote a letter to his foster mother, Shirley, in which he mused on the importance of self-sufficiency: "Everyone says that only the People's Government can help the people solve their difficulties. It is right to use our own abilities to overcome disaster. Depending on other people is not a fundamental solution. Don't you agree?"[113]

It is unclear whether Da-Chwen appreciated the irony of writing such a letter to the foreign woman who financially supported him. Regardless, his words were prescient. China's intervention in the Korean War in October 1950 lent new urgency to a campaign to achieve national self-sufficiency in providing for social welfare needs. In this context, Chinese officials, intellectuals, and child welfare workers revived the Marxist argument that humanitarian programs facilitated imperialism in China by rendering its most vulnerable people dependent on imperialist largesse. Among the most prominent humanitarian programs in China, the adoption plan emerged as a focal point of this critique—with profound consequences for the future of global humanitarianism in China and across East Asia.

# 5

## THE HUMANITARIAN CLOAK

In 1947 Generalissimo and Madame Chiang Kai-shek donated their former wartime residence—a hundred-acre estate consisting of twenty-one stone buildings in the picturesque hills overlooking the Yangzi River in Chongqing—to serve as the location for an orphanage to be named Chiang Memorial Children's Village (Zhongzheng Fu You Cun).[1] They entrusted the operation of the orphanage to an American Southern Baptist missionary named Dr. J. R. Saunders, who had previously worked with China's Children Fund. Saunders founded a new organization, the American-Oriental Friendship Association (AOFA), to fundraise for Chiang Memorial Children's Village and other Christian orphanages in China through its own version of the adoption plan. In one typical fundraising brochure, Saunders encouraged American donors to "adopt" Chinese children and "rear them as your own":

> Through the adoption plan, individuals, families, and groups in the United States and Canada can adopt children in China. They can write to the children they are sponsoring and receive replies; many parents take out adoptions for their children and through correspondence build up a lasting friendship. Our Homes emphasize the Adoption Plan with its possibilities for understanding, goodwill, and mutual benefit to both the child adopted and the child's sponsor.[2]

While the AOFA's adoption plan celebrated affective bonds of friend-ship and family across national, racial, and cultural lines, such transna-tional intimacies were infused with urgent political significance in the context of the Chinese Civil War and the emerging Cold War. A Septem-ber 1948 AOFA newsletter asked, "Can you think what will be the dan-ger to Christianity and Democracy if the 15,000,000 orphan children of China are allowed to become Communist? When you say you can do nothing to prevent the spread of Communism, ARE YOU SURE?"[3] After China's Communist revolution in 1949, the political significance of the AOFA's adoption plan soon became apparent to the new Communist authorities in Chongqing. When the Chongqing Branch of the People's Relief Administration of China investigated Chiang Memorial Children's Village in 1951, it was appalled to find that children still "carried around pictures and letters from their American parents and from foreign chil-dren." Its report framed the effects of the adoption plan in alarmist terms as compromising the political loyalty and even the very Chinese-ness of the children: "They look down upon their own fatherland, lose respect for their own nationality, and despise their fellow compatriots." It quoted one child named Ssu-Chun—who had been "adopted" by a man named John from Marion, Virginia—as telling investigators, "I would rather be an American's dog than a Chinese person."[4]

Throughout the summer and fall of 1951, the PRAC Chongqing Branch waged a campaign to reverse the effects of the adoption plan by getting the children at Chiang Memorial Children's Village to recognize that "the kind of harm the American imperialists had done to their thinking was even more sinister than physical abuse." The campaign culminated with children participating in a mass denunciation meeting in which they renounced the intimate ties they had forged with foreigners through the adoption plan. A boy named Er-hsiang, who had been "adopted" by a couple in Perry, Georgia, was among the first to speak: "Before I did not know that they had come to poison and deceive us, and I even thought that they had come to give us help and be good to us. Only now do I know that Saunders is an imperialist element. He insulted our dignity and poisoned our character. I truly hate him!" Shortly thereafter, a boy named Ling-yung, who had been adopted by a man named King See in Manila, the Philippines, also rose to speak: "In the past I listened to the imperialists' rumors and hated the Communist Party and the People's Liberation Army. Now I understand

FIGURE 5.1 Advertisement for the AOFA's adoption plan. *Asia Calling* 1, no. 8 (1947): 2.

that I had drank his poison." One by one, other children followed suit in making their denunciations. After each child spoke, they took out the photographs and letters they had saved from their foster parents and tore them up before their classmates and teachers. Er-hsiang's letters from his foster father Geo, Ling-yung's photograph of his sponsor King See—all ended up with the ripped remains of global intimacy accumulating by the fistful on the ground beneath the children's feet.[5]

The striking image of the children of Chiang Memorial Children's Village ripping their former sponsors' letters and photographs to shreds at a mass denunciation meeting provides one dramatic illustration of the processes through which China systematically dismantled foreign-funded humanitarian institutions during the early 1950s. In the immediate aftermath of the revolution, Chinese Communist Party leaders had endorsed the PLAN China Branch's efforts to use the adoption plan to transform children into "people's diplomats" who could secure material and ideological support for the revolution abroad (chapter 4). In the context of the Korean War, however, the adoption plan instead appeared to have created a sizable group of children emotionally and economically indebted to China's greatest military and ideological enemy—the United States. Paradoxically, the very aspect of the adoption plan that had made it seem such a promising program for forging a new "revolutionary humanitarianism"—the transnational intimate relationships developed between Chinese children and foreign adults—also made it a dangerous example of how "imperialist humanitarianism" might subvert the revolution from within. As the CCP's efforts to erase the effects of the adoption plan make clear, the emotional loyalties of children were an important battleground on the affective terrain of Cold War China.

Focusing on two especially controversial orphanages supported by the adoption plan—the AOFA's Chiang Memorial Children's Village in Chongqing and the CCF's Canaan Children's Home in Beijing—this chapter analyzes how humanitarian work on behalf of China's children became a fraught arena for testing the limits of Sino-American cooperation in the midst of the quickly descending Cold War. At the time of the Chinese Communist revolution, tens of thousands of Chinese children lived in foreign-funded orphanages—many of them missionary-affiliated institutions that were far less "progressive" than those supported by the PLAN China Branch. While the CCP often accused American aid organizations of "cultural imperialism," they were hesitant to shut down institutions on which so many vulnerable children depended. Against this backdrop, Chinese and foreign relief workers engaged in serious efforts to integrate private humanitarian aid from abroad into the embryonic social welfare system of the People's Republic of China. Emphasizing the CCP's ideological commitment to combatting imperialism, scholars of Cold War China have long contended that, by the time of the Communist revolution, there existed little possibility of developing positive Sino-American ties.[6] Shifting focus from high-level diplomacy to international humanitarian work offers a new perspective on Sino-American relations in the early years of the Cold War, revealing a messy reality of compromise and negotiation taking place just behind the sharply drawn ideological battle lines. During the Korean War, however, even Sino-American cooperation in the realm of child welfare work became untenable. The uprooting of humanitarian institutions from China in the early 1950s would ultimately reshape the geopolitics of humanitarianism across East Asia, foreclosing the possibility of a humanitarianism of international solidarity and paving the way toward a new age of Cold War humanitarianism.

## "ALL HONEST PEOPLE": HUMANITARIANISM AND INTERNATIONAL SOCIALISM BEFORE 1950

Debates over humanitarianism in postrevolution China were shaped by the uneasy partnerships forged between humanitarian organizations and international socialist groups during the first half of the twentieth century. Marxist critiques of humanitarianism date back to the *Manifesto of the Communist Party*, in which Marx and Engels list humanitarianism as one instance of what they term "bourgeois socialism."[7] According to Marxist logic, humanitarianism reinforced global inequalities by sanding the roughest edges off of imperialism and colonialism. By providing services like orphanages and famine relief, humanitarians sought to convince colonized people to associate imperial powers with noble benevolence while ignoring the imperialist exploitation that created the conditions of near-constant humanitarian crisis in the first place. As Sam Moyn observed, Marx-inspired critiques of how humanitarianism reinforces global inequality remain the "near orthodox view of humanitarianism" among scholars today.[8]

Despite their presumed ideological hostility, humanitarianism and international socialism developed a surprisingly symbiotic relationship as they both grew into globally significant movements during the first half of the twentieth century. During the Russian famine of 1921–1922, Lenin and the Bolsheviks actively courted humanitarian aid.[9] In a dramatic appeal "to all honest people" published in U.S. newspapers, Russian writer Maxim Gorky declared, "Russia's misfortune offers humanitarians a splendid opportunity to demonstrate the vitality of humanitarianism. . . . I ask all honest European and American people for prompt aid to the Russian people."[10] Despite virulent anticommunism in Europe and the United States during the early 1920s, both the International Committee of the Red Cross and Herbert Hoover's American Relief Administration (ARA) answered the call, launching what was at the time "the greatest humanitarian aid program in the history of the world, involving dozens of nations and as many charitable organizations." To overcome American resistance to donate to Bolshevik Russia, the ARA helped pioneer the use of photography and film to cultivate sympathy for the victims of humanitarian crises. Not only did humanitarian aid during the Russian famine help the Bolsheviks survive a major crisis of their early rule, the famine was also "a major turning point in the emergence of a feeling of international solidarity in response to natural disasters."[11] During the 1930s the American left became increasingly involved in humanitarian efforts. In the midst of the Great Depression, photographers such as Dorothea Lange of the Farm Security Administration depicted the suffering of migrant women and children to combat anti-immigrant sentiment and bolster the moral case for economic relief. At the same time, heart-rending images of child refugees fleeing conflicts in China, Spain, and Germany dramatized the human toll of the rise of fascism.[12] By the late 1930s, humanitarians and socialists had become frequent allies in efforts to combat fascism in Europe and Asia.

After the outbreak of the Sino-Japanese War in 1937, Chinese causes once again ascended to the forefront of the global humanitarian conscience, and China became one of the primary fields for humanitarian-socialist cooperation. In response to the devastation of Chinese industry wrought by the Japanese invasion of coastal China, a group of prominent left-wing figures in China—including New Zealander Rewi Alley; Americans Edgar Snow, Helen Foster Snow, and Ida Pruitt; and British Ronald Hall—promoted the Chinese Industrial Cooperative Movement as a way to alleviate poverty and unemployment.[13] Contributions from foreigners and overseas Chinese poured in from at least ten countries, totaling approximately US$5 million during the course of the war.[14] Thanks in particular to the insistence of Soong Ching-ling and Rewi Alley, a significant portion of funds was directed to the Communist base area at Yan'an. By 1941 the area was home to forty-one industrial cooperatives with 1,041 members. In a September 1939 letter to Ronald Hall praising the cooperative movement, Mao Zedong wrote, "The size of its contribution to our struggle is beyond measure."[15]

In addition to the Industrial Cooperatives Movement, Soong Ching-ling's China Defence League also deployed the rhetoric of international solidarity to advocate for humanitarian aid to the Chinese Communists.

In 1943 the China Defence League published an English-language book, *In Guerilla China*, that combined forceful appeals for humanitarian aid to the Communist-controlled "Border Regions" with heroic descriptions of Communist "guerillas" as "the forces that have bitten deepest into the Japanese Fascist lines."[16] In a February 8, 1944, letter "To American Workers," Soong asked them to "openly express their hope that the people fighting fascism behind the lines of the Japanese invaders are also able to receive a share of supplies befitting of their combat mission."[17]

The most celebrated symbol of humanitarian selflessness in China during World War II was Canadian Communist medical doctor Norman Bethune. After briefly serving in the Spanish Civil War, Bethune worked as a medical volunteer in Mao's Eighth Route Army for two years before dying of blood poisoning on November 12, 1939, from a cut on his finger sustained while performing surgery on the battlefield. On December 12, 1939, Mao wrote a memorial titled "In Memory of Norman Bethune" that cemented his heroic status among the Chinese Communists.[18] By the early 1950s, Bethune was lionized as the embodiment of the new ideal of "revolutionary humanitarianism" (*geming rendao zhuyi*). In a December 1952 essay titled "Learn from Comrade Norman Bethune's Spirit of Revolutionary Humanitarianism," the president of the Chinese Medical Association, Fu Lianzhang, praised Bethune as having "manifested the noble spirit of communism and internationalism."[19] The celebration of Bethune's "revolutionary humanitarianism" provided an ideological and rhetorical framework through which humanitarian aid could be incorporated into the PRC's emerging social welfare system.

When the Chinese Communists criticized humanitarian organizations during the post–World War II period, it was primarily to complain that they were not receiving a share of humanitarian aid commensurate with their needs and contributions to the war effort. The Communists were especially frustrated by the paltry portion of UNRRA aid to China that was distributed to Communist-controlled regions. In the aftermath of the war, the CCP formed the Chinese Liberated Areas Relief Association (CLARA) to oversee relief efforts and administer UNRRA aid in the Communist-controlled areas of North China.[20] Yet despite the UNRRA's promise to provide aid on the basis of need and without political discrimination, CLARA representatives claimed that while Communist-controlled areas were home to approximately 60 percent of China's war refugees, they received only about 2 percent of UNRRA supplies.[21] In June 1946 an article on the front page of the *People's Daily* complained, "[We] only ask for that portion of outside help that we are supposed to receive. . . . This is a reasonable request and an appeal for justice that should receive the sympathy and support of fair-minded people in China and abroad."[22] By the summer of 1947, CLARA had become even more scathing in its criticisms of the UNRRA, issuing a report arguing that UNRRA aid had become a tool for "camouflaging American assistance to Chiang's civil war as postwar relief." Nevertheless, the CCP continued to maintain that the original humanitarian mission of the UNRRA was just and worthy—if only it were faithfully implemented. The same report concluded by thanking "the sincere and honest efforts of many UNRRA individuals . . . on behalf of the people in the Liberated Areas."[23] On the eve of the Chinese Communist revolution, the CCP remained fully in favor of global humanitarian aid—as long as it received its fair share.

## STRANGE BEDFELLOWS:
## CHRISTIAN HUMANITARIANISM IN COMMUNIST CHINA

Inheriting these global and local histories of fraught cooperation between humanitarian organizations and socialist movements, the PRC leadership was initially divided over whether and under what conditions China should continue to accept humanitarian aid from abroad. The nature of this divide is well-illustrated by the very different speeches delivered by PRAC chair Soong Ching-ling and Vice Premier Dong Biwu at the Chinese People's Relief Congress in April 1950. Soong forcefully articulated her vision for a new model of humanitarianism as "people's diplomacy" that could secure much-needed aid while also forging people-to-people links with progressive forces abroad.[24] In contrast, Dong accused the United States in particular of using the "cloak of humanitarianism" (*rendao waiyi*) as cover for a "reactionary political plot" to destroy the revolution. Situating American humanitarianism in the context of the "so-called Asia policy" of the United States, he quoted Secretary of State Dean Acheson as calling relief aid to China "a great opportunity to win back the Chinese people's hearts and strike a blow to the Soviet Union."[25] While Soong emphasized how aid from abroad could help the PRC, Dong warned that aid could be a Trojan horse undermining the revolution from within.

In the meantime, humanitarian institutions and local officials were already taking the initiative to negotiate how to continue humanitarian work across the ideological battle lines of the emerging Cold War. The CCF's efforts to carve out a role as an American Christian philanthropy in Communist China are emblematic of this brief but significant moment in which humanitarian organizations sought to integrate their programs into the fabric of the PRC's social welfare system. The CCF has been described as "the most politically conservative" international child welfare organization in the postwar period, deploying its "Christian identity" as a "weapon in the Cold War battle."[26] Nevertheless, characterizing the CCF as a dyed-in-the-wool anticommunist organization fails to account for its concerted efforts throughout 1949–1950 to court the support of Chinese Communist officials and alter its programs to meet Communist demands. The CCF's experiences during this period illustrate both the possibilities and limitations of practicing Christian humanitarianism in Communist China.

After the Chinese Communist revolution, the CCF was faced with the delicate task of simultaneously justifying its work in the rapidly polarizing political climates of Mao Zedong's China and Joseph McCarthy's America. Within China, the CCF used its monthly Chinese-language publication, *Blessed Children*, to convince Chinese audiences that its humanitarian programs were appropriate for China's new ideological climate. For example, on the front page of the December 1950 issue are two brief articles, "Instructions from Chairman Mao" and the "Pu Kong Orphanage Christian's Pledge," their parallel placement inviting careful comparison. Highlighting the overlap between Maoist ideology and Christian principles, the instructions from Chairman Mao call for a "spirit of mutual help" and "pursuing a simple lifestyle."[27] Likewise, the "Christian's pledge" adopts a Maoist vocabulary to demand that children "imitate the spirit of Christ in assiduously serving the masses."[28] By selectively quoting from both Mao and its own Christian tracts, the CCF implied that communists and Christians held shared principles that could underpin the practice of Christian charity in Communist China.

The CCF also sought to convince Chinese readers that its adoption plan was suitable for the children of new China. To this effect, *Blessed Children* published an article titled "Lessons from Incoming Letters" that attempted to apply a facade of equality to the highly paternalistic relationships between Chinese children and their American benefactors. The article reminded CCF children that "many sponsors are groups of ordinary Sunday school children who might even be younger than you all!" It also encouraged children to avoid using formalistic expressions of gratitude in their letters, such as "please frequently favor me with your instructions," which it dismissed as "social niceties of the old society." Moreover, the article included a Chinese translation of a letter sent by a group of American children in which each had written a "life lesson" to share with their Chinese counterparts. These lessons focused on uncontroversial values like perseverance ("no matter what happens, never lose faith") and helping others ("don't laugh at other people, instead you should help them").[29] By selecting this particular letter for translation and publication, the CCF implied that the letters children received through the adoption plan were innocuous missives that might even inculcate them with values that would help them become productive citizens of the PRC.

However, the CCF deployed strikingly different rhetoric when justifying its continued work in the PRC to American audiences. In late 1949 CCF founder Calvitt Clarke penned an article for *China News* entitled "Can We Do Business with Communist China?" His answer was a resounding "yes":

> As for CCF operating Chinese orphanages both within and without Communist China, our concern is the Chinese people and especially the children of China. We ask for the privilege of serving them wherever they desperately need us. Our thinking may differ from the beliefs of Communist officials but we Americans have learned in our country to cooperate with different races and beliefs. A child forms a common bond. And we believe that Christ died for us all, for all the round world.[30]

By invoking universal Christian love as well as the familiar notion that humanitarianism was above politics, the CCF argued that to stop its work in China would amount to punishing innocent children for the sins of their government.

Other *China News* articles implied that the gravest threat facing children in CCF orphanages was not Communist oppression but rather abandonment by their erstwhile American sponsors. The CCF assured donors that Communist officials were permitting its work to continue "without interruption," while also emphasizing that "no funds pass through any government official's hands" and "not one dollar has been lost."[31] In contrast to these measured reassurances about Chinese Communist rule, the CCF harshly criticized those Americans who had recently canceled their adoptions:

> So frequently of late the office receives letters from former contributors stating, "We have decided to drop the adoption of our Chinese child. We do not want to support any Communist." In the first place, the child isn't a Communist. . . . In the second place, that child, deserted by the friend he prayed for, is much less apt to become a Communist if he is cared for in our orphanage, where he is taught the same things he was taught before the Communists came, including Christianity, than if he is thrown out into the street.[32]

Dramatizing the life-or-death stakes of Americans dropping their adoptions, Clarke wrote, "Unless there is a marked improvement in income in the next few months I shall have to cable instructions to either turn out a percentage of children in all of our orphanages located in Communist territory or close up some of the orphanages completely. Such a cable will be a death warrant to thousands of children."[33]

As such articles demonstrate, by 1950 the CCF was increasingly forced to defend itself against accusations that its work benefited the Communist Party. In response to these allegations, it began developing the argument that its work in China was actually *anti*-Communist because it instilled children with Christianity and love for the United States. In a letter to the State Department's director for Chinese affairs, O. Edmund Clubb, Clarke estimated that only one in one hundred letters "shows propaganda or influence upon the child on the part of the Communists." On the other hand, "many" letters were "full of wishes to see America and appreciation for what America has done." The CCF also used children's letters with content favorable to the United States to assuage the worries of State Department officials who came to investigate their office.[34]

The CCF pursued conflicting public relations strategies in different national and linguistic contexts—emphasizing its ability to *strengthen* Communist rule in Chinese publications and ability to *weaken* Communist control in American publications. This reflected the very different functions of the CCF China office in Guangzhou—tasked with securing continued support from local Communist officials—and the CCF headquarters in Richmond—which was responsible for fundraising among an increasingly anti-Communist American public. As a result, the CCF's Chinese- and English-language publications both presented deliberately oversimplified characterizations of the organization's relationship with the Chinese Communist government. However, the interactions among CCF employees, local officials, and orphanage children on the ground in China reveal a messier reality marked by negotiation, conflict, and compromise.

In the months after the revolution, the CCF negotiated with Guangzhou municipal authorities over the conditions under which it could continue operating in China. At the November 15, 1949, meeting of the CCF's China Executive Committee in Guangzhou, Chairman Calvin Lee summarized the initial compromise they reached: "The People's Liberation Army has not interfered in any way with C.C.F. work and [our] religious program will not be interfered with if it is carried out on a voluntary and not compulsory basis. Orphans have been asked to join in the propaganda work of the P.L.A. but only on a voluntary basis and a few orphans have joined this kind of work on their own free will."[35] As the CCF had always made religious instruction central to its philanthropic mission, Lee's reassuring language belied major concessions: CCF children and staff would *not* be required to participate in religious activities, and they *would* be permitted to participate in propaganda work for the Communist government. As a result of this compromise, Communist ideology gradually came to replace Christianity in the instruction offered at CCF orphanages. In February 1950 Superintendent Hai Lau Ming of the CCF's Kiu Kong Orphanage reported, "Compulsory Bible classes have been abolished."[36] By late 1950, children at the CCF-supported Lingnan Industrial School were participating in a variety of explicitly political activities, including welcoming returning soldiers from the People's Volunteer Army, attending an exhibition on the "Resist America, Aid Korea" movement, and celebrating the anniversary of the founding of the Chinese Communist Party.[37]

The CCF also proved willing to embrace aspects of the Chinese Communists' inchoate pedagogical philosophy. At the July 1950 meeting of the CCF South China District Orphanages Conference (SCDOC), a wide range of fundamental changes to the CCF's program were discussed, including "how to implement a democratic style of looking after children," "how to adapt to the religious life of the liberated areas," and issues regarding the writing and translation of children's letters.[38] At an SCDOC study meeting held on December 2, 1950, participants were encouraged to consult a series of reference materials, including a book titled *Fostering and Educating a New Generation*, which argued, "The goal of our education is to raise the new generation to possess correct ideology and revolutionary disposition."[39] Nevertheless, the book also criticized "extreme" practices, such as struggle sessions that left uncomprehending children in tears and teachers who let students ("little cadres") grade their own exams in the name of democracy.[40] While the CCF embraced Chinese Communist ideas like "new democracy" and "ideological education," the practical meaning of these concepts was still in flux, and moderate interpretations compatible with the CCF's own pedagogical practices often still prevailed.

The CCF's efforts to continue funding orphanages via the adoption plan during the early years of the PRC were not without considerable difficulties. Most pressing was a lack of funds. In November 1949 the CCF's China Office announced that, due to declining fundraising in the United States, the CCF would be cutting all staff salaries and all grants to affiliated orphanages by one third.[41] While CCF orphanages attempted to make up for decreased funding by increasing children's productive labor, such activities rarely made much of a dent in budget deficits.[42] Furthermore, the high turnover of children made coordinating the adoption plan increasingly difficult. In February 1950 the China Executive Committee decided to send a list of children who had withdrawn to Clarke in Richmond "so he can decide what to do about the sponsors of these children."[43]

Despite these problems, as 1950 drew to a close, the CCF's adoption plan appeared to all involved to have weathered the tumultuous postrevolution period and carved out a role in early PRC society. In June 1950 Calvin Lee made a tour of several CCF orphanages in South China and reported that they were "running smoothly."[44] On June 26 the Pu Kong Orphanage sent 327 letters and hand-drawn cards from its children to the CCF office in Guangzhou to be forwarded to their foster parents in the United States.[45] These were apparently received in Richmond, where in September 1950 the Executive Committee reported that "our work in China is continuing as usual, without interference from the Communist Government. Much of the Christmas mail from China has already been received."[46] There were also indications that both Americans and Chinese were willing to continue their support for the adoption plan. Clarke remarked at one meeting, "It would appear from the correspondence that the general public throughout America is sympathetic to the needs of the orphan children whom we are helping—regardless of the attitude of the State Department."[47] And on December 13, 1950, a meeting of the teachers, students, and staff of the Lingnan Industrial School voted to continue receiving CCF aid through the adoption plan. As their decision put it, "this is the aid of American friends and does not have any relationship with imperialism."[48]

## "A LIVING DR. NORMAN BETHUNE": LAURA RICHARDS AND THE CANAAN CHILDREN'S HOME

In at least one case, Chinese Communist authorities were so impressed with an orphanage funded by the CCF's adoption plan that they offered to transform it into a model of revolutionary humanitarianism. Founded in 1929 by an American Presbyterian missionary named Laura Richards, the Canaan Children's Home in Beijing had been funded by the CCF's adoption plan since 1946.[49] Like other CCF orphanages, the Canaan Home coexisted with the new Communist authorities for more than two years after the liberation of Beijing. In fact, in a spring 1950 letter to CCF sponsors, Richards conveyed the impression that the Canaan Home had flourished with the birth of the PRC: "Never before have we had so many teachers"; "Our clothing is now better than it used to be"; "The place in which we now live is quite suitable for our family."[50] Richards's optimistic tone, however, masked her tense relationship with the local cadres assigned to monitor the orphanage. Beginning in February 1949 Communist cadres regularly gathered the children at the Canaan Home for evening political study sessions in which they were instructed on themes such as "economic exploitation" and "Americans are imperialists."[51] One month later the Canaan Home moved to the former site of the Peking American School, where three Communist cadres set up a permanent office from which to inspect the orphanage's operations.[52] They interviewed the children one by one, probing for evidence of mistreatment or that Richards harbored ill will toward the Communists. At least according to Richards's unpublished memoirs, however, the children remained steadfast in their support of her and refused to renounce their Christian faith.[53]

In the course of their surveillance, the cadres apparently developed a begrudging respect for Richards's work providing for more than two hundred children. Richards was famously Spartan in her living habits. As one child, "Zechariah," later recalled, "She lived the same life as the children, eating carrots, wild vegetables, the leaves and stems of sweet potatoes. . . . The better parts of the food, like the sweet potato plant, she saved for the feeble men and babies."[54] Richards's friend and former colleague Florence Logan remembered that "Laura's way of life gave the Communists no grounds for their usual accusations against foreigners."[55] As Logan put it, "Poverty was her greatest protection, really. They couldn't accuse her of mistreating servants, things like that. She was a servant herself."[56] Like other CCF-sponsored orphanages, the Canaan Home also incorporated "daily labor" into the orphanage's routine, and its publicity materials emphasized the spiritual and physical benefits of performing labor.[57] Finally, Laura Richards was apparently well liked by neighbors and local community members interviewed by the cadres.[58]

In early 1951 the cadres who had spent two years observing Richards's work at Canaan Children's Home made her an extraordinary offer. They called the entire orphanage together for a meeting and began by generously praising Richards: "She served the Chinese people with all her mind and soul. She gave her life to the cause of the Chinese people. We admire her. We realize that she has no hostility toward the Chinese government. It is our wish to cooperate with her to run this orphanage." And then they offered her a deal. If Richards would discontinue religious education and publicly criticize U.S. imperialism, she could continue running the orphanage and would be honored as a "living Dr. Norman Bethune."[59] The Communists' willingness to make a CCF-funded orphanage into a model of revolutionary humanitarianism stands as a testament to the real if fleeting possibilities for humanitarian collaboration across Cold War lines.

The moment, however, would soon pass. For the deeply religious Richards, who viewed Canaan Home first and foremost as an endeavor of Christian faith, the Communists' offer was impossible to accept. She went immediately to the British Embassy to request help securing an exit visa and left China to return to the United States via Hong Kong shortly thereafter.[60]

Spurned by Richards, the Communists launched an all-out rhetorical assault on the Canaan Home, denouncing it as an imperialist institution in a flurry of newspaper articles, mass denunciation meetings, and propaganda materials. Once imagined as a model of revolutionary humanitarianism, the CCF-funded Canaan Children's Home would instead gain notoriety as a symbol of how humanitarian institutions served as a "cloak" for imperialist encroachment.

It is important to avoid reading the virulent anticommunism of humanitarian organizations like the CCF—and the virulent antihumanitarianism of the CCP—backward into the early years of the PRC. Near the end of 1950 it appeared as if the CCF's flexible approach to dealing with Communist authorities—and the Communists' own moderate approach to humanitarian institutions—had made it possible for the adoption plan to survive as a global humanitarian program in Communist China. Within a matter of days, however, the situation would change dramatically.

## "JUST SHORT OF A DECLARATION OF WAR": DEFUNDING THE HUMANITARIAN PROJECT

The Chinese government's decision to reverse course and systemically cut off foreign funding for philanthropic activities in China originated in the context of reciprocal economic sanctions between the United States and China during the Korean War. In a move the *New York Times* called "just short of a war declaration," on December 16, 1950, the U.S. government froze all Chinese assets in the United States and barred U.S. ships from calling at Chinese ports.[61] Retaliating in kind, on December 28 Premier Zhou Enlai announced the freezing of all American assets in China, including all public and private American funds in Chinese bank accounts.[62] As the United States was China's largest provider of humanitarian aid, the decision to freeze all American funds immediately threatened the financial viability of humanitarian institutions in China. At Chiang Memorial Children's Village the effects were immediate. By January 3, 1951, less than one week after Zhou's order, a significant portion of its funds had already been frozen.[63] By the end of January, only 3,500 yuan remained accessible—enough to maintain the orphanage for only another three months.[64]

Korean War economic sanctions help explain the specific timing of China's decision to begin defunding humanitarian work in December 1950, as well as why U.S.-funded institutions were targeted earliest and most vociferously. Nevertheless, tit-for-tat retaliation for U.S. sanctions was only a proximate reason for targeting foreign philanthropy. More significantly, Chinese officials and intellectuals had come to identify global humanitarianism as an insidious tool of economic exploitation. On December 29, 1950, the famous writer Guo Moruo, in his new capacity as vice-premier of the Government Administration Council, delivered a report titled "Guiding Principles for Dealing with Cultural, Educational, and Relief Institutions as well as Religious Organizations That Accept American Funds."[65] Unanimously approved by the Government Administration Council and published the following day on the front page of the *People's Daily*, Guo's report sketched the historical and ideological logic behind the decision to bar all American philanthropy in China.[66] It was the opening salvo in what would become a widespread campaign to expose the pernicious effects of humanitarian aid in China.

Tracing the history of American philanthropy in modern China, Guo's report argued that it was a form of "cultural encroachment" with the singular purpose to "deceive, corrupt, and instill a slave-like mentality" in the Chinese people to facilitate economic exploitation. Guo located the origins of American cultural encroachment in China with the early twentieth-century Boxer Indemnity Scholarship Program that funded Chinese students to study in the United States. He quoted a memorandum from 1906 by the president of the University of Illinois, Edmund J. James, arguing for educational aid to China on the basis that "trade tends to follow moral and spiritual domination far more inevitably than it follows the flag."[67] For Guo, this quote was smoking-gun evidence that the true motive behind American aid programs was capitalist exploitation: "This is an imperialist's own most candid and straightforward recognition of the aim of cultural encroachment." According to Guo, American "cultural encroachment" intensified during the period of Nationalist rule, when half of all foreign aid to China came from the United States, the largest portion of which was directed to "religious and relief activities," including funding more than two hundred orphanages. After liberation, Guo contended, these American-funded institutions in China engaged in a variety of tactics to sabotage the revolution, including "spreading rumors, committing libel, engaging in reactionary propaganda . . . and even going so far as to hide weapons, collaborate with Nationalist special agents, and engage in espionage."[68]

In the wake of Guo's report, a deluge of editorials, essays, and publicity materials echoed his arguments in decrying American aid to China. For example, on December 30, 1950, a front-page editorial in the *People's Daily* titled "Eliminate the American Imperialists' Forces of Economic and Cultural Encroachment in China" deployed evocative metaphors to conceptualize the relationship between humanitarianism and imperialism. "American imperialists use economic encroachment to extract the blood and sweat of the Chinese people, and then they vainly attempt to use a small bit of the blood and sweat they have extracted from the Chinese people to purchase back their loyalty." The editorial then proceeds to liken humanitarians to image-conscious robbers: "There exists in this world a certain kind of thief. He pillages your property and then afterward gives you back a few unimportant items and asks you to consider him your 'benefactor.' The American imperialists are just this kind of thief." The editorial concludes that of all forms of U.S. encroachment in China, philanthropy was the most "venomous": "The American imperialists' huge investment in financial aid to China's religious, cultural, and relief enterprises is for the simple purpose of using these methods to strangle the spirits of the Chinese people, cause the Chinese people to mistake enemies for friends, and willingly become their slaves. This is the American imperialists' most venomous encroachment policy."[69]

As many foreign-funded charitable institutions had connections to Protestant and Catholic missions, efforts to delegitimize humanitarian aid to China also overlapped with the Three Selfs Patriotic Movement, which aimed to sever ties between Chinese Christians and foreign missions and bring religion under state control. The concept of the "three selfs" (self-support, self-government, self-propagation) dates back to mid-nineteenth-century discussions within the American Board of Commissioners for Foreign Missions and the British Church Missionary Society on how to develop the native church. In the early 1950s, however, Chinese Communist authorities adapted the three selfs idea to appeal to the patriotism of Chinese Christians while encouraging them to confront their historical connections to imperialism. To this effect, a group of left-leaning Christian leaders worked with Zhou Enlai to prepare a "Christian

Manifesto" that called for rapidly achieving independence from foreign money and personnel while resolutely opposing imperialism.[70] The director of Chiang Memorial Children's Village, Zhang Junci, was among the first group of 1,527 Chinese Christians who had signed the manifesto as of August 1950.[71]

The chorus of prominent intellectuals and officials who criticized humanitarian aid during the final days of 1950 provided an ideological justification for the economic sanctions that defunded American-supported philanthropic institutions in China. Based on a Marxist analysis of how Chinese people had become dependent on imperialist charity, they argued that China could only be truly independent if it stopped accepting aid from abroad. Throughout 1949–1950 local officials had tolerated—and in some cases even enthusiastically embraced—the adoption plan as a useful humanitarian program safe from accusations of imperialist influence. In the fateful year of 1951, however, the new ideological framework provided by Guo's report would lead to a thorough reevaluation of the effects of the adoption plan on the children of new China.

## "THE CRIMES OF IMPERIALISM AGAINST CHINA'S CHILDREN"

Over the course of 1951 these high-level critiques of humanitarianism morphed into a mass movement to systematically discredit and dismantle all American-funded humanitarian institutions in China. A January 9, 1951, directive from the East China Military and Administrative Committee instructed, "Without exception, all relief institutions that receive American aid are to be taken over by the local branch of the People's Relief Administration of China according to the regulations of the general office." The directive further emphasized that in addition to taking over operation of American-funded institutions, PRAC officials should "launch anti-American patriotic mass movements, so as not only to break off economic connections to American imperialism, but also to completely sweep away the deceiving influence of imperialism from political thinking."[72]

In the spring, as local branches of the PRAC mobilized to investigate foreign-funded child welfare institutions across China, they publicized horror stories of gross neglect and maltreatment of children—transforming "the crimes of imperialism against China's children" into a national scandal. On March 7 the *People's Daily* ran an exposé about the Holy Infant Home for Babies, operated by Canadian Catholic nuns in Guangzhou, alleging that 2,116 babies had died in the past two years, a death rate of 94 percent.[73] Two days later another exposé made similar charges of gross neglect leading to astronomical death rates at two orphanages run by Catholic nuns in Nanjing.[74] These and similar claims also circulated through materials published and distributed by the PRAC, including two booklets in 1951 titled *The Crimes of Imperialism Against China's Children* and *The Crimes of Imperialism Against China's Children (Continued)*.[75] These accusations provoked an emotionally charged nationwide backlash. As of early April *People's Daily* had received 112 letters from individuals and groups expressing outrage over the abuse of children at foreign-funded child welfare institutions.[76]

While these scathing indictments helped discredit the humanitarian motives of foreign orphanages, by highlighting only the most shocking instances of abuse, such articles left open the possibility of distinguishing between good and bad humanitarians. If the children at a foreign-funded orphanage were well nourished and kindly treated, was it still guilty of imperialist crimes? As many of the orphanages funded by the adoption plan provided for children's material welfare at comparatively high standards, Communist authorities needed a new line of attack to show that these institutions also inflicted serious harm on China's children. In this context, the intimate relationships forged between Chinese children and foreign adults via the adoption plan emerged as explosive symbols of how the emotional and psychological damage wrought by dependency on humanitarian aid could be even more dangerous than physical abuse.

The CCF-funded Canaan Children's Home had first come to the attention of Beijing municipal authorities in the summer of 1949, when the students of the Tongzhou Agricultural Association Training Class filed a complaint accusing the Canaan Home of preventing three children from joining their youth study group. In response, the Beijing Municipal Civil Affairs Bureau launched an investigation that would last nearly two months and uncover problems far beyond those raised in the initial complaint. In addition to criticizing the Canaan Home for "prohibiting students from joining the study group," the Civil Affairs Bureau report also lambasted Canaan for its "dark reactionary rule," under which children were not permitted to leave the premises, converse with the opposite sex, or receive family visits, and in which they were coerced into accepting religion.[77] No immediate punishments were inflicted on the Canaan Home, and Laura Richards gradually managed to win over the cadres stationed there for observation. However, after Richards turned down their offer to continue running the orphanage as a "living Dr. Norman Bethune," the old accusations against the Canaan Home would come pouring forth again—this time in public.

After Richards's abrupt departure, the PRAC Beijing Branch immediately began preparations for assuming control of the Canaan Children's Home, and their investigations revealed the alarming consequences of children's perceived debt to their American benefactors. In early 1951 Wang Tongxun of Fu Jen University inspected the Canaan Home and was shocked to find it a world apart, where it was as if the revolution had never occurred: "The children amazingly do not even know who the leader of China is. They ask, how come we do not hear about 'Chairman Chiang' these days?" Even more troubling, Wang found that the children's deep affection for their American patrons had rendered them politically disloyal. When Wang tried to teach the children songs such as "The East Is Red," they resisted and even erased the lyrics from the blackboard when he left the room. As the children explained to him, "Americans saved our lives, so we must repay their kindness." As far as Wang was concerned, the Canaan Home was unassailable evidence of how humanitarianism served American imperialism. He concluded, "Does this not clearly illustrate what American imperialism's so-called 'relief' and 'friendship' as well as the 'philanthropic undertakings' they operate in China actually are in the final analysis?"[78]

Others who inspected the Canaan Children's Home likewise made explicit the political stakes of the children's intimate ties to the United States. Highlighting the fact that children were given biblical names like "John" and "Eve," one report claimed that the orphanage "made children slowly forget their own parents, their own country."[79] As a consequence, such reports argued, children felt political loyalty to the United States over China. A member of the Beijing YMCA recounted an incident in which an official from the Beijing Civil Affairs Bureau asked a child at Canaan, "Is America better, or is China better?" The child responded, "America is better!" The official then asked, "If America and China went to war, whom would you help?" Again, the child answered, "I would help America."[80] Published when China and the United States were, in fact, at war in Korea, the story underscored the high stakes of children's emotional attachment to the United States.

Even more so than at the Canaan Children's Home, the representatives of the PRAC Chongqing Branch sent to investigate Chiang Memorial Children's Village focused almost obsessively on the intimate relationships forged between Chinese children and their American foster parents through the adoption plan. The report they produced described with palpable scorn how the adoption plan worked to "stupefy" children:

> Every child is introduced to an "American father," an "American mother," and an "American child" to be its friend. . . . These "foreign fathers and mothers" then use this opportunity to write letters to the children and to send photographs, American picture postcards, pictorials, and all kinds of gifts to stupefy China's children. Through Saunders, the children's life circumstances are also regularly reported to the "foreign fathers and mothers." At that time, each Chinese child would carry around pictures and letters from their American parents and from foreign children.

In "just this way," the report concluded, the adoption plan "harms the thinking of Chinese children and causes them to forget their own fatherland." The report quoted individual children to demonstrate the psychological damage wrought by their participation in the adoption plan. In addition to Ssu-Chun, who had told investigators he "would rather be an American's dog than a Chinese person," it quoted a child named Guoqing who said, "I really wish I could turn into a mosquito and fly to America."[81] By including quotes in which children compared themselves to dogs and insects, the report implied that the adoption plan debased and dehumanized children by alienating them from their Chinese identity. Echoing accounts of the Canaan Children's Home, the report added that the adoption plan also caused children to "adopt a hostile attitude to the Chinese Communist Party and the People's Liberation Army." If the former superintendent of Chiang Memorial Children's Village, J. R. Saunders, could have seen this report about the children who were formerly his charges, he doubtlessly would have felt gratified. AOFA publications had often asserted that the adoption plan would hinder the development of communism in China by securing children's loyalty to the United States. One pamphlet claimed, "Your contribution will go far towards preventing the advent of Communism by more firmly cementing the friendly relations between the people of this country and those of China." Beneath a picture of smiling AOFA-supported children, the pamphlet added, "These children will never forget America."[82] Ironically, the best evidence for these claims would come from the observations of the PRAC Chongqing Branch as it prepared to assume control of the orphanage and purge it of American influence. Saunders had left China two years prior, but PRAC officials found that many children still carried around photographs of their American foster parents.[83]

FIGURE 5.2 "Glimpses of Chiang Memorial Children's Village," *Asia Calling* 2, no. 5 (1948): 26.

## CHILDREN'S NARRATIVES IN THE CAMPAIGN TO DISCREDIT HUMANITARIANISM

These startling findings at the Canaan Children's Home and Chiang Memorial Children's Village gained national notoriety as they circulated through letters, newspaper reports, publicity pamphlets, and mass denunciation meetings. Across all these media, the firsthand testimony of children who received aid from abroad emerged as a privileged form of evidence in the campaign to discredit global humanitarian work in China. To be sure, like "speak bitterness" sessions and other uses of personal narrative in public discourse in the early PRC, children's testimonials were often generic and accessible to broader publics only through the mediation of the newspaper editors who published their letters and the local officials who solicited their participation in denunciation meetings.[84] Nevertheless, the broad circulation of children's narratives reveals how the emotional loyalties of children became a key battleground in the campaign to uproot the humanitarian project in China.

On March 21, 1951, the *People's Daily* published a letter from a boy named Enguang who had lived at the Canaan Children's Home for more than ten years before entering a vocational school attached to Yenching University. Enguang's letter made the explosive (and, it turned out, true) allegations that Laura Richards's husband, Nie Shouguang, who handled the orphanage's administration and finances, had raped two female children in addition to embezzling orphanage funds.[85] While these were certainly the most shocking and damning accusations, Enguang's criticisms of the Canaan Home were not limited to the physical abuse of children. Framing his personal observations in the stock phrases that had begun circulating in condemnations of humanitarian institutions, he added, "The American imperialist elements not only abuse them, they also provide them with an education of enslavement that causes them to forget their own fatherland."[86] Enguang's letter spoke to how foreign humanitarian institutions endangered both the bodies and minds of Chinese children.

The Canaan Children's Home also played a significant role in the PRAC's broader publicity campaign to discredit foreign humanitarian work in China. For example, the PRAC's book, *The Crimes of Imperialism Against China's Children*, included a lengthy section accusing the Canaan Home of attempting to "destroy China's next generation" through "a false ideological education to make children resent their biological parents, resent society, resent their own fatherland, and even forget their fatherland." Emphasizing the children's intimate, familial ties to Americans, the book recorded one child's response when asked to write an essay on the topic "my knowledge of American imperialism." Refusing the assignment altogether, the child retorted, "We were brought up by Americans. Mother Richards was an American. How could I write such a thing?"[87]

Orphanages supported by the adoption plan were also prominently targeted through the mass denunciation meetings that were frequent spectacles of the Three Selfs Patriotic Movement and the campaign to eliminate foreign-funded philanthropy in China. Chiang Memorial Children's Village gained nationwide notoriety at the Meeting for Dealing with Christian Organizations That Accept American Funds held in Beijing in April 1951. Attended by 151 delegates representing Christian organizations from across China, the meeting aimed to "completely sever all relations between Chinese Christianity and American imperialism."[88] After three days of speeches and small group discussions, the floor was opened for "indignant denunciations" of imperialists and their collaborators within the Chinese Church. Some of the harshest denunciations were reserved for a reactionary "guilty of the most heinous crimes"—the chairman of the Chiang Memorial Children's Village Board of Directors, Bishop W. Y. Chen.[89]

Bishop Chen was among the most prominent Chinese Christians in the United States. A March 1944 profile in *Time* magazine referred to him as "China's No. 1 Protestant" and dubbed him the "unofficial ambassador of another famed Chinese Methodist, Generalissimo Chiang Kai-shek."[90] After the Chiang family donated their former wartime residence to serve as the location of Chiang Memorial Children's Village, it was Chen who traveled to New York to present the deed to the president of the Division of Foreign Missions, Bishop Garfield Bromley Oxnam.[91] By April 1951, however, Chen's American celebrity and close connections to the Nationalist government had become his greatest liabilities. At the meeting, the Methodist bishop of North China, Z. T. Kaung, accused Chen of "calling himself the Bandit Chiang's unofficial ambassador and everywhere asking for 'American aid' in order to serve as [the Americans'] helper in slaughtering the Chinese people."[92]

Even more threatening than Chen's personal ties to the United States were his efforts to forge affective bonds between Americans and Chinese children through his work at Chiang Memorial Children's Village. At the same meeting, Lutheran pastor Li Muqun also rose to accuse Chen of "using 'donations' from the war criminal Soong Mei-ling and American imperialists . . . to implement an education of enslavement for China's children." Pastor Li read out loud the accusations against Chiang Memorial Children's Village leveled by a twelve-year-old child at a previous denunciation meeting:

> They often publicize how rich and good America is and talk about how poor and bad China is. They often show American movies for us to watch, to see the American kids in the movie eating bread with butter and drinking milk with white sugar. They also show movies shot in Chinese villages or famine areas for us to watch, to see how Chinese kids suffer. It made many of us kids envy and love America and not love our own fatherland.[93]

Framing the receipt of global humanitarian aid as compromising the national loyalty of Chinese children, Pastor Li lent power and credibility to his denunciation by quoting at length from a child's own personal recollections.

The children of the Canaan Children's Home also participated in mass denunciation meetings. On April 28, 1951, more than twenty current and former Canaan children attended a mass denunciation session as part of the Meeting for Dealing with Relief Organizations That Accept American Funds in Beijing. Speaking on their behalf, the young writer of the letter to the editor of *People's Daily*, Enguang, repeated many of his earlier accusations, reserving especially harsh words for Canaan's American superintendent, Laura Richards, a woman he had grown up calling "mamma."[94]

## TATTERED REMAINS

The investigations of the Canaan Children's Home and Chiang Memorial Children's Village—and the national publicity campaigns these inspired—culminated with the formal takeover of the orphanages by local branches of the PRAC. In the process of assuming control of these institutions formerly funded through the adoption plan, the PRAC placed particular emphasis on severing children's affective ties to Americans and rebuilding their emotional bonds with China.

The PRAC Beijing Branch formally took over control of the Canaan Home in March 1951. Contemporary accounts of the takeover narrated the event as simultaneously reinstilling children with proper familial *and* political sentiments. A recurring theme in critiques of the Canaan Home had been that it sought to permanently sever children's relationships to their birth parents, many of whom were still alive. On April 6, 1951, the *People's Daily* published a letter from a woman named Yumei, who fourteen years earlier had sent her three-month-old daughter to the Canaan Home due to economic distress after her husband lost his job. After sending her child to the orphanage, Yumei realized that she might never be permitted to take her daughter back. "After my child entered the orphanage," she wrote, "it was just the same as if I had sold her."[95] Yumei's account is consistent with CCF policy as described in internal documents. A February 1946 document outlined CCF policy regarding parents who wanted to resume custody of their children: "For the purposes of nurturing them to become useful adults, all orphans who are accepted by this organization cannot be taken back part way through. If there is a need to take a child back, a guarantor must be responsible for repaying all expenses for the period when the child was taken in by this organization."[96] Some children apparently greeted their parents' attempts to retake custody with hostility. When her father came to reclaim her, a girl named "Magdalene" was quoted saying to him, "How cheap! Before you didn't support me, and now you want to take me back. Nothing is that easy!"[97] In this context, the PRAC Beijing Branch's takeover of the Canaan Home was portrayed as reinscribing children's proper loyalties to family, country, and party. Finally reunited with her daughter after the takeover, Yumei's letter concluded, "If it weren't for the Communist Party and Chairman Mao, my daughter and I never would have been able to reunite."

The PRAC Chongqing Branch likewise viewed its most important task in effecting the takeover of Chiang Memorial Children's Village as severing the transnational intimacies forged through the adoption plan and cultivating children's emotional attachment to the new China. On November 15, 1951, the PRAC Chongqing Branch sent a telegram to the superintendent of Chiang Memorial Children's Village, Zhang Junci, announcing that it was dispatching its representative, Sun Litai, to formally assume control of the orphanage. Echoing the language of Guo Moruo's December 1950 report, the telegram justified the takeover by citing how the "education of enslavement" provided at Chiang Memorial Children's Village had turned children into "docile servants of imperialism."[98] Another report detailing specific plans for the takeover invoked the "cloak" metaphor previously used by Dong Biwu at the People's Relief Congress in April 1950 and repeated in many critiques of humanitarianism thereafter: "For the past several years, the American imperialist element Saunders has used the cloak of 'relief aid' to inflict harm on the thinking of China's

FIGURE 5.3 "After the Canaan Orphanage was taken over by the People's Relief Administration of China, the children were given new life." *Diguo zhuyi canhai Zhongguo ertong de zuixing* [The crimes of imperialism against China's children] (Beijing: Renmin jiuji zonghui, 1951), 24.

children that is even more sinister than physical abuse while deeply inculcating the enslaved reactionary ideology of befriending and worshipping America."[99] By deploying familiar language from national-level attacks on humanitarianism, the PRAC Chongqing Branch presented its takeover of Chiang Memorial Children's Village as part of a nationwide struggle to reverse the psychological effects of humanitarianism on China's children.

Having framed the adoption plan as causing children to "worship" America and "despise" China, the PRAC Chongqing Branch could consider its work complete only when the children of Chiang Memorial Children's Village had renounced their ties to their American benefactors and expressed their loyalty to China and the Communist Party. The PRAC Chongqing Branch began its campaign to win back children's affection by educating them on the "Resist America, Aid Korea" movement and organizing other activities designed to "expose the facts of American imperialism's cultural invasion." These initial efforts did not meet with much success. While children expressed outrage at America's "imperialist crimes," they did not think such crimes had taken place at their own orphanage, where all children ate their fill and wore warm clothes, and some apparently believed the orphanage's relationship with the United States would continue after the takeover. On August 20, 1951, however, representatives from Chiang Memorial Children's Village attended a meeting for American-funded institutions convened by the Southwest District Military and Political Affairs Committee. Upon returning from the meeting, an orphanage employee named Hu Decheng presided over intensified efforts to reeducate children's emotional loyalties.[100] The successful conclusion of his campaign was marked by the mass denunciation meeting described in the introduction to this chapter—when the children of Chiang Memorial Children's Village denounced their American sponsors and ripped their letters and photographs to pieces.

The PRAC Chongqing Branch officially took control of Chiang Memorial Children's Village on November 19, 1951. To mark the occasion, the children and staff organized an elaborate "Welcome the Takeover" celebration attended by more than two hundred people. After speeches by representatives of the PRAC, the women's federation, and local community members, the child Er-hsiang spoke on behalf of the eighty-six children remaining in the orphanage. We cannot know what he felt as he addressed the audience gathered before him, or whether the tattered remains of his foster father Geo's photograph were still seared into his memory. But according to his speech, he and his classmates were filled with joy: "We have never been as happy as we are today! We have long desired to return to our fatherland's embrace. Today it really has been achieved. We feel extremely happy in our hearts!"[101] As far as the PRAC Chongqing Branch was concerned, it was the "happily ever after" punctuating the end of the tale of Chiang Memorial Children's Village.

## MADAME CHIANG'S LITTLE SPIES

During the early 1950s virtually all foreign-funded child welfare institutions in China were shut down or taken over by local authorities.[102] But for the children who had lived in these facilities, escaping the past was not so simple. The fate of the tens of thousands of "warphans" who had been supported by the NARC during World War II provides an illustrative example of the hardships that the former child recipients of humanitarian aid faced as adults in Mao's China.

At first glance, it may seem surprising that having lived at an NARC warphanage would become politically problematic in the Communist era. After all, the NARC was a "united front" organization that counted several prominent Communist women—including Zhou Enlai's wife, Deng Yingchao—among its leadership. Virtually all the CCP's top leaders, including Mao Zedong, Zhou Enlai, and Zhu De, were listed as "honorary members" of the NARC executive council. Moreover, the NARC supported the creation of a large warphanage in the Communists' wartime capital of Yan'an, providing it with funding for five hundred children throughout the duration of the war.[103] Nevertheless, the NARC's publicity materials downplayed the Communists' role in the organization in favor of emphasizing the personal contribution of Madame Chiang Kai-shek. In fact, the CCP itself had helped promote Madame Chiang's image as the heroic "mother of the nation" responsible for rescuing China's warphans. For instance, on June 24, 1940, *Xinhua ribao*, the official newspaper of the CCP, published a fawning letter from the children of the Yan'an warphanage addressed to "our most beloved mother—Madame Chiang." The letter began, "We are truly lucky. Growing up under your nurturing and care, we are progressing every day. You are not only providing for us but also making it so that we can learn in peace. We are extremely grateful!"[104] The Yan'an warphanage even had a portrait of Madame Chiang hanging on the wall.[105] As these examples show, during World War II the Communists had celebrated the NARC's work as a great humanitarian undertaking—and allowed Madame Chiang Kai-shek to claim full credit.

After the establishment of the PRC, however, the NARC's close association with Madame Chiang would bring immense suffering to former warphans. As the Chinese Civil War intensified during the late 1940s, Madame Chiang quickly became one of the Communists' most despised public enemies. In December 1948 the CCP labeled her a war criminal, and after the establishment of the PRC she was often referred to in the press as "the war criminal Soong Mei-ling."[106] Once proudly referred to as "Madame Chiang's children," former warphans were described by a litany of epithets, including "running dogs of the Chiang family dynasty" (*Jiang jia wangchao de zougou*) and "Soong Mei-ling's little spies" (*Song Meiling de xiao tewu*).[107] These labels severely damaged the employment prospects of former warphans. During the Mao era, the Chinese government developed an extensive dossier system in which detailed biographical records were compiled on individual citizens and used to inform personnel decisions.[108] The mere mention of the NARC or Madame Chiang in a worker's dossier could derail their career. In an oral history interview, former warphan Gao Zongjun recalled how his fateful choice to mention Madame Chiang in his file would continue to haunt him for decades: "Those who had the name Soong Mei-ling in their files were all out of luck—couldn't get promoted, couldn't get a raise, always complaining of suffering. I was muddle-headed and wrote Soong Mei-ling and have been out of luck the rest of my life."[109]

Former NARC warphans were subjected to especially cruel violence and persecution during the Cultural Revolution. The son of one former warphan recalled that it was not until well after Mao's death that his father dared to gather with former warphanage classmates to share tearful reminiscences about those who had not survived the Cultural Revolution: "That night in my house they talked about so many people who had died. Some had committed suicide, others had been persecuted to death, beaten to death. Too many."[110] Li Hongfang was one of the former warphans who had been killed during the Cultural Revolution. His son, Li Linping, recalled: "My father only lived to the age of forty-nine. He was a warphan in the National Association for Refugee Children. . . . He died during the

'Cultural Revolution.' During the 'Cleansing the Class Ranks' campaign, he wrote dozens of confessions, but he was never able to adequately explain his history."[111] Such cases were not rare. During the early 1990s a group of alumni researching the history of the NARC No. 7 Warphanage near Chongqing tracked down hundreds of former warphans and discovered that many of them had suffered during the Cultural Revolution for their association with the warphanage.[112]

In this atmosphere, prominent Communists who had played important roles in the NARC went to extraordinary lengths to conceal their past participation. During World War II, Cao Mengjun was a prominent editor of women's magazines and an underground CCP member who served on the NARC executive council. After the founding of the PRC, she remained a well-respected public figure as a longtime member of the Standing Committee of the All-China Women's Federation. Throughout this time, Cao had kept a rare photograph of the founders of the NARC taken in Wuhan in 1938. Terrified of persecution during the Cultural Revolution, and yet unwilling to part with the photograph, she used scissors to cut Madame Chiang Kai-shek out of the picture. It was not enough. Red Guards found the photograph in a raid of Cao's home, and she died shortly thereafter in the midst of severe persecution.[113] As it turns out, the only other extant copy of this photograph in China was locked away in the personal archives of Zhou Enlai, where it had been marked "top secret." Apparently, Zhou feared that if a photograph of his wife, Deng Yingchao, standing together with "the war criminal Madame Chiang Kai-shek" and other leaders of the NARC were to become public, it could be ruinous for both of their political careers.[114] It was not until 1985, when Deng Yingchao first publicly affirmed the role of the Communist Party in the NARC and praised its wartime humanitarian work, that the NARC's image was rehabilitated—setting off a flurry of academic research and public commemorations.[115]

---

The dismantling of the humanitarian project in postrevolution China fundamentally reshaped the politics of humanitarianism in East Asia, ending once commonplace collaborations between humanitarian organizations and socialist groups and ushering in a new age of Cold War humanitarianism. The adoption plan played a key role in this transformation. For the Chinese

Communist government, the sentimental bonds between Chinese children and their foreign foster parents symbolized how humanitarianism had rendered China's most vulnerable citizens emotionally and economically dependent on its enemies. For humanitarian organizations like the CCF, which had attempted to accommodate its work to the demands of Communist authorities, being lambasted as agents of American imperialism made it virtually impossible to avoid taking sides in the zero-sum politics of the new Cold War order. After it was forced out of China in 1951, the CCF refocused its humanitarian work on places like Japan and Korea, explicitly reconceptualizing the adoption plan as a way to strengthen ties between Americans and U.S. Cold War allies in East Asia.

In most histories of humanitarianism, the recipients of aid in the non-Western world appear only as victims, either rescued or forsaken by the Western actors at the center of the story. However, it was the Chinese critics of humanitarianism—from prominent figures like Guo Moruo to the children who condemned their former foster parents at mass denunciation meetings—who drove organizations like the CCF to abandon their work in China and remake their programs to align with U.S. Cold War foreign policy interests in East Asia. The Chinese intellectuals who attacked global humanitarianism as a tool of American imperialism had framed their argument as a historical critique. From the perspective of hindsight, however, it was a self-fulfilling prophecy.

# 6

## COLD WAR HUMANITARIANISM

The more things stay the same, the more they change. Between 1968 and 1969 a boy named Yoon Tae sent eighteen letters to his foster father, an American named Jackson who lived in Tuckerton, New Jersey. In letters over the years, Yoon Tae wrote to Jackson, "I miss you very much"; "I think of you every day and pray for you"; and "I love you very much. I am very proud of you."[1] By all appearances, the two built a mutually meaningful relationship. Yoon Tae's "personal history" indicated that his favorite game was football, so Jackson sent him a football along with a pump to inflate it for his twelfth birthday.[2] Rooted in a prolonged and often substantive correspondence, the relationship recalled those forged between countless other foreign sponsors and Chinese children in earlier decades. But Yoon Tae was not Chinese. He was Korean—living in the CCF-funded Jin Yang Bo Yook Won Home in southeastern South Korea. Since the outbreak of the Korean War, the CCF had begun supporting dozens of orphanages across South Korea, which had become one of the most important U.S. allies in East Asia.[3] While Yoon Tae's relationship with Jackson may have been similar to those between Chinese children and foreign foster parents in years past, the new transnational circuits along which such intimate exchanges took place during the 1950s and 1960s speak to the lasting changes to the geopolitics of humanitarianism wrought by the Chinese Communist revolution.

In the aftermath of the Communist government's decision to cut off all humanitarian aid from abroad, China underwent a rapid decoupling from the U.S.-led global humanitarian order. Forced to leave China, humanitarian organizations such as the CCF, PLAN, and the AOFA redistributed aid to East Asian Cold War hotspots such as Hong Kong, Taiwan, Japan, and South Korea, where they reimagined the adoption plan as building sentimental bonds between the United States and its Cold War allies. By the mid-1950s, the adoption plan had enmeshed ordinary Americans and the children of U.S. Cold War allies in a vast web of intimate relationships sustained by the transnational circulation of photographs, gifts, letters, and money. In 1957 it was estimated that the CCF's Korea Office alone handled fifty thousand letters between children and their sponsors each year. By the end of the decade, the adoption plan had become one of the largest humanitarian fundraising sources for child welfare work in East Asia and across much of the world. As of 1960 the CCF and PLAN ranked as the seventh and eighth largest private voluntary associations in the United States by total annual revenue, bringing in US$25.6 million and $25.4 million, respectively.[4] It was also during this period that the first large-scale programs for legal international adoption took shape in Japan and Korea. Once ambivalent about explicitly acknowledging the political objectives of their humanitarian work, during the 1950s and 1960s organizations like the CCF and PLAN actively promoted the adoption plan and international adoption as ways for ordinary citizens to support U.S. Cold War foreign policy in East Asia. In effect, they became the vectors of American empire and anticommunism that Chinese Marxist critics like Dong Biwu and Guo Moruo claimed they always had been. Their prophecy had been fulfilled. A new era of Cold War humanitarianism had dawned.

Back in China, all eyes were on Soong Ching-ling. As the head of both the People's Relief Administration of China and the China Welfare Fund, she was the public face of the discredited argument that humanitarian aid from the capitalist West could serve the needs of the Chinese Communist revolution. Her sister, Madame Chiang, the other most prominent champion of humanitarian work on behalf of China's children, had been labeled a war criminal and fled with the Nationalists to Taiwan. As Sun Yat-sen's widow and a longtime ally of the Communists, Soong Ching-ling had a considerable reservoir of political capital. But could the progressive social welfare circles she led avoid being caught up in the vitriolic backlash against U.S.-funded humanitarianism in China? After the decision to ban all foreign philanthropic aid to China in December 1950, the Chinese and foreign workers who had administered humanitarian programs like the adoption plan were left looking for new ways to leverage their cosmopolitan backgrounds into viable careers in Mao's China while also reaffirming their political loyalties. For Soong Ching-ling and many others who had worked under her, the rapidly growing importance of international propaganda, and the accompanying demand for people with the skills to produce and distribute it, provided the best opportunity to accomplish these goals. During the 1950s and 1960s many former humanitarian workers played crucial roles in constructing the Mao-era international propaganda industry, particularly in the field of foreign-language print media. Nevertheless, transitioning into international propaganda work required former humanitarian administrators to use the multilingual skills and transnational social networks they had gained from decades in the discredited fields of humanitarian and missionary work to create propaganda that was deeply critical of their former vocations. There was an irony at the heart of Mao-era international propaganda: it relied on missionary and humanitarian networks to propagate its critique of the missionary and humanitarian enterprises in China.

This chapter analyzes how the collapse of the humanitarian aid industry in China shaped the global soft power competition between China and the United States during the Cold War. The first half traces how former employees of the humanitarian sector in China—including almost the entire staff of the PLAN China Branch—used their international connections and multicultural knowledge to produce much of China's most widely circulated international propaganda during the Mao era. Building on recent scholarship challenging characterizations of Mao's China as closed off from the world, it illustrates how transnational humanitarian networks inherited from the Nationalist era were reconstituted to serve new ideological ends during the Mao period.[5] The second half of the chapter follows the CCF's expansion to Hong Kong, Taiwan, Japan, and Korea during the 1950s—where it also played a crucial role in supporting the first systematic programs for legal international adoption. It shows how the CCF repurposed the adoption plan—a humanitarian fundraising strategy developed over decades in "semicolonial" China—as an important tool of the informal U.S. empire in East Asia and beyond.

## FROM HUMANITARIANISM TO PROPAGANDA

After coming to power in 1949, China's new Communist government sought to establish itself on the world stage by competing with the United States for status and influence in the Third World. However, as China lacked the capacity to project economic and military power on a global scale, it would need to rely on cultural diplomacy, and especially foreign-language print media, to promote a positive image of China abroad.[6] But who had the skills and connections to produce propaganda capable of shaping global opinion of China? Soong Ching-ling, whose decades-long efforts to attract humanitarian aid to the Communists had been shut down with the stroke of a pen, played a leading role in guiding former humanitarian administrators from the China Welfare Fund and the PLAN China Branch into the burgeoning field of international propaganda.

On December 30, 1950, only two days after Premier Zhou Enlai announced the freezing of all American assets in China, Soong released a statement endorsing the decision. Her support was crucial to the policy's success. After all, Soong's China Welfare Fund, and the many social welfare and relief institutions throughout China that it supported, were among those that would be most adversely affected by the loss of American funds. Nevertheless, Soong insisted that the policy was ultimately to the benefit of philanthropic institutions and those who depended on them:

> According to this order, of course, all American relief and welfare institutions in China will be thoroughly invested in and supervised by the People's Government. This is entirely in accordance with the interests of the Chinese people and with the interests of all of the men, women, elderly, and children who have been nurtured by relief aid. In the relief and welfare work that America has carried out in China for more than 100 years, although a certain number of kind-hearted American people did indeed have the desire to help China, objectively they were all used directly or indirectly by American imperialism for the purposes of covering up aggression, colluding with special agents, numbing the people's will to fight, and buying the people's support.

Soong called on her colleagues to "enthusiastically support this order of the People's Government" and "publicize and explain" the new policy to the recipients of humanitarian aid. Nevertheless, she concluded by reiterating the distinction between the friendly American people and the imperialist American government that she had previously used to justify accepting private voluntary aid from the United States. In a strikingly conciliatory note, she asked those who worked in the humanitarian sector to "explain clearly the traditional friendship between the people of China and America and to carry out education in internationalism."[7] Her insistence on the importance of "internationalism" and continued collaboration between Chinese people and their allies within imperialist countries hinted at where she and the broader humanitarian sector in China would devote their energies after international aid was no longer available.

Soong wasted little time plotting her next moves. During the summer of 1950, the China Welfare Fund had undergone a thorough reorganization, expanding beyond the provision of relief aid to engage in a variety of activities, including cultural diplomacy. Renamed the China Welfare Institute (CWI), the organization's new regulations called for "publishing all kinds of propaganda information and materials sufficient to show all of the Chinese people's efforts in relief work" as well as for "establishing connections with all progressive actors overseas in order to disseminate our organization's propaganda materials."[8] The December 1950 decision to freeze all American funds in China accelerated the CWI's shift from soliciting humanitarian aid to producing international propaganda. On December 31, 1950, the day after she released her statement, Soong met with Zhou Enlai to discuss founding an "English-language overseas propaganda magazine" under the auspices of the CWI.[9] Zhou signaled his approval, and Soong immediately began preparations for creating a magazine. At a meeting held at the CWI's Shanghai headquarters on August 31, 1951, it was decided that "the target readers of this bimonthly magazine are progressive actors and free entrepreneurs in capitalist and colonized countries as well as those who sympathize or might sympathize with the people of China."[10] They eventually settled on the title *China Reconstructs*, as it conveyed both the sense of China reconstructing itself and China helping to reconstruct other societies around the world.[11] After a year of preparation work, the first issue of *China Reconstructs* was published in January 1952.

The closing of the PLAN China Branch in November 1950 and the founding of *China Reconstructs* just over one year later reveal the extent to which former humanitarian aid administrators were responsible for expanding China's international propaganda capacities. Besides Soong Ching-ling, many of the PLAN China Branch's top staff members worked for *China Reconstructs* in various capacities. Director Gerald Tannebaum participated in planning meetings for the magazine, assisted with overseas promotion and distribution, and later also worked on the editorial team.[12] Lu Ping, who had headed the PLAN China Branch's translation department, held a number of important roles at *China Reconstructs* over the years, including office manager and assistant editor-in-chief. Zou Lüzhi, who had been in charge of the education department, also served as an office manager at *China Reconstructs*, and Lin Debin, who ran the PLAN China Branch's general affairs office, worked in the magazine's promotion department.[13] Former superintendents of PLAN-supported institutions, such as Zhao Puchu of Shanghai Boystown and Ren Deyao of the Children's Theatre, contributed articles.

In addition to high-level staff from the PLAN China Branch, many of the other key figures in publishing *China Reconstructs* also had backgrounds in transnational philanthropy. Li Dequan, former vice-chair of the National Association for Refugee Children, and Wu Yaozong, an American-educated Chinese Christian who had worked for the YMCA in China, both served on the editorial board.[14] Soong Ching-ling selected an American named Talitha Gerlach, who had worked as a YWCA secretary in China and for the China Welfare Fund before returning to the United States to found an aid organization called China Welfare Appeal, to serve as head of the sales promotion department.[15] Writing personally to Zhou Enlai to obtain permission for Gerlach to return to China, Soong explained how Gerlach's career in humanitarianism qualified her for international propaganda work: "First, she has a deep understanding of both China and the United States. Second, because she worked in the YWCA's international department, she has connections in many countries in a variety of different fields, from fundraising work to project management. . . . Over the past decades she has always been a core force inside the China Welfare Fund. She is familiar with the China Welfare Fund's history, and since its founding she has also become a part of that history."[16] Soong invited Israel Epstein, a veteran of the China Defence League who had become one of the most prominent foreign champions of the Chinese Communist Party, to serve as editor-in-chief—a post he would hold until his retirement in 1985.[17] These veterans of transnational philanthropy, both Chinese and foreign, possessed the multicultural knowledge to publish an English-language magazine that would appeal to a diverse international audience—as well as the transnational social networks necessary to build a global readership base.

*China Reconstructs* was an instant success. After initially printing 7,700 copies of its inaugural issue, the CWI almost immediately had to print an additional 2,000 copies to meet demand. By the end of its first year of publication, the magazine's circulation had reached 18,000 copies, distributed to an astonishing 107 countries, including 20 in Asia, 26 in Europe, 28 in the Americas, and 28 in Africa.[18] Converted to a monthly magazine in 1955, by 1956 its circulation had reached approximately 52,000 copies per issue.[19] Articles from *China Reconstructs* were also translated and reprinted in newspapers and magazines across the world.[20] In 1960 the CWI began publishing *China Reconstructs* in a variety of foreign languages, including Spanish, French, Arabic, Russian, German, and Portuguese—as well as commencing publication of a Chinese edition for domestic circulation. Throughout the 1950s and 1960s *China Reconstructs* stood out as one of the PRC's most influential international propaganda publications, "especially in the countries of the Third World, where it had a broad and deep influence."[21]

The humanitarian backgrounds of its editorial staff were clearly reflected in the content of *China Reconstructs*. One of the main topics covered throughout the inaugural issue was China's recent decision to cut off aid from abroad. A feature article on the People's Relief Administration of China rearticulated many of the criticisms of American charity that had been made domestically during the campaign to uproot foreign-funded relief institutions. It explained, "To attain its own purposes, American imperialism directly or indirectly carried on various 'charities' in China. . . . Obviously, the aim of such manoeuvres was not really to further the welfare of the Chinese people, but rather to smooth the road to U.S. domination over China." At the same time, the article was also careful to reassure readers that this decision had not negatively affected the former recipients of aid. It continued, "In place of the funds which stopped coming from America, PRAC has financed those institutions which have continued to operate, as well as guided them in the improvement of their work."[22] To complement *China Reconstructs*, the CWI also published other English-language propaganda materials that reproduced for foreign audiences the attacks on orphanages supported by the adoption plan that had already circulated within China. One booklet titled *Children's Tears* accused foreign-sponsored orphanages in China of having "deceived well-meaning contributors in their home countries who thought that their gifts were really relieving suffering in China." The booklet argued:

> The complete disregard shown by these institutions for the lives and health of the children under their charge are eloquent evidence of the fact that they were founded to serve imperialist aims, with "charity" as a convenient form rather than a genuine aim. This is confirmed by the fact that those children who did not die of malnutrition or other causes were educated in a spirit of subservience to everything foreign and alienation from their own families and countrymen.

The booklet included a translated statement by a child named Enguang, who had become something of a spokesperson for children who had lived in the CCF-supported Canaan Home, in which he claimed that the institution "even tried to poison our minds against our families."[23]

Despite being written, edited, and published by former humanitarian aid administrators, *China Reconstructs* deliberately minimized the extent to which aid from abroad had contributed to the "unprecedented progress of welfare work" for which CWI took credit.[24] To illustrate the vitality of social welfare work in China, the first issue featured profiles of two of the most prominent institutions to have been supported by the PLAN China Branch's adoption plan: Shanghai Boystown and the China Welfare Fund Children's Theatre. In an article titled "Urban Relief and Rehabilitation," Zhao Puchu, superintendent of Shanghai Boystown, continued the attack on "imperialist relief" that "even in the 'best' cases" caused its recipients to feel "subservience to the very forces whose exploitation of China was responsible for their widespread poverty." Instead, he praised the work that institutions like Shanghai Boystown had done in the two years since liberation, which had "kicked the last props from under the moth-eaten slander that China has not the resources to move ahead without imperialist 'advice' or 'philanthropy.' "[25] Similarly, an article by Ren Deyao, one of the founders of the Children's Theatre, proclaimed that "since liberation, the Children's Theatre has settled down to become one of the main cultural influences among the children of Shanghai and the whole nation."[26] Neither article mentioned that both of these institutions were funded almost entirely by Americans through the adoption plan, including during the majority of the two-year period that had elapsed since liberation. In its pivot to international propaganda work, the CWI had to minimize the extent to which its proudest accomplishments had depended on the humanitarian aid it now needed to disavow.

Nevertheless, the creators of *China Reconstructs* drew deeply on their experiences conducting "people's diplomacy" through the adoption plan in their new international propaganda work. The editorial guidelines that *China Reconstructs* issued to authors reiterated almost verbatim the prescriptions on style and tone that the PLAN China Branch had provided to children writing letters to their foster parents through the adoption plan. For instance, the instructions provided to writers included: "Don't use high-minded language"; "the political nature should not be too strong"; and "consider the level of receptiveness of foreign readers."[27] With regard to content, writers were instructed to avoid "the original texts of documents and political reports, theory, and articles about politics and the military" and instead focus on concrete examples of the "social, economic, cultural, educational, and relief and social welfare aspects of China's development." As Mao himself commented in 1958, "*China Reconstructs* speaks through facts. This is how overseas propaganda should be done." By eschewing overtly political content and an excessively polemical tone, the editors sought to ensure that *China Reconstructs* could not "easily be mistaken for 'official propaganda' in capitalist countries."[28]

The editors of *China Reconstructs* also relied on the transnational exchange of letters to gauge and influence foreign opinion of China. From the first issue, the magazine encouraged its foreign readers to write letters sharing their responses to its articles.[29] By the end of the 1950s the magazine's office was receiving well over one hundred letters per month.[30] The editorial staff went to considerable lengths to maintain personal ties with readers by responding quickly to their letters and adjusting the tone and content of articles to suit their tastes.[31] The high volume of reader letters allowed the *China Reconstructs* staff to carry out a version of a project they had initially conceptualized at the PLAN China Branch. In June 1950 the latter had launched an ambitious project to create a comprehensive catalog of "sponsor information records." The plan was to comb through sponsors' letters to compile information about their "class status, family situation, economic situation, profession, faith, etc." Once compiled, such records could then be used to help children tailor their letters to their foster parents' personal backgrounds—and thereby better "educate and persuade" them.[32] However, largely because the PLAN China Branch closed only five months later, these "sponsor information records" were mostly incomplete and never put to use. Several years later, many of the same staff members revived a similar version of this project at *China Reconstructs*. The magazine's office translated reader letters into Chinese, categorized them by subject matter, and used them to produce reports analyzing international opinion on a variety of topics. Such reports were in turn used to inform the content and tone of future issues so as to influence global opinion of China more effectively.

In many cases, CWI reports optimistically confirmed that *China Reconstructs* was successfully portraying China's socialist development as a beacon of hope for people across the Third World and within the Euro-American left. A couple of examples of reader letters excerpted in CWI reports are illuminating. One student from Uganda wrote in response to an article called "The Development of the People's Commune Movement": "To me this article was very inspiring, because it made me think that the African people can also do this if we also have the opportunity." An Indonesian reader replied to the article "Tibet's Bumper Harvest": "I was very happy to read about the situation in Tibet. I hope these poor, unfortunate people now can live a socialist life. This is what the selfless People's Liberation Army and the new social system have given them." These letters—and many more like them—confirmed to the CWI that *China Reconstructs* was helping to promote a positive image of China abroad.

Beyond collecting self-affirming praise, reader letters also alerted the CWI to broad-based dissent against Chinese policies, even among the very friendly international audience represented by readers of *China Reconstructs*. One of the most controversial incidents among readers was the Sino-Indian border dispute surrounding the Aksai Chin plateau—an area claimed by India where China had recently constructed a road linking Xinjiang and Tibet. To be sure, some readers endorsed China's position as articulated through extensive coverage in *China Reconstructs*. One reader from Ceylon wrote, "I feel that China must peacefully maintain the current status and must not let the imperialist and reactionary faction peel off one inch of territory." More disconcerting, however, was the volume of letters from across the world questioning China's position in the dispute. One reader from the Netherlands wrote, "I do not understand why China, as a peace-loving country, cannot let India have one 90,000-square-kilometer mountainous district." Unsurprisingly, the most critical letters came from India itself. One letter from an Indian reader described how the conflict had destroyed his faith in China:

> For a long time I have sincerely admired China and the Chinese people. All along I have read your magazine with deep interest and firm conviction. At the same time, I have felt pride in your many victories. We, the people of India, take you as a people of action who live for genuine peace. But your occupation of India, our homeland's sacred territory, has dispelled all of the value I placed on you in the past. What's even worse, you cleverly call those who have been invaded the "invaders." This not only destroys your reputation, it will make you into one of the few countries in the world with which any country that possesses some amount of reason and honesty will refuse to have relations.

While the CWI noted that the number of letters expressing negative reactions to China's position on the border dispute with India had declined from 1959 to 1960, its reports warned of a major public relations problem in explaining China's stance to the world.[33]

Almost all the key figures from the PLAN China Branch—including Soong Ching-ling, Gerald Tannebaum, Lu Ping, Zou Lüzhi, and Lin Debin—played crucial roles in making *China Reconstructs* one of the most powerful tools for understanding and influencing international opinion of China during the Cold War. Distributed to more than one hundred countries and reaching a peak circulation of more than fifty thousand copies, the magazine reached far more people than the PLAN China Branch's adoption plan. Rather than retreating from the mission of using personal stories and transnational letter exchange to transform global attitudes toward China, these pioneers of people's diplomacy pivoted to the field of international propaganda, where they continued their work, albeit in a very different form, on an even greater scale. However, there was one important member of the PLAN China Branch staff who was not involved in the CWI's work on *China Reconstructs*. Zhang Zong'an, the assistant director of the PLAN China Branch and second in authority behind only Gerald Tannebaum, instead chose to work on a very different form of foreign-language propaganda.

## "ENEMY PROPAGANDA"

During the early years of the PRC, many of the older children who had participated in the adoption plan joined the People's Liberation Army, and some soon found themselves fighting the compatriots of their former foster parents on the battlefield in Korea. Zhang Zong'an joined the fight as well. During the mid-1940s Zhang had attended the American-founded Baptist Shanghai University, where she also joined the Chinese Communist Party and participated in underground party work. In 1947 she was hired by the China Welfare Fund, serving as Soong Ching-ling's secretary and conducting translation work before her appointment as assistant director of the PLAN China Branch. As a Communist Party member who was also well connected within American missionary and philanthropic circles, Zhang had been crucial to the PLAN China Branch's ability to navigate the delicate politics of working with an American humanitarian organization in the midst of the Chinese Communist revolution. For example, in early 1950, when Soong Ching-ling discovered PLAN's ties to more conservative American relief agencies, it was Zhang in whom she confided. The same qualities that made Zhang so valuable to the PLAN China Branch— her excellent English-language skills, political credibility, and experience working with a wide variety of Americans—would also serve her well in her next line of work.[34]

After the PLAN China Branch closed in late 1950, Zhang Zong'an went to work for the Enemy Propaganda Division of the General Political Department of the People's Liberation Army. As an "intellectual cadre," she worked with a small team of approximately ten people to create and disseminate propaganda aimed at American and British soldiers in Korea. One of the main forms of propaganda they produced were English-language leaflets—sometimes called "paper bullets"—that were fired out of mortars to shower down on foreign troops. Frequently deploying images of distraught children, these leaflets exploited the trauma of family separation to convince soldiers that they were better off surrendering to ensure they returned home to their children alive. At the top of one leaflet was a photograph of a group of American children with the caption, "Where are our Daddies and Brothers?" Beneath it was a cartoon drawing of a rotund man labeled "big business" telling a group of upset children, "Mustn't be sad, kiddies. After all, your daddies and brothers are fighting for a good cause—me."[35] Another leaflet adopted the voice of an American child pleading, "Daddy, Dear Daddy, Come Home to Us Now." It went on to ask, "Aren't you a family man? Haven't you a darling sweetheart and kiddies?"[36] Yet another exhorted, "Those who love you want you back home, safe and sound. Don't get killed and fill one of these permanent graves in Korea."[37] Widely covered in the American press, the Enemy Propaganda Division's leaflets received mixed appraisals from American commentators. An article in the *Baltimore Afro-American* reported that U.S. soldiers saw the leaflets as a "big joke," quoting Sergeant Major Josh Cunningham of Mobile, Alabama, as calling one leaflet "a gem" that could not be "any funnier."[38] Other reports, however, suggested that many U.S. soldiers found the propaganda deeply affecting. Hal Boyle, a prominent Associated Press journalist, reported on the emotional effect such leaflets had on U.S. troops. In one article, he quoted from a letter that an "upset" and "disturbed" soldier wrote to him asking how he should respond to such propaganda: "We realize that enemy propaganda is one of their greatest weapons. . . . But in our position how can we help but believe parts of this?"[39]

The work of the Enemy Propaganda Division also drew indirectly on the techniques of "people's diplomacy" pioneered by Zhang Zong'an and her colleagues at humanitarian organizations such as the PLAN China Branch. In some regards, these leaflets were like a distorted mirror image of the adoption plan advertisements that Zhang had helped produce just a couple of years earlier. They deployed images of distraught and pleading children—figured as potential war orphans—to appeal to the familial and humanitarian sentiments of their intended American audiences. Moreover, they sought to mobilize the affective ties between parents and children divided across national and geographic boundaries to shape international opinion of China and its role in the world order. In this case, however, it was the American parents who were in war-torn East Asia, and the kids anxiously awaiting word of them on the other side of the Pacific Ocean were their own children.

In addition to her colleagues' work in foreign-language print media, Zhang Zong'an's work with the Enemy Propaganda Division offers an extraordinary example of how former humanitarian workers in China went on to important careers within the burgeoning field of international propaganda. But while former humanitarian administrators in China carved out new careers in propaganda work, the international humanitarian organizations for which they had once worked charted a very different course after being kicked out of China. For the CCF in particular, which had sought to remain in China after the Communist revolution and went to considerable lengths to adapt its humanitarian program to the ideological environment of the PRC, the provision of aid through the adoption plan became a means of furthering the U.S. Cold War agenda in East Asia.

## THE BIRTH OF COLD WAR HUMANITARIANISM IN EAST ASIA

After being forced out of China in 1951, humanitarian organizations worked quickly to transfer funds, personnel, and even children from China to U.S. Cold War allies in East Asia. The transformation of China's Children Fund during the 1950s exemplifies how the uprooting of humanitarian organizations from China reshaped the geopolitics of global humanitarianism across East Asia. On February 6, 1951, the Board of Directors renamed the organization "Christian Children's Fund" (retaining the acronym CCF) and began a dramatic global expansion.[40] By 1955 approximately 16,227 children in twenty-four countries across Asia, the Middle East, and Europe were enrolled in the CCF's adoption plan. In a testament to the geopolitical significance of East Asia in the early Cold War, South Korea, Japan, Hong Kong, and Taiwan combined to account for 80 percent of all children supported.[41] As the CCF reallocated humanitarian aid from China to these new Cold War hotspots, it also reconceptualized the adoption plan as creating emotional and economic ties between Americans and their new Cold War allies.

In early 1951 the CCF moved its overseas headquarters from Guangzhou to Hong Kong and refocused its efforts on the rapidly growing population of Chinese refugees flowing to the British colony. The CCF also made concerted efforts to transfer children out of its South China orphanages, and approximately three hundred eventually made it to new CCF-funded institutions in Hong Kong.[42] By 1953 the CCF sponsored 2,131 children at nine orphanages throughout the colony, many of them recent refugees from China.[43] It also began publicizing its work in Hong Kong as rescuing child refugees from a cruel and incompetent Chinese Communist regime. Heart-rending stories of children left to starve by callous Communist cadres replaced the CCF's earlier reassurances that the Communists were permitting the normal operation of its orphanages. The CCF's assistant international director, Edmund Janss, recounted a tragic tale of what happened to the children who could not be relocated to Hong Kong:

> Reports soon leaked out of Red China that these youngsters had been ousted from CCF Homes by soldiers of the "People's Republic." A heartbreaking letter from one such youngster, Kwang San Sun, was sent to Richmond a few months later: "A soldier gave me a small bag of rice and told me to leave. I asked him, 'But where shall I go?' He snapped at me gruffly, 'Wherever you want!'" The saddest and most poignant part of the letter, however, was the closing, where the child said, "Please, dear friend, remember that I will never forget your kindness. Tell my dear sponsor also that I will never forget his goodness to me, no matter what happens!"[44]

The CCF also circulated stories of Chinese children orphaned by Communist cruelty only to be rescued by the adoption plan in Hong Kong. For example, John C. Caldwell's book *Children of Calamity* (1957) relayed the tale of Chan Kak Shing, "a bright and attractive boy now in the CCF Agricultural Settlement in Hong Kong": "My father owned a little land and a shop in the Poo Yue district of South China. Shortly after the communists came into power he was arrested. . . . He hanged himself in prison, using strips of bedding and blankets which mother had taken to prison for him. . . . My mother died of shock soon after Father's death. I was able to escape to Hong Kong."[45] In such materials, the CCF rebranded itself as a beacon of hope for the child victims of Communist oppression in China.

The CCF also published Chinese-language materials that sought to instill appreciation and gratitude for its work among the local population in Hong Kong. In October 1951 the organization founded a bimonthly

Chinese-language magazine called *Children's Voice* (*Tong sheng*) that detailed the work at CCF orphanages in Hong Kong and included many firsthand testimonials from local children. A December 1951 article titled "What Is the Christian Children's Fund?" noted that fifty-five thousand Americans had contributed to the CCF and challenged local readers, "Can we not also be as warmhearted and devoted in fulfilling our duties?"[46] *Children's Voice* also published examples of letters that CCF-supported children sent to their sponsors overseas, such as one letter that began, "My dear friend: It has been several months since I have written a letter to you. I am very sorry. I hope that you are in good health, just like I have wished."[47] By publicizing these letters to a local audience, *Children's Voice* sought to create a sense of intimacy and gratitude toward the United States among the people of Hong Kong.

The extent to which Cold War politics—more than demonstrated need—came to shape the political geography of humanitarian aid distribution is well-illustrated by the CCF's work in Taiwan. By 1953 it sponsored two orphanages in Taiwan that had enrolled 120 children in the adoption plan.[48] However, as the missionary in charge of establishing a CCF-funded orphanage in Taichung noted, there simply was not much need for its services on the island. "Our big problem is that we are starting an orphanage in a place that is really not in need and for this reason it will take some time. . . . It does not seem right to take children from good homes and put them in an institution just because they are orphans."[49] Why would the CCF put so much effort into implementing its adoption plan in a place where it was not needed? The Cold War logic underlying its expansion into Taiwan is clearly revealed in a pamphlet advertising its work on the island. Entitled "The Most Anti-Communistic Spot in Asia," its cover depicts a Chinese child spooning rice into her mouth above the caption: "Russia did not supply the rice in this child's bowl, nor did the Communists in China. America supplied it."[50] The message could not be clearer: providing for the needs of Chinese children through CCF would ensure their loyalty to the United States rather than the Soviet Union or the PRC.

In addition to working with Chinese refugee children in Hong Kong and Taiwan, by the early 1950s the CCF was also devoting a great portion of its resources to Japan and South Korea, two of the most important U.S. allies in East Asia. By 1953 the CCF supported 1,760 children in Japan through the adoption plan, many of them mixed-race children of

FIGURE 6.1 Advertisement for the CCF's work in Taiwan. L. Nelson Bell, "The Most Anti-Communistic Spot in Asia" (undated). Courtesy of ChildFund International.

American soldiers and Japanese women being housed at institutions such as the Elizabeth Saunders Home, which was operated by Sawada Miki, an heiress to the Mitsubishi fortune who was outspoken on the issue of Japan's "mixed-blood children" (*konketsuji*).[51] The CCF saw the incorporation of these children into the adoption plan as complementing U.S. efforts to transform Japan from World War II enemy into Cold War ally. As John Caldwell noted in 1957, the CCF's Japan office handled "some one thousand letters between children and their sponsors plus between three and four hundred gift packages a year."[52] The CCF explicitly connected this flow of money, letters, and gifts between Americans and Japanese children to the overall U.S.-Japan relationship. At an executive committee meeting on July 28, 1952, Overseas Director Verent Mills proclaimed, "The Japanese Government is friendly and favorable to the work being done by CCF."[53] Both publicly and privately, the organization framed the adoption plan as serving the interests of U.S. foreign policy in Japan.

It was South Korea, however, that emerged in the mid-1950s as by far the largest recipient of CCF aid. By the time the Korean Armistice Agreement ended hostilities in the Korean War in July 1953, the CCF was supporting 4,000 children in twenty-three homes across South Korea. As of 1955, 8,863 Korean children were enrolled in its adoption plan—approximately 55 percent of all children enrolled worldwide.[54] While the CCF had long cooperated with U.S. military forces in China and Japan, it developed a particularly close relationship with U.S. forces in Korea. In 1954 it dispatched William Asbury to conduct a detailed survey of Korean orphanages for the U.S. Army chief of chaplains.[55] In return, the army provided large amounts of material aid to CCF programs in Korea. That same year, the organization constructed a new orphanage called the Nam Buk Home with US$26,000 worth of building materials donated by the army. Financial support from the U.S. military was so important to the CCF's Korea program that an internal report warned that the withdrawal of a majority of troops in the fall of 1954 would cause "a considerable drop in income for many orphanages."[56] When promoting its Korea program in the United States, the CCF again foregrounded anticommunist politics. One typical advertisement, titled "This Picture Is as DANGEROUS as It Is PITIFUL," displayed an image of an emaciated Korean child next to the warning: "The road to communism is paved with hunger, ignorance, and lack of hope." Implying that "adopting" such starving children would save them from succumbing to communism, the advertisement concluded, "Christian Children's Fund did something about the boy in the picture. It fed him and saved his life and will give him schooling and teach him a trade."[57]

As the CCF expanded its adoption plan across East Asia, some of its former employees also moved on to create successful international child sponsorship programs for other humanitarian organizations. In 1953, Erwin Raetz, who had been the CCF's general superintendent of orphanages in China, left the organization to create a child sponsorship program on behalf of a new humanitarian organization called World Vision, which had been founded by American Baptist minister Bob Pierce in 1950 to provide emergency relief aid during the Korean War. Pierce had first been inspired to aid Asian children when he visited China in 1947. According to World Vision lore, a Dutch missionary in Xiamen confronted Pierce with the story of a girl named White Jade who had been kicked out of her home for converting to Christianity. Moved by the story of White Jade's plight, Pierce gave the missionary five dollars—all the money he had in his pocket—to help pay for her care. It was also in China that Pierce met Erwin Raetz and became acquainted with the work of CCF. As the Korean War came to a close, Pierce hired Raetz to create a child sponsorship program for World Vision that would provide a stable source of funding for long-term child welfare work in South Korea. By 1960 World Vision was sponsoring 13,215 children, and child sponsorship constituted by far the largest portion of its annual income.[58] It remains one of the largest NGOs in the world today.

During the 1950s, as the adoption plan emerged as one of the most popular humanitarian programs throughout East Asia, legal international adoption was also increasing in popularity as a means for Western (and especially American) families to rescue Asian children. The little-known historical connections between the adoption plan for international child sponsorship and legal international adoption provide insights into how the intimate turn in global humanitarianism provided a new set of tools for the conduct of Cold War foreign policy in East Asia.

## THE CCF AND LEGAL ADOPTION IN CHINA

It was not until the 1950s that the CCF began actively assisting American families in legally adopting children from the orphanages it sponsored in Asia—particularly in Japan and Korea. Yet from its earliest days in China, it had fielded inquiries from sponsors about the possibility of legally adopting children. For example, on September 5, 1948, a woman named Lucille from Durham, North Carolina wrote to the organization to inquire about whether she and her mother might legally adopt children from its orphanages: "I know the children are well taken care of at the various Orphanages but mother and I would, simply, adore having the companionship of one or two Little Ones."[59] The CCF had leant some encouragement to such requests by hinting at the possibility of legal adoption in its publicity materials. One advertisement for the adoption plan in 1949 claimed, "Some of these adopted children will be brought to America eventually by their foster parents."[60] Nevertheless, actually coordinating legal international adoption from China during the 1940s was all but impossible. While the Chinese Exclusion Act was repealed in 1943, Chinese immigration to the United States remained restricted to a miniscule quota of 105 people annually.[61] In 1948 Clarke wrote to the Immigration and Naturalization Service inquiring into the possibility of facilitating legal adoptions of sponsored children in China, but he was informed that "the adopted child of an American citizen is not entitled to nonquota or preference status in the issuance of an immigration visa."[62] As the Chinese immigration quota was already oversubscribed, adopting children from China was effectively impossible. Clarke wrote to another woman who had requested to legally adopt two Chinese children: "It so happens that their quota is filled for the next 10 years. . . . I am sorry that I have to write this, what may seem to you to be a very disappointing reply, but the powers that be seem to have made it as hard as possible with government red tape."[63]

Although the CCF could not yet facilitate international adoption to the United States, it did regularly arrange for domestic adoptions within China—both to extended relatives and to strangers looking to adopt a son to serve as their heir, a common practice with a long history in China.[64] The archives of CCF-supported orphanages in China are peppered with examples of "good" local families adopting children by paying back a portion of the funds the CCF expended in raising them.[65] For example, the records of departures from the Morning Star Orphanage in Guangzhou regularly list children as "taken for adoption by good family" or "adopted by Chinese family."[66] Often the CCF facilitated adoptions to local people explicitly seeking to adopt a boy for the traditional purpose of securing a male heir. For example, in June 1949 a family surnamed Huang approached the CCF office in Guangzhou about adopting an heir. The office in turn wrote to the Morning Star Orphanage asking them to select an orphan "without any relatives" so that the two sides could meet and determine whether they were amenable to an adoption.[67]

In other cases, the CCF coordinated adoptions across national boundaries through overseas Chinese family networks spanning South China, Southeast Asia, and the United States. Many of the CCF's South China orphanages were filled with the children of overseas Chinese migrants whose transnational families had been torn asunder by the Pacific War. After Japan's surrender, as people sought to reconstruct families after years of war, some children in CCF orphanages were found and adopted by relatives who had survived the war overseas. In January 1947 the CCF-supported En Kwang School in Kunming reported the departure of nine children, seven of whom had been adopted by relatives living in Burma.[68] In another case, a woman requested to adopt her nephew, Yanhua, from the Kiu Kong Orphanage. She explained that Yanhua's cousin had gone to the United States and been very successful in business, and she planned to send Yanhua to the United States to work with him. She was permitted to adopt him after agreeing to pay 500 Hong Kong dollars as reimbursement for his living and educational expenses. The records do not indicate whether he ever made it to America.[69] The CCF even permitted children to be adopted by diasporic Chinese to whom they were not related. In February 1948 a Taishanese man named Shurong, who was working as a merchant in the United States, and his wife, who was living with her son-in-law in Guangzhou, asked the organization for permission to adopt a two-year-old boy "to carry on the family line as heir." The CCF agreed to the adoption on the condition that the boy would be raised as a Christian and educated in Christian schools.[70] Combining the Chinese tradition of adopting boys as heirs to continue the family line with the new American Christian practice of facilitating transnational adoptions in order to place children in Christian homes, the case symbolizes how the CCF served as a link between two very different historical eras of adoption in East Asia.

The CCF had long been sympathetic to inquiries from individual American families interested in adopting Chinese children, and it had willingly facilitated the adoption of children to local and diasporic Chinese families. Nevertheless, it was not until it expanded into Japan and Korea in the 1950s that it came to see legal international adoption as a necessary humanitarian measure for a very particular group of children: the mixed-race children of American soldiers and local women, whom they feared would face discrimination growing up in East Asian societies. In retrospect, then, there was one population of children who curiously escaped the notice of the CCF and other international humanitarian institutions working in post–World War II China: the mixed-race children of American soldiers and Chinese women who began to appear in cities like Chongqing, Chengdu, and Shanghai in the aftermath of the war. Why did "Eurasian" children in postwar China never become a "problem" that demanded the solution of international adoption?

## JEEP BABIES

In the summer of 1946 a woman named Chen, who lived in a lane house off Avenue Dubail in the former French concession of Shanghai, gave birth to a son with "blue eyes, blonde hair, and a tanned complexion." Immediately recognizable as "the fruit of an Asian and white biracial union," the child was quite clearly not her husband's. As rumors and recriminations swirled among her relatives and friends, it eventually came out that Chen—young, pretty, and conversant in English thanks to her education in mission schools—had been prostituted to a U.S. military officer stationed in China by her husband, who had hoped to secure the officer's support for his business dealings. But even while Chen was berated by her mother-in-law as a "dirty whore," the whole family quickly fell head over heels for the mixed-race child, whom they all showered with extra love and affection.[71]

Chen was not the only Chinese woman to give birth to a mixed-race child fathered by an American soldier in the aftermath of World War II. In the months after Japan's surrender, more than 100,000 U.S. military personnel were stationed in China, and sexual relations between U.S. soldiers and Chinese women, both consensual and coerced, provoked widespread controversy in Chinese society. In reference to the sight of Chinese women riding in U.S. military jeeps, women who socialized with American servicemen came to be known derisively as "jeep girls."[72] And shortly after the emergence of jeep girls, some Chinese media outlets began predicting that "jeep babies" would be soon to follow. As one January 1946 article put it, "Last year gave rise to jeep girls. Beginning this year, there will certainly be blue-eyed, blonde-haired jeep babies and jeep kids who appear adorning women's arms or in trashcans."[73] Sure enough, by the spring of 1946 mixed-race babies were increasingly noticeable in Chinese cities that hosted large numbers of American soldiers. According to one estimate, as of April 1946 there were at least 110 jeep babies in Chengdu and approximately 260–270 in the wartime capital of Chongqing.[74]

While Chen's in-laws eventually welcomed her mixed-race child into their home, many Chinese women who gave birth to babies by American soldiers faced strong social pressure to give them up. U.S. War Department policy effectively prohibited marriage between U.S. soldiers and Chinese women, and many of the American servicemen who fathered children with local women would have already departed China before they were born.[75] The women who gave birth to jeep babies were often unmarried, and many likely feared that bringing a mixed-race child home would lead to social ostracization and dim their future marriage prospects. As a result, many women who had become pregnant by U.S. soldiers simply left their babies in the hospitals where they gave birth, "as if they were compensation for medical services." In Chongqing, this phenomenon was so widespread that several hospitals joined together to create a makeshift "jeep nursery" and hired several wet nurses to feed the babies.[76] By the summer of 1946, as the number of jeep babies quickly exceeded the hospitals' ability to care for them, Chongqing-area hospitals started placing notices in local newspapers advertising the babies as available for adoption. Much to their surprise, local families vied with each other for a chance to adopt these mixed-race children. Initially, the hospitals had asked for a fee of several thousand yuan to adopt a jeep baby, but in light of the overwhelming demand, the price of adopting one of these babies eventually rose to over 100,000 yuan. In reference to the large sums paid for jeep babies, one article remarked sarcastically, "The reason for this is probably because foreign goods are superior to domestically produced goods."[77] Other commentators pointed to stereotypes that mixed-race "Eurasian" children were smarter and more attractive.[78]

In retrospect, what is perhaps most remarkable about the phenomenon of jeep babies in post–World War II China is that they attracted so little attention. After receiving limited coverage in Chinese newspapers and periodicals during the first half of 1946, jeep babies quickly disappeared from public discourse in China. Raised by their mothers or adopted into local families, jeep babies did not attract the attention of major Chinese or international child welfare organizations. The children of American

FIGURE 6.2 Cartoon image of an American serviceman, a Chinese "jeep girl," and their "jeep baby," published in a Chinese newspaper. Chun Yan, "Shengli kuanghuan xia de jiejing: Zhongmei hunxie'er chongchi Chongqing" [Fruits of victorious revelry: Chongqing is full of Chinese American mixed-race children], *Haifeng*, no. 22 (April 13, 1946): 1.

soldiers and Chinese women also went unnoticed in the United States. Decades later, during 1982 congressional hearings about extending preferential immigration rights to the children (many of them already adults) who had been fathered by U.S. soldiers in Asia, speakers acknowledged the existence of such individuals in Korea, Vietnam, Laos, Thailand, Japan, the Philippines, and Taiwan. No one seemed aware that American soldiers had also fathered children in China.[79]

There are several reasons why the children of U.S. soldiers and Chinese women did not elicit national or international controversy. Relative to the large numbers of U.S. troops stationed in Japan—and later in Korea and Vietnam—the number of American military personnel in China was comparatively small, and as a result there were fewer children fathered by American soldiers. The exorbitant prices that local families were willing to pay to adopt jeep babies in part resulted from a powerful strain of social Darwinist thought in China that promoted "Sino-Western intermixing as a eugenic vehicle for improving the Chinese race."[80] And unlike in Japan, Korea, and Vietnam, where the children of local women and Black soldiers were often the focal point of controversy, Chiang Kai-shek had banned Black American soldiers from serving in China, so the fathers of jeep babies were almost exclusively white.[81] Moreover, in December 1946 a nationwide wave of mass protests against the presence of the U.S. military in China broke out in response to an American Marine raping a nineteen-year-old student named Shen Chong in Beijing. In this atmosphere, many families likely found it prudent to remain quiet about children fathered by U.S. soldiers.[82] For all these reasons, jeep babies were never placed in the international spotlight—and they never became a target of humanitarian intervention.

As it turns out, however, the little-noticed phenomenon of jeep babies in postwar China was only a brief prelude to a series of major international controversies that would transform international adoption of the mixed-race children of U.S. soldiers and East Asian women into one of the most popular humanitarian causes of the Cold War. In the early 1950s, in the wake of the Allied occupation of Japan, the "mixed-blood" children of American soldiers and Japanese women ignited an intense moral panic that consumed the Japanese media and government, leading many Japanese commentators to call for their mass deportation to the United States.[83] After the Korean War, the children of American soldiers and Korean women became a cause célèbre in the United States, and many Americans appealed to exaggerated descriptions of the plight of "Amerasian" children in Korea to argue that it was Americans' moral duty to take them in.[84] Later, in the 1980s, the plight of Vietnamese Amerasians fathered by U.S. soldiers also became a prominent humanitarian cause, eventually leading to the passage of the Amerasian Homecoming Act in 1987 to facilitate their migration to the United States.[85] In response to the transnational moral panics sparked by the children of American military personnel and East Asian women, many Americans came to see to legal international adoption as a form of moral atonement for the sins of U.S. soldiers abroad—as well as a way for the United States to demonstrate benevolent concern for important East Asian allies. The CCF, which already supported thousands of children across East Asia through the adoption plan, played a crucial but little-appreciated role in the rise of legal international adoption as one of the most celebrated and debated forms of humanitarian action in Cold War East Asia.

## FROM THE ADOPTION PLAN
## TO INTERNATIONAL ADOPTION

In recent years, scholars have written extensively about the historical origins of international adoption in Japan and Korea. While these works sometimes mention the adoption plan in passing as having helped popularize the idea of adopting Asian children in the United States, the CCF's key role in furnishing funds, facilities, personnel, and expertise to support the development of legal international adoption remains largely unknown.[86] Although the CCF advertised child sponsorship as a form of "virtual adoption," international child sponsorship and legal international adoption aimed to achieve very different philanthropic and political goals. As Sara Fieldston has argued, while international adoption aimed to transform the lives of individual children, child sponsorship programs had the "loftier" aim to "mold children, and, through them, to remake nations."[87] The CCF's publicity materials made clear that its goal was to raise a generation of Asian children who would transform their home countries into Westernized, Christian democracies. For example, one article employed the classic colonialist language of the "civilizing mission" in suggesting how the adoption plan could effect change in Japan: "Unless a little child leads Japan to civilization she is forever doomed. . . . If there could be planted in every Japanese child's heart the seed of kindness we would solve the problem. Yes, it is as simple as that. A religion of love could transform Japan. The children of Japan could be taught it. We would like to see a thousand China's Children Fund orphanages and schools established in Japan."[88] Or, as another CCF advertisement crudely put it: "America has conquered Japan physically. Now, with God's help, may we conquer her spiritually."[89] In an article for the *Korea Times* in 1954, the director of the CCF's Korea program, Ernest Nash, explained that "the making of good *Korean* citizens out of homeless orphans is the primary aim of the many thousands of Americans" who participate in the CCF's adoption plan in Korea. Therefore, although the adoption plan created a "very near approximation of parent-child relationships," Nash stated that the CCF's "generous contributors consider that the Korean children they wish to help had best be left in Korea, and not adopted into homes in America."[90]

Nevertheless, as the CCF expanded its operations in Japan and Korea, it became one of the leading organizations promoting legal international adoption as a solution to the particular "problem" posed by the sizable populations of mixed-race children born to U.S. soldiers and local women. At first it had simply sought to incorporate these children into its adoption plan. In 1950 the CCF's Verent Mills traveled to Japan, where he was impressed with the plight of these "GI babies"—as well as with their special claim on American help. A CCF article describing Mills's visit emphasized the importance of incorporating these children into the adoption plan for the future of U.S. relations with Japan: "There is a feeling in Japan—the Japan we are so anxious to impress with our American Way of Life and with our justice and fairness—that the children have a claim on America. They did not ask to be born and deserted. CCF is perfectly willing to assume this responsibility, if the American public will support such a program."[91] Before long, however, Mills and CCF leadership became convinced that even if they were raised and educated in CCF institutions, these children faced bleak futures in Japan. Rather than blame the plight of GI babies on the American fathers who abandoned them (or the U.S. military policy of discouraging marriages with Japanese women), the CCF placed the blame squarely on Japanese racism: "The Japanese have been taught that their race is unusual in that it is 'pure and unmixed for over 6,000 years' . . . so deeply ingrained is the legend that the mixed-blood child is unacceptable to the average Japanese."[92]

In this context, the CCF somewhat reluctantly embraced the idea of U.S. couples legally adopting "mixed-blood" children from Japan and Korea. Internally, Calvitt Clarke acknowledged, "CCF will suffer losses in income when CCF children who are 'adopted' under our sponsorship plan are removed from our orphanages to be brought to the United States." Nevertheless, he instructed offices in Korea and Japan to cooperate fully in facilitating international adoptions: "CCF cannot be selfish in this matter. I realize that the life of a Korean GI [baby] will not be easy and if his or her life will be better in America, then I would be an insincere person if I did anything to discourage legal adoptions."[93] Overcoming this initial reluctance, CCF leadership soon began publicly promoting the mass adoption of mixed-race children from Japan and Korea to the United States. In 1952 Verent Mills called for the "mass adoption of GI babies by American families."[94] Implicitly acknowledging that racism against these mixed-race children might also become a problem in the United States, Clarke offered the alternative suggestion of shipping mixed-race children en masse to racially diverse areas like Hawaii or Puerto Rico. "There would be no racial problems in Hawaii," he wrote. "For that matter, there would be none in Puerto Rico either, but Puerto Rico is already overpopulated."[95]

In Japan, the CCF helped make the international adoption of mixed-race children possible through its financial support of Sawada Miki's Elizabeth Saunders Home, which Sawada had founded in 1948 for the specific purpose of caring for Japan's "mixed-blood" children. Informed by a strong racial nationalism, Sawada actively sought to convince Japanese mothers to give their mixed-race children over to the orphanage. Once the children were under her care, she helped arrange for many of them to be adopted by American families, but she did not permit Japanese families to adopt children from the home.[96] A very high percentage of the mixed-raced children in Japan who were adopted by American families during the 1950s came from the Elizabeth Saunders Home. As of 1957 an estimated 1,222 children from Japan had been adopted by Americans through special nonquota visas made available through the Refugee Relief Act of 1953.[97] According to Sawada, the Elizabeth Saunders Home alone had facilitated international adoptions for approximately 800 of these children.[98] Sawada was able to carry out her program for mixed-race children in large part due to the generous financial support of the CCF. The organization began supporting the Elizabeth Saunders Home through the adoption plan in 1950, and for the next two decades it remained the home's most consistent source of financial support.[99] By 1953 the CCF was sponsoring 101 children at the Elizabeth Saunders Home, which it provided with a greater monthly allocation of funds than for any of the other eighteen orphanages it supported in Japan.[100] The CCF took considerable pride in its role in facilitating the mass removal of mixed-race children from Japan to the United States. In his book *Yankee Si!* (1961), the CCF's Edmund Janss declared, "The mixed-blood child in Japan has been taken to the heart of America."[101]

It was in South Korea, however, where international adoption was first institutionalized on a mass scale, and it was also in Korea where the CCF played the most active role in providing financial and logistical support to facilitate the adoption of mixed-race children by American families. In 1956 the organization agreed to construct a special annex at its Seoul Choong Hyun Babies' Home to serve as a reception center for mixed-race children awaiting adoption into American homes.[102] Opened on June 29, 1956, as the Lemnitzer-Doughty-Clarke Wing of the Seoul Choong Hyun Babies' Home, by the fall of 1957 the reception center was hosting dozens of children at a time as they awaited the processing of their adoptions.[103] The CCF went to great lengths to prepare these children for their journey to the United States:

> Here they are clothed as American children, eat an American diet, and are in all things trained in American ways of living. Their health is cared for by Western trained Korean nurses. Ladies of Seoul's international community volunteer their services to teach the children English and to play American games with them. Thus the children who pass through our CCF home are conditioned to be suited to the environment of the homes in America to which they are going, and the task of the adoptive parents is made that much the easier.[104]

In building and operating the reception center in Seoul, the CCF was also making a substantial financial commitment to facilitating international adoption. It invested US$7,000 in the construction of the new wing.[105] Moreover, as children were generally removed from the sponsorship program once someone had committed to legally adopting them, the CCF estimated that it "would be out of pocket some US$4,000 to $5,000 annually" for the care of children in the reception center.[106]

Much like it had since its earliest days in China, the CCF received frequent letters from donors requesting to legally adopt the children they sponsored in Korea. By the mid-1950s, however, the organization could help make the legal adoption of Korean children a reality. As the volume of requests grew (at one point Clarke estimated that it received "a few requests" for adoptions every day), it worked out standard procedures for handling serious inquiries into the adoption of specific children.[107] For example, in 1958 an American couple named the Kelloggs wrote to the CCF hoping to adopt a Korean girl named Chung Cha, whom they had already sponsored for several years through the adoption plan. Nash quickly referred the request to Hong Oak Soon, director of Child Placement Services in Seoul, who in turn sent the following reply back to the Kelloggs: "Enclosed are "Application for Adoption" form and general information which is self-explanatory of our procedure in adoption process. While your home is being studied we will look into the condition of the child whether she is good enough for adoption and immigration and will let you know of it."[108] Although the outcomes of such requests depended on home evaluations of prospective adopters as well as medical examinations of the children they hoped to adopt, by the late 1950s the adoption plan had become an increasingly common stepping stone to legal international adoption. As of July 1957, sixty-nine children from the CCF's adoption plan in South Korea had been legally adopted into American homes.[109]

Nevertheless, the adoption plan and legal international adoption did not always coexist so easily. One issue was that donors to the CCF's adoption plan often specifically requested to sponsor mixed-race "GI children," who were in increasingly short supply because so many were in the process of being legally adopted. As Clarke wrote in a letter to Nash, "This creates quite a problem because the sponsors are dissatisfied if the children assigned are not mixed-blood children."[110] In one extraordinary case, a woman from Washington, D.C., was startled to see a *Life* magazine story indicating that a boy named Kang Yong, the very boy she sponsored through the CCF's adoption plan, had been legally adopted into a home in the United States. A CCF investigation revealed that because of a problem with the paperwork when the boy left his Korean orphanage, they had failed to inform his sponsor of his departure.[111]

The CCF's involvement in caring for children being processed for international adoption also caused it to become embroiled in a sharp controversy over "proxy" adoptions. Under the proxy method, U.S. citizens designated an agent to adopt a child on their behalf in a foreign court. Popular independent adoption organizations like the Holt Adoption Program and Pearl Buck's Welcome House favored the proxy method because it allowed for adoptions to be completed quickly and without the endorsement of a social service agency. The International Social Service (ISS), on the other hand, vehemently opposed proxy adoptions and argued that professional investigations into the backgrounds of the child and the prospective adoptive parents were necessary to ensure the best interests of the child were protected.[112] The CCF's stake in this debate was financial. The children awaiting adoption in its reception center were being processed through the ISS, and the longer its background investigations stretched on, the longer the CCF had to support the children at its own expense. By early 1958 Nash was venting his frustration with the "financially painful" "stagnating" of children in the reception center. On behalf of the CCF, he began advocating for greater use of proxy adoptions within the Child Placement Service Committee organized by the Korean Ministry of Social Affairs.[113] The CCF had helped build a vast bureaucracy capable of coordinating both the adoption plan and legal international adoption across East Asia on a mass scale. But as far as Nash was concerned, excessive adherence to bureaucratic procedure was beginning to hinder, rather than facilitate, the formation of transnational intimate relationships between Americans and Asian children as a form of humanitarian rescue and Cold War politics.

---

On August 17, 1971, Gerald Tannebaum, the former director of the PLAN China Branch, left China after twenty-six years, stopping in Europe for several months before arriving back in the United States early in 1972.[114] One of a small number of American citizens who chose to remain in China after the Communist revolution, Tannebaum had worked in relative obscurity for the China Welfare Institute and *China Reconstructs* before experiencing an improbable career revival playing foreign characters in some of the most prominent films of the Mao period—including portraying notorious British opium dealer Lancelot Dent in *Lin Zexu* (1959) and the titular role of the Canadian Communist hero in *Dr. Bethune* (1964).[115] In 1962 he married a Chinese actress named Chen Yuanchi, and when she accompanied him to the United States in 1972 she was widely reported to be the first private citizen from the PRC to receive a visa to immigrate to the United States.[116] Shortly after Tannebaum returned from his decades-long sojourn in China, another American made the trip in the opposite direction. President Richard Nixon touched down in China on February 21, 1972, and he met with Chairman Mao in Beijing later that afternoon.

Against the backdrop of Nixon's historic trip to China, the romance of Gerald Tannebaum and Chen Yuanchi became a powerful symbol of the possibility of renewed Sino-American ties. Back in the United States, Tannebaum published frequent articles about his easy intimacy with ordinary Chinese people. In one article, he wrote of the apartment complex where he and Chen lived in Shanghai: "Almost everyone in the apartment house called me Lao Tan. Tan is my Chinese surname, and lao, which means old, is a term of intimacy and friendliness. It was a sign that my relations with the neighbors were easy and informal, and there were few barriers between us."[117] Chen Yuanchi wrote of her marriage to an American as a model for improved U.S.-China relations. Shortly after arriving in the United States, she published a lengthy essay in the *New York Times* titled "Why I Married an American." Chen wrote, "It was the love and faith he had in the Chinese people that moved me. I never imagined a foreigner could be so devoted to another people's cause." She held out the success of their relationship as evidence of the possibility of a transformed world order: "The fact that he was an American touched me even more because this gave me, a Chinese citizen, the confidence that real friendship between the peoples of the world is possible."[118] Chen and Tannebaum's transnational marriage was widely lauded in American newspapers as "a symbol of the improved ties between China and the United States."[119]

At the moment of the "opening to China" by the United States, the love story of Gerald Tannebaum and Chen Yuanchi offered a compelling way to imagine how ordinary people could participate in healing the deep divide between these Cold War adversaries. For decades, transnational intimate relationships between American and Chinese citizens had been all but impossible. Despite Tannebaum's protestations, both the United States and China had viewed even the affective bonds forged between Americans and Chinese children through the adoption plan as politically problematic. American humanitarian organizations instead sought to promote intimate ties between American citizens and the children of U.S. allies like Japan and Korea. In China, Tannebaum and his former colleagues at the PLAN China Branch had transitioned into producing international propaganda, some of it geared toward renouncing the kind of humanitarian work to which they had once dedicated their careers. On one level, the political significance attached to Tannebaum and Chen's marriage was a throwback to the early days of the revolution, when the PLAN China Branch sought to transform Americans' views of China, one family at a time. It was also a preview of things to come. Since the 1990s, the intimate relationships forged between Chinese citizens and people across the world—most prominently through transnational romance and international adoption—have again become highly contested issues through which China's role in the world order is renegotiated on a grassroots level.

# CONCLUSION

In the spring of 2007, nine-year-old Nicole was preparing to return to China.[1] Born in 1998, as an infant she had been found outside the entrance of an orphanage in rural Jiangxi Province. Before her first birthday, she was adopted by an American couple, and she grew up in the United States with no memory of her earliest days in China. Like many adoptive parents of Chinese children, Nicole's parents decided to take their daughter on a three-week trip to China to visit her orphanage and establish a connection to the country and culture of her birth. In an interview with a researcher prior to the trip, Nicole said, "I am excited about seeing my orphanage and the nanny that took care of me." She added, "I think China is going to be very different now. Many people are helping [orphanages], and so, it can make life better. . . . We might see the person [a local foster child] that we are helping." As part of an American family that was sponsoring another child back in China, Nicole looked forward to the prospect of meeting the child who benefited from her family's support—someone with whom she shared a similar background, but whose life must have seemed unfathomably different from her own middle-class childhood in the United States. Only nine years old, Nicole set out for China with a complicated mix of identities—Chinese and American, adoptee and sponsor, beneficiary and benefactor—amid another wave of global humanitarian interest in China's children.

Nicole's story reveals several salient features of global humanitarianism in the twenty-first century. First, it highlights how the promise of an intimate relationship with an individual child has continued to drive humanitarian engagement. Nicole was one of approximately 160,000 Chinese children who were adopted by foreign families after China began allowing international adoption in the 1990s.[2] The Chinese foster child that her family sponsored was one among millions of children around the world supported by international child sponsorship, which had become a multibillion-dollar industry by the turn of the millennium. However, the enormous gulf between Nicole's life in the United States and the life of institutionalized children in China also points to criticisms that adoption and sponsorship programs have done little to address global inequality. Witnessing the poor conditions at the orphanage where she had been found, Nicole felt an uneasiness that she could not fully articulate. "It felt kind of strange," she told her interviewer.[3] Finally, Nicole's story shows that after decades cut off from humanitarian aid, by the early twenty-first century China's children had once again become quintessential victims of the humanitarian imagination, with important consequences for both China and the humanitarian aid industry. Bringing the intertwined stories of international adoption and child sponsorship up to the present, this conclusion analyzes how global humanitarianism has transformed China, and how China has in turn transformed global humanitarianism.

## THE STAYING POWER OF SPONSORSHIP

Since the 1960s, the progress of decolonization, the persistence of global inequality, and the continued improvement of communication and transportation technologies have only heightened the conditions that gave rise to global humanitarianism's intimate turn. As a result, international child sponsorship has exploded in popularity—even as it has endured unremitting criticism on both political and ethical grounds.[4] Increasingly sensitive to accusations of paternalism, humanitarian organizations have long stopped referring to child sponsorship as "adoption." CCF removed the term "adoption" from all publicity materials in the 1960s to "correct the assumption of complete possession."[5] Moreover, as the atrocities of the Vietnam War led many Americans to question whether U.S. power was a force for good in the world, humanitarian organizations reconsidered their earlier embrace of jingoistic Cold War rhetoric. During the Vietnam War, the CCF, PLAN, and World Vision all used child sponsorship to fundraise for child welfare work in Vietnam, initially framing their work as crucial to the U.S. goal of winning Vietnamese hearts and minds. But as the war grew increasingly unpopular, the reputation of humanitarian organizations working alongside the U.S. military suffered as well. By 1968 CCF sponsorships for Vietnamese children had begun to decline, and World Vision was criticized for being a "pawn of the American military," complicit in an immoral war that was causing children to suffer.[6] As a result, sponsorship agencies abandoned Cold War rhetoric and reasserted their independence and neutrality. In 1969 the CCF insisted that it had "no position whatsoever regarding the war in Vietnam. Our ministry is to assist children without regard to the circumstances motivating their need."[7] The close association with U.S. foreign policy that organizations like the CCF and PLAN had cultivated after being kicked out of China in 1951 had become a liability rather than an asset to their fundraising.

During the final decades of the twentieth century, numerous high-profile exposés revealed systematic problems with how child sponsorship agencies raised and distributed money. In 1974 a federal investigation led by Senator Walter Mondale criticized large sponsorship agencies, and especially the CCF, for insufficient oversight of the programs they funded around the world.[8] In May 1982 the *New Internationalist* devoted an entire issue to investigating child sponsorship agencies. Printed across the magazine's cover was a call to boycott: "Please do not sponsor this child: There are better ways to help." The *New Internationalist*'s critiques of child sponsorship included high overhead costs, creating division and inequality within local communities, and failing to address root causes of poverty.[9] In one article about a CCF sponsorship program in Madhya Pradesh, India, a former volunteer described bitter animosities stemming from some children receiving personal gifts that exceeded the area's average monthly wage while other children received nothing.[10] Instead, the *New Internationalist* encouraged donors to give to programs that would empower whole communities and reduce inequality, such as agricultural cooperatives and village-operated health centers.[11]

In response to such criticisms, many major humanitarian organizations accelerated their embrace of "community development" as the best use of the humanitarian funds collected through child sponsorship. In the late 1970s World Vision joined other major humanitarian organizations in committing to pool funds received from child sponsorship for use on development projects that benefited entire communities rather than spending the money for the benefit of individual children. In 1983, one year after the *New Internationalist* exposé, World Vision briefly discontinued its child sponsorship program in favor of marketing materials that emphasized helping children by helping their communities. After witnessing a steep decline in donations, however, World Vision quickly returned to child sponsorship as its primary fundraising tool.[12] These changes to how organizations spent the money they raised from child sponsorship were not enough to satisfy a growing chorus of critics. In 1998 the *Chicago Tribune* published a special report on child sponsorship titled, "The Miracle Merchants: Myths of Child Sponsorship." Its investigations discovered shocking instances of philanthropic malpractice, including misleading marketing, bloated administrative expenses, shoddy financial practices, and poor oversight. For example, they uncovered numerous instances in which sponsors were sending money and letters to children who had in fact been dead for years.[13] Most damning of all was the finding that despite ubiquitous claims that small monthly donations were sufficient to dramatically improve children's lives, child sponsorship programs often provided few substantial benefits to sponsored children or their communities.[14]

Despite this endless string of stinging critiques, child sponsorship continued to grow in popularity as a form of humanitarian giving. According to a report by the Organization for Economic Co-Operation and Development, by the end of the twentieth century child sponsorship had become "*the* most successful fundraising tool" for humanitarian work in the Global South.[15] As of 2013, donors contributed approximately US$3.29 billion through child sponsorship programs each year, which flowed to approximately 9.14 million internationally sponsored children throughout the world. By far the largest child sponsorship program, as of 2013 World Vision sponsored approximately 4.1 million children worldwide. Plan International (formerly Foster Parents Plan for War Children) remained the second largest international child sponsorship program (approximately 1.5 million sponsorships), and ChildFund (formerly CCF) was the fourth largest (approximately 510,000 sponsorships).[16] The enduring popularity of international child sponsorship is testament to the staying power of global humanitarianism's intimate turn. Child sponsorship has long been criticized as paternalistic, wasteful, and unable to address the root causes of child suffering. Nevertheless, humanitarian organizations from the NARC to World Vision have tried and failed to sustain their fundraising without child sponsorship. The promise of a personal relationship with an individual child remains the most powerful humanitarian fundraising pitch in the world today.

## AROUND THE WORLD AND BACK:
## LEGAL INTERNATIONAL ADOPTION IN CHINA

During the 1950s, child sponsorship organizations like CCF and PLAN left China to focus their work elsewhere across East Asia and the world. In the 1990s things came full circle as international adoption agencies that had originally operated in places such as South Korea and Vietnam shifted global humanitarian attention back to China. Since the 1950s, legal international adoption has been a popular form of humanitarian rescue and transnational family formation. Since 1953, approximately 200,000 children from South Korea have been adopted by families abroad, causing South Korea to be dubbed the world's biggest "baby exporter" in international media.[17] Other East Asian countries have also played a significant role in the history of international adoption. From 1953 to 1957, American families adopted more than 1,200 children from Japan. During the late 1950s and early 1960s, more than 500 Chinese children in Hong Kong were adopted by families in the United States through a project operated by International Social Service–USA.[18] And in the weeks leading up to the fall of Saigon in 1975, approximately 3,000 children were evacuated from South Vietnam via "Operation Babylift," ultimately destined for adoption by families in North America, Europe, and Australia.[19] In more recent decades, countries like Russia, Guatemala, and Ethiopia have also sent large numbers of children abroad through international adoption.[20] Yet after the turn of the twenty-first century, China became by far the most popular destination for Western families looking to adopt a child overseas.

For decades after opening to international adoption in 1992, China was consistently the top "sending country" of children to families abroad. Among the approximately 160,000 children who were adopted internationally from China, around 83,000 of them (52 percent) were adopted by families in the United States.[21] International adoption from China has also been highly gendered, with girls constituting about 90 percent of adoptees.[22] While international adoption from China peaked in 2005, when more than 14,000 Chinese children were adopted by foreign families, until the outbreak of the COVID-19 pandemic China continued to send a considerable number of children abroad through international adoption each year. In 2017 more than 2,200 children were internationally adopted from China—86 percent of them to the United States.[23]

International adoption from China during the twenty-first century was as deeply intertwined with international politics as the adoption plan was during World War II and the Cold War. And similar to the adoption plan, it is precisely because international adoption is often viewed as an apolitical act of humanitarian rescue that it can be so effectively mobilized in the service of political aims. In the United States, international adoption from China has generally been represented in a very positive light. Countless news articles and documentaries have depicted adoption from China as an ideal way of forming global families while also rescuing an orphan girl from institutional care.[24] A cottage industry of children's books, including titles such as *The Red Thread: An Adoption Fairy Tale* and *When You Were Born in China*, portray international adoption as a way of forming happy, multicultural families and building affective bonds between China and the United States.[25] Even HBO's popular series *Sex and the City* positively depicts one of the main characters adopting a Chinese baby girl.

How was the spectacle of large numbers of Chinese girls being adopted into primarily white American families portrayed in China? In 1995 British filmmakers Brian Woods and Kate Blewett produced *The Dying Rooms*, a documentary film that aimed to expose the inhumane conditions in China's state-run orphanages. Widely seen and discussed across Europe and the United States, the film created the impression that untold numbers of baby girls, unwanted by their parents, were languishing in Chinese orphanages that callously neglected their well-being. *The Dying Rooms* played a significant role in galvanizing humanitarian interest in China's "lost girls" and coincided with a dramatic uptick in Chinese international adoption.[26] However, the film was met with outrage in China. Within months the China Intercontinental Communication Center had released an English-language rebuttal film that attempted to debunk *The Dying Rooms* as a misleading portrait of orphan care in China created by deceptive editing and outright fabrication. The rebuttal film concludes by interviewing several Swedish couples that had adopted children from China, all of whom reported that they had personally observed the good conditions in Chinese orphanages. That film's final frame shows a white couple holding two Chinese babies as the narrator intones: "The fabrications invented by Kate Blewett and her colleagues may deceive people for a while, but not for long. China has opened her doors to millions of foreign visitors every year. They all have the opportunity to witness the truth, which is a complete contradiction to what they have seen in the British TV program."[27] As the response to the *Dying Rooms* made clear, rather than view international adoption as shameful, Chinese authorities instead viewed it as an opportunity to mold global opinion of China.[28]

The rise of international adoption was portrayed positively in Chinese society. The popular Chinese TV series *Ode to Joy* (*Huanle song*), which has been described as "China's answer to *Sex and the City*," depicted the contrasting fates of a Chinese woman named Andy, who had been adopted by American parents, and her younger brother, Xiao Ming, a child with special needs who was left behind in a Chinese orphanage.[29] While Andy becomes a precociously successful Wall Street executive, her brother remains institutionalized into adulthood. Despite offering some somber reflections on how gender, ability, and citizenship shape the highly unequal life chances of children in a globalizing China, *Ode to Joy* ultimately depicts Andy as a poster child for the good fortune of Chinese adoptees in the United States. Chinese state-run newspapers have likewise covered international adoption in a mostly positive light. One article in 2009 described international adoption as a contemporary manifestation of the ancient Chinese philosopher Mozi's principle of "universal love."[30] Many ordinary Chinese people also viewed international adoption favorably. According to a survey of both urban and rural Chinese people's views of international adoption published in 2010, the majority of respondents considered international adoption to be a "positive trend." In particular, respondents believed that adopted Chinese children were "lucky" because of the good education, material comforts, and economic opportunities it was believed they would enjoy in the United States.[31] International adoption was a privileged form of global intimacy that was widely celebrated in mainstream Chinese and American society.

## THE POLITICS OF INTERNATIONAL ADOPTION IN CHINA

In the United States, international adoption from China is often framed as a form of humanitarian rescue for "unwanted" Chinese girls. According to this narrative, China's one-child policy, in combination with a patriarchal Confucian culture that values sons over daughters, caused many Chinese families to abandon baby girls, who were fated to languish in squalid orphanages unless adopted into loving American homes.[32] To be sure, both the one-child policy and a cultural preference for sons are crucial to explaining why so many Chinese girls landed in state-run orphanages. However, this narrative obscures how the Chinese government deliberately manufactured the "need" for international adoption. In the 1980s domestic adoption in China increased along with stricter enforcement of the one-child policy—from an estimated 158,500 adoptions in 1980 to 562,000 in 1987, nearly 80 percent of them of girls.[33] Throughout the 1980s, domestic adoption was highly effective as an informal, grassroots solution to the problem of families that, in the context of harsh enforcement of the one-child policy, made the "coerced choice" to relinquish a daughter in the hopes of having a son.[34] Beginning in the 1990s, however, Chinese state authorities simultaneously suppressed domestic adoption and encouraged international adoption. China's 1991 National Adoption Law, well known for legalizing international adoption, also sharply restricted domestic adoption.[35] Kay Ann Johnson has persuasively argued that the "creation of a pool of children available for international adoption was closely related to, if not wholly caused by, active government suppression of customary adoption practices."[36]

Why would the Chinese government deliberately suppress domestic adoption in favor of international adoption? As with the adoption plan in earlier decades, Chinese child welfare institutions and state authorities viewed international adoption as a powerful tool through which to attract material and ideological support for their own political projects abroad.

Most immediately, authorities worried that families were using domestic adoption to circumvent the one-child policy, either by giving up daughters for adoption in the hopes of having a son or by falsely "adopting" their own biological children. By making adopted children count against a family's birth quota under the one-child policy, the 1991 adoption law closed this "loophole" in family planning regulations.[37] The national adoption law was revised in 1999 to exempt adoptions from social welfare institutions from counting against birth quotas, but many child welfare institutions continued to prefer international adoption for financial reasons. In total, adopting a child from China typically cost between US$15,000 and $30,000, approximately $6,000 of which was given directly to the orphanage as a mandatory "donation." As the rise of international adoption brought the plight of Chinese children back to the forefront of global humanitarian concern, new international NGOs also infused significant quantities of money, technology, expertise, and volunteer labor into China's child welfare system. In doing so, they both improved the quality of care for institutionalized children and relieved the Chinese state from much of its responsibility to provide adequate child welfare services on a permanent basis.[38]

Mandatory donations to child welfare institutions, typically required only of foreign adopters, created a strong incentive to channel children into international rather than domestic adoption. A 2006 study of Chinese orphanages that regularly provided children for international adoption found that more than 80 percent of the orphanages informed prospective Chinese adopters (who met all the legal requirements) that they had no healthy babies available for adoption. Among the minority that did acknowledge having babies available for adoption, some demanded fees even higher than the donations required of foreigners, creating a bidding war between local and foreign families for healthy Chinese babies.[39] In the most extreme cases, the potential profits from international adoption have led to the creation of baby trafficking schemes. In 2005 news broke that the Hengyang Social Welfare Institute in Hunan Province had been buying babies from traffickers and selling them to orphanages that then put them up for international adoption.[40] It is difficult to know the extent of baby trafficking for international adoption in China, and Chinese authorities severely punished those traffickers who were caught. Still, it was China's policy of financially incentivizing international adoption that created the "demand" for baby girls that made trafficking lucrative in the first place.

Finally, international adoption was also a powerful means through which the Chinese state obtained not only material resources but also positive publicity abroad. Organizations such as Families with Children from China sponsor cultural events that promote a positive image of China and Chinese culture within the United States.[41] According to Chinese scholar Fan Ke, adoptive parents constitute an important constituency within American society that can counter negative media coverage of China: "After adopting a Chinese child, many American guardians begin to have a deeper understanding of China. . . . After seeing some unfair or one-sided reporting, some people take up their pens and demand that those who work in the media maintain fair-minded professional integrity."[42] More recently, China has also begun promoting highly supervised "homeland tours" for adoptees and their families to visit China and tour famous cultural heritage sites.[43] By carefully scripting how adoptees and their families experience China, homeland tours provide another means of promoting a positive image of China abroad.[44]

Beginning in the early 1990s, international adoption provided an effective way for the Chinese state to shore up its population policies, channel foreign money and resources to state-operated child welfare institutions, and cultivate favorable views of China abroad. As sociologist Leslie Wang concluded, "As Western child-savers devote personal resources to caring for and rehabilitating the PRC's unwanted kids, they also bolster Chinese state authority through their willing participation in outsourced intimacy."[45] To be sure, the contemporary phenomenon of international adoption from China had many differences from the adoption plan of the 1930s–1950s. Most important, whereas the adoption plan involved sending money, letters, and gifts to children who remained in China, international adoption involved assuming full responsibility for them as parents. The level of financial, legal, and emotional commitment involved in international adoption was orders of magnitude greater. Nevertheless, from a Chinese perspective, international adoption fulfilled many of the same functions as the adoption plan did in an earlier era. As the plight of Chinese children once more became an international cause célèbre, the promise of an intimate, familial relationship with an individual child again proved among the most effective strategies for attracting global humanitarian resources to China. With the backing of state authorities, Chinese child welfare institutions mobilized these emotional and economic ties between Chinese children and foreign adults to attract international support for their social welfare and political goals.

CONCLUSION 237

# TRANSFORMING CHINA,
## TRANSFORMING HUMANITARIANISM

More than 150 years of humanitarian aid transformed China in numerous ways. Humanitarian organizations provided meaningful quantities of life-saving aid to Chinese people, even if it amounted to only a small portion of overall need. Yet despite limited material impact, transnational aid organizations played an essential role in sustaining a new form of semi-colonialism in China. Humanitarian aid groups provided moral cover for foreign exploitation of China while enabling foreign powers to engage in imperialism on the cheap by outsourcing relief work to private donors. Through their quest to save China's children, humanitarian organizations also transformed the roles of children in Chinese society. By calling on children to serve as "people's diplomats" capable of representing China to international audiences, the adoption plan illustrated how children could be mobilized as effective political actors precisely because their presumed innocence imbued their words with authenticity and moral authority.[46] Moreover, many Chinese aid workers developed valuable language skills, multicultural knowledge, and transnational social connections through their participation in global humanitarian networks. Even after China shut down foreign-funded aid organizations in the early 1950s, these cosmopolitan individuals continued to play important roles in mediating China's relationship with the world, especially by helping to build the Mao-era international propaganda system. The return of foreign humanitarian groups to China beginning in the 1990s also had a significant impact on Chinese society, reinforcing China's population policies, alleviating its social welfare burdens, and fostering transnational cultural connections.

The rise of global humanitarianism in China in turn produced a series of profound changes to the moral logic, geographical distribution, and political uses of humanitarian aid, which cumulatively constitute one of the most important transformations in the history of humanitarianism. In the context of semicolonialism, Chinese children became the subjects of new global humanitarian fundraising campaigns that attracted small contributions from large numbers of private donors across the world. Yet Chinese people were not simply passive victims around whom a new global humanitarian system coalesced. Chinese relief organizations actively cultivated global interest in China's children by tapping into Chinese diasporic networks that stretched from Oceania and Southeast Asia to Europe and North America to solicit and coordinate aid to China. Moreover, the success of humanitarian programs like the adoption plan depended largely on the invisible labor of Chinese administrators, caretakers, and teachers. It was these unheralded Chinese workers who made the adoption plan into a sustainable fundraising strategy, providing the proof of concept necessary for groups like the CCF, PLAN, and World Vision to expand the adoption plan across the world during the latter half of the twentieth century. However, as aid organizations expanded the geographical scope of humanitarian action, they also diluted humanitarian responsibility. Under the ideology of global humanitarianism that took shape in China, humanitarian organizations provided aid on a purely voluntary basis, and they received praise for saving even a small number of lives. Global humanitarianism came to exemplify psychologist Albert Bandura's theory that the diffusion of responsibility causes moral disengagement. In Bandura's words, "When everyone is responsible, no one is really responsible."[47]

China also played a significant role in global humanitarianism's intimate turn. Rooted in the notion of human sympathy, humanitarian ideals inherited from the Enlightenment offered little practical guidance for how to navigate a competitive global marketplace for humanitarian attention. During World War II, Chinese relief institutions turned to the adoption plan as a strategy for getting concerned foreigners to donate—and keep donating—to the specific cause of China's children despite the many other worthy causes competing for their charity. While child sponsorship had previously been used in both Chinese and Western philanthropy, the adoption plan exploded in popularity only after the war, when improved global communications infrastructure made it both possible and necessary for humanitarian organizations to create a sense of personal connection between donors and the causes they hoped donors would support. The adoption plan was a particularly important strategy for cultivating humanitarian interest in places like China, Japan, and South Korea, which were not colonized by Western powers and fell outside traditional networks of colonial humanitarianism. Many of the largest child sponsorship agencies in the world today have historical ties to China and worked extensively in East Asia before expanding across the world.

The Chinese recipients of humanitarian aid via the adoption plan keenly appreciated how global humanitarianism's intimate turn transformed its political possibilities. From the Nationalist-affiliated NARC to the Communist-affiliated PLAN China Branch, Chinese relief organizations mobilized the emotional ties between Chinese children and foreign foster parents to cultivate international support for their own political priorities. Although U.S.-based humanitarian organizations like the CCF aimed to use the adoption plan to promote pro-American sentiment, their ability to do so was constrained by shifting political conditions in China. Ultimately, the CCF agreed to cede control over the curriculum at the orphanage-schools it supported to local authorities as a condition for remaining in China after the Communist revolution. Often invisible in the Western-language archives of humanitarian organizations held overseas, uncovering how Chinese institutions shaped the adoption plan to their own interests required extensive research with local Chinese sources. It falls to other scholars with different language skills and areas of expertise to investigate whether local actors were able to adapt humanitarian aid programs to serve their own priorities in different geographical and historical contexts.

After 1950, Chinese Communist officials rejected the global humanitarian system their predecessors had helped construct. Alarmed that many Chinese children still harbored fond feelings toward their American sponsors, Communist intellectuals made the adoption plan into an explosive symbol of how global humanitarianism served as a tool of American imperialism. By the early 1950s, China had fully decoupled from the U.S.-led global humanitarian order. Organizations like the CCF and PLAN responded by redistributing resources to U.S. Cold War allies and explicitly reconceptualizing humanitarian aid as a tool of U.S. Cold War foreign policy. Yet the rise of Cold War humanitarianism was not inevitable. For decades humanitarian organizations had worked successfully across ideological lines, providing crucial aid to groups such as the Bolsheviks in Russia, the Republicans in Spain, and the Communists in China. For better or worse, it was the Chinese Communists' decision to reject humanitarian aid from abroad that closed the door on the era of humanitarian-socialist cooperation and brought about a new age of Cold War humanitarianism.

## 240 CONCLUSION

## GLOBAL INTIMACY, GLOBAL POLITICS

It's the spring of 2016, and a new propaganda poster has appeared in subway stops across Beijing. Released for China's first annual "National Security Education Day" on April 15, 2016, the poster is titled "Dangerous Love" (*weixian de aiqing*), and it consists of a sixteen-panel cartoon illustrating the romance between a Chinese woman named Xiao Li and an auburn-haired man named David from an unspecified "foreign country." David meets Xiao Li at a party and tells her that he is living in China as a visiting scholar. After Xiao Li informs him that she is a civil servant whose work involves compiling internal documents for use in central policymaking decisions, David pursues a romantic relationship with her. Smitten by David's flattering attention, Xiao Li agrees to let him see some internal documents for an academic article he is writing. Shortly thereafter, David runs off with the documents and is never heard from again. Finally, Xiao Li is apprehended by the Ministry of State Security, which informs her that David is a spy. The cartoon ends with Xiao Li crying, "I didn't know he was a spy! I've been used!"[48] It is difficult to imagine that posting this cartoon in Beijing subway stations enhanced China's national security. As one Beijinger commented when interviewed about the poster, "How could ordinary people know anything about state secrets?"[49] Rather, the poster campaign served a more general function of fostering suspicion about Western men pursuing romantic relationships with Chinese women—and of shaming Chinese women who date foreign men. The poster reveals that even after four decades of "reform and opening up" had enabled Chinese people to form various kinds of intimate relationships with foreigners on an unprecedented scale, the Chinese state still viewed transnational romance as a gendered form of potentially subversive activity.

Such fears are not limited to China. The U.S. government has also produced cautionary tales warning U.S. citizens traveling to China about the risks of forming relationships with secret government agents. Like many Americans who travel to China as researchers or on study abroad programs, before going to China to conduct research in 2016 I was asked to watch a film called *Game of Pawns* produced by the FBI's Counterintelligence Unit. The film is based on the true story of Glenn Duffie Shriver, an American study abroad student in Shanghai who was convicted of conspiracy to spy for China. As depicted in the film, Shriver is befriended by a "pretty and smart" Chinese woman named Amanda, who invites him to write paid articles on U.S.-China relations. In a neat inversion of the Chinese "Dangerous Love" story, Amanda works for the Chinese Ministry of State Security and gradually ropes Shriver into a scheme in which he will pursue employment with the CIA in order to transfer classified materials to China.[50] Although based on a true story, the film traffics in Orientalist stereotypes and appears designed to leave Americans traveling to China skeptical of the motives of any Chinese person seeking to pursue a close relationship.

While transnational romance continues to conjure fears of spying and shady business dealings, the phenomenon of international adoption from China was largely immune from such concerns. In part because of the presumed childhood innocence of the adoptees and humanitarian motives of the adopters, international adoption has been celebrated as an idealized form of migration and multiracial family-making and a positive symbol of globalization. Moreover, because Asian children are viewed as docile and "racially flexible," adoptive parents in the Global North often believe that they can be seamlessly integrated into mainstream, white society without threatening its fundamental character.[51] Steeped in time-honored discourses of humanitarian benevolence and childhood innocence, international adoption remained a privileged form of global intimacy even as other kinds of transnational intimate ties were viewed as suspect.

Yet even international adoption was not immune to the pressures created by the COVID-19 pandemic and escalating hostility between China and the United States. The number of Chinese children adopted by American families had been steadily declining for fifteen years prior to the outbreak of COVID-19, when international adoption from China ground to a complete halt. According to the U.S. State Department, no Chinese children were adopted to the United States from 2021 to 2022, and only sixteen were adopted by families in the United States in 2023.[52] Many reasons for the decline in international adoption from China over the past two decades were positive, including declining poverty, the end of the one-child policy, and the relaxation of restrictions on domestic adoption. As China under Xi Jinping seeks to cultivate the image of a global superpower, the large-scale "export" of baby girls through international adoption increasingly contradicts the image of strength and prosperity that China aims to project on the world stage. In 2017 China implemented a new law regulating and restricting the work of foreign

NGOs in China, which was justified using rhetoric that recalled 1950s attacks on humanitarianism as a tool of imperialism.[53] And in September 2024, China's Foreign Ministry confirmed that China had officially banned all international adoptions, except for stepchildren and the children of blood relatives.[54] The era of international adoption from China is over. China no longer wants its children to be quintessential victims of the humanitarian imagination.

After nearly two hundred years as a recipient of humanitarian aid, in recent years China has begun increasing the amount of aid it provides to developing countries around the world. As early as the 1960s, it began sending medical missions to Africa as a way to build its global soft power and compete with the Soviet Union and the United States for international influence.[55] While China has not traditionally emphasized relief aid as an element of its foreign policy, under Xi Jinping it has provided emergency aid during the West African Ebola epidemic of 2014, the Nepal earthquake in 2015, and the ongoing Syrian refugee crisis. During the COVID-19 pandemic, China made high-profile donations of medical supplies to help rehabilitate its international image amid widespread criticism of its response to the initial outbreak in Wuhan.[56] Following in the footsteps of other imperialist powers, China hopes to use humanitarianism as a tool for advancing its geopolitical and economic interests. If China's own history is any guide, it may find that the recipients of its aid have other ideas.

# GLOSSARY OF SELECTED CHINESE NAMES AND TERMS

| English / Hanyu Pinyin | Chinese Characters |
| --- | --- |
| American-Oriental Friendship Association (AOFA) | 中美友誼協會 |
| Bailie School | 山丹培黎工業學校 |
| *bo ai* | 博愛 |
| *bu du zi qi zi* | 不獨子其子 |
| Cai Tinggan | 蔡廷幹 |
| Canaan Home | 迦南孤兒院 |
| Cao Mengjun | 曹孟君 |
| Central China Famine Relief Committee | 江皖華洋義賑會 |
| Central China Famine Relief Fund | 華洋義賑會 |
| Chang yue juan | 常月捐 |
| Chen Suk-ying (Madame Sun Fo) | 陳淑英 |
| *chi du* | 尺牘 |
| Chiang Memorial Children's Village | 中正福幼村 |
| China Defense League | 保衛中國同盟 |
| China International Famine Relief Commission (CIFRC) | 中國華洋義賑救災總會 |

| | |
|---|---|
| *China Reconstructs* | 中國建設 |
| China Welfare Fund (CWF) | 中國福利基金會 |
| China Welfare Fund Children's Theatre | 中國福利基金會兒童劇團 |
| China Welfare Institute (CWI) | 中國福利會 |
| China's Children Fund (CCF) | 美華兒童福利會 |
| Chinese Liberated Areas Relief Association (CLARA) | 中國解放區救濟總會 |
| Chinese National Relief and Rehabilitation Administration (CNRRA) | 行政院善後救濟總署 |
| Chinese People's Relief Congress | 中國人民救濟代表會議 |
| Christian Children's Fund | 基督教兒童福利會 |
| Chun Yun School | 從雲小學 |
| *ci you* | 慈幼 |
| *cong ganqing dao lixing* | 從感情到理性 |
| cooperating organization | 協助團體 |
| Cultural Workers Corps | 文工隊 |
| Dao yuan | 道院 |
| Ding Zan | 丁瓚 |
| Du Junhui | 杜君慧 |
| East China Military and Administrative Committee | 華東軍政委員會 |
| emotional stability | 情緒穩定性 |
| Enemy Propaganda Division | 對敵宣傳處 |
| Foster Parents Plan for War Children (PLAN) China Branch | 戰災兒童義養會中國分會 |
| Fu Lianzhang | 傅連暲 |
| *geming rendao zhuyi* | 革命人道主義 |
| Guo Xiuyi | 郭秀儀 |
| *guoji jian de qinggan* | 國際間的情感 |
| Holy Infant Home for Babies | 聖嬰育嬰院 |
| Hsiang Shan Orphanage | 香山慈幼院 |

## GLOSSARY OF CHINESE NAMES AND TERMS 245

| | |
|---|---|
| Huang zheng | 荒政 |
| hypo-colony | 次殖民地 |
| infant protection society | 保嬰社 |
| jeep babies | 吉普嬰孩 or 吉普嬰兒 |
| jeep girls | 吉普女郎 |
| *jia shu* | 家書 |
| *jiang jia wangchao de zougou* | 蔣家王朝的走狗 |
| Jingye Foundling | 淨業教養院 |
| Kiu Kong Orphanage | 僑光院 |
| Li Muqun | 李牧群 |
| *Liang you* | 良友 |
| Liao Tsuifeng (Madame Lin Yutang) | 廖翠鳳 |
| Lin Debin | 林德彬 |
| Lingnan Industrial School | 嶺南兒童工藝所 |
| *Little Snowflake* | 小雪花 |
| Lu Ping | 魯平 |
| Ministry of Social Affairs Beibei Experimental Child Welfare Center | 社會部北碚兒童福利實驗區 |
| Morning Star Orphanage | 童光院 |
| National Association for Refugee Children (NARC) | 戰時兒童保育會 |
| National Child Welfare Association (NCWA) | 中華慈幼協會 |
| National Institute of Health Mental Hygiene Laboratory | 中央衛生實驗院心理衛生室 |
| National Relief Commission | 振濟委員會 |
| Oei Hui-lan (Madame Wellington Koo) | 黃蕙蘭 |
| Peh Chuan Orphanage | 北泉慈幼院 |
| Peking United International Famine Relief Committee | 北京國際統一救災總會 |
| people's diplomacy | 人民外交 |
| People's Relief Administration of China (PRAC) | 中國人民救濟總會 |

## 246 GLOSSARY OF CHINESE NAMES AND TERMS

| | |
|---|---|
| personal data sheet | 個人事實表格 |
| Pu Kong Orphanage | 普光院 |
| *qiao pi* | 僑批 |
| *qingxu shenghuo* | 情緒生活 |
| Ren Deyao | 任德耀 |
| *rendao waiyi* | 人道外衣 |
| *renyu zhi* | 認育制 |
| *ru mu zhi qing* | 孺慕之情 |
| semicolony | 半殖民地 |
| *shan tang* | 善堂 |
| Shanghai Boystown Orphanage | 上海少年村 |
| Shanghai Home for Destitute Children | 上海災兒教養所 |
| Shen Dunhe | 沈敦和 |
| Shi Jianqiao | 施劍翹 |
| *Song Meiling de xiao tewu* | 宋美齡的小特務 |
| South China District Orphanages Conference (SCDOC) | 華南區孤兒院聯合會 |
| Three Selfs Patriotic Movement | 三自愛國教會運動 |
| Tianjin Massacre | 天津教案 |
| W. Y. Chen | 陳文淵 |
| *wai ruan nei ying* | 外軟內硬 |
| *wan e zhi yuan* | 萬惡之源 |
| Wang Chonghui | 王寵惠 |
| Wang Feng | 汪豐 |
| warphan | 難童 |
| *warphanage* | 保育院 |
| *weixian de aiqing* | 危險的愛情 |
| Work for the Suffering Children | 為苦難兒童而工作 |
| World Red Swastika Society | 世界紅卍字會 |

## GLOSSARY OF CHINESE NAMES AND TERMS   247

| | |
|---|---|
| Wu Aizhuang (Madame Feng Wang) | 吳靄莊 |
| Wu Chaoshu | 伍朝樞 |
| Xiao Xiaorong | 蕭孝嶸 |
| Xie Enqi | 謝恩祈 |
| *xinli weisheng* | 心理衛生 |
| Xu Shiying | 許世英 |
| *yi zhen* | 義賑 |
| *yin xin* | 銀信 |
| *you you suo zhang* | 幼有所長 |
| Yu Tsai School | 育才學校 |
| Z. T. Kaung | 江長川 |
| Zhang Aizhen | 張藹真 |
| Zhang Junci | 張君慈 |
| Zhang Zong'an | 張宗安 |
| Zhao Juntao | 趙君陶 |
| Zhao Puchu | 趙樸初 |
| Zhu Zhixin | 朱執信 |
| Zou Lǔzhi | 鄒綠芷 (鄒尚錄) |

# NOTES

## INTRODUCTION

1. Case File C211, Box 47, Folder 42, Records of Foster Parents Plan International, Inc., Volume 2, University of Rhode Island Special Collections Department (FPP).

2. Letter from Gerald Tannebaum, April 19, 1949, Box 47, Folder 42, FPP.

3. Letter from Feng-ming, November 9, 1949, Box 115, Folder 86, FPP.

4. Chen Jian, *Mao's China and the Cold War* (Chapel Hill: University of North Carolina Press, 2001), 17–48; Niu Jun, *Lengzhan yu xin Zhongguo waijiao de yuanqi, 1949–1955* [The Cold War and the origins of foreign relations of the People's Republic of China] (Beijing: Shehui Kexue Wenxian Chubanshe, 2013), 26–131.

5. Leslie Wang, *Outsourced Children: Orphanage Care and Adoption in Globalizing China* (Stanford, Calif.: Stanford University Press, 2016); Kay Ann Johnson, *China's Hidden Children: Abandonment, Adoption, and the Human Cost of the One-Child Policy* (Chicago: University of Chicago Press, 2016).

6. On female infanticide, see Michelle King, *Between Birth and Death: Female Infanticide in Nineteenth-Century China* (Stanford, Calif.: Stanford University Press, 2014). On footbinding, see Dorothy Ko, *Cinderella's Sisters: A Revisionist History of Footbinding* (Berkeley: University of California Press, 2005). On child trafficking, see Johanna S. Ransmeier, *Sold People: Traffickers and Family Life in North China* (Cambridge, Mass.: Harvard University Press, 2017). On famine relief, see Pierre Fuller, *Famine Relief in Warlord China* (Cambridge, Mass.: Harvard University Asia Center, 2019).

7. Emily Baughan: *Saving the Children: Humanitarianism, Internationalism, and Empire* (Oakland: University of California Press, 2022); Abosede George, *Making Modern Girls: A History of Girlhood, Labor, and Social Development in Colonial Lagos* (Athens: Ohio University Press, 2014).

250 INTRODUCTION

8. Rana Mitter, *Forgotten Ally: China's World War II, 1937–1945* (Boston: Houghton Mifflin Harcourt, 2013), 5; Sun Yankui, *Kunan de renliu: Kangzhan shiqi de nanmin* [People in misery: Refugees in the War of Resistance] (Guilin: Guangxi shifan daxue chubanshe, 1994), 57–80.

9. Ben Goldberger, Paul Moakley, and Kira Pollack, eds., *100 Photographs: The Most Influential Images of All Time* (New York: Time Books, 2015), 102–3.

10. Major synthetic accounts of the history of humanitarianism include Michael Barnett, *Empire of Humanity: A History of Humanitarianism* (Ithaca, N.Y.: Cornell University Press, 2011); and Silvia Salvatici, *A History of Humanitarianism, 1755–1989: In the Name of Others*, trans. Philip Sanders (Manchester, UK: Manchester University Press, 2019).

11. "Humanitarian Response," ChildFund Alliance, accessed May 3, 2024, https://childfundalliance.org/humanitarian-response/; "What Is Humanitarianism?," British Red Cross, accessed May 3, 2024, https://www.redcross.org.uk/get-involved/teaching-resources/what-is-humanitarianism.

12. Jean-Luc Blondel, "The Meaning of the Word 'Humanitarian' in Relation to the Fundamental Principles of the Red Cross and Red Crescent," *International Review of the Red Cross*, no. 273 (1989): 507, 511.

13. For a discussion of the definition of humanitarianism, see Michael Barnett and Janice Gross Stein, "Introduction: The Secularization and Sanctification of Humanitarianism," in *Sacred Aid: Faith and Humanitarianism*, ed. Michael Barnett and Janice Gross Stein (New York: Oxford University Press, 2012), 11–15. On the relationship between humanitarianism and human rights, see Samuel Moyn, "Human Rights and Humanitarianization," in *Humanitarianism and Human Rights: A World of Differences?*, ed. Michael Barnett (Cambridge: Cambridge University Press, 2020), 33–48. Numerous scholars, including Thomas Haskell and Peter Stamatov, have focused on the figure of the far-away stranger as the target of humanitarian aid. Thomas L. Haskell, "Capitalism and the Origins of Humanitarian Sensibility," *American Historical Review* 90, no. 2 (1985): 339–61; Peter Stamatov, *The Origins of Global Humanitarianism: Religion, Empires and Advocacy* (New York: Cambridge University Press, 2013).

14. The roots of this historiography can be traced to Eric Williams, *Capitalism and Slavery* (London: Andre Deutsch, 1944). A classic example of this argument is David Brion Davis, *The Problem of Slavery in the Age of Revolution, 1770–1823* (Ithaca, N.Y.: Cornell University Press, 1975). For an insightful summary and critique of this argument, see Haskell, "Capitalism and the Origins of Humanitarian Sensibility." Peter Stamatov rejects the fundamental premise of this historiography, arguing instead that the "moral dimension" of humanitarianism "cannot be explained as deriving from the logic of economic transformations." Peter Stamatov, "Beyond and Against Capitalism: Abolitionism and the Moral Dimension of Humanitarian Practice," *International Social Science Journal* 65, no. 215/216 (2014): 33.

15. For a critique of social science literature that views postwar global humanitarianism as "a distinctly novel phenomenon with no history," see Stamatov, *The Origins of Global Humanitarianism*, 8–11.

# INTRODUCTION 251

16. Kevin O'Sullivan, *The NGO Moment: The Globalization of Compassion from Biafra to Live Aid* (Cambridge: Cambridge University Press, 2021).

17. Stamatov, *The Origins of Global Humanitarianism*.

18. Rob Skinner and Alan Lester, "Humanitarianism and Empire: New Research Agendas," *Journal of Imperial and Commonwealth History* 40, no. 5 (2012): 730.

19. Helen Gilbert and Chris Tiffin, eds., *Burden or Benefit? Imperial Benevolence and Its Legacies* (Bloomington: Indiana University Press, 2008); Salvatici, *A History of Humanitarianism*, 35–52.

20. Kathryn Edgerton-Tarpley, "Tough Choices: Grappling with Famine in Qing China, the British Empire, and Beyond," *Journal of World History* 24, no. 1 (2013): 135–76.

21. Joanna Simonow, "Famine Relief in Colonial South Asia, 1858–1947: Regional and Global Perspectives," in *Routledge Handbook of the History of Colonialism in South Asia*, ed. Harald Fischer-Tiné and Maria Framke (New York: Routledge, 2021), 499.

22. J. P. Daughton, "Behind the Imperial Curtain: International Humanitarian Efforts and the Critique of French Colonialism in the Interwar Years," *French Historical Studies* 34, no. 3 (2011): 515.

23. Andrew Porter, "Trusteeship, Anti-Slavery, and Humanitarianism," in *The Oxford History of the British Empire, Volume III: The Nineteenth Century*, ed. Andrew Porter (New York: Oxford University Press, 1999), 218–20. See also Adam Hochschild, *King Leopold's Ghost: A Story of Greed, Terror, and Heroism in Colonial Africa* (Boston: Houghton Mifflin, 1999), 185–291.

24. Daughton, "Behind the Imperial Curtain," 517–22.

25. Baughan, *Saving the Children*.

26. Ian Tyrell, *Reforming the World: The Creation of America's Moral Empire* (Princeton, N.J.: Princeton University Press, 2010); Merle Curti, *American Philanthropy Abroad: A History* (New Brunswick, N.J.: Rutgers University Press, 1963).

27. Bruno Cabanes, *The Great War and the Origins of Humanitarianism, 1918–1924* (New York: Cambridge University Press, 2014), 193.

28. Davide Rodogno, "Non-state Actors' Humanitarian Operations in the Aftermath of the First World War: The Case of Near East Relief," in *The Emergence of Humanitarian Intervention: Ideas and Practices from the Nineteenth Century to the Present*, ed. Fabian Klose (Cambridge: Cambridge University Press, 2016), 185–207.

29. Emily Baughan, "International Adoption and Anglo-American Internationalism, c. 1918–1925," *Past & Present* 239, no. 1 (2018): 181–217.

30. Dong Wang, *China's Unequal Treaties: Narrating National History* (Lanham, Md.: Lexington Books, 2005), 10.

31. Shu-mei Shih, *The Lure of the Modern: Writing Modernism in Semicolonial China, 1917–1937* (Berkeley: University of California Press, 2001), 33.

32. Madeline Hsu, *Dreaming of Gold, Dreaming of Home: Transnationalism and Migration Between the United States and South China, 1882–1943* (Stanford, Calif.: Stanford University Press, 2000); Adam McKeown, *Chinese Migrant Networks and Cultural Change: Peru, Chicago, Hawaii, 1900–1936* (Chicago: University of Chicago Press, 2001); Shelly Chan,

*Diaspora's Homeland: Modern China in the Age of Global Migration* (Durham, N.C.: Duke University Press, 2018).

33. Hillary Kaell, *Christian Globalism at Home: Child Sponsorship in the United States* (Princeton, N.J.: Princeton University Press, 2020).

34. Akira Iriye, "A Century of NGOs," *Diplomatic History* 23, no. 3 (1999): 421–35.

35. John Pomfret, *The Beautiful Country and the Middle Kingdom: America and China, 1776 to the Present* (New York: Holt, 2016), 106–21.

36. Michael Hunt, *The Making of a Special Relationship: The United States and China to 1914* (New York: Columbia University Press, 1983), x–xi, 177–83, 190–202, 270, 304.

37. Harold R. Isaacs, *Scratches on Our Minds: American Views of China and India* (Armonk, N.Y.: M. E. Sharpe, 1980), 193.

38. John K. Fairbank, *Chinese-American Interactions: A Historical Summary* (New Brunswick, N.J.: Rutgers University Press, 1975), 55.

39. A. L. Warnshuis, "Christian Missions and the Situation in China," *Annals of the American Academy of Political and Social Science* 132 (1927): 80; Daniel H. Bays, *A New History of Christianity in China* (Malden, Mass.: Wiley-Blackwell, 2012), 94.

40. Huang Wende, *Feizhengfu zuzhi yu guoji hezuo zai Zhongguo: Huayang Yizhenhui zhi yanjiu* [Nongovernmental organizations and international cooperation in China: Research on the China International Famine Relief Commission] (Taipei: Xiu wei zixun, 2004), 255.

41. Central China Famine Relief Committee, *Reports and Accounts from October 1, 1911, to June 30, 1912* (Shanghai: North-China Daily News & Herald, 1912), 47–48; Peking United International Famine Relief Committee, *The North China Famine of 1920–1921 with Special Reference to the West Chihli Area* (Beijing: Commercial Press Works, 1922), 17–19, 48.

42. Mary Brown Bullock, *The Oil Prince's Legacy: Rockefeller Philanthropy in China* (Stanford, Calif.: Stanford University Press, 2011), 72.

43. Karen Lynn Brewer, "From Philanthropy to Reform: The American Red Cross in China, 1906–1930" (PhD diss., Case Western Reserve University, 1983), 386. See also Julia Irwin, *Making the World Safe: The American Red Cross and a Nation's Humanitarian Awakening* (New York: Oxford University Press, 2013), 42–45.

44. James Hevia, *English Lessons: The Pedagogy of Imperialism in Nineteenth-Century China* (Durham, N.C.: Duke University Press, 2003). Ruth Rogaski has also proposed the term "hyper-colonialism" to describe the multiplicity of imperialist power in treaty-port Tianjin. Ruth Rogaski, *Hygienic Modernity: Meanings of Health and Disease in Treaty-Port China* (Berkeley: University of California Press, 2004).

45. Shih, *Lure of the Modern*, 30–40. See also Anne Reinhardt, *Navigating Semi-colonialism: Shipping, Sovereignty, and Nation-Building in China, 1860–1937* (Cambridge, Mass.: Harvard University Asia Center, 2018).

46. Barnett, *Empire of Humanity*, 118.

47. Arissa Oh, *To Save the Children of Korea: The Cold War Origins of International Adoption* (Stanford, Calif.: Stanford University Press, 2015); Catherine Ceniza Choy, *Global Families: A History of Asian International Adoption in America* (New York: New York

# INTRODUCTION 253

University Press, 2013); Eleana Kim, *Adopted Territory: Transnational Korean Adoptees and the Politics of Belonging* (Durham, N.C.: Duke University Press, 2010).

48. Sara Fieldston, *Raising the World: Child Welfare in the American Century* (Cambridge, Mass.: Harvard University Press, 2015), 80. See also Christina Klein, *Cold War Orientalism: Asia in the Middlebrow Imagination, 1945–1961* (Berkeley: University of California Press, 2003).

49. Some recent scholarship has begun to challenge this Eurocentric approach to the history of humanitarianism. For example, Mark R. Frost, "Humanitarianism and the Overseas Aid Craze in Britain's Colonial Straits Settlements, 1870–1920," *Past & Present* 236, no. 1 (2017): 169–205; Pierre Fuller, "North China Famine Revisited: Unsung Native Relief in the Warlord Era, 1920–1921," *Modern Asian Studies* 47, no. 3 (2013): 820–50.

50. Matthew Hilton et al., "History and Humanitarianism: A Conversation," *Past & Present* 241, no. 1 (2018): e15–28.

51. Barnett, *Empire of Humanity*, 14.

52. On humanitarian relief during the Armenian genocide, see Rodogno, "Non-state Actors' Humanitarian Operations." On the Great Kantō Earthquake, see Janet Borland, *Earthquake Children: Building Resilience from the Ruins of Tokyo* (Cambridge, Mass.: Harvard University Press, 2020); and J. Charles Schencking, *The Great Kantō Earthquake and the Chimera of National Reconstruction in Japan* (New York: Columbia University Press, 2013).

53. Angela Ki Che Leung, "Relief Institutions for Children in Nineteenth-Century China," in *Chinese Views of Childhood*, ed. Anne Behnke Kinney (Honolulu: University of Hawaii Press, 1994), 260.

54. Kaell, *Christian Globalism at Home*, 20–70.

55. Baughan, "International Adoption." See also Kaell, *Christian Globalism at Home*, 103.

56. Kaell, 117.

57. "Proposed Agreement Between the National Child Welfare Association of China and China Child Welfare," 1929, Box 4, Folder 8, United China Relief Records, New York Public Library (UCRR). On China Child Welfare, see Margaret Tillman, "Precocious Politics: Preschool Education and Child Protection in China, 1903–1953" (PhD diss., University of California, Berkeley, 2013), 131–39.

58. For example, "Bringing Health to China's Little Ones," *Frederick News-Post*, March 20, 1930, 11.

59. Letter to Garfield Huang, August 27, 1928, Box 4, Folder 5, UCRR.

60. Peggy Dougherty, "Report of My Trip to China in the Interest of the China Child Welfare, Inc.," H. H. Kung Papers, Hoover Institute (HHK). Thank you to Margaret Tillman for sharing this source.

61. Yuri W. Doolan, *The First Amerasians: Mixed Race Koreans from Camptowns to America* (Oxford: Oxford University Press, 2024).

62. Rachel McCleary, *Global Compassion: Private Voluntary Organizations and U.S. Foreign Policy Since 1939* (New York: Oxford University Press, 2009), 68–69.

63. Larry E. Tise, *A Book About Children: The World of Christian Children's Fund, 1938–1991* (Falls Church, Va.: Hartland, 1993), 301.

## 254 INTRODUCTION

64. Didier Fassin, *Humanitarian Reason: A Moral History of the Present Times* (Berkeley: University of California Press, 2012), 247–48.

65. Sabine Frühstück, *Playing War: Children and the Paradoxes of Modern Militarism in Japan* (Oakland: University of California Press, 2017), 114.

66. Letter from Cheng-ho, July 8, 1949, Box 115, Folder 84, FPP.

67. Letter from Jin-chun, November 4, 1950, Box 46, Folder 39, FPP.

68. Viviana Zelizer, *The Purchase of Intimacy* (Princeton, N.J.: Princeton University Press, 2005).

69. Peter N. Stearns, "Challenges in the History of Childhood," *Journal of the History of Childhood and Youth* 1, no. 1 (2008): 35–42.

70. Major works addressing the significance of children in modern Chinese history include Jon L. Saari, *Legacies of Childhood: Growing Up Chinese in a Time of Crisis, 1890–1920* (Cambridge, Mass.: Harvard University Asia Center, 1990); Ping-chen Hsiung, *A Tender Voyage: Children and Childhood in Late Imperial China* (Stanford, Calif.: Stanford University Press, 2008); Andrew Jones, *Developmental Fairy Tales: Evolutionary Thinking and Modern Chinese Culture* (Cambridge, Mass.: Harvard University Press, 2011); Maura Cunningham, "Shanghai's Wandering Ones: Child Welfare in a Global City, 1900–1953" (PhD diss., University of California, Irvine, 2014); Margaret Mih Tillman, *Raising China's Revolutionaries: Modernizing Childhood for Cosmopolitan Nationalists and Liberated Comrades, 1920s–1950s* (New York: Columbia University Press, 2018).

71. Huang, *Feizhengfu zuzhi yu guoji hezuo zai Zhongguo*; Xu Fenghua, *Shenfen, zuzhi yu zhengzhi: Song Qingling he Baomeng—Zhongfuhui yanjiu (1938–1958)* [Identity, organization, and politics: Research on Soong Ching-ling and the China Defense League—China Welfare Institute] (Shanghai: Shanghai Shudian Chubanshe, 2013); Zhang Chun, *Kangri Zhanzheng shiqi Zhan Shi Ertong Baoyuhui yanjiu* [Research on the National Association for Refugee Children During the War of Resistance Against Japan] (Beijing: Tuanjie chubanshe, 2015).

72. A noteworthy exception is Aaron Moore, "Growing Up in Nationalist China: Self-Representation in the Personal Documents of Children and Youth, 1927–1949," *Modern China* 42, no. 1 (2016): 73–110. In the context of modern Japanese history, Janet Borland also makes extensive use of child-produced sources such as essays and drawings. Borland, *Earthquake's Children*.

73. Tillman, *Raising China's Revolutionaries*, xiii.

74. Fieldston, *Raising the World*.

75. Sarah Maza, "The Kids Aren't All Right: Historians and the Problem of Childhood," *American Historical Review* 125, no. 4 (2020): 1261–85.

## 1. CHINA AND THE BIRTH OF GLOBAL HUMANITARIANISM

1. Sun Yat-sen, *Guofu quanji* [Complete works of Sun Yat-sen], vol. 1 (Taipei: Jindai zhongguo chubanshe, 1989), 15. This translation is from Wm. Theodore de Bary, *Sources of Chinese Tradition*, vol. 2, 2nd ed. (New York: Columbia University Press, 2000), 321–22.

2. Sun Yat-sen, *Guofu quanji*, 15–16.

# 1. CHINA AND THE BIRTH OF GLOBAL HUMANITARIANISM   255

3. Michael N. Barnett, *Empire of Humanity: A History of Humanitarianism* (Ithaca, N.Y.: Cornell University Press, 2011), 117.

4. Pierre Fuller, "'Barren Soil, Fertile Minds': North China Famine and Visions of the 'Callous Chinese' Circa 1920," *International History Review* 33, no. 3 (2011): 453–72.

5. Quoted in Joanna Handlin Smith, *The Art of Doing Good: Charity in Late Ming China* (Berkeley: University of California Press, 2009), 3.

6. Examples include Liang Qizi [Angela Ki Che Leung], *Shishan yu jiaohua: Ming Qing shiqi de cishan zuzhi* [Charitable works and moral education: Benevolent institutions during the Ming and Qing dynasties] (Taipei: Lian jing chuban shiye gongsi, 1997); Fuma Susumu, *Chūgoku zenkai, zendō shi kenkyu* [Research on the history of China's benevolent societies and benevolent halls] (Kyoto: Dōhōsha shuppan, 1997); Lilian M. Li, *Fighting Famine in North China: State, Market, and Environmental Decline, 1690s–1990s* (Stanford, Calif.: Stanford University Press, 2007); Smith, *The Art of Doing Good*; Xia Shi, *At Home in the World: Women and Charity in Late Qing and Early Republican China* (New York: Columbia University Press, 2018); Pierre Fuller, *Famine Relief in Warlord China* (Cambridge, Mass.: Harvard University Asia Center, 2019).

7. Joanna Handlin Smith, "Benevolent Societies: The Reshaping of Charity During the Late Ming and Early Ch'ing," *Journal of Asian Studies* 46, no. 2 (1987): 309–37.

8. Joanna Handlin Smith, "Social Hierarchy and Merchant Philanthropy as Perceived in Several Late-Ming and Early-Qing Texts," *Journal of Economic and Social History of the Orient* 41, no. 3 (1998): 420.

9. Yang Jianli, "Wanqing shehui zaihuang jiuzhi Gongneng de yanbian—yi 'dingwu qihuang' de liang zhong zhenji fangshi weili" [Changes in social disaster relief in the late Qing: Taking two kinds of relief methods during the "incredible famine of 1877–1878" as examples], *Qingshi yanjiu*, no. 4 (2000): 59–64.

10. On the Taiping Civil War, see Tobie Meyer-Fong, *What Remains: Coming to Terms with Civil War in 19th Century China* (Stanford, Calif.: Stanford University Press, 2013). On the North China Famine of 1876–1879, see Kathryn Edgerton-Tarpley, *Tears from Iron: Cultural Responses to Famine in Nineteenth-Century China* (Berkeley: University of California Press, 2008).

11. Michelle Tien King, *Between Birth and Death: Female Infanticide in Nineteenth-Century China* (Stanford, Calif.: Stanford University Press, 2014), 151–55. See also Zhu Hu, *Difangxing liudong ji qi chaoyue: Wanqing yizhen yu jindai Zhongguo de xinchen daixie* [The fluidity and transcendence of localism: Late-Qing charitable relief and the supersession of the old by the new in modern China] (Beijing: Zhongguo renmin daxue chubanshe, 2006).

12. Quoted in Vivienne Shue, "The Quality of Mercy: Confucian Charity and the Mixed Metaphors of Modernity in Tianjin," *Modern China* 32, no. 4 (2006): 426.

13. Shue, 428–32.

14. Andrea Janku, "Sowing Happiness: Spiritual Competition in Famine Relief Activities in Late Nineteenth-Century China," *Minsu quyi*, no. 143 (2004).

15. Caroline Reeves, "The Power of Mercy: The Chinese Red Cross Society, 1900–1937" (PhD diss., Harvard University, 1998).

## 256  1. CHINA AND THE BIRTH OF GLOBAL HUMANITARIANISM

16. Thomas David DuBois, "The Salvation of Religion? Public Charity and the New Religions of the Early Republic," *Minsu quyi* 172, no. 6 (2011): 73–126.
17. Shi, *At Home in the World*.
18. Pierre Fuller, "North China Famine Revisited: Unsung Native Relief in the Warlord Era, 1920–1921," *Modern Asian Studies* 47, no. 3 (2013): 831–37.
19. William Rowe, *China's Last Empire: The Great Qing* (Cambridge, Mass.: Harvard University Press, 2009), 165–74.
20. King, *Between Birth and Death*.
21. Henrietta Harrison, "'A Penny for the Little Chinese': The French Holy Childhood Association in China, 1843–1951," *American Historical Review* 113, no. 1 (2008): 73, 80, 73.
22. "Classement par diocèses des diverses sommes reçues," *Annales de l'oeuvre de la Sainte-Enfance* 51, no. 314 (June 1900): 154–79; King, *Between Birth and Death*, 121.
23. King, *Between Birth and Death*, 145–48.
24. King, 155–58; Harrison, "A Penny for the Little Chinese," 89–90.
25. Satadru Sen, "The Savage Family: Colonialism and Female Infanticide in Nineteenth-Century India," *Journal of Women's History* 14, no. 3 (2002): 53–79.
26. Edgerton-Tarpley, *Tears from Iron*.
27. A. F. Parrott, "For the Young: A Letter from Shan-Si," *China's Millions*, no. 53 (November 1879), 145–46.
28. On the history international famine relief committees in China, see Huang, *Feizhengfu zuzhi yu guoji hezuo zai Zhongguo: Huayang Yizhenhui zhi yanjiu* [Nongovernmental organizations and international cooperation in China: Research on the China International Famine Relief Commission] (Taipei: Xiu wei zixun, 2004); Fuller, *Famine Relief in Warlord China*; Andrew Nathan, *A History of the China International Famine Relief Commission* (Cambridge, Mass.: East Asian Research Center, Harvard University), 1965.
29. "The Central China Famine Relief Fund," *North-China Herald and Supreme Court & Consular Gazette*, December 7, 1906, 540–41.
30. Central China Famine Relief Committee, *Reports and Accounts from October 1, 1911, to June 30, 1912* (Shanghai: North China Daily News & Herald, 1912), 17–19.
31. Peking United International Famine Relief Committee, *The North China Famine of 1920–1921 with Special Reference to the West Chihli Area* (Beijing: Commercial Press Works, 1922), 167–68.
32. China International Famine Relief Commission (CIFRC), *History, Organization & Policy* (Beijing: China International Famine Relief Commission, 1923), 8–10.
33. Central China Famine Relief Committee, *Reports and Accounts*, 6.
34. American National Red Cross, *Report of the China Famine Relief, American Red Cross, October, 1920—September, 1921* (Shanghai: Commercial Press, 1921).
35. Peking United International Famine Relief Committee, *The North China Famine of 1920–1921*, 59, 61, 87–92.
36. Peking United International Famine Relief Committee, 26.
37. Fuller, "North China Famine Revisited," 822–23.
38. Fuller, *Famine Relief in Warlord China*, 236.

# 1. CHINA AND THE BIRTH OF GLOBAL HUMANITARIANISM  257

39. Central China Famine Relief Committee, *Reports and Accounts*, 34.

40. Central China Famine Relief Committee, 16, 35.

41. Central China Famine Relief Committee, 36.

42. Peking United International Famine Relief Committee, *The North China Famine of 1920–1921*, 31, 33, 41, 53.

43. Zhu Zhixin, "Qinlüe zhuquan yu rendaozhuyi" [The violation of sovereignty and humanitarianism], in *Zhu Zhixin xiansheng wenji* [Collected writings of Mr. Zhu Zhixin] (Taipei: Zhongyang wenwu zongjingxiao, 1985), 300–301.

44. Wang Chung-hui, "Zhongguo lilai duiwai taidu" [China's attitude to the outside world throughout history], in *Wang Chonghui xiansheng wenji* [Collected writings of Mr. Wang Chung-hui] (Taipei: Zhongyang wenwu zongjingxiao, 1981), 463. Wang Chung-hui's and Zhu Zhixin's critiques of humanitarianism in China are also analyzed in Huang, *Feizhengfu zuzhi yu guoji hezuo zai zhongguo*, 5–6.

45. Lujunbu, ed., *Lujun xingzheng jiyao* [Minutes on army administration], vol. 609 (Taipei: Wenhai chubanshe, 1981), 278–79.

46. Caroline Reeves, "Sovereignty and the Chinese Red Cross Society: The Differentiated Practice of International Law in Shandong, 1914–1916," *Journal of the History of International Law* 13, no. 1 (2011): 173.

47. Lujunbu, *Lujun xingzheng jiyao*, 278–79.

48. Karen Lynn Brewer, "From Philanthropy to Reform: The American Red Cross in China, 1906–1930" (PhD diss., Case Western Reserve University), 222–35; Caroline Reeves, "Holding Hostages in China, Holding China Hostage: Sovereignty, Philanthropy, and the 1923 'Lincheng Outrage,'" *Twentieth-Century China* 21, no. 1 (2001): 46–50; Zhou Qiuguang, *Hongshizihui zai Zhongguo (1904–1927)* [The Red Cross in China] (Beijing: Renmin chubanshe, 2008), 165–70; Alexandra Pfeiff, "Two Adoptions of the Red Cross: The Chinese Red Cross Society and the Red Swastika Society from 1904 to 1949" (PhD diss., European University Institute, 2018), 61–64.

49. "Lujunbu fouren Meiguo Honghui zai Hua sheli fenhui" [Ministry of the Army rejects the American Red Cross establishing a branch in China], *Shenbao*, May 1, 1918, 10.

50. Reeves, "Holding Hostages in China," 49.

51. Zhou, *Hongshizihui zai Zhongguo*, 170–72.

52. Quoted in Reeves, "Holding Hostages in China," 50.

53. Li Liangming, "Beifa zhanzheng yu Wuhan gongren yundong" [The Northern Expedition and the workers' movement in Wuhan], *Huazhong shifan daxue xuebao*, no. 4 (1987): 57–62.

54. CIFRC, *Annual Report 1927* (Beijing: CIFRC, 1928), 42–43.

55. CIFRC, *History, Organization & Policy*, 7.

56. CIFRC, *Annual Report 1930* (Beijing: CIFRC, 1931), 62.

57. CIFRC, *Annual Report 1928* (Beijing: CIFRC, 1929), 35–36.

58. CIFRC, *Annual Report 1929* (Beijing: CIFRC, 1930), 39.

59. American National Red Cross, *The Report of the American Red Cross Commission to China* (Washington, D.C.: American National Red Cross, 1929), 29–30.

258  1. CHINA AND THE BIRTH OF GLOBAL HUMANITARIANISM

60. CIFRC, *Famine in China's Northwest: American Red Cross Commission's Findings and Rejoinders Thereto* (Beijing: China International Famine Relief Commission, 1930), 18, 22.

61. "Waijiaobu dian ling Wu Chaoshu xiang Meiguo Hong Shizi Hui yanzhong zewen qi laihua diaochatuan baogao Huazai yuanyin Shijian" [Foreign Ministry instructs Wu Chaoshu to demand an explanation from American Red Cross on the reasons for its China investigation committee report on famine in China], November 5, 1929, 002-060100-00024-005, Academia Historica (AH).

62. "Xu Shiying jiuzheng Meihonghui dui hua zai miulun" [Xu Shiying corrects the American Red Cross's falsehoods about famine in China], *Shen bao*, December 12, 1929, 16.

63. "Meihonghui cha zai baogaoshu zhi jiaoxun" [The lessons of the American Red Cross's famine investigation report], *Da gong bao*, October 2, 1929, 2.

64. "Waijiaobu kangyi diaochatuan cha zai baogao" [Foreign Ministry protests famine investigation committee report], *Minguo ribao*, November 7, 1929, 4.

65. Adam McKeown, *Melancholy Order: Asian Migration and the Globalization of Borders* (New York: Columbia University Press, 2008), 43–65.

66. Yu Chenzi, "Lun shijie jingji jingzheng zhi dashi (xu di shi yi hao)" [On the grand trend of world economic competition (continued from issue 11)], *Xinmin congbao*, no. 14 (1902): 50–51. See also Guanhua Wang, *In Search of Justice: The 1905–1906 Chinese Anti-American Boycott* (Cambridge, Mass.: Harvard University Asia Center, 2001), 38–61; and Mae Ngai, *The Chinese Question: The Gold Rushes and Global Politics* (New York: Norton, 2021), 289–92.

67. Lin Jiajin, *Jindai Guangdong qiaohui yanjiu* [Research on remittances in modern Guangdong] (Guangzhou: Zhongshan daxue chubanshe, 1999), 27–40.

68. Glen Peterson, "Overseas Chinese and Merchant Philanthropy in China: From Culturalism to Nationalism," *Journal of Chinese Overseas* 1, no. 1 (2005): 94–95.

69. John Fitzgerald and Mei-fen Kuo, "Diaspora Charity and Welfare Sovereignty in the Chinese Republic: Shanghai Charity Innovator William Yinson Lee (Li Yuanxin, 1884–1965)," *Twentieth-Century China* 41, no. 1 (2017): 72–96.

70. Yong Chen, "Chinese Charity in Early Chinese American History," in *Chinese Diaspora Charity and the Cantonese Pacific, 1850–1949*, ed. John Fitzgerald and Hon-ming Yip (Hong Kong: Hong Kong University Press, 2020), 132.

71. Clarence Glick, *Sojourners and Settlers: Chinese Migrants in Hawaii* (Honolulu: University of Hawaii Press, 1980), 242–77.

72. Ren Guixiang, *Haiwai Huaqiao yu zuguo Kangri Zhanzheng* [Overseas Chinese and the motherland's War of Resistance Against Japan] (Beijing: Tuanjie chubanshe, 2015), 116–21.

73. On the monthly donation quota system, see Jack Neubauer, "Destroying the Family to Save the Nation: Rethinking the Role of Overseas Chinese in China's War of Resistance Against Japan," in *Melancholy Borders*, ed. Andrew B. Liu, Owen Miller, and Meha Priyadarshini (New York: Columbia University Press, forthcoming).

74. "Chinese Show Raises $5,000 for Relief," *Straits Times*, November 14, 1937, 2.

75. "Chinese Art Treasures," *Evening Telegraph and Post* (Dundee, Scot.), January 15, 1938, 4.

# 1. CHINA AND THE BIRTH OF GLOBAL HUMANITARIANISM  259

76. "Chinese Relief Fund," *Otago Daily Times* (Dunedin, N.Z.), July 23, 1938; "Children's Work for Chinese Refugees," *Evening Post* (Wellington, N.Z.), September 2, 1939; "Benefit Concert," *Auckland Star*, July 4, 1939.

77. "Chinese Relief Fund," *Daily News* (Sydney, Aus.), March 4, 1939, 3; Derham Groves, *Anna May Wong's Lucky Shoes: 1939 Australia Through the Eyes of an Art Deco Diva* (Ames, Iowa: Culicidae Press, 2011), 32.

78. Renqiu Yu, *To Save China, to Save Ourselves: The Chinese Hand Laundry Alliance of New York* (Philadelphia: Temple University Press, 1992), 94–95.

79. "Chain of Parties for China Relief Set for June 17: Dinners in 1,561 Cities to Get $1,000,000 Aid; Canton Fair Is Planned in New York Chinatown," *New York Herald Tribune*, June 7, 1938, 4.

80. "Roosevelt Pleased by Chinese Benefits: Colonel Now Estimates More than 1,000,000 Attended," *New York Times*, June 19, 1938, 24.

81. "6,500 Reserve Tickets for 'Rice Party' Tonight: Chinatown to Entertain Visitors with Dinner and Outdoor Performances in Drive to Aid Refugees," *New York Herald Tribune*, June 17, 1938, 8.

82. "200,000 Attend Rice Bowl Parties," *North-China Herald*, June 22, 1938.

83. On the history of the NARC, see Zhang Chun, *Kangri Zhanzheng shiqi Zhanshi Ertong Baoyuhui yanjiu* [Research on the National Association for Refugee Children During the War of Resistance Against Japan] (Beijing: Tuanjie chubanshe, 2015); Lin Jia-hui, "Zhanshi Ertong Baoyuhui de jianli yu zuzhi yunzuo" [The establishment and organizational operations of the National Association for Refugee Children," *Shi-Hui*, No. 10 (2006): 269–320; Norman Apter, "Saving the Young: A History of the Child Relief Movement in Modern China" (PhD diss., University of California, Los Angeles, 2013), 149–181.

84. Zhang, *Kangri Zhanzheng shiqi Zhanshi Ertong Baoyuhui yanjiu*, 51–70; Helen M. Schneider, "Mobilising Women: The Women's Advisory Council, Resistance, and Reconstruction During China's War with Japan," *European Journal of East Asian Studies* 11, no. 2 (2012): 220–23.

85. Rana Mitter, *Forgotten Ally: China's World War II, 1937–1945* (Boston: Houghton Mifflin Harcourt, 2013), 182.

86. Zhang, *Kangri Zhanzheng shiqi Zhanshi Ertong Baoyuhui yanjiu*, 130.

87. Soong Mei-ling, "Jin wei nantong qingming" [A sincere appeal to save the children], *Funü shenghuo*, no. 11 (March 1938): 2.

88. Tang Guozhen, "Zhongguo Funü Weilao Ziwei Kangzhan Jiangshi Zonghui Zhanshi Ertong Baoyuhui gongzuo baogao" [National Chinese Women's Association for War Relief Association for Refugee Children work report], in *Funü tanhuahui gongzuo baobao* [Women's Symposium work report] (1939), 23.

89. Zhang Aizhen, "Ertong Baoyuhui liu zhounian jinian ganyan" [Reflections on the sixth anniversary of the National Association for Refugee Children], in *Zhanshi Ertong Baoyuhui liu zhounian jiniankan* [Memorial volume for the sixth anniversary of the National Association for Refugee Children] (Chongqing: Zhanshi ertong baoyuhui: 1944), 22.

260   1. CHINA AND THE BIRTH OF GLOBAL HUMANITARIANISM

90.  "Zhanshi Ertong Baoyuhui baoguan weiyuanhui shouzhi jisuan shu [National Association for Refugee Children Treasury Committee Income and Expense Calculations]," in *Zhanshi Ertong Baoyuhui liu zhounian jiniankan*, 68.

91.  "Rules for Adoption of Refugee Children by Foreign Nationals," *Malaya Tribune*, October 14, 1939, 4.

92.  "25,000 Throng to Chinatown for Rice Bowl Party: Mme. Chiang, in Greeting, Appeals to Americans to Adopt Chinese Orphans to 'Acquire Merit on Earth,'" *New York Herald Tribune*, June 18, 1938, 5.

93.  "Chinese Orphans: Proposed 'Adoption' by New Zealanders—Madame Chiang Kai-shek's Appeal," *Press* (Christchurch, N.Z.), June 4, 1938.

94.  "Adoption Plan Helping Chinese Children: Appeal Launched in Wellington," *Press*, June 24, 1938.

95.  Letter from F. W. Furkert, October 13, 1948, Papers Relating to Chinese Orphans, MS-Papers-5960-8, Alexander Turnbull Library, Wellington, New Zealand (PRCO).

96.  "Chinese Orphans."

97.  "Broadcasting: Today's Programmes," *Evening Post*, August 5, 1938; "Funds for Chinese Refugees," *Press*, September 21, 1938. On Wu Aizhuang's fundraising activities in New Zealand, see also Wu Minchao, "Cong linshi nanmin dao luodi shenggen: erzhan qianhou de xinxilan huaqiao nüxing" [From temporary refugees to permanent residents: Chinese women in New Zealand around World War II], *Jindaishi yanjiu*, no. 6 (2018): 89–103.

98.  "'Adoption' Plan—Chinese Children: Appeal by Consul's Wife," *Evening Post*, Aug. 6, 1938.

99.  "An Attraction: Madame Feng Wang to Speak," *Evening Post*, November 22, 1939.

100.  Letter from Madame Feng Wang to Madame Chiang Kai-shek, October 3, 1938, 11-4230, 109–111, Second Historical Archives of China, Nanjing (SHAC).

101.  Zhanshi Ertong Baoyuhui renyang ertong jiguan tongji biao [Statistical table of NARC adopted children by native place], March 1938–March 1940, 11-4034, 6, SHAC.

102.  Renyang ertong xiezhu tuanti baogao biao [Cooperating organizations report form for adopted children], 11-4228, 103–4, SHAC.

103.  Letter from Tsuifeng Lin to Madame Chiang, July 7, 1938, 11-4229, 49–51, SHAC.

104.  Letter from Mrs. V. K. W. Koo to Madame Chiang, June 8, 1938, 11-4233, 147–48, SHAC.

105.  Letter from Tsuifeng Lin to Madame Chiang, October 4, 1938, 11-4229, 54–55, SHAC.

106.  Letter from Tsuifeng Lin to Madame Chiang, November 8, 1938, 11-4229, 56–57, SHAC.

107.  "Wellesley Receives a Commencement Gift from China's First Lady," *Bee* (Danville, Va.), June 23, 1938, 8; "Many Present at N.Y. Party for Dr. Kung: C. H. Wang, Manager of Bank of China, Is Cocktail Host," *China Press* (Shanghai), July 24, 1937, 5.

108.  Wei han gao shou dao 360 zhang xiangpian bing qing ling ji nühai xiangpian, fu renyang ertong zhe mingdan you [To inform that 360 photos have been received and also request photos of girls, list of adopted children attached], May 23, 1939, 11-4234, 119–25, SHAC.

109.  Letter from Wang Sheng Chih to Madame Chiang, January 8, 1940, 11-4234, 130–31, SHAC; Wang Sheng Chih, "Refugee Children in China," *Malaya Tribune*, October 14, 1939, 4.

110.  Letter from Ann Chung to Madame Chiang, August 29, 1938, 11-4235, 192–93, SHAC.

111.  "Maliujia funü mujuan tuan jinxing jiuji nantong jue xian jiang suo cun yikuan hui zuguo jiuji tuanyuan jinli renyang wai fu xiang quanmu" [Malacca women's fundraising

group conducts relief for refugee children, resolves to send existing funds for relief in the fatherland, members undertake sponsorships to the best of their means and solicit donations], *Nanyang siang pau* (Singapore), May 14, 1938, 16.

112. "Jinbao Huashang ge huiyou renyang zuguo nantong nian ming bing jiang xiang qiaojie quanmu yi hong jiuji" [Friends of the Kampar Chinese Merchants Association adopt 20 refugee children in the fatherland and will solicit contributions among overseas Chinese community to expand relief work], *Nanyang siang pau*, July 27, 1939, 32.

113. "K. C. Li Dies at 68; Tungsten Expert: President of Wah Chang Smelting and Refining—'Richest Chinese' in U.S.," *New York Times*, March 8, 1961, 33.

114. Letter from Twinem to K. C. Li, January 22, 1940, 11-4230, 32–38, SHAC.

115. Letter from K. C. Li to Twinem, February 24, 1940, 11-4230, 24–26, SHAC.

116. Hong Kong Branch of the National Association for the Care of Warphans, 11-4235, 64–70, SHAC.

117. Letter from Madame Chiang Kai-shek to F. W. Furkert, June 7, 1940, PRCO.

118. Letter from Madame Feng Wang to Madame Chiang, November 8, 1938, 11-4230, 112, SHAC.

119. Kenneth Pomeranz, *The Great Divergence: China, Europe, and the Making of the Modern World Economy* (Princeton, N.J.: Princeton University Press, 2000), 25.

120. On the Mandarin Paradox, see Eric Hayot, *The Hypothetical Mandarin: Sympathy, Modernity, and Chinese Pain* (New York: Oxford University Press, 2009); and Carlo Ginzburg, "Killing a Chinese Mandarin: The Moral Implications of Distance," *Critical Inquiry* 21, no. 1 (1994): 46–60.

121. Hayot, *The Hypothetical Mandarin*, 3–7.

122. Quoted in Ginzburg, "Killing a Chinese Mandarin," 53.

## 2. GLOBAL HUMANITARIANISM'S INTIMATE TURN

1. Letter from Gladys to Chi-ming, December 1, 1939, 11-4238, 46–59, SHAC.

2. Letter from Kuo-hwa to Hilda, January 29, 1941, 11-4238, 184–88, SHAC.

3. Ann Stoler, *Carnal Knowledge and Imperial Power: Race and the Intimate in Colonial Rule* (Berkeley: University of California Press, 2002).

4. Emmanuelle Saada, *Empire's Children: Race, Filiation, and Citizenship in the French Colonies* (Chicago: University of Chicago Press, 2012).

5. Jane Hunter, *The Gospel of Gentility: American Women Missionaries in Turn-of-the-Twentieth Century China* (New Haven, Conn.: Yale University Press, 1984).

6. "Rules for Adoption of Refugee Children by Foreign Nationals," *Malaya Tribune*, October 14, 1939, 4.

7. Colette M. Plum, "Unlikely Heirs: War Orphans During the Second Sino-Japanese War, 1937–1945" (PhD diss., Stanford University, 2006), 9; H. L. Mencken, "War Words in England," *American Speech* 19, no. 1 (1944): 15.

8. May-ling Soong Chiang, *A Letter from Madame Chiang Kai-shek to Boys and Girls Across the Ocean* (Chongqing: China Information Pub. Co., 1940), 14. In Chinese,

262  2. GLOBAL HUMANITARIANISM'S INTIMATE TURN

NARC-operated orphanage-schools were called *baoyu yuan*, and the children who resided in them were most commonly referred to as *nantong*.

9.  Zhang Chun, *Kangri Zhanzheng shiqi Zhanshi Ertong Baoyuhui yanjiu* [Research on the National Association for Refugee Children During the War of Resistance Against Japan] (Beijing: Tuanjie chubanshe, 2015), 227–29.

10.  Zhang Chun, 220–26.

11.  Guo Xiuyi, "Wo yuan xianshen yu zhanshi ertong bayou shiye" [I am willing to dedicate myself to the cause of wartime child welfare], *Funü shenghuo* 5, no. 11 (1939): 4.

12.  On letter-writing manuals for children in Republican China, see Danni Cai, "Power, Politeness, and Print: Children's Letter Writing in Republican China," *Journal of the History of Childhood and Youth* 13, no. 1 (2020): 38–62.

13.  Cai Danni [Danni Cai], "Minguo xuesheng shuxin jiaoyu yanjiu—yi xuesheng chidu ben wei zhongxin" [Research on epistolary education for students in the Republican period—using student letter writing manuals as a focal point] (MA thesis, Xiamen University, 2014), 27.

14.  *Xuesheng xin chidu* [New letter writing manual for students] (Hong Kong: Chen xiang ji shuju, n.d.), 13–14.

15.  Letter from Chia-chin to Helen, May 27, 1941, 11-4237, 47–49, SHAC.

16.  Letter from Hew-wei to Bethea, November 15, 1940, 11-4239, 56–57, SHAC.

17.  "Wei zhuanji gai yuan ertong renyang ren laihan you" [Forwarding sponsor letters to children in the orphanage], March 2, 1940, 11-4239, 61, SHAC.

18.  "Wei chengbao ertong Li Yijia shenghuo qingxing ji jiaoyu zhuangkuang qi jianhe" [Respectfully reporting on the living conditions and educational progress of child Li Yijia], December 27, 1940, 11-4237, 121, SHAC.

19.  Letter from E. T. to Li-chiang, December 6, 1939, 11-4232, 112–19, SHAC.

20.  Letter from Joan to Yuen-lan, February 15, 1940, 11-4231, 58–69, SHAC.

21.  Letter from Joan to Yuen-lan.

22.  Letter from Alice to Kwang Foo, December 1, 1939, 11-4237, 33–43, SHAC.

23.  Letter from Hsio-djen to Alice, February 14, 1941, 11-4231, 118–21, SHAC. As explained later in this chapter, though Alice had initially written to a boy named Kwang Foo, another boy, named Hsio-djen, was the eventual recipient of her letter.

24.  Letter from Dorothy to Chia Cheng, February 17, 1940, 11-4232, 166–71, SHAC.

25.  Letter from Hsio-djen to Alice, February 14, 1941.

26.  Letter from Leska to I-Cha, February 18, 1940, 11-4231, 95–101, SHAC.

27.  Letter from Lillias to Madame Chiang, June 24, 1939, 11-4236, 97–100, SHAC.

28.  Letter from Maria to Ren, January 1940, 11-4238, 81–89, SHAC.

29.  Letter from E. T. to Li-chiang, December 6, 1939.

30.  Letter from Bethea to Hew-wei, July 1, 1940, 11-4239, 42–47, SHAC.

31.  Letter from Bethea to Hew-wei, July 10, 1941, 11-4229, 88–89, SHAC.

32.  Letter from Gladys to Chi-ming, December 1, 1939.

33.  Letter from Dorothy to Tao-chuan, March 2, 1940, 11-4232, 152–56, SHAC.

34.  Letter from Tao-chuan to Dorothy, June 30, 1940, 11-4232, 145–46, SHAC.

35.  Letter from Bethea to Madame Chiang, May 24, 1940, 11-4239, 53–54, SHAC.

36. Letter from Bethea to Hew-wei, July 1, 1940.

37. Letter from Twinem to Bethea, May 8, 1941, 11-4239, 58, SHAC.

38. Letter from Bethea to Hew-wei, May 21, 1941, 11-4229, 81–85, SHAC.

39. Letter from Twinem to Lillias, March 7, 1940, 11-4236, 102, SHAC.

40. Letter from Twinem to Gladys, April 13, 1940, 11-4236, 22–23, SHAC.

41. "Wei ertong Yan Qimingi yi tao jiang yuan han ji zhaopian tuihuan qing" [Returning original letter and photograph because child Yan Qiming has fled the orphanage], March 14, 1940, 11-4234, 18–20, SHAC.

42. Letter from Gladys to Twinem, June 30, 1940, 11-4232, 161–62, SHAC.

43. Du Junhui, "Baoyuyuan ertong taowang de yanjiu" [Research on children running away from warphanages], *Funü xinyun* 2, no. 8 (1940): 1.

44. Additional examples are recorded in 11-4234, 113–17; and 11-4238, 176–88, SHAC.

45. Letter from Chen-shih to Gladys, January 25, 1941, 11-4232, 163–64; letter from Twinem to Gladys, May 27, 1941, 11-4232, 165, SHAC.

46. Letter from Alice to Kwang Foo, December 1, 1939.

47. Madeline Yuan-yin Hsu, *Dreaming of Gold, Dreaming of Home: Transnationalism and Migration Between the United States and South China, 1882–1943* (Stanford, Calif.: Stanford University Press, 2000).

48. Gregor Benton and Hong Liu, *Dear China: Emigrant Letters and Remittances, 1820–1980* (Oakland: University of California Press, 2018).

49. On the significance of *qiaopi* for maintaining family ties, see Liu Jin, *Wuyi yinxin* [Silver letters from Wuyi] (Guangzhou: Guangdong renmin chubanshe, 2009), 63–74.

50. Benton and Liu, *Dear China*, 7.

51. Jiangmenshi dang'an ju, Jiangmenshi zazhi ban, Wuyi Daxue Guangdong Qiaoxiang Wenhua Yanjiu Zhongxin, eds., *Qingxi qiaoxiang: Wuyi yinxin dang'an tu'ce* [Maintaining connections with an overseas Chinese village: Archival photographs of silver letters from Wuyi] (Jiangmen: Jiangmenshi dang'an ju, 2010), 46. Tan's story is also discussed in Liu, *Wuyi yinxin*, 65–66.

52. Benton and Liu, *Dear China*, 9, 13.

53. Zhou Chuan, ed., *Zhongguo jinxiandai gaodeng jiaoyu renwu cidian* [Biographical dictionary of higher education in modern China] (Fuzhou: Fujian jiaoyu chubanshe, 2018), 579–80.

54. On the history of the mental hygiene movement in China, see Emily Baum, *The Invention of Madness: State, Society, and the Insane in Modern China* (Chicago: University of Chicago Press, 2018), 137–58; and Wen-ji Wang, "Yufang, shiying yu gaizao: Minguo shiqi de xinli weisheng" [Prevention, adaptation, and transformation: Mental hygiene during the Republican Period], in *Jiankang yu shehui: Huaren weisheng xinshi* [Health and society: A new history of Chinese hygiene], ed. Zhu Pingyi (Taipei: Lianjing, 2013), 237–57.

55. Colin Koopman, *How We Became Our Data: A Genealogy of the Informational Person* (Chicago: University of Chicago Press, 2019), 79–82.

56. Ellen Mathews, "A Study of Emotional Stability in Children by Means of a Questionnaire," *Journal of Delinquency* 8, no. 1 (1923): 1–40.

264  2. GLOBAL HUMANITARIANISM'S INTIMATE TURN

57. Xiao Xiaorong, "Xiao shi dingzheng geren shishi biaoge di yi zhong zhi chongding" [First kind of reformulation of Xiao Xiaorong's amended personal data sheet], *Jiaoyu tongxun* 4, no. 6 (1941): 7–11.

58. Xiao shi dingzheng geren shishi biaoge (di yi zhong) [Xiao Xiaorong's amended personal data sheet (type one), 11-3318, 64–65, SHAC.

59. Xiao Xiaorong, *Renshi xinli wenti* [Issues in personnel psychology] (Shangahi: Shangwu yinshuguan, 1944), 264–66.

60. Fan Tingwei, "Ding Zan yu Kangzhan shiqi de xinli jiankang jiaoyu" [Ding Zan and mental health education during the War of Resistance], *Haixia jiaoyu yanjiu*, no. 1 (2014): 73–74; Wen-ji Wang and Hsuan-Ying Huang, "Mental Health," in *The Making of the Human Sciences in China: Historical and Conceptual Foundations*, ed. Howard Chiang (Boston: Brill, 2019), 469.

61. Ding Zan, "Ertong xingwei zhidao wo jian" [My views on children's behavioral guidance], *Jia*, no. 13 (1947): 49.

62. On the Mental Hygiene Laboratory and its work with children during World War II, see Su Hua, "Kangzhan shiqi nantong de yichang xinli wenti" [Abnormal psychological problems of refugee children during the War of Resistance], *Minguo dang'an*, no. 3 (1995): 121–29; and Hu Qing, "Minguo shiqi de ertong zhidao lilun yu shijian yanjiu" [Research on the theory and practice of child guidance during the Republic of China] (MA thesis, Suzhou University, 2020), 30–32.

63. Ding Zan, *Xinli weisheng luncong* [Collected essays on mental hygiene] (Taipei: Taiwan shangwu, 1966), 49–51.

64. Qian Ping, "Di yi baoyuyuan ji baoyuhui liaoyangyuan xinli weisheng diaocha baogao" [Report on investigation of mental hygiene at the NARC No. 1 orphanage and sanatorium], 1943, 11-3318, 55–63, SHAC.

65. Xiong Zhi, "Liu nian lai ben hui gongzuo zongjie baogao" [Summary report of this organization's work over the past six years], in *Zhanshi Ertong Baoyuhui liu zhounian jiniankan*, 3.

66. Zhang Chun, *Kangri Zhanzheng Shiqi Zhanshi Ertong Baoyuhui yanjiu*, 239.

67. Zhang Chun, 141–43.

68. "Zhanshi Ertong Baoyuhui zhishu di san baoyuyuan gongzuo ziliao" [NARC No. 3 Warphanage work materials], February 1946, in *Zhao Juntao jiaoyu sixiang lunwen ji* [Zhao Juntao's collected essays on education], ed. Teng Jiuming (Chongqing: Chongqing Chubanshe, 2003), 3–77.

69. "Li Guoqi xiansheng fangwen jilu" [Record of interview with Mr. Kuo-chih Lee], in *Guo Tingyi xiansheng mensheng gu jiu yi wang lu* [The reminiscences of Mr. Kuo Ting-yee by his disciples and friends], ed. Chen Yi-shen et al. (Taipei: Zhongyang yanjiuyuan jindaishi yanjiusuo, 2004), 133–37.

70. Tara Zahra, *The Lost Children: Reconstructing Europe's Families After World War II* (Cambridge, Mass.: Harvard University Press, 2011), 64–65.

71. Sara Fieldston, *Raising the World: Child Welfare in the American Century* (Cambridge, Mass.: Harvard University Press, 2015), 12–53.

72. Ding Zan, *Xinli weisheng luncong*, 51–52.

73. Susan Glosser, *Chinese Visions of Family and State, 1915–1953* (Berkeley: University of California Press, 2003); Sean Hsiang-lin Lei, "Xiguan cheng siwei: Xin Shenghuo Yundong yu feijiehe fangzhi zhong de lunli, jiating yu shenti" [Habituating the four virtues: ethics, family, and the body in the antituberculosis campaigns and the New Life Movement], *Zhongyang yuanjiuyuan jindaishi yanjiusuo jikan*, no. 74 (2011): 133–77.

74. Ding Zan, *Xinli weisheng luncong*, 52.

75. Letter from Madame Chiang to Mrs. M. Fong, September 30, 1938, 11-4234, 89–90, SHAC.

76. May-Ling Soong Chiang, *A Letter from Madame Chiang Kai-Shek*, 16, 26.

77. Letter from Chen-shih to Gladys, January 25, 1941.

78. Arlie Russell Hochschild, *The Managed Heart: Commercialization of Human Feeling* (Berkeley: University of California Press, 2012), 25.

79. Kristine Alexander, "Agency and Emotion Work," *Jeunesse: Young People, Texts, Cultures* 7, no. 2 (2015): 120–28.

80. Letter from Maria to Ren, January 1940.

81. Qian Ping, "Di yi baoyuyuan ji baoyuhui liaoyangyuan xinli weisheng diaocha baogao."

82. Letter from Emma DeLong Mills to Soong Mei-ling, May 9, 1938, Box 9, Papers of Emma DeLong Mills, MSS.2, Wellesley College Archives (EDM).

83. Letter from Emma DeLong Mills to Soong Mei-ling, May 17, 1938, Box 9, EDM.

84. Letter from Emma DeLong Mills to Soong Mei-ling, June 28, 1938; letter from Soong Mei-ling to Emma DeLong Mills, July 22, 1938, Box 9, EDM.

85. Letter from W. E. Barnard to Madame Chiang, August 15, 1938, 11-4235, 126–27, SHAC.

86. Letter from Madame Chiang to W. E. Barnard, May 3, 1939, 11-4235, 132, 11-4236, 53, SHAC.

87. Letter from NARC to Van Wessem, March 5, 1940, 11-4234, 162–65, SHAC.

88. Letter from Twinem to Wang Sheng-chih, April 16, 1940, 11-4234, 135, SHAC.

89. Letter from Twinem to W. E. Barnard, August 7, 1939, 11-4236, 58, SHAC.

90. Letter from Twinem to Lillias, March 7, 1940.

91. Letter from Han to K. S., May 27, 1941, 11-4239, 97–100, SHAC.

92. Letter from Cheng Zur to Katherine, July 10, 1940, 11-4237, 117–19, SHAC.

93. Letter from Kate to Yon Hung, April 10, 1940, 11-4231, 37–44, SHAC.

94. Letter from Gung-hsing Wang to Madame Chiang, December 29, 1939, 11-4239, 115–20, SHAC.

95. Letter from Twinem to Gung-hsing Wang, April 16, 1940, 11-4239, 112–14, SHAC.

96. Letter from Chung-ya to A Class, Kemper Hall, March 27, 1940, 11-4239, 129–30, SHAC.

97. Correspondence between K. Tong and NARC, May 27–30, 1941, 11-4232, 125–26; letter from NARC Child Representative to the Children of America, May 30, 1941, 11-4232, 149–51, SHAC.

98. Letter from Madame Chiang to W. E. Barnard, July 18, 1938, 11-4236, 52; 11-4235, 123–24, SHAC.

99. Letter from W. E. Barnard to Madame Chiang, August 15, 1938.

100. Letter from Lillian Thomason to Madame Chiang, February 13, 1939, 11-4234, 78, SHAC.

101. Madame Quo Tai-chi to Madame Chiang, September 3, 1938, 11-4228, 31–32, SHAC.

## 266 2. GLOBAL HUMANITARIANISM'S INTIMATE TURN

102. "Rules for Adoption of Refugee Children by Foreign Nationals."
103. Letter from NARC to McCelland, April 14, 1943, 11-4239, 184, SHAC.

## 3. INSTITUTIONALIZING THE INTIMATE TURN

1. On the CCF's activities in South China in the postwar period, see Zhu Aiqin, "Meihua ertong fulihui zai huanan diqu de huodong yanjiu: 1945–1952" [Research on the activities of China's Children Fund in the South China region: 1945–1952] (MA thesis, Sun-Yat-sen University, 2005); Lei Jiachun, "Minguo shiqi de Guangzhou jidujiao cishan huodong yanjiu (1912–1949)" [Research on Christian philanthropic activities in Republican era Guangzhou] (MA thesis: Guangzhou University, 2019).
2. Larry E. Tise, *A Book About Children: The World of Christian Children's Fund, 1938–1991* (Falls Church, Va.: Hartland, 1993), 24.
3. Edmund W. Janss, *Yankee Si! The Story of Dr. J. Calvitt Clarke and His 36,000 Children* (New York: William Morrow, 1961), 9.
4. J. Calvitt Clarke III, *Fifty Years of Begging: Dr. J. Calvitt Clarke and Christian Children's Fund* (Bloomington, Ind.: Archway, 2018), xix.
5. J. Calvitt Clarke III, "The Literary Life of Dr. J. Calvitt Clarke," *Paperback Parade: The Magazine for Paperback Readers and Collectors*, March 2014, 20–49; Clarke, *Fifty Years of Begging*, 86–166.
6. Richard Grant, *Eurasian Girl* (New York: Universal, 1935), 59.
7. Grant, 114.
8. Grant, 115. On discourses concerning "Eurasian" children in the United States and China during the era of Chinse exclusion, see Emma Teng, *Eurasian: Mixed Identities in the United States, China, and Hong Kong, 1842–1943* (Berkeley: University of California Press, 2013).
9. Grant, *Eurasian Girl*, 106.
10. Hrishi Karthikeyan and Gabriel J. Chin, "Preserving Racial Identity: Population Patterns and the Application of Anti-Miscegenation Statutes to Asian Americans, 1910–1950," *Asian Law Journal* 9, no. 1 (2002): 1–40. The U.S. Supreme Court declared antimiscegenation laws unconstitutional in the case of *Loving v. Virginia* (1967). On the history of such laws in the United States, see Peggy Pascoe, *What Comes Naturally: Miscegenation Law and the Making of Race in Modern America* (New York: Oxford University Press, 2009).
11. Warren I. Cohen, *America's Response to China: A History of Sino-American Relations* (New York: Columbia University Press, 2010); Hunt, *The Making of a Special Relationship*.
12. Division of Liberated Areas, Foreign Economic Administration, *The United Nations Relief and Rehabilitation Administration* (Washington, D.C.: The Administration, 1943), 1.
13. On the UNRRA, see Jessica Reinisch, "Internationalism in Relief: The Birth (and Death) of UNRRA," *Past & Present* 210, Issue Supp. 6 (2010): 258–89; Silvia Salvatici, *A History of Humanitarianism, 1775–1989: In the Name of Others* (Manchester, UK: Manchester University Press, 2019), 116–40.

3. INSTITUTIONALIZING THE INTIMATE TURN   267

14. On the CNRRA, see Rana Mitter, "Imperialism, Transnationalism, and the Reconstruction of Post-War China: UNRRA in China, 1944–7," *Past & Present* 218, Supp. 8 (2013): 51–69.

15. "CNRRA: Its Purpose, Functions, and Organization," 1946, FO 371/53581, Foreign Office Records, National Archives, Kew (FO).

16. Hans Van de Ven, *China at War: Triumph and Tragedy in the Emergence of the New China* (Cambridge, Mass.: Harvard University Press, 2018), 227.

17. Quoted in Mitter, "Imperialism, Transnationalism," 60.

18. Rachel M. McCleary, *Global Compassion: Private Voluntary Organizations and U.S. Foreign Policy Since 1939* (New York: Oxford University Press, 2009), 68–69.

19. Zhang Chun, *Kangri Zhanzheng shiqi Zhanshi Ertong Baoyuhui yanjiu* [Research on the National Association for Refugee Children During the War of Resistance Against Japan] (Beijing: Tuanjie chubanshe, 2015), 87–102.

20. Tise, *A Book About Children*, 301.

21. "Yi jiu si wu nian ben hui kaiban zhi shi zhilüe" [Brief account of the establishment of this organization after 1945], 17-1-121-51, Guangzhou Municipal Archives (GMA).

22. "Qiaoguang zhi jinxi" [Kiu Kong Orphanage past and present], *Fu er* 1, no. 1 (July 1946): 7; "200 Still Die Daily in Swatow Famine: Kwantung Relief Group Labors to Cut Starvation Toll," *New York Times*, February 2, 1944, 4. On the Taishan famine of the early 1940s, see Huang Jianyun, *Taishan gujin gailan* [A Survey of Taishan from antiquity to the present] (Guangzhou: Guangdong Renmin Chubanshe, 1992), 214.

23. Edmund W. Janss, *A Brief History of Christian Children's Fund, Inc.* (Richmond, Va.: Christian Children's Fund, 1967), 28–29; Margaret Mih Tillman, *Raising China's Revolutionaries: Modernizing Childhood for Cosmopolitan Nationalists and Liberated Comrades, 1920s–1950s* (New York: Columbia University Press, 2018), 152.

24. "The CCF Adoption Plan," *China News* 7, no. 2 (Winter 1949–1950): 2–3.

25. Advertisement, *China News* 4, no. 3 (Spring 1946): 3.

26. "A Recipe for Children," *China News* 2, no. 4 (Summer 1944): 2.

27. "Will China Choose Democracy or Communism?," *China News* 5, no. 1 (Spring 1947): 4.

28. On the link between Cold War politics and the role of consumer goods in defining idealized family life, see Elaine Tyler May, *Homeward Bound: American Families in the Cold War Era* (New York: Basic Books, 1988).

29. Daniel H. Bays, *A New History of Christianity in China* (Malden, Mass.: Wiley-Blackwell, 2012), 94.

30. Nancy Bernkopf Tucker, "An Unlikely Peace: American Missionaries and the Chinese Communists, 1948–1950," *Pacific Historical Review* 45, no. 1 (February 1976): 101.

31. Pearl S. Buck, "Is There a Case for Foreign Missions?" *Harper's Magazine*, December 1, 1932, 155.

32. On the "evangelical-ecumenical divide" at this time, see David A. Hollinger, *Protestants Abroad: How Missionaries Tried to Change the World but Changed America* (Princeton, N.J.: Princeton University Press, 2017), 10–11, 83–88.

33. "The CCF Adoption Plan," 2.

34. "Statement of Policy with Reference to Christian Teaching as Voted by the Executive Committee of China's Children Fund," *China News* 5, no. 2 (Fall 1947): 4.

35. "Will China Choose Democracy or Communism?" 1.
36. Letter from Maddry to Saunders, February 20, 1939, AR 551-2, Box 51, Folder 1939–1943, Southern Baptist Historical Library and Archives (SBHLA).
37. Letter from Maddry to Saunders, May 30, 1939, AR 551-2, Box 51, Folder 1939–1943, SBHLA.
38. Charles E. Maddry, "Concerning Orphanage Work in China," *Baptist Record*, April 6, 1944, 3.
39. Letter from Saunders to Maddry, July 10, 1940, AR 551-2, Box 51, Folder 1939–1943, SBHLA.
40. Letter from Saunders to Crawley, October 23, 1956, AR 551-2, Box 51, Folder 1935–1967, SBHLA.
41. Kathryn Joyce, *The Child Catchers: Rescue, Trafficking, and the New Gospel of Adoption* (New York: PublicAffairs, 2013).
42. "Will China Choose Democracy or Communism?," 1. Emphasis added.
43. Arissa H. Oh, *To Save the Children of Korea: The Cold War Origins of International Adoption* (Stanford, Calif.: Stanford University Press, 2015), 79–80.
44. Janss, *Yankee Si*, 30–31. The phrase "un-ugly Americans" references Eugene Burdick and William Lederer's novel *The Ugly American* (1958), which critiqued the ignorance of the U.S. diplomatic corps in Asia.
45. "The Influence of These 'Adoptions,'" *China News* 1, no. 2 (Fall 1943): 3.
46. F. C. Liu, "This Century Is for the Children," *China News* 4, no. 1 (Summer 1945): 1–2.
47. "From an Adoptee in China to His Foster Mother in America," *China News* 2, no. 1 (Winter 1944): 4.
48. "The Adoption Plan," *China News* 8, no. 1 (Winter 1950–1951): 4; Minutes of Meeting of Executive Board of China's Children Fund, Incorporated, October 10, 1950, Box IA, Folder 9, Archival Materials Re Christian Children's Fund, ChildFund International (CCF).
49. May, *Homeward Bound*, 135–42.
50. Stephanie Coontz, *The Way We Never Were: American Families and the Nostalgia Trap* (New York: Basic Books, 1992); Sarah Potter, *Everybody Else: Adoption and the Politics of Domestic Diversity in Postwar America* (Athens: University of Georgia Press, 2014).
51. Quoted in Laura Briggs, *Somebody's Children: The Politics of Transracial and Transnational Adoption* (Durham, N.C.: Duke University Press, 2012), 6–7.
52. "A Letter from a Sponsor Regarding Her 'Adopted' Boy," *China News* 5, no. 2 (Fall 1947): 3.
53. "The CCF Adoption Plan," 3.
54. Eleana Jean Kim, *Adopted Territory: Transnational Korean Adoptees and the Politics of Belonging* (Durham, N.C.: Duke University Press, 2010); Catherine Ceniza Choy, *Global Families: A History of Asian International Adoption in America* (New York: New York University Press, 2013); Oh, *To Save the Children of Korea*.
55. Christina Klein, *Cold War Orientalism: Asia in the Middlebrow Imagination, 1945–1961* (Berkeley: University of California Press, 2003); Sara Fieldston, *Raising the World: Child Welfare in the American Century* (Cambridge, Mass.: Harvard University Press, 2015).
56. Hollinger, *Protestants Abroad*, 59–92.

57. Hollinger, 61–63. On the history of the indigenization movement in China, see Albert Monshan Wu, "The Quest for an 'Indigenous Church': German Missionaries, Chinese Christians, and the Indigenization Debates of the 1920s," *American Historical Review* 122, no 1 (2017): 85–114.

58. Jun Xing, "The American Social Gospel and the Chinese YMCA," *Journal of American-East Asian Relations* 5, no. 3/4 (1996): 277–304.

59. Yan Yongqi, "Ertong jiaxun" [Children's family precepts], *Fu er*, no. 32 (December 1950): 10.

60. Si Tuxian, "Ka boshi shicha Guangzhou gu'er yuan ji" [Notes from Dr. Clarke's inspection of Guangzhou orphanages], *Fu er* 1, no. 1 (July 1946): 3; "Ka boshi xiang ge yuan ertong xunhua" [Dr. Clarke's instructions to the children of each orphanage], *Fu er* 1, no. 1 (July 1946): 3.

61. For example, Meihua Ertong fuli hui Guangzhou Tongguang Gu'er Yuan gaikuang biao [CCF Guangzhou Morning Star Orphanage general information form], October 20, 1948, 10-4-634-33, GMA.

62. Huang Mingyuan, "Yesu de bo'ai" [Jesus's universal love], *Fu er* 2, no. 1 (August 1947): 6.

63. Bai Heng, "Jiang sai huaxu" [Tidbits from the speech competition], *Fu er* 2, no. 9 (July 1948): 10.

64. "Yesu jidu bo'ai jingshen: Pu Sheng Yuan yanjiang bisai di yi ming Xu Haoxin (chu zhong zu)" [Jesus Christ's spirit of universal love: Pu Kong Orphanage speech competition first place winner Xu Haoxin (middle school division)], *Fu er* 2, no. 9 (July 1948): 10.

65. Janss, *Yankee Si*, 48–49.

66. Letter from Chau Ho, February 1949, Kiu Kong Orphanage Folder, CCF.

67. Chen Duxiu, "Jidujiao yu Zhongguoren" [Christianity and the Chinese people], *Xin qingnian* 7, no. 3 (February 1920): 15–22.

68. Rana Mitter, *Forgotten Ally: China's World War II, 1937–1945* (Boston: Houghton Mifflin Harcourt, 2013); Zach Fredman, *The Tormented Alliance: American Servicemen and the Occupation of China, 1941–1949* (Chapel Hill: University of North Carolina Press, 2022).

69. U.S. Department of State, *United States Relations with China with Special Reference to the Period 1944–1949* (Washington, D.C.: U.S. Government Printing Office, 1949), 694.

70. Fredman, *Tormented Alliance*, 135–62.

71. Chunmei Du, "Rape in Peking: Injured Woman, Microhistory and Global Trial," *Gender & History* (2023): 1–19; Robert Shaffer, "A Rape in Beijing, December 1946: GIs, Nationalist Protests, and U.S. Foreign Policy," *Pacific Historical Review* 69, no. 1 (2000): 31–64.

72. U.S. Department of State, *United States Relations with China*, 354.

73. Mao Zedong, "Bie le, Si Tu Lei Deng" [Farewell, Leighton Stuart], April 18, 1949, in *Mao Zedong xuanji* [Selected writings of Mao Zedong], vol. 4 (Beijing: Renmin chubanshe, 1960), 1491–98.

74. "Shishi ceyan zongbaogao" [Summary report on current affairs survey], *Da gong bao*, February 10, 1947, 10; C.Y.W. Meng, "Two Chinese Papers Conduct Poll on GI, Civil War, Government," *China Weekly Review*, February 22, 1947, 323.

75. The magazine originally used the English-language title "Children's Aid" before switching to "Blessed Children" in July 1948. For the sake of consistency, I refer to the magazine as *Blessed Children* throughout.

76. "Meihua Ertong Fulihui huananqu banshichu zhiyuan mingbiao" [CCF South District Orphanages Conference office staff list], *Fu er* 1, no. 1 (July 1946): 2.

77. Li Qirong, "Fakanci" [Introduction to the magazine], *Fu er* 1, no. 1 (July 1946): 1.

78. Si Tuxian, "Meihua Ertong Fulihui yu suoshu ge yuan" [China's Children Fund and its affiliated orphanages], *Fu er* 1, no. 2 (August 1946): 5.

79. "Jiang Zhuxi Zhongzheng yishi—guxiang yu younian" [Anecdotes of Chairman Chiang Kai-shek—Hometown and Childhood], *Fu er* 1, no. 2 (August 1946): 6; Li Jielian, "Guofu geming fendou shi" [History of Sun Yatsen's revolutionary struggle], *Fu er* 2, no. 9 (July 1948): 11.

80. Letter from Clarke to Mills, September 9, 1946, Kiu Kong Orphanage Folder, CCF.

81. "General Instructions Re Adoptions," 17-1-117-70, GMA.

82. Letter from Clarke to Mills, September 9, 1946.

83. "General Instructions Re Adoptions."

84. Joseph Ho, *Developing Mission: Photography, Filmmaking, and American Missionaries in Modern China* (Ithaca, N.Y.: Cornell University Press, 2021).

85. Karen Halttunen, "Humanitarianism and the Pornography of Pain in Anglo-American Culture," *American Historical Review* 100, no. 2 (1995): 330.

86. Heide Fehrenbach and Davide Rodogno, "The Morality of Sight: Humanitarian Photography in History," in *Humanitarian Photography: A History*, ed. Rodogno and Fehrenbach (New York: Cambridge University Press, 2015), 4.

87. Susan Sontag, *Regarding the Pain of Others* (New York: Picador, 2003), 117.

88. "Meihua Ertong Fulihui huanan qu gu'er shenqing jiaoyang jianze" [CCF South China District general regulations for orphans applying for education and upbringing], February 12, 1946, 17-1-121-87, GMA.

89. "General Instructions Re Adoptions."

90. "A Letter from a Sponsor Regarding Her 'Adopted' Boy," 3.

91. "Children's Histories with Photographs, Canaan Home for Children," February 17, 1947, 17-1-116-1, GMA.

92. Foochow City Orphanage Case Files, J. Calvitt Clarke Box 2, CCF.

93. Meihua Ertong Fulihui guanyu huiji 1947 nian 12 yuefen buzhu gu'er yuan jingfei bing yizhao guiding banli ru hui shiyi zhi Shijie Hongwanzi Hui Beiquan Ciyou Yuan de gonghan [CCF official letter to World Red Swastika Society Peh Chuan Orphanage regarding remitting orphanage funding for December 1947 and handling matters for joining the organization according to the regulations], December 9, 1947, 0105-0002-00008-0000-053-000, Chongqing Municipal Archives (CMA).

94. Meihua Ertong Fulihui huanan qu gu'er . . . qingqiu ru Shijie Hongwanzi Hui Beiquan Ciyou Yuan shenqing biao ji fubiao [Application forms and attachments for CCF South China District Orphans . . . requesting to enter the World Red Swastika Society Peh Chuan Orphanage], 0105-0005-00003-0000-001-000, CMA.

# 3. INSTITUTIONALIZING THE INTIMATE TURN 271

95. Shehuibu Beibei Ertong Fuli Shiyan Qu . . . zhi Shijie Hongwanzi Hui Beiquan Ciyou Yuan Xuexiao de gonghan [Official letter from Ministry of Social Affairs Beibei Experimental Child Welfare Center to the World Red Swastika Society Peh Chuan Orphanage], July 1948, 0105-0002-00008-0000-082-000, CMA.

96. "Meihua Ertong Fulihui Zhongguo banshichu zhi quanguo suo shu ge yuan gonghan san ze" [Three official letters from the CCF China Office to all affiliated orphanages in China], *Fu er* 2, no. 5 (1948): 2.

97. "Wei 38 nian ertong yu renyangren tongxun xu yu 7 yue 1 ri zhi qian bantuo you" [Re: correspondence between children and their sponsors for the year 1949 must be completed before July 1], April 20, 1949, 17-1-120-27, GMA.

98. "Meihua Ertong Fulihui gonghan" [CCF official letter], *Fu er* 2, no. 12 (January 1949): 2.

99. "Meihua Ertong Fulihui Zhongguo banshichu zhi quanguo suo shu ge yuan gonghan san ze."

100. "Wei 38 nian ertong yu renyangren," 17-1-120-27, GMA.

101. "Wei chengbao ben yuan liu qi yuefen yuanwu banli qingxing ji shouzhi qingxing qi jianhe beian you" [Re: Submitting report for inspection and approval on orphanage affairs and revenues and expenditures for the months of June and July], August 16, 1949, 17-1-115-35, GMA.

102. Li Qirong, "Xie xin de yishu" [The art of letter writing], *Fu er* 2, no. 7 (1948): 5.

103. Li Kaowen, "Xie shenme xin?" [What kind of letter to write?], *Fu er* 2, no. 12 (1949): 5.

104. On the relationship between translation and modernity in China, see Lydia Liu, *Translingual Practice: Literature, National Culture, and Translated Modernity—China, 1900–1937* (Stanford, Calif.: Stanford University Press, 1995).

105. "Meihua Ertong Fulihui huanan qu zhi suoshu ge gu'er yuan gonghan" [Official letter from CCF South China District Conference to affiliated orphanages], *Fu er* 1, no. 2 (1946): 2.

106. "Meihua Ertong Fulihui zhi suoshu ge gu'er yuan gonghan" [Official letter from China's Children Fund to affiliated orphanages], *Fu er* 1, no. 11 (1947): 2.

107. "Hanfu suo shi si dian chu di yi dian yu you dongshihui taolun ling xing hanfu wai qiyu san dian ye jun zunzhao banli you" [Re: Replying to the four points of instruction, except for the first point, which will be responded to separately after it is discussed by the board of directors, the remaining three points have already been handled in accordance with the instructions], January 25, 1948, 17-1-124-85, GMA; "Meihua Ertong Fulihui guanyu gaozhi Shijie Hongwanzi hui Beiquan Ciyou Yuan xianqi huiji renyangzhe zhong ying wen mingce ji lingqu jingfei biaozhun gonghan" [CCF official letter regarding informing the World Red Swastika Society Peh Chuan Orphanage of the deadlines for sending Chinese and English sponsor name register and standards for receiving funds], January 2, 1948, 0105-0002-00008-0000-061-000, CMA.

108. "Lingnan Ertong Gongyisuo di yi ci jiaodao huiyi lu" [Records of the first Lingnan Industrial School teachers' meeting], March 18, 1947, 20-3-6-1, GMA.

109. "Wei 38 nian ertong yu renyangren," 17-1-120-27, GMA.

110. "Meihua Ertong Fulihui Zhongguo banshichu zhi quanguo suo shu ge yuan gonghan san ze."

## 272 3. INSTITUTIONALIZING THE INTIMATE TURN

111. "Meihua Ertong Fulihui gonghan" [CCF official letter], August 24, 1946, 17-1-118-43, GMA.

112. "General Instructions Re Adoptions."

113. "Zhi Rui Tang jian han" [Letter to Rui Tang], February 4, 1949, 零18-44-8, GMA.

114. Helen Clarke to Mills, February 13, 1951, Box IB1, Folder 2, CCF.

115. Gregor Benton and Liu Hong, *Dear China: Emigrant Letters and Remittances, 1820–1980* (Oakland: University of California Press, 2018), 33–40.

116. Benton and Liu, 7–8, 46–47.

# 4. ADOPTING REVOLUTION

1. Letter from Yin-ho to Esther, July 1, 1949, Box 114, Folder 82, FPP.

2. Michael N. Barnett, *Empire of Humanity: A History of Humanitarianism* (Ithaca, N.Y.: Cornell University Press, 2011); Sara Fieldston, *Raising the World: Child Welfare in the American Century* (Cambridge, Mass.: Harvard University Press, 2015); Emily Baughan, *Saving the Children: Humanitarianism, Internationalism, and Empire* (Oakland: University of California Press, 2022).

3. Henry D. Molumphy, *For Common Decency: The History of Foster Parents Plan, 1937–1983* (Warwick, UK: Foster Parents Plan International, 1984), 2, 17, 4–7.

4. Molumphy, 104–5. It was not until the mid-1950s, in the increasingly polarized political climate of the high Cold War, that PLAN was forced to abandon its commitment to political neutrality and publicly align itself with anticommunist causes. See Fieldston, *Raising the World*, 88–90.

5. The China Welfare Fund has gone by three different names during its history: China Defense League (Baowei Zhongguo Tongmeng), 1938–1945; China Welfare Fund (Zhongguo Fuli Jijinhui), 1945–1950; and China Welfare Institute (Zhongguo Fulihui), 1950–present. For clarity and simplicity, I use the name China Welfare Fund (CWF) throughout this chapter. On the history of the CWF, see Xu Fenghua, *Shenfen, zuzhi yu zhengzhi: Song Qingling He Baomeng—Zhongfuhui Yanjiu (1938–1958)* [Identity, organization, and politics: Song Qingling and the China Defense League—China Welfare Institute] (Shanghai: Shanghai Shudian Chubanshe, 2013).

6. "Gei Zhongguo zai haiwai de pengyoumen de gongkai xin" [An open letter to China's friends overseas], September 18, 1943, in *Song Qingling xuanji, shang juan* [Selected works of Soong Ching-ling, vol. 1] (Beijing: Renmin chubanshe, 1992), 377.

7. Xu, *Shenfen, zuzhi yu zhengzhi*, 86–90.

8. Bart Barnes, "6 Months in China Ended at 26 Years: Baltimorean's 26-Year Stay in China Ended," *Washington Post*, November 11, 1974, C1.

9. "Tanningbang tan Zhongguo Fuli Jijinhui" [Tannebaum discusses the China Welfare Fund], in *Wangshi huimou: Zhongguo Fulihui shizhi ziliao huicui* [Glancing back on the past: Selected historical records of the China Welfare Institute], ed. Gu Linmin (Shanghai: Zhongguo Fulihui chubanshe, 2011), 260–61.

# 4. ADOPTING REVOLUTION 273

10. "Staff History," Box 115, Folder 88, FPP.

11. *Wei kunan ertong er gongzuo: Zhanzai Ertong Yiyanghui Zhongguo Fenhui gongzuo baogao* [Work for the suffering children: Foster parents' plan for war children China Branch work report] (Shanghai: Zhanzai ertong yiyanghui zhongguo fenhui, 1949), 10.

12. "China: Program Review (1949)," Box 114, Folder 81, FPP; *Wei kunan ertong er gongzuo*, 36.

13. Drew Pearson, "The Merry-Go-Round," *Palm Beach (Fla.) Post*, December 8, 1947, 4; "Mme. Sun Yat-sen's Romance," *Times of India*, December 9, 1947, 3.

14. "Madame Sun Denies Report of Romance," *Los Angeles Times*, December 10, 1947, 1; "Mei jizhe hunao—Sun furen piyao—yaoqiu Piersen zidong gengzheng" [American journalist spews nonsense—Madame Sun denies rumors, demands Pearson correct the record], *Da gong wan bao*, December 13, 1947, 1.

15. Zheng Peiyan, "1947 nian Song Qingling zao e'yi feibang" [In 1947 Soong Ching-ling encountered malicious slander], *Shiji*, no. 6 (2013): 14–17.

16. See, for example, "Eyes That Trust, Plead, and Accuse," *Chicago Daily Tribune*, October 26, 1947, 35.

17. "China: Program Review (1949)."

18. Initially the PLAN China Branch provided institutions with a monthly allotment of US$10 per foster child, but the allotment was reduced to $7 in September 1949 to accommodate more children and in view of stabilizing commodity prices. "China: Program Review (1949)."

19. Apart from the cost of adopting a foster child, many foster parents sent additional cash gifts to their foster children for birthdays and holidays. These gifts were given directly to the individual children, but the recipients were encouraged to share with classmates or spend the money in ways that benefited the entire institution. "China: Program Review (1949)." See also "Zhan zai ertong yiyang hui Zhongguo fenhui yi jiu si jiu nian nianbao" [PLAN China Branch 1949 annual report], C45-2-4-4, 1949, Shanghai Municipal Archives (SMA).

20. "China: Program Review (1949)."

21. "Zhongguo fuli jijinhui 1949 nian zongganshi nianbao" [China Welfare Fund 1949 annual report of the secretary-general], C45-1-2-1, SMA.

22. "Zhongguo fuli jijinhui guanyu Tanningbang zongganshi lü ping de bagao" [China Welfare Fund report regarding Secretary-General Tannebaum's trip to Beiping], C45-1-2-5, SMA.

23. On policy regarding private charities in the early PRC, see Li Xiaowei, "Yi jiu si jiu nian zhi yi jiu wu liu nian guojia zhengquan yu minjian cishan zuzhi de guanxi jiexi" [Analysis of the relationship between state power and nongovernmental charity organizations in 1949–1956], *Zhonggong dangshi yanjiu*, no. 9 (2012): 66–73. On the gradual demise of private charities over the course of the New Democracy period (1949–1953), see Nara Dillon, "New Democracy and the Demise of Private Charity in Shanghai," in *Dilemmas of Victory: The Early Years of the People's Republic of China*, ed. Jeremy Brown and Paul G. Pickowicz (Cambridge, Mass.: Harvard University Press, 2007), 80–102.

24. "Zhongguo Renmin Jiuji Daibiao Huiyi kaimu" [The Chinese People's Relief Congress opens], *Renmin ribao*, April 26, 1950.

# 274 4. ADOPTING REVOLUTION

25. "Minutes of the Third Meeting for the Year of 1950 of the Corporation of Foster Parents' Plan for War Children, Inc.," November 2, 1950, Box 1, Folder 5, FPP.

26. "Zai Zhongguo Renmin Jiuji Daibiao Da Huiyi shang: Song Qingling zhi bimu ci" [Soong Ching-ling's Closing Remarks before the Chinese People's Relief Congress], *Renmin ribao*, May 5, 1950; "Zhongguo Renmin Jiuji Zonghui zhangcheng" [People's Relief Administration of China by-laws], *Renmin ribao*, May 5, 1950. For an account of the founding and early history of the People's Relief Administration of China, see Wen Jian, "Xin Zhongguo chengli chuqi Zhongguo Renmin Jiuji Zonghui yanjiu" [Research on the People's Relief Administration of China in the early days of new China] (MA thesis, Hebei Normal University, 2012).

27. "Zhongguo Fulijijin Hui Gongzuo de baogao—yi jiu wu ling nian si yue er shi wu ri zai Zhongguo Renmin Jiuji Daibiao Huiyi shang" [The China Welfare Fund Work Report—April 25, 1950, at the Chinese People's Relief Congress], *Renmin ribao*, May 7, 1950.

28. "Zhongguo Fulijijin Hui Gongzuo de baogao."

29. "Zhi Zhou Enlai" [Letter to Zhou Enlai], May 25, 1950, in *Song Qingling shuxin ji* [Collected letters of Soong Ching-ling] (Beijing: Renmin chubanshe, 1999), 275–78. "Zhongguo Renmin Jiuji Zonghui zhijian weiyuanhui juxing huiyi [The Chinese People's Relief Administration executive and supervisory committees hold a meeting], *Renmin ribao*, May 6, 1950.

30. "U.S. Helps Looms in China for Private Relief Groups," *Christian Science Monitor*, April 24, 1950.

31. "Zhi Zhang Zongan" [Letter to Zhang Zong'an], in *Song Qingling shuxin ji*, 266–67.

32. *Wei kunan ertong er gongzuo*, 32–34. In addition to monthly letters, children were further required to write a thank you letter whenever they received a gift from their foster parents.

33. "Zhan zai ertong yiyang hui Zhongguo fenhui yi jiu si jiu nian nianbao"; "Zhan zai Ertong Yiyanghui Zhongguo fenhui 1950 nian shang ban nian gongzuo zongjie" [PLAN China Branch work summary for the first half of 1950], 1950, C45-2-9-13, SMA.

34. "Zhengjiu beifang gu'er: Sun furen paiyuan lai ping shicha xiezhu xun ren waiji de fumu" [Rescuing orphans in the North: Madame Sun Yatsen sends staff member to Beiping to conduct inspections, help search for foreign foster parents], *Da gong bao*, July 12, 1948, 3.

35. "Zhan zai ertong yiyang hui Zhongguo fenhui yi jiu si jiu nian nianbao."

36. "Zhan zai ertong yiyang hui Zhongguo fenhui yi jiu si jiu nian nianbao."

37. *Wei kunan ertong er gongzuo*, 15, 16.

38. "China: Program Review (1949)."

39. "Zhan zai ertong yiyang hui Zhongguo fenhui yi jiu si jiu nian nianbao."

40. Quoted in Matthias Messmer, "China's Realities from the Viewpoints of 'Foreign Experts,'" in *The Jewish-Chinese Nexus: A Meeting of Civilizations*, ed. M. Avrum Ehrlich (New York: Routledge, 2008), 25.

41. *Wei kunan ertong er gongzuo*, 13.

42. *Wei kunan ertong er gongzuo*, 9–10.

# 4. ADOPTING REVOLUTION 275

43. "Zhan zai ertong yiyang hui Zhongguo fenhui yi jiu si jiu nian nianbao."
44. "Zhan zai ertong yiyang hui Zhongguo fenhui yi jiu si jiu nian nianbao."
45. "Zhan zai Ertong Yiyanghui Zhongguo fenhui 1950 nian shang ban nian gongzuo zongjie."
46. Letter from Ping-wei to Ruth, July 1949, Box 115, Folder 84, FPP; Case File C367, Box 48, Folder 45, FPP.
47. Letter from Ping-wei to Ruth, August 10, 1949, Box 115, Folder 84, FPP.
48. Case File C488, Box 48, Folder 47, FPP.
49. Letter by Cheng-chung, July 8, 1950, Box 46, Folder 38, FPP.
50. Letter from Pao to Phyllis, February 17, 1949, Box 115, Folder 86, FPP; Case File C145, Box 47, Folder 41, FPP.
51. Letter from Chi-Hai to C. D., February 3, 1949, Box 115, Folder 86, FPP.
52. "A Child's-Eye View of War in China," *New York Herald Tribune*, March 6, 1949.
53. *Wei kunan ertong er gongzuo*, 24–26, 32.
54. "Zhan Zai Ertong Yiyanghui Zhongguo fenhui 1950 nian shang ban nian gongzuo zongjie."
55. Case File C263, Box 47, Folder 43, FPP; letter from Hsiu-yun to Mrs. D. B., June 15, 1949, Box 114, Folder 80, FPP.
56. Letter from Chih-sun to Jeanette, July 12, 1949, Box 114, Folder 83, FPP.
57. *Wei kunan ertong er gongzuo*, 15.
58. "Zhan zai ertong yiyang hui Zhongguo fenhui yi jiu si jiu nian nianbao."
59. Case File C552, Box 48, Folder 49, FFP.
60. Letter by Chih-kao, August 8, 1950, Box 46, Folder 39, FPP; English translation, August 25, 1950, Box 46, Folder 39, FPP.
61. Laura Briggs, *Somebody's Children: The Politics of Transracial and Transnational Adoption* (Durham, N.C.: Duke University Press, 2012), 129–35.
62. See, for example, "New Foster Parents Project," *New York Times*, October 1, 1947, 32; "China's Starving Children," *New York Herald Tribune*, November 17, 1947, 22.
63. "Eyes That Trust, Plead, and Accuse," *New York Herald Tribune*, October 24, 1948, F48.
64. "Eyes That Trust, Plead, and Accuse," *Daily Boston Globe*, November 16, 1947, A31.
65. "Politics Is Decried in Aid to Children: Head of Foster Parents Plan Tells of Tour, Defends Help in Satellite Countries," *New York Times*, August 18, 1948, 22.
66. See, for example, William Fulton, "Push 'Do-Good' Schemes Over Radio, in Press: Some Are Drum Beaters for Trumanism," *Chicago Daily Tribune*, March 19, 1951, 10.
67. *Wei kunan ertong er gongzuo*, 11–12.
68. "Zhan zai ertong yiyang hui Zhongguo fenhui yi jiu si jiu nian nianbao."
69. *Wei kunan ertong er gongzuo*, 19–21.
70. "Zhan zai Ertong Yiyanghui Zhongguo fenhui 1950 nian shang ban nian gongzuo zongjie."
71. "Zhan zai Ertong Yiyanghui Zhongguo fenhui 1950 nian shang ban nian gongzuo zongjie."
72. Case File C388, Box 48, Folder 45, FPP.
73. Eugenia Lean, *Public Passions: The Trial of Shi Jianqiao and the Rise of Popular Sympathy in Republican China* (Berkeley: University of California Press, 2007), 198–201.
74. "Zhan zai ertong yiyang hui Zhongguo fenhui yi jiu si jiu nian nianbao."

## 276  4. ADOPTING REVOLUTION

75. Xu Shiqi, "Xiang shi dajie xuexi" [Learn from big sister Shi], *Yiyanghui tongxun*, no. 14 (March 1950): 2.

76. "Zhan zai ertong yiyang hui Zhongguo fenhui yi jiu si jiu nian nianbao."

77. "Yi zhi shaonian ertong wenyi gongzuozhe de duiwu—Zhongguo Fulihui guanyu Zhongguo Fulihui Ertong Jutuan shengzhang qingkuang de jieshao" [A children's art and culture workers army—the China Welfare Institute's introduction to the China Welfare Institute Children's Theatre's development], October 9, 1950, C45-1-26-10, SMA; "Zhongguo Fulihui Ertong Jutuan lishi yange" [The historical development of the China Welfare Institute Children's Theatre], December 1950, C45-2-10-47, SMA.

78. "Zhongguo Fulihui guanyu liang nian lai chengjiu qingkuang de baogao" [Report regarding the accomplishments and state of affairs of the China Welfare Institute over the past two years], October 1951, C45-1-54-4, SMA.

79. "Zhongguo Fulihui Ertong Jutuan lishi yange."

80. "Yi zhi shaonian ertong wenyi gongzuozhe de duiwu."

81. Letter by Yu-li, July 4, 1950, Box 46, Folder 39, FPP; Case File C470, Box 48, Folder 47, FPP.

82. "Yi zhi shaonian ertong wenyi gongzuozhe de duiwu"; "Zhongguo Fulihui 1950 nian gongzuo baogao (xiuzheng ban)" [China Welfare Institute 1950 work report (revised version)], 1950, C45-1-18-27, SMA; "Zhongguo Fulihui guanyu liang nian lai chengjiu qingkuang de baogao"; "Zhongguo Fulihui Ertong Jutuan 1950 nian shangbanye nian gongzuo zongjie" [Summary report on the China Welfare Institute Children's Theatre's work in the first half of 1950], August 1950, C45-2-7-25, SMA.

83. "Yi zhi shaonian ertong wenyi gongzuozhe de duiwu."

84. Letter by Su-ping, July 20, 1950, Box 46, Folder 39, FPP; Case File C475, Box 48, Folder 47, FPP.

85. "Yi zhi shaonian ertong wenyi gongzuozhe de duiwu."

86. Letter by Yu-li, July 4, 1950; Case File C470.

87. Letter from Chung-lan to Mrs. A. I., July 22, 1950, Box 46, Folder 39, FPP; Case File C209, Box 47, Folder 42, FPP.

88. "Yi zhi shaonian ertong wenyi gongzuozhe de duiwu."

89. Jingye Jiaoyangyuan, *Liulang ertong jiaoyang wenti: Jingye Jiaoyangyuan di yi ci baogao* [The problem of educating street urchins: The first report of the Jingye Reformatory] (Shanghai: Jingye Jiaoyangyuan, 1942), 5; Normal D. Apter, "Saving the Young: A History of the Child Relief Movement in Modern China" (PhD diss., University of California, Los Angeles, 2013), 102–11.

90. "Shanghai Shaoniancun—liulang ertong de da jiating" [Shanghai Boystown: A big family for street urchins], *Shen bao*, May 23, 1946, 8.

91. Zhang Dawei, ed., *Xue di hongqi fei hou—cong Jingye Jiaoyangyuan dao Shanghai Shaoniancun* [A red flag flies above the snowy ground—from the Jingye Foundling to Shanghai Boystown] (Shanghai: Shanghaishi baoshanqu fojiao xiehui, 2001), 7–8.

92. "Zhan zai ertong yiyang hui Zhongguo fenhui yi jiu si jiu nian nianbao."

93. Wang Juan, "Zhao Puchu xiansheng yanhu women dixia dang" [Teacher Zhao Puchu provided cover for our underground party], in *Xue di hongqi fei hou*, 50.

5. THE HUMANITARIAN CLOAK  277

94. "Hu Shaoniancun feidang jiaoyuan Wang Danren deng panchu tuxing" [Shanghai Boystown Communist bandit teacher Wang Danren and others sentenced to jail], *Shen bao*, September 16, 1948.

95. Wang, "Zhao Puchu xiansheng yanhu women dixia dang," 50.

96. *Wei kunan ertong er gongzuo*, 18–19.

97. Letter from Lien-shoo to Mrs. J. S., August 11, 1949, Box 114, Folder 82, FPP.

98. Zhang Weizhong, "Wei Shanghai jiefang zuo gongxian" [Contributing to the liberation of Shanghai]," in *Xue di hongqi fei hou*, 88–89.

99. Song Jianhua, "Women canjia le renmin jiefangjun" [We joined the People's Liberation Army], in *Xue di hongqi fei hou*, 89–90.

100. Letter from Teh-san to John, Summer 1949, Box 114, Folder 83, FPP.

101. Letter by Chai-po, July 13, 1949, Box 115, Folder 87, FPP.

102. Song, "Women canjia le renmin jiefangjun," 90–91.

103. Letter from Gun-chun to the Macauleys, June 1949, Box 114, Folder 83, FPP.

104. Ren Zhenbei, "Shaoniancun tongxue xue sa chaoxian zhanchang—zhuiji Wang Tianwen, Sun Gunquan tongxue" [The blood of our Boystown classmates spilled on the battlefield of Korea—remembering classmates Wang Tianwen and Sun Gunquan], in *Xue di hongqi fei hou*, 93–94.

105. Wang Wenxiang, "Yi Zhanyou—ji zai Kangmei Yuanchao zhanchang shang fu shang he xisheng de ji wei Shaoniancun tongxue" [In memory of comrades-in-arms—remembering several Boystown students who were injured or sacrificed on the battlefield of the War to Resist America and Aid Korea], in *Xue di hongqi fei hou*, 92.

106. "Zhongguo Fulihui zhangcheng (cao an)" [China Welfare Institute regulations (draft)], C45-1-12-4, SMA.

107. "Minutes of the Third Meeting for the Year of 1950 of the Corporation of Foster Parents' Plan for War Children, Inc."

108. Molumphy, *For Common Decency*, 104–5.

109. Quoted in Matthias Messmer, "China's Realities from the Viewpoints of 'Foreign Experts,'" 25.

110. "Zhongguo Fulihui guanyu Meiguo Yiyang Hui shixiang de chuli yijian xiang jiuji zonghui de baogao" [China Welfare Fund report to the People's Relief Administration regarding its opinions for handling the matter of the American Foster Parents Plan], C45-1-27, SMA.

111. Du Shuzhen, ed., *Zhongguo Fulihui zhi* [Records of the China Welfare Institute], (Shanghai: Shanghai Shehui Kexue Xueyuan Chuabanshe, 2002), 28.

112. Molumphy, *For Common Decency*, 28–30, 111.

113. Letter from Da-Chwen to Shirley, July 3, 1950, Box 46, Folder 38, FPP; Case File C251, Box 47, Folder 43, FPP.


## 5. THE HUMANITARIAN CLOAK

1. "Chiangs Donate Wartime Headquarters to Methodist Church to House Orphans," *New York Times*, September 23, 1947; "Zhonghua Jidujiao Weili Gonghui Zhongzheng

## 278 5. THE HUMANITARIAN CLOAK

Fu You Cun 1950 nian 1 yue baogao shu" [January 1950 report for Chinese Methodist Chiang Memorial Children's Village], January 1950, 0105-0006-00010-0000-001-000, CMA.

2. "Salient Facts About the Pu Kong Orphanage and Similar Children's Homes in China," AR 551-2, Box 52, Folder 1945–1960, SBHLA.

3. Newsletter of the American-Oriental Friendship Association, September 10, 1948, Series 4, Box 3, Folder 6, Charles Luther Boynton Papers, Missionary Research Library Archives, Burke Library, Union Theological Seminary (CLB).

4. "Zhonghua Jidujiao Weili Gonghui Zhongzheng Fu You Cun qingkuang chubu liaojie baogao" [Preliminary report on understanding the circumstances at the Chinese Methodist Church's Chiang Memorial Children's Village], 0105-0006-00018-0000-005-000, CMA; "Zhonghua Jidujiao Weili Gonghui Zhongzheng Fu You Cun 1949 nian juankuan ren ming dan" [1949 list of sponsors for Chinese Methodist Chiang Memorial Children's Village], 105-0006-00007-0000-102-000, CMA.

5. "Zhonghua Jidujiao Weili Gonghui Zhongzheng Fu You Cun 1949 nian juankuan ren ming dan"; "Zhonghua Jidujiao Weili Gonghui Zhongzheng Fu You Cun qingkuang chubu liaojie baogao."

6. Jian Chen, *Mao's China and the Cold War* (Chapel Hill: University of North Carolina Press, 2001); Odd Arne Westad, *Restless Empire: China and the World Since 1750* (New York: Basic Books, 2012).

7. Karl Marx and Friedrich Engels, *Manifesto of the Communist Party* (Moscow: Progress Publishers, 1977), 67–69.

8. Samuel Moyn, "Theses on Humanitarianism and Human Rights," *Humanity Journal*, September 23, 2016, http://humanityjournal.org/blog/theses-on-humanitarianism-and-human-rights/.

9. Bruno Cabanes, *The Great War and the Origins of Humanitarianism, 1918–1924* (New York: Cambridge University Press, 2014), 189–246.

10. "Help or Millions Die—Gorky: Reds, Starving, Agree to Free All Americans, Appeal Via Soviets to 'Honest People,'" *Chicago Daily Tribune*, July 31, 1921, 1.

11. Cabanes, *The Great War*, 240, 216–22, 243.

12. Laura Briggs, *Somebody's Children: The Politics of Transracial and Transnational Adoption* (Durham, N.C.: Duke University Press, 2012), 131–35.

13. Xu Fenghua, *Shenfen, zuzhi yu zhengzhi: Song Qingling he Baomeng—Zhongfuhui yanjiu (1938–1958)* [Identity, organization, and politics: Song Qingling and the China Defense League—China Welfare Institute] (Shanghai: Shanghai Shudian Chubanshe, 2013), 154–69.

14. Nym Wales, *China Builds for Democracy: A Story of Cooperative Industry* (New York: Modern Age Books, 1941), 191; Xu, *Shenfen, zuzhi yu zhengzhi*, 163–64.

15. Xu Fenghua, *Shenfen, zuzhi yu zhengzhi*, 164–65.

16. China Defence League, *In Guerrilla China: Report of the China Defence League* (New York: China Aid Council, 1943), 6.

17. "Zhi Meiguo gongrenmen" [To American workers], February 8, 1944, in *Song Qingling xuanji* [Selected works of Song Qingling] (Beijing: Renmin chubanshe, 1992), 381–83.

# 5. THE HUMANITARIAN CLOAK 279

18. Mao Zedong, "Jinian Bai Qiu En" [In memory of Norman Bethune], December 12, 1939, in *Mao zedong xuanji* [Selected works of Mao Zedong] (Beijing: Renmin chubanshe, 1960), vol. 2, 620–22.

19. Fu Lianzhang, "Xuexi Bai Qiu En tongzhi de geming rendao zhuyi jingshen—jinian Bai Qiu En tongzhi shishi shi san zhounian" [Learn from Comrade Norman Bethune's spirit of revolutionary humanitarianism—commemorating the thirteenth anniversary of the death of Norman Bethune], *Zhonghua yixue zazhi* 38, no. 2 (1952): 1027.

20. Rana Mitter, "Relocation and Dislocation: Civilian, Refugee, and Military Movement as Factors in the Disintegration of Postwar China, 1949–49," *Itinerario* 46, no. 2 (2022): 193–213.

21. Chinese Liberated Areas Relief Association (CLARA), *UNRRA Relief for the Chinese People: A Report* (Shanghai: Information Department of the Chinese Liberated Areas Relief Association, 1947), 6–9.

22. "Yaoqiu gongping jiuji" [Demand fair relief aid], *Renmin ribao*, June 11, 1946, 1.

23. CLARA, *UNRRA Relief for the Chinese People*, 29–30.

24. "Zhongguo Fuli Jijinhui gongzuo de baogao."

25. Dong Biwu, "Xin Zhongguo de jiuji fuli shiye" [The relief and welfare undertaking in New China], *Renmin ribao*, May 5, 1950, 1.

26. Sara Fieldston, *Raising the World: Child Welfare in the American Century* (Cambridge, Mass.: Harvard University Press, 2015), 10, 83.

27. "Mao zhuxi xunci" [Instructions from Chairman Mao], *Fu er*, no. 32 (December 1950): 1.

28. "Puguang Yuan Jidutu gongyue" [Pu Kong Orphanage Christian's pledge], *Fu er*, no. 32 (December 1950): 1.

29. "Lai xin de jiaoxun" [The lessons of incoming letters], *Fu er*, no. 32 (December 1950): 9.

30. J. Calvitt Clarke, "Can We Do Business with Communist China?," *China News* 7, no. 2 (Winter 1949–1950): 4.

31. "The World Can't Exist Half Stuffed and Half Starved," *China News* 7, no. 3 (Spring 1950): 4.

32. "What About CCF Orphanages in Communist China?," *China News* 8, no. 1 (Winter 1950–1951): 4.

33. Clarke, "Can We Do Business with Communist China?," 3.

34. Letter from J. Calvitt Clarke to O. Edmund Clubb, November 16, 1950, Box IB21, Folder 16, CCF.

35. "Minutes of Meeting the China's Children Fund, China Executive Committee—Session 23," November 15, 1949," 17-1-116-137, GMA.

36. "Minutes of Meeting of the China Executive Committee of the China's Children Fund—Session 26," February 21, 1950, 17-1-116-146, GMA.

37. "Yi jiu wu ling niandu xia xueqi Lingnan Ertong Gongyisuo gongzuo zongjie baogao" [Lingnan Industrial School summary work report for second semester 1950], July 24, 1951, 038-003-19-093, Guangdong Provincial Archives (GPA).

38. "Meihua Ertong Fulihui Huananqu Gu'er Yuan Lianhui di wu jie nianhui" [Fifth annual meeting of the CCF South China District Orphanages Conference], 17-1-120-22, GMA.

39. "Huanan Qu Gu'er Yuan Lianhehui xuexi jiaoyi hui di er ci xuexi xiang mu zenyang shishi minzhu guanli" [South China District Orphanages Conference study meeting, topic

#2, how to implement democratic management], 17-1-120-16, GMA; Zhongguo Shao-nian Ertong She, *Peiyang jiaoyu xin de yi dai: di yi ci Quanguo Shaonian Ertong Gongzuo Ganbu Dahui wenxian* [Fostering and educating a new generation: Documents from the first National Conference for Children's Work Cadres] (Beijing: Qingnian chubanshe, 1950), 2.

40. Zhongguo Shaonian Ertong She, *Peiyang jiaoyu xin de yi dai*, 2–3.

41. "Zhi Huananqu ge yuan jianhan" [Letter to South China District orphanages], Novem-ber 18, 1949, 零18-44-68, GMA.

42. "Minutes of Meeting of the China Executive Committee," February 21, 1950.

43. "Minutes of Meeting of the China Executive Committee of the China's Children Fund—Session 25," February 3, 1950, 17-1-116-144, GMA.

44. "Minutes of Meeting of the China's Children Fund, China Executive Committee—Session 29," June 29, 1950, 17-1-116-128, GMA.

45. "Meihua Ertong Fuli Hui Puguang Gu'er Yuan gonghan" [CCF Pu Kong Orphanage offi-cial letter], June 26, 1950, 17-1-124-68, GMA.

46. "Minutes of the Meeting of the Executive Committee of China's Children Fund," Septem-ber 27, 1950, Box IA1, Folder 9, CCF.

47. "Minutes of the Meeting of the Executive Committee of China's Children Fund," Febru-ary 1, 1950, Box IA1, Folder 9, CCF.

48. "1950 niandu er ci huiyi lu" [Minutes of second meeting of 1950], 20-3-2-25, GMA.

49. Becky Cerling Powers, *Laura's Children: The Hidden Story of a Chinese Orphanage* (Vin-ton, Tex.: Canaan Home Communications, 2010), 2, 253–55; "Letter written by Florence Logan on Laura Richards' Behalf," January 1947, provided to the author by Becky Powers. I thank Powers for sharing numerous primary sources regarding Laura Richards and the Canaan Children's Home from her personal collection.

50. Laura Richards, "Canaan Children's Home News Letter," spring 1950, provided by Becky Powers.

51. Powers, *Laura's Children*, 270–73.

52. Laura Richards, "Moving from the Dowager's Boat House to the American School," undated, provided by Becky Powers.

53. "Moving from the Dowager's Boat House to the American School."

54. Zechariah, "The Memory of Our Dear Mother Laura May Richards," 1988, provided by Becky Powers.

55. Letter from Florence Logan to Becky Powers, January 28, 1985, provided by Becky Powers.

56. Becky Cerling Powers, "Interview with Florence Logan, June 3, 1987," provided by Becky Powers.

57. "Canaan Children's Home News Letter."

58. Powers, *Laura's Children*, 280.

59. Zechariah, untitled memoirs, 2001, provided by Becky Powers. On the uses of Bethune's legacy in the PRC, see Christos Lynteris, *The Spirit of Selflessness in Maoist China: Social-ist Medicine and the New Man* (New York: Palgrave Macmillan, 2013).

60. Powers, *Laura's Children*, 318–33.

61. Walter H. Waggoner, "Red China's Assets in U.S. Are Frozen: Washington Takes Unilateral Action—Tightens Ban on Shipping to Mainland," *New York Times*, December 17, 1950, 1.

62. "Suqing Meidi zai Zhongguo de jingji he wenhua qinlüe shili" [Eliminate the American imperialists' forces of economic and cultural aggression in China], *Renmin ribao*, December 30, 1950, 1; Henry R. Lieberman, "Red China Seizes American Assets: Order Confiscates Property, Freezes Public and Private Funds in Reprisal Move," *New York Times*, December 29, 1950, 1.

63. "Zhonghua Jidujiao Weili Gonghui Fu You Cun 1951 nian Zhongwen di shi yi ci jilu (baogao fuyoucun zhi yuanqi, chouhua juankuan deng)" [Chinese Methodist Children's Village Eleventh Chinese Minutes for 1951 (Reporting on Children's Village's origins, planning, donations, etc.)], 0105000600017000051000, CMA.

64. "Zhonghua Jidujiao Weili Gonghui Zhongzheng Fu You Cun 1950 nian 1 yue baogaoshu" [Chinese Methodist Chiang Memorial Children's Village January 1950 report], 010500060001000000001000, CMA, incorrectly dated; it is actually from January 1951.

65. On Guo Moruo's intellectual biography, see Pu Wang, *The Translatability of Revolution: Guo Moruo and Twentieth-century Chinese Culture* (Cambridge, Mass.: Harvard University Asia Center, 2018).

66. "Guanyu chuli jieshou meiguo jintie de wenhua jiaoyu jiuji jiguan ji zongjiao tuanti fangzhen de baogao" [Report on guiding principles for dealing with cultural, educational, and relief institutions as well as religious organizations that accept American funds], *Renmin ribao*, December 30, 1950, 1.

67. Edmund J. James, "Memorandum Concerning the Sending of an Educational Commission to China," Folder IL1, Broadsides and Ephemera Collection, Duke University Libraries Digital Collections.

68. "Zhongyang Renmin Zhengfu Zhengwuyuan guanyu chuli jieshou Meiguo jintie de wenhua jiaoyu jiuji jiguan ji zongjiao tuanti fangzhen de jueding" [Central People's Government Government Administration Council resolution regarding guiding principles for dealing with cultural, educational, and relief institutions as well as religious organizations that accept American funds], B1-1-1996-1, SMA.

69. "Suqing Meidi zai Zhongguo de jingji he wenhua qinlüe shili."

70. Daniel H. Bays, *A New History of Christianity in China* (Malden, Mass.: Wiley-Blackwell, 2012), 158–68.

71. "Fangzhi diguo zhuyi liyong jiaohui weihai Zhongguo renmin" [Guard against imperialism utilizing the church to harm the Chinese people], *Renmin ribao*, September 23, 1950, 1, 7–8.

72. "Huadong Junzheng Weiyuanhui guanyu zhixing 'Zhongyang Renmin Zhengfu Zhengwuyuan guanyu chuli jieshou Meiguo jintie de wenhua jiaoyu jiuji jiguan ji zongjiao tuanti fangzhen de jueding' de zhishi" [East China Military and Administrative Committee directive regarding implementation of the "Central People's Government Government Administration Council Resolution regarding guiding principles for dealing with cultural, educational, and relief institutions as well as religious organizations that accept American funds"], B1-1-1996-10, SMA.

# 282  5. THE HUMANITARIAN CLOAK

73. "Diguo zhuyi 'cishan shiye' zai wo guo zao xia taotian zuixing!" [Imperialist "charitable undertaking" creates monstrous crimes in our nation!], *Renmin ribao*, March 7, 1951, 1.

74. "Nanjing 'Sheng Xin Ertong Yuan,' 'Ci'ai Yuying Yuan' waiji xiunü canhai Zhongguo ertong" [Foreign nuns harm China's children at Nanjing "Sacred Heart Home for Children," "Benevolent Love Home for Babies"], *Renmin ribao*, March 9, 1951, 3.

75. Contemporary scholars have questioned the veracity of charges of abuse and neglect at foreign-run child welfare institutions in Shanghai. See Beatrice Leung and William T. Liu, *The Chinese Catholic Church in Conflict: 1949–2001* (Boca Raton, Fla.: Universal Publishers, 2004), 62.

76. "Duzhe fen fen zhi han ben bao tongchi diguo zhuyi fenzi canhai wo guo ertong zuixing" [Numerous readers send letters to this paper denouncing the imperialist elements' crime of cruelly slaughtering our nation's children], *Renmin ribao*, April 6, 1951, 2.

77. "Beijing Shi Renmin Zhengfu Minzheng ju diaocha Jia Nan Gu'er Yuan zongjie" [Summary of Beijing People's Government Civil Affairs Bureau investigation of Canaan Orphanage], October 18, 1949, 002-001-00055, Beijing Municipal Archives (BMA).

78. "Baowei zuguo ke'ai de ertong" [Defend the lovable children of our fatherland], *Renmin ribao*, March 21, 1951, 6.

79. "Zhongguo Renmin Jiuji Zonghui Beijing shi fenhui jieguan Mei zi banli de san ge 'jiuji jiguan' " [Beijing branch of the Chinese People's Relief Administration takes over control of three 'relief institutions' operated with American Capital], *Renmin ribao*, March 29, 1951, 1.

80. " 'Sheng Ying Ying Yuan' deng shijian jiqi guangda qunzhong fennu" ['Holy Infant Home for Babies' and other incidents arouse indignation of the broad masses], *Renmin ribao*, March 12, 1951, 1.

81. "Zhonghua Jidujiao Weili Gonghui Zhongzheng Fu You Cun qingkuang chubu liaojie baogao."

82. "I'm Wondering," Box 267, Folder 1896 (Records of the American-Oriental Friendship Association), Missionary Pamphlet Collection, Yale Divinity Library Special Collections (AOFA).

83. "Zhonghua Jidujiao Weili Gonghui Zhongzheng Fu You Cun qingkuang chubu liaojie baogao."

84. Gail Hershatter, *The Gender of Memory: Rural Women and China's Collective Past* (Berkeley: University of California Press, 2011).

85. "Baowei zuguo ke'ai de ertong." During the early 1940s, Nie Shouguang raped two teenage girls at the orphanage, embezzled the largest donation in the orphanage's history, and fled to his ancestral home in Anhui Province. His crimes were reported to Laura Richards by members of the orphanage staff as well as by one of the victims. Nevertheless, Nie returned to the orphanage in 1944 and remained until 1951. Although Richards apparently never doubted his guilt, she allowed him to stay, both out of Christian forgiveness and because his political connections were crucial to allowing the orphanage to continue operating in occupied Beijing. Powers, *Laura's Children*, 210–36.

86. "Baowei zuguo ke'ai de ertong."

87. *Diguo zhuyi canhai Zhongguo ertong de zuixing* [The crimes of imperialism against China's children] (Beijing: Renmin jiuji zonghui, 1951), 22, 25.

88. "Zhengwuyuan Wen Jiao Weiyuanhui Zongjiao Shiwuchu zhaoji huiyi—chuli jieshou Meiguo jintie de Jidujiao tuanti" [The Religion Office of the Government Administration Council Cultural and Education Committee convenes a meeting on dealing with Christian organizations that accept American funds], *Renmin ribao*, April 17, 1951, 1.

89. "Chuxi chuli jieshou Meiguo jintie de Jidujiao tuanti huiyi de daibiao kongsu diguo zhuyi liyong zongjiao qinlüe zhongguo" [Delegates in attendance at the meeting for dealing with Christian organizations that accept American funds denounce imperialists using religion to encroach upon China], *Renmin ribao*, April 24, 1951, 1.

90. "Bishop from China," *Time* 43, no. 11 (March 13, 1944): 79.

91. "Chiangs Donate Wartime Headquarters to Methodist Church to House Orphans."

92. Jiang Changchuan, "Wo kongsu Jiudujiao bailei Chen Wenyuan" [I denounce Christian scum Chen Wenyuan], *Renmin ribao*, April 25, 1951, 6.

93. Li Muqun, "Kongsu Mei diguo zhuyi zougou Chen Wenyuan" [Denounce the American imperialist running dog Chen Wenyuan], *Renmin ribao*, April 25, 1951, 6.

94. Chuxi chuli jieshou Meiguo jintie jiuji jiguan huiyi daibiao kongsu diguo zhuyi liyong 'cishan shiye' canhai Zhongguo renmin [Representatives in attendance at the meeting for dealing with relief organizations that accept American funds denounce American imperialism using "charitable endeavors" to cruelly harm the Chinese people], *Renmin ribao*, May 5, 1951, 3.

95. "Wo he wo de nü'er tuanyuan le—An Jia Yu Mei ganxie zhengfu jieguan 'Jia Nan Gu'er Yuan'" [My daughter and I reunited—An-Jia Yu-Mei thanks the government for taking control over Canaan Orphanage], *Renmin ribao*, April 6, 1951, 2.

96. 17-1-121-87, GMA.

97. *Diguo zhuyi canhai Zhongguo ertong de zuixing*, 26.

98. "Zhongguo Renmin Jiuji Zonghui Chongqing Shi fenhui guanyu Zhonghua Jidujiao Weili Gonghui Zhongzheng fu you cun you ben hui jieban bing pai Sun Litai wei jieguan daibiao dian" [People's Relief Administration of China Chongqing Branch telegram regarding our organization taking over Chinese Methodist Chiang Memorial Children's Village and sending Sun Litai as representative for the takeover], November 15, 1951, 0105-0006-00018-0000-001-000, CMA.

99. "Jieban Zhonghua Jidujiao Weili Gonghui Fu You Cun baogao" [Report on taking over control of Chinese Methodist Children's Village], 0105-0006-00018-0000-005-000, CMA.

100. "Jieban Zhonghua Jidujiao Weili Gonghui Fu You Cun baogao."

101. "Jieban Zhonghua Jidujiao Weili Gonghui Fu You Cun baogao."

102. Li Xiaowei, "Yi jiu si jiu nian zhi yi jiu wu liu nian guojia zhengquan yu minjian cishan zuzhi de guanxi jiexi" [Analysis of the relationship between state power and nongovernmental charity organizations in 1949–1956], *Zhonggong dangshi yanjiu*, no. 9 (2012): 66–73.

## 284 5. THE HUMANITARIAN CLOAK

103. Zhang Chun, *Kangri Zhanzheng shiqi Zhanshi Ertong Baoyuhui yanjiu* [Research on the National Association for Refugee Children During the War of Resistance Against Japan] (Beijing: Tuanjie chubanshe, 2015), 68, 195–97.

104. "Shan Gan Ning bianqu ertong zhi Jiang furen de xin" [Letter from the children of the Shaan-Gan-Ning border region to Madame Chiang], *Xinhua ribao*, June 24, 1940, 4.

105. Margaret Mih Tillman, *Raising China's Revolutionaries: Modernizing Childhood for Cosmopolitan Nationalists and Liberated Comrades, 1920s–1950s* (New York: Columbia University Press, 2018), 106.

106. "Shanbei mou weiquan renshi tan zhanfan mingdan wenti" [An authoritative person in northern Shaanxi discusses the issue of the war criminal list] *Renmin ribao*, December 27, 1948, 1.

107. Zhang Chun, *Kangri Zhanzheng shiqi Zhanshi Ertong Baoyuhui yanjiu*, 19, 53.

108. J. M. Chris Chang, "Paper Affairs: Discipline by the Dossier in a Mao-Era Work Unit," *Administory* 4, no. 1 (2019): 125–40.

109. "Zhanshi ertong baoyusheng Gao Zongjun jiangshu: bei jiandiao de lishi" [Cut out of history: Narrated by NARC warphan Gao Zongjun], Sun TV (2022), accessed April 12, 2023, https://www.youtube.com/watch?v=qEww60Pehaw&list=PL1Flk3ukUUwa7ELqkj corcndcrgnSM5Lx&index=126&t=1227s.

110. Quoted in Zhang Chun, *Kangri Zhanzheng shiqi Zhanshi Ertong Baoyuhui yanjiu*, 5–6.

111. Quoted in Zhang Chun, 6.

112. Zhishu di qi baoyuyuan yuanshi bianweihui and Zhonggong sichuan sheng nanchuan shiwei dangshi yanjiushi, eds., *Zhongguo Zhanshi Ertong Baoyuhui zhishu di qi baoyuyuan shiliao xuanji* [Selected historical materials from the NARC No. 7 Warphanage] (Hubei: Hubeisheng chubanju, 1994), 246.

113. Cheng Ronghua, "Zhuang Jing yu Zhongguo Zhanshi Ertong Baoyuhui" [Zhuang Jing and the NARC], in *Xuzhou wenshi ziliao*, vol. 27 [Xuzhou literary and historical materials], ed. Zhongguo renmin zhengzhi xieshang huiyi jiangsu sheng xuzhou shi weiyuanhui wenshi weiyuanhui (Xuzhou: Zhengxie jiangsu sheng xuzhou shi weiyuanhui wenshi wenyuanhui, 2007), 105–7.

114. Cheng Ronghua, 106–7; "Zhanshi ertong baoyusheng gao zongjun jiangshu: Bei jiandiao de lishi."

115. Zhang Chun, *Kangri Zhanzheng shiqi Zhanshi Ertong Baoyuhui yanjiu*, 18–19.

## 6. COLD WAR HUMANITARIANISM

1. English translations of letters from Yoon Tae to Jackson, 1968, unprocessed documents, CCF.

2. "Yoon Tae Personal Information Folder," February 21, 1968, CCF; "Designated Funds," March 20, 1968, unprocessed documents, CCF.

3. Letter from Vernon Kemp to Jackson, February 21, 1968, unprocessed documents, CCF.

4. Rachel M. McCleary, *Global Compassion: Private Voluntary Organizations and U.S. Foreign Policy Since 1939* (New York: Oxford University Press, 2009), 27.

5. For example, see Alexander Cook, ed., *Mao's Little Red Book: A Global History* (Cambridge: Cambridge University Press, 2013); Gregg Brazinsky, *Winning the Third World: Sino-American Rivalry During the Cold War* (Chapel Hill: University of North Carolina Press, 2017); Matthew Galway, *The Emergence of Global Maoism: China's Red Evangelism and the Cambodian Communist Movement, 1949–1979* (Ithaca, N.Y.: Cornell University Press, 2022).

6. Brazinsky, *Winning the Third World*.

7. "Yonghu guanzhi qingcha Meiguo caichan dongjie Meiguo gongsi cunkuan" [Support the supervision and investigation of American property and the freezing of American funds], December 30, 1950, in *Song Qingling xuanji shang juan* [Selected works of Song Qingling] (Beijing: Renmin chubanshe, 1992), 588–89.

8. "Zhongguo Fulihui zhangcheng (cao an)" [China Welfare Institute regulations (draft)], C45-1-12-4, SMA.

9. Du Shuzhen, ed., *Zhongguo Fulihui zhi* [Records of the China Welfare Institute] (Shanghai: Shanghai shehui kexue xueyuan chubanshe, 2002), 28.

10. Lu Ping, "Wo qinli de Zhongguo Jianshe chuangban shimo" [The story of my experience of the founding of *China Reconstructs*], *Jinri Zhongguo* 61, no. 2 (February 2012): 39.

11. Xu Fenghua, "Zhongguo Jianshe de chuangban yu xin Zhongguo chengli chuqi de duiwai xuanchuan" [The establishment of *China Reconstructs* and foreign propaganda in the initial period of the PRC], *Zhonggong dangshi yanjiu*, no. 5 (2016): 62.

12. Lu Ping, "Zai Song Qingling lingdao xia chuangban Zhongguo Jianshe zazhi" [Founding *China Reconstructs* magazine under the leadership of Soong Chingling], *Bai nian chao*, no. 4 (2012): 54, 57; "Zhongguo Fulihui Zhongguo Jianshe she guanyu liu Tanningbang zai Beijing bangzhu gaigao de baogao" [Report on the China Welfare Institute *China Reconstructs* office retaining Tannebaum in Beijing to help with editing manuscripts], December 12, 1962, C45-2-338-21, SMA.

13. Lu Ping, "Zai Song Qingling lingdao xia," 53; Yan Juanzhen, "Bu gai hushi de shige fanyijia Zou Lǔzhi" [The poetry translator who should not be overlooked: Zou Lǔzhi], *Mudanjiang daxue xuebao* 21, no. 9 (2012): 118.

14. Xu Fenghua, "Zhongguo Jianshe de chuangban," 62.

15. Xiao Gang, *Geng Lishu* [Talitha Gerlach] (Shenyang: Liaoning Renmin Chubanshe, 1993).

16. "Zhi Zhou Enlai" [To Zhou Enlai], May 1950, in *Song Qingling shuxin ji (xia)*, 287–88.

17. "Israel Epstein, Prominent Chinese Communist, Dies at 90," *New York Times*, June 2, 2005.

18. "Zhongguo Fulihui Zhongguo Jianshe She Yewubu guanyu Zhongguo Fulihui yingwen shuangyue kan Zhongguo Jianshe 1952 nian bianji gongzuo de baogao" [China Welfare Institute China Reconstructs Office Business Department 1952 report regarding editorial work of the China Welfare Institute's English bimonthly magazine *China Reconstructs*], 1952, C45-2-50-58, SMA.

286  6. COLD WAR HUMANITARIANISM

19. Xu Fenghua, "Zhongguo Jianshe de chuangban," 64.

20. "Zhongguo Fulihui guanyu Zhongguo Jianshe jiankuang de jieshao" [China Welfare Institute short introduction on *China Reconstructs*], 1958, C45-2-213-34, SMA.

21. Xu Fenghua, "Zhongguo Jianshe de chuangban," 67, 59.

22. "The People's Relief Administration of China," *China Reconstructs*, no. 1. (January–February 1952): 48.

23. *Children's Tears* (Shanghai: China Welfare Institute, 1952), 3–5, 20.

24. Soong Ching-ling, "Welfare Work and World Peace," *China Reconstructs*, no. 1 (January–February 1952): 2.

25. Chao Pu-chu, "Urban Relief and Rehabilitation," *China Reconstructs*, no. 1 (January–February 1952): 28–31.

26. Jen Teh-yao, "The Children's Own Theatre," *China Reconstructs*, no. 1 (January–February 1952): 35–37.

27. Lu Ping, "Wo qinli de Zhongguo Jianshe chuangban shimo," 40.

28. Xu Fenghua, "Zhongguo Jianshe de chuangban," 61–62, 66.

29. "Introducing 'China Reconstructs,'" *China Reconstructs*, no. 1 (January–February 1952): 1.

30. "Zhongguo Fulihui Zhongguo Jianshe guowai laixin zongshu" [China Welfare Institute *China Reconstructs* summary of letters from abroad], 1960, C45-2-298, SMA.

31. Lu Ping, "Wo qinli de Zhongguo Jianshe chuangban shimo," 40.

32. "Zhan zai Ertong Yiyanghui Zhongguo fenhui 1950 nian shang ban nian gongzuo zongjie."

33. "Zhongguo Fulihui Zhongguo Jianshe guowai laixin zongshu."

34. *Zhongguo Fulihui zhi*, 527.

35. Cheng Shaokun and Huang Jiyang, *Meijun zhanfu—Chaoxian zhanzheng huoxian jishi* [American prisoners of war—a record of facts from the front lines of the Korean War] (Beijing: Hua Yi chubanshe, 2013), 1, 5–6, 2.

36. "Red 'Dear Daddy' Propaganda Barrage Just Dud to Korea GIs," *Newsday*, February 29, 1952, 2.

37. Cheng Shaokun and Huang Jiyang, *Meijun zhanfu*, 4–5.

38. Bradford Laws, "Chinese Propaganda Big Joke to GI's in Korea," *Baltimore Afro-American*, June 30, 1951, 1.

39. Hal Boyle, "Communist Leaflets in Korea Designed to Upset GIs: Told to 'Go Home,'" *Christian Science Monitor*, April 5, 1951, 6.

40. "Minutes of Special Meeting of the Board of Directors of China's Children Fund, Incorporated," February 6, 1951, Box IA1, Folder 10, CCF.

41. "Proposed Budget for 1955," Box IA1, Folder 12, CCF.

42. Larry E. Tise, *A Book About Children: The World of Christian Children's Fund, 1938–1991* (Falls Church, Va.: Hartland, 1993), 30.

43. "Proposed Budget for 1953," Box IA1, Folder 11, CCF.

44. Edmund W. Janss, *Yankee Si! The Story of Dr. J. Calvitt Clarke and His 36,000 Children* (New York: Morrow, 1961), 38.

45. John C. Caldwell, *Children of Calamity* (New York: John Day, 1957), 52.

46. Zhang Ande, "Shenme shi Jiudujiao Ertong Fulihui" [What is the Christian Children's Fund], *Tong sheng*, no. 2 (December 1951): 1.

47. "Zhi yi wei waiguo pengyou—gongxi Shengdan bing su jinkuang [Letter to a foreign friend—Christmas wishes and descriptions of the recent situation]," *Tong sheng*, no. 1 (October 1951): 5.

48. "Proposed Budget for 1953."

49. Fisher to Mills, January 5, 1951, Box IB1, Folder 1, CCF. See also Sara Fieldston, *Raising the World: Child Welfare in the American Century* (Cambridge, Mass.: Harvard University Press, 2015), 84.

50. L. Nelson Bell, "The Most Anti-Communistic Spot in Asia," J. Calvitt Clarke Box 2, CCF.

51. "Proposed Budget for 1953"; Tise, *A Book About Children*, 37–38. On Sawada Miki's work with the children of American soldiers and Japanese women, see Elizabeth Anne Hemphill, *The Least of These: Miki Sawada and Her Children* (New York: Weatherhill, 1980).

52. Caldwell, *Children of Calamity*, 73.

53. "Minutes of the Meeting of the Executive Committee of Christian Children's Fund," July 28, 1952, Box IA1, Folder 11, CCF.

54. "Proposed Budget for 1955."

55. "Report of the International Director for Christian Children's Fund for 1954," Box IA1, Folder 13, CCF.

56. "Overseas Director's Report for 1954," Box IA1, Folder 13, CCF; "Proposed Budget for 1955."

57. Reproduced in Christina Klein, *Cold War Orientalism: Asia in the Middlebrow Imagination, 1945–1961* (Berkeley: University of California Press, 2003), 157.

58. David P. King, *God's Internationalists: World Vision and the Age of Evangelical Humanitarianism* (Philadelphia: University of Pennsylvania Press, 2019), 35–36, 73.

59. Letter from Lucille to Calvitt Clarke, September 5, 1948, Box IB21, Folder 16, CCF.

60. "The CCF Adoption Plan," *China News* 7, no. 2 (Winter 1949–1950): 3.

61. Erika Lee, *At America's Gates: Chinese Immigration During the Exclusion Era, 1882–1943* (Chapel Hill: University of North Carolina Press, 2003), 214.

62. "General Information Regarding Visas for Immigrants," Box IB21, Folder 16, CCF.

63. Clarke to Mullins, February 28, 1950, Box IB26, Folder 1, CCF.

64. Ann Waltner, *Getting an Heir: Adoption and the Construction of Kinship in Late Imperial China* (Honolulu: University of Hawaii Press, 1990); James L. Watson, "Agnates and Outsiders: Adoption in a Chinese Lineage," *Man* 10, no. 2 (1975): 293–306.

65. "I have some interesting news for you—news about your little adoptee," Kiu Kong Orphanage Folder, CCF.

66. "Records of Departures and Substitutes from Morning Star Orphanage," Morning Star Orphanage 1948 Folder, CCF.

67. "Zhi Tongguang Yuan Wu Xuchuan jianhan" [Letter to Wu Xuchuan of Morning Star Orphanage], June 27, 1949, 零18-44, GMA.

68. Letter from Pearl C. Y. Hsu to Erwin Raetz, January 26, 1947, Kiu Kong Orphanage Folder, CCF.

69. "Zhi qiaoquang yuan gonghan" [Official letter to the Kiu Kong Orphanage], February 16, 1949, 零18-44-11, GMA.

70. "Baozheng shu" [Letter of guarantee], February 25, 1948, 17-1-115, 6, GMA.

71. Tai er, "Jipu nülang de bei'ai" [The sorrow of a jeep girl], *Feng guang*, no. 23 (August 23, 1946): 3.

72. On the controversies surrounding relations between U.S. soldiers and Chinese "jeep girls," see Chunmei Du, "Jeep Girls and American GIs: Gendered Nationalism in Post-World War II China," *Journal of Asian Studies* 81, no. 2 (2022): 341–63; Zach Fredman, *Tormented Alliance* (Chapel Hill: University of North Carolina Press, 2022), 135–62.

73. "Jipu yinghai" [Jeep babies], *Jing hua*, no. 20 (January 11, 1946): 1. I am grateful to Chunmei Du for calling my attention to newspaper coverage about the children of U.S. soldiers and Chinese women.

74. Chun Yan, "Shengli kuanghuan xia de jiejing: Zhongmei hunxie'er chongchi Chongqing" [Fruits of victorious revelry: Chongqing is full of Chinese-American mixed-race children], *Haifeng*, no. 22 (April 13, 1946): 1.

75. Fredman, *Tormented Alliance*, 137–38.

76. Jiang Tiansheng, "Qihuo keju de jipu ying'er" [Jeep babies: A rare commodity worth hoarding], *Feng guang*, no. 15 (June 17, 1946): 8.

77. Fang Cao, "Chongqingshi shang zhenggou jipu nülang da pi sishengzi" [A rush to buy the large number of illegitimate children of jeep girls in Chongqing], *Haiguang zhoubao*, no. 9 (January 29, 1946): 8

78. Gong Zhiyang, "Jipu yinghai biaojia chuhuo" [Jeep babies priced and sold], *Haifeng*, no. 17 (March 9, 1946): 12.

79. U.S. Congress, *Amerasian Immigration Proposals: Hearing Before the Subcommittee on Immigration and Refugee Policy of the Committee on the Judiciary*, Ninety-seventh Congress, Second session (Washington, D.C.: U.S. Government Printing Office, 1982).

80. Emma Teng, *Eurasian: Mixed Identities in the United States, China, and Hong Kong, 1842–1943* (Berkeley: University of California Press, 2013), 12.

81. Fredman, *Tormented Alliance*, 5.

82. Chunmei Du, "Rape in Peking: Injured Woman, Microhistory and Global Trial," *Gender & History*, 2023, 1–19.

83. Kristin Roebuck, "Orphans by Design: 'Mixed-Blood' Children, Child Welfare, and Racial Nationalism in Postwar Japan," *Japanese Studies* 36, no. 2 (2016): 191–212.

84. Yuri Doolan, "The Cold War Construction of the Amerasian, 1950–1982," *Diplomatic History* 46, no. 4 (2022): 782–807.

85. Jane K. Lipman, "'The Face Is the Road Map': Vietnamese Amerasians in U.S. Political and Popular Culture, 1980–1988," *Journal of Asian American Studies* 14, no. 1 (2011): 33–68.

86. Catherine Ceniza Choy, *Global Families: A History of Asian International Adoption in America* (New York: New York University Press, 2013), 79–81; Arissa H. Oh, *To Save the Children of Korea: The Cold War Origins of International Adoption* (Stanford, Calif.: Stanford University Press, 2015), 204.

87. Fieldston, *Raising the World*, 5–6.
88. "Armament and a Little Child," *China News* 4, no. 2 (Fall 1945): 4.
89. "Printed By Request," *China News* 5, no. 1 (Spring 1947): 3.
90. Ernest T. Nash, "From Orphan to Good Citizen," *Korea Times*, April 12, 1954, Box IB9, Folder 2, CCF.
91. "GI Babies in Japan," *China News* 8, no. 1 (Winter 1950–1951): 1–2.
92. Janss, *Yankee Si!*, 45.
93. Calvitt Clarke to Ernest Nash, May 7, 1956, Box IB9, Folder 2, CCF.
94. Peter Kalischer, "Madame Butterfly's Children," *Collier's*, September 20, 1952, 18. See also Yukiko Koshiro, *Trans-Pacific Racisms and the U.S. Occupation of Japan* (New York: Columbia University Press, 1999).
95. Quoted in Oh, *To Save the Children of Korea*, 73.
96. Roebuck, "Orphans by Design."
97. Choy, *Global Families*, 24.
98. William R. Burkhardt, "Institutional Barriers, Marginality, and Adaptation Among the American-Japanese Mixed Bloods in Japan," *Journal of Asian Studies* 42, no. 3 (1983): 519.
99. Robert A. Fish, "The Heiress and the Love Children: Sawada Miki and the Elizabeth Saunders Home for Mixed-Blood Orphans in Postwar Japan" (PhD diss., University of Hawaii, 2002), 131.
100. "Proposed Budget for 1953."
101. Janss, *Yankee Si!*, 45.
102. Nash to Clarke, May 7, 1956, Box IB9, Folder 2, CCF.
103. "Annual Report of the Korea Office for the Year Ending July 31, 1957," Box IB9, Folder 9; "Director's Report Upon Activities of Korea Office," Box IB9, Folder 10; CCF.
104. Nash to Clarke, January 30, 1958, Box IB10, Folder 2, CCF.
105. "Annual Report on Korea Operations (Year Ending July 1956)," Box IB9, Folder 4, CCF.
106. Nash to Clarke, May 7, 1957, Box IB9, Folder 7, CCF.
107. Oh, *To Save the Children of Korea*, 229.
108. Nash to Hong, February 18, 1958; Hong to Kellogg, February 25, 1958, Box IB10, Folder 2, CCF.
109. "Annual Report of the Korea Office for the Year Ending July 31, 1957."
110. Clarke to Nash, September 13, 1956, Box IB9, Folder 3, CCF.
111. Nash to Clarke, November 3, 1956, Box IB9, Folder 5, CCF.
112. On debates over proxy adoptions, see Choy, *Global Families*, 82–95; and Oh, *To Save the Children of Korea*, 95–131.
113. Nash to Clarke, January 14, 1958, Box IB10, Folder 2, CCF.
114. Amei Wallach, "True Believers from the East," *Newsday*, May 22, 1972, 3A.
115. Bart Barnes, "6 Months in China Ended at 26 Years: Baltimorean's 26-Year Stay in China Ended," *Washington Post*, November 11, 1974, C1.
116. Chen Yuanchi, "Why I Married an American," *New York Times*, January 22, 1972, 29; Wallach, "True Believers from the East."
117. Gerald Tannebaum, "I Was an American in China—in the Years When It Wasn't Supposed to Exist," *Los Angeles Times*, March 11, 1974, A5.

118. Chen, "Why I Married an American."

119. "Chinese Actress Receives Visa to Live in U.S.," *Los Angeles Times*, December 17, 1971, E2. See also "Actress Reflects Better Feelings of U.S.-China," *Hartford Courant*, December 17, 1971, 40.

# CONCLUSION

1. This paragraph is based on Iris Chin Ponte, Leslie Kim Wang, and Serena Pen-Shian Fan, "Returning to China: The Experiences of Adopted Chinese Children and Their Parents," *Adoption Quarterly* 13, no. 2 (2010): 100–124.

2. John James Kennedy and Yaojiang Shi, *Lost and Found: The "Missing Girls" in Rural China* (New York: Oxford University Press, 2019), 84.

3. Ponte, Wang, and Fan, "Returning to China," 113.

4. For a critical analysis of the child sponsorship industry, see Peter Ove, *Change a Life, Change Your Own: Child Sponsorship, the Discourse of Development, and the Production of Ethical Subjects* (Halifax, Can.: Fernwood, 2018).

5. Quoted in Sara Fieldston, *Raising the World: Child Welfare in the American Century* (Cambridge, Mass.: Harvard University Press, 2015), 166.

6. Fieldston, 190; David P. King, *God's Internationalists: World Vision and the Age of Evangelical Humanitarianism* (Philadelphia: University of Pennsylvania Press, 2019), 133–39.

7. Quoted in Fieldston, *Raising the World*, 196.

8. Fieldston, 200–202.

9. Peter Stalker, "Please Do Not Sponsor This Child," *New Internationalist*, no. 111 (May 1982): 7–9.

10. Derek Williams, "Mountains of Paper," *New Internationalist*, no. 111 (May 1982): 12–13.

11. "The Way to Help," *New Internationalist*, no. 111 (May 1982): 16–17.

12. King, *God's Internationalists*, 203–4.

13. Lisa Anderson, "The Miracle Merchants: Myths of Child Sponsorship," *Chicago Tribune*, March 15, 1998, 1, 3–5.

14. Michael Tackett and David Jackson, "The Miracle Merchants: Myths of Child Sponsorship," *Chicago Tribune*, March 22, 1988, 1, 3–4.

15. Ian Smillie, "Optical & Other Illusions: Trends and Issues in Public Thinking About Development Co-Operation," in *Public Attitudes and International Development Co-Operation*, ed. Ian Smillie and Henny Helmich (Paris: Organization for Economic Co-Operation and Development, 1998), 30–31.

16. Bruce Wydick, Paul Glewwe, and Laine Rutledge, "Does International Child Sponsorship Work? A Six-Country Study of Impacts on Adult Life Outcomes," *Journal of Political Economy* 121, no. 2 (2013): 400–401.

17. Choe Sang-hun, "World's Largest 'Baby Exporter' Confronts Its Painful Past," *New York Times*, September 17, 2023.

18. Catherine Ceniza Choy, *Global Families: A History of Asian International Adoption in America* (New York: New York University Press, 2013), 24, 47–73.

CONCLUSION 291

19. Dana Sachs, *The Life We Were Given: Operation Babylift, International Adoption, and the Children of War in Vietnam* (Boston: Beacon Press, 2010).

20. On the history of international adoption from Guatemala, see Rachel Nolan, *Until I Find You: Disappeared Children and Coercive Adoptions in Guatemala* (Cambridge, Mass.: Harvard University Press, 2024).

21. U.S. Department of State, "Adoption Statistics," accessed September 7, 2024, https://travel .state.gov/content/travel/en/Intercountry-Adoption/adopt_ref/adoption-statistics-esri .html.

22. Leslie K. Wang, *Outsourced Children: Orphanage Care and Adoption in Globalizing China* (Stanford, Calif.: Stanford University Press, 2016), 14.

23. Peter Selman, "International Adoptions from the People's Republic of China, 1992–2017," Working Paper, New Castle University, 2019.

24. See, for example, "Bringing Kids All the Way Home," *Newsweek*, June 15, 1997; Andy Newman, "Journey from a Chinese Orphanage to a Jewish Rite of Passage," *New York Times*, March 8, 1997.

25. Grace Lin, *The Red Thread: An Adoption Fairy Tale* (Park Ridge, Ill.: Albert Whitman, 2007); Sara Dorow and Stephen Wunrow, *When You Were Born in China: A Memory Book for Children Adopted from China* (St. Paul, Minn.: Yeong & Yeong, 1997). On the theme of the "red thread" in international adoption stories, see Wang, *Outsourced Children*, 12–13.

26. Kate Blewett and Brian Woods, dirs., *The Dying Rooms* (Lauderdale Productions, 1995).

27. "*The Dying Rooms*: A Patchwork of Lies," China Intercontinental Communication Center, August 10, 1995, https://www.truevisiontv.com/films/the-dying-rooms-and-return.

28. Wang, *Outsourced Children*, 10–12.

29. Zhang Xingjian, "TV Drama Ode to Joy Sparks Virginity Debate in China," *Telegraph* (London), September 27, 2017.

30. Jiao Xiang, "Kuaguo de ai" [Transnational love], *Renmin ribao*, November 3, 2009, 13.

31. Tony Xing Tan and Xiaohui Fan, "Chinese Views on International Adoption," in *From Home to Homeland: What Adoptive Families Need to Know Before Making a Return Trip to China*, ed. Debra Jacobs, Iris Chin Ponte, and Leslie Wang (St. Paul, Minn.: Yeong & Yeong, 2010), 327–37.

32. On the history of the one child-policy, see Kay Ann Johnson, *Wanting a Daughter Needing a Son: Abandonment, Adoption, and Orphanage Care in China* (St. Paul: Yeong and Yeong, 2004); Susan Greenhalgh, *Just One Child: Science and Policy in Deng's China* (Berkeley: University of California Press, 2008); Sarah Mellors Rodriquez, *Reproductive Realities in Modern China: Birth Control and Abortion, 1911–2021* (Cambridge: Cambridge University Press, 2023).

33. Sten Johansson and Ola Nygren, "The Missing Girls of China: A New Demographic Account," *Population and Development Review* 17, no. 1 (1991): 35–41.

34. Arthur P. Wolf and Chieh-shan Huang, *Marriage and Adoption in China, 1854–1945* (Stanford, Calif.: Stanford University Press, 1980). On the decision to relinquish daughters under China's one-child policy as a "coerced choice," see Kay Ann Johnson, *China's*

*Hidden Children: Abandonment, Adoption, and the Human Costs of the One-Child Policy* (Chicago: University of Chicago Press, 2016), 17–18.

35. Kay Ann Johnson, "Politics of International and Domestic Adoption in China," *Law & Society Review* 36, no. 2 (2002): 389.

36. Johnson, *China's Hidden Children*, 57.

37. Nili Luo and David M. Smolin, "Intercountry Adoption and China: Emerging Questions and Developing Chinese Perspectives," *Cumberland Law Review* 35, no. 3 (2004-2005): 610–16.

38. Wang, *Outsourced Children*, 14.

39. Brian Stuy, "Domestic Adoption in China's Orphanages," January 19 2006, http://research -china.blogspot.com/2006/01/domestic-adoption-in-chinas-orphanages.html. See also Wang, *Outsourced Children*, 64–67.

40. Patricia J. Meier and Xiaole Zhang, "Sold Into Adoption: The Hunan Baby Trafficking Scandal Exposes the Vulnerabilities in Chinese Adoptions to the United States," *Cumberland Law Review* 39, no. 1 (2008): 87–130.

41. Wang, *Outsourced Children*, 69–70.

42. Fan Ke, "Kuaguo lingyang yu kua wenhua de 'jia'—yi laihua lingyang de Meiguo gongmin weili" [Transnational adoption and transcultural "family"—the case study of American citizens who adopt from China], *Huaqiao Huaren lishi yanjiu*, no. 1 (2011): 9.

43. Ponte, Wang, and Fan, "Returning to China."

44. Wang, *Outsourced Children*, 73–75, 155–59.

45. Wang, 154.

46. On the mobilization of children as political actors in twentieth-century China, see Jack Neubauer, "Save the Adults: The Little Teacher System and the Politics of Childhood in Modern China," *Journal of the History of Childhood and Youth* 16, no. 2 (2023): 266–86.

47. Albert Bandura, "Selective Activation and Disengagement of Moral Control," *Journal of Social Issues* 46, no. 1 (1990): 36–37.

48. "Weixian de aiqing" [Dangerous love], accessed June 20, 2023, https://www.chinala wtranslate.com/nsed/.

49. Didi Kristen Tatlow, "China's 'Dangerous Love' Campaign, Warning of Spies, Is Met with Shrugs," *New York Times*, April 21, 2016.

50. Tom Feliu, dir., *Game of Pawns* (Federal Bureau of Investigation, 2013).

51. On American views of the "racial flexibility" of Chinese children in the context of international adoption, see Sara K. Dorow, *Transnational Adoption: A Cultural Economy of Race, Gender, and Kinship* (New York: New York University Press, 2006).

52. U.S. Department of State, "Adoption Statistics."

53. Edward Wong, "Clampdown in China Restricts 7,000 Foreign Organizations," *New York Times*, April 28, 2016.

54. "2024 nian 9 yue 5 ri waijiaobu fayanren Mao Ning zhuchi lixing jizhehui" [Foreign Ministry spokesperson Mao Ning holds regular press conference on September 5, 2024], September 5, 2024, https://www.mfa.gov.cn/web/wjdt_674879/fyrbt_674889/202409

/t20240905_11485842.shtml; Alexandra Stevenson and Zixu Wang, "China Stops Foreign Adoptions, Ending a Complicated Chapter," *New York Times*, September 6, 2024.

55. Dongxin Zou, "Socialist Medicine and Maoist Humanitarianism: Chinese Medical Missions to Algeria, 1963–1984" (PhD diss., Columba University, 2019).

56. Lina Gong, "Humanitarian Diplomacy as an Instrument for China's Image-Building," *Asian Journal of Comparative Politics* 6, no. 3 (2021): 238–52.

# BIBLIOGRAPHY

## ARCHIVES

| | |
|---|---|
| AH | Academia Historica 國史館 |
| AOFA | Records of the American-Oriental Friendship Association, Yale Divinity Library Special Collections |
| BMA | Beijing Municipal Archives 北京市檔案館 |
| CCF | Archival Materials Regarding Christian Children's Fund, ChildFund International |
| CLB | Charles Luther Boynton Papers, Missionary Research Library Archives, Burke Library, Union Theological Seminary |
| CMA | Chongqing Municipal Archives 重慶市檔案館 |
| EDM | Papers of Emma DeLong Mills, MSS.2, Wellesley College Archives |
| FO | Foreign Office Records, National Archives, Kew |
| FPP | Records of Foster Parents Plan International, Inc., Vol. 2, University of Rhode Island Library, University Archives and Special Collections |
| GMA | Guangzhou Municipal Archives 廣州市檔案館 |
| GPA | Guangdong Provincial Archives 廣東省檔案館 |
| HHK | H. H. Kung Papers, Hoover Institution Library and Archives |
| PRCO | Papers Relating to Chinese Orphans, MS-Papers-5960-8, Alexander Turnbull Library, Wellington, New Zealand |
| SBHLA | Southern Baptist Historical Library and Archives |
| SHAC | Second Historical Archives of China, Nanjing 中國第二歷史檔案館 |
| SMA | Shanghai Municipal Archives 上海市檔案館 |
| UCRR | United China Relief Records, New York Public Library |

## BOOKS, ACADEMIC ARTICLES, AND OTHER SOURCES

Alexander, Kristine. "Agency and Emotion Work." *Jeunesse: Young People, Texts, Cultures* 7, no. 2 (2015): 120–28.

American National Red Cross. *Report of the China Famine Relief, American Red Cross, October, 1920—September, 1921*. Shanghai: Commercial Press, 1921.

Apter, Norman D. "Saving the Young: A History of the Child Relief Movement in Modern China." PhD dissertation, University of California, Los Angeles, 2013.

Bandura, Albert. "Selective Activation and Disengagement of Moral Control." *Journal of Social Issues* 46, no. 1 (1990): 27–46.

Barnett, Michael N. *Empire of Humanity: A History of Humanitarianism*. Ithaca, N.Y.: Cornell University Press, 2011.

——, ed. *Humanitarianism and Human Rights: A World of Differences?* Cambridge: Cambridge University Press, 2020.

Barnett, Michael N., and Janice Gross Stein, eds. *Sacred Aid: Faith and Humanitarianism*. New York: Oxford University Press, 2012.

Baughan, Emily. "International Adoption and Anglo-American Internationalism, c. 1918–1925." *Past & Present* 239, no. 1 (2018): 181–217.

——. *Saving the Children: Humanitarianism, Internationalism, and Empire*. Oakland: University of California Press, 2022.

Baum, Emily. *The Invention of Madness: State, Society, and the Insane in Modern China*. Chicago: University of Chicago Press, 2018.

Bays, Daniel H. *A New History of Christianity in China*. Malden, Mass.: Wiley-Blackwell, 2012.

Benton, Gregor, and Liu Hong. *Dear China: Emigrant Letters and Remittances, 1820–1980*. Oakland: University of California Press, 2018.

Blewett, Kate, and Brian Woods, dirs. *The Dying Rooms*. Lauderdale Productions, 1995.

Blondel, Jean-Luc. "The Meaning of the Word 'Humanitarian' in Relation to the Fundamental Principles of the Red Cross and Red Crescent." *International Review of the Red Cross*, no. 273 (1989): 507–15.

Borland, Janet. *Earthquake Children: Building Resilience from the Ruins of Tokyo*. Cambridge, Mass.: Harvard University Asia Center, 2020.

Brazinsky, Gregg. *Winning the Third World: Sino-American Rivalry During the Cold War*. Chapel Hill: University of North Carolina Press, 2017.

Brewer, Karen Lynn. "From Philanthropy to Reform: The American Red Cross in China, 1906–1930." PhD dissertation, Case Western Reserve University.

Briggs, Laura. *Somebody's Children: The Politics of Transracial and Transnational Adoption*. Durham, N.C.: Duke University Press, 2012.

Brown, Jeremy, and Paul Pickowicz, eds. *Dilemmas of Victory: The Early Years of the People's Republic of China*. Cambridge, Mass.: Harvard University Press, 2007.

Bullock, Mary Brown. *The Oil Prince's Legacy: Rockefeller Philanthropy in China*. Stanford, Calif.: Stanford University Press, 2011.

Burkhardt, William R. "Institutional Barriers, Marginality, and Adaptation Among the American-Japanese Mixed Bloods in Japan." *Journal of Asian Studies* 42, no. 3 (1983): 519–44.

Cabanes, Bruno. *The Great War and the Origins of Humanitarianism, 1918–1924.* New York: Cambridge University Press, 2014.

Cai Danni. "Minguo xuesheng shuxin jiaoyu yanjiu—yi xuesheng chiduben wei zhongxin" [Research on epistolary education for students in the Republican period—using letter-writing manuals as a focal point]. MA thesis, Xiamen University, 2014.

——. "Power, Politeness, and Print: Children's Letter Writing in Republican China." *Journal of the History of Childhood and Youth* 13, no. 1 (Winter 2020): 38–62.

Caldwell, John C. *Children of Calamity.* New York: John Day, 1957.

Central China Famine Relief Committee. *Reports and Accounts from October 1, 1911, to June 30, 1912.* Shanghai: North China Daily News & Herald, 1912.

Chan, Shelly. *Diaspora's Homeland: Modern China in the Age of Global Migration.* Durham, N.C.: Duke University Press, 2018.

Chang, J. M. Chris. "Paper Affairs: Discipline by the Dossier in a Mao-Era Work Unit." *Administory* 4, no. 1 (2019): 125–40.

Chen, Jian. *Mao's China and the Cold War.* Chapel Hill: University of North Carolina Press, 2001.

Chen Yi-shen, ed. *Guo Tingyi xiansheng mensheng gu jiu yi wang lu* [The reminiscences of Mr. Kuo Ting-Yee by his disciples and friends]. Taipei: Zhongyang yanjiuyuan jindaishi yanjiusuo, 2004.

Cheng Shaokun and Huang Jiyang. *Meijun zhanfu—Chaoxian zhanzheng huoxian jishi* [American prisoners of war—a record of facts from the front lines of the Korean War]. Beijing: Hua Yi Chubanshe, 2013.

Chiang, May-ling Soong. *A Letter from Madame Chiang Kai-Shek to Boys and Girls Across the Ocean.* Chungking: China information Pub. Co, 1940.

China Defence League. *In Guerilla China; Report of China Defence League.* New York: China Aid Council, 1943.

China International Famine Relief Commission (CIFRC). *Annual Report 1927.* Beijing: China International Famine Relief Commission, 1928.

——. *Annual Report 1928.* Beijing: China International Famine Relief Commission, 1929.

——. *Annual Report 1929.* Beijing: China International Famine Relief Commission, 1930.

——. *Annual Report 1930.* Beijing: China International Famine Relief Commission, 1931.

——. *Famine in China's Northwest: American Red Cross Commission's Findings and Rejoinders Thereto.* Beijing: China International Famine Relief Commission, 1930.

——. *History, Organization & Policy.* Beijing: China International Famine Relief Commission, 1923.

Chinese Liberated Areas Relief Association. *UNRRA Relief for the Chinese People: A Report.* Shanghai: Information Department of the Chinese Liberated Areas Relief Association, 1947.

Choy, Catherine Ceniza. *Global Families: A History of Asian International Adoption in America.* New York: New York University Press, 2013.

Clarke, Calvitt, III. *Fifty Years of Begging: Dr. J. Calvitt Clarke and Christian Children's Fund.* Bloomington, Ind.: Archway, 2018.

——. "The Literary Life of Dr. J. Calvitt Clarke." *Paperback Parade: The Magazine for Paperback Readers and Collectors,* March 2014, 20–49.

"Classement par diocèses des diverses sommes reçues." *Annales de L'Oeuvre de La Sainte-Enfance* 51, no. 314 (June 1900): 154–79.

Cohen, Warren I. *America's Response to China: A History of Sino-American Relations.* New York: Columbia University Press, 2010.

Cook, Alexander C., ed. *Mao's Little Red Book: A Global History.* Cambridge: Cambridge University Press, 2014.

Coontz, Stephanie. *The Way We Never Were: American Families and the Nostalgia Trap.* New York: Basic Books, 2000.

Cunningham, Maura Elizabeth. "Shanghai's Wandering Ones: Child Welfare in a Global City, 1900–1953." PhD dissertation, University of California, Irvine, 2014.

Curti, Merle. *American Philanthropy Abroad.* New Brunswick, N.J.: Rutgers University Press, 2016.

Daughton, J. P. "Behind the Imperial Curtain: International Humanitarian Efforts and the Critique of French Colonialism in the Interwar Years." *French Historical Studies* 34, no. 3 (2011): 503–28.

Davis, David Brion. *The Problem of Slavery in the Age of Revolution, 1770–1823.* Ithaca, N.Y.: Cornell University Press, 1975.

*Diguo zhuyi canhai Zhongguo ertong de zuixing* [The crimes of imperialism against China's children]. Beijing: Renmin jiuji zonghui, 1951.

Ding Zan. *Xinli weisheng luncong* [Collected essays on mental hygiene]. Taipei: Taiwan shangwu, 1966.

Division of Liberated Areas, Foreign Economic Administration. *The United Nations Relief and Rehabilitation Administration.* Washington, D.C.: The Administration, 1943.

Doolan, Yuri W. "The Cold War Construction of the Amerasian, 1950–1982." *Diplomatic History* 46, no. 4 (September 1, 2022): 782–807.

——. *The First Amerasians: Mixed Race Koreans from Camptowns to America.* New York: Oxford University Press, 2024.

Dorow, Sara. *Transnational Adoption: A Cultural Economy of Race, Gender, and Kinship.* New York: New York University Press, 2006.

——. *When You Were Born in China: A Memory Book for Children Adopted from China.* St. Paul, Minn.: Yeong & Yeong, 1997.

Du, Chunmei. "Jeep Girls and American GIs: Gendered Nationalism in Post–World War II China." *Journal of Asian Studies* 81, no. 2 (May 2022): 341–63.

——. "Rape in Peking: Injured Woman, Microhistory and Global Trial." *Gender & History* (2023): 1–19.

Du Shuzhen, ed. *Zhongguo Fulihui zhi* [Records of the China Welfare Institute]. Shanghai: Shanghai Shehui Kexue Xueyuan Chubanshe, 2002.

DuBois, Thomas David. "The Salvation of Religion? Public Charity and the New Religions of the Early Republic." *Minsu quyi* 172, no. 6 (2011): 73–126.

Edgerton-Tarpley, Kathryn. *Tears from Iron: Cultural Responses to Famine in Nineteenth-Century China.* Berkeley: University of California Press, 2008.

——. "Tough Choices: Grappling with Famine in Qing China, the British Empire, and Beyond." *Journal of World History* 24, no. 1 (2013): 135–76.

# BIBLIOGRAPHY 299

Ehrlich, M. Avrum, ed. *The Jewish-Chinese Nexus: A Meeting of Civilizations*. New York: Routledge, 2008.

Fairbank, John King. *Chinese-American Interactions: A Historical Summary*. New Brunswick, N.J: Rutgers University Press, 1975.

Fan Ke. "Kuaguo lingyang—dui Meiguoren lingyang Zhongguo yinghai ji xiangguan xianxiang de kaocha [Transnational adoption—an examination of Americans adopting Chinese babies and associated phenomena]." *Shijie minzu*, no. 3 (2004): 39–48.

——. "Kuaguo lingyang yu kua wenhua de 'jia'—yi lai Hua lingyang de Meiguo gongmin weili" [Transnational adoption and transcultural "family"—case study of American citizens who adopt from China]. *Huaqiao Huaren lishi yanjiu*, no. 1 (2011): 1–11

Fan Tingwei. "Ding Zan yu Kangzhan shiqi de xinli jiankang jiaoyu" [Ding Zan and mental health education during the War of Resistance]. *Haixia jiaoyu yanjiu*, no. 1 (2014): 73–77.

Fassin, Didier. *Humanitarian Reason: A Moral History of the Present Times*. Berkeley: University of California Press, 2012.

Fehrenbach, Heide, and Davide Rodogno, eds. *Humanitarian Photography: A History*. New York: Cambridge University Press, 2015.

Feliu, Tom, dir. *Game of Pawns: The Glenn Duffie Shriver Story*. N.p.: Federal Bureau of Investigation, 2013.

Fieldston, Sara. *Raising the World: Child Welfare in the American Century*. Cambridge, Mass.: Harvard University Press, 2015.

Fish, Robert A. "The Heiress and the Love Children: Sawada Miki and the Elizabeth Saunders Home for Mixed-Blood Orphans in Postwar Japan." PhD dissertation, University of Hawai'i at Manoa, 2002.

Fitzgerald, John, and Mei-fen Kuo. "Diaspora Charity and Welfare Sovereignty in the Chinese Republic: Shanghai Charity Innovator William Yinson Lee (Li Yuanxin, 1884–1965)." *Twentieth-Century China* 42, no. 1 (2017): 72–96.

Fredman, Zach. *Tormented Alliance*. Chapel Hill: University of North Carolina Press, 2022.

Frost, Mark R. "Humanitarianism and the Overseas Aid Craze in Britain's Colonial Straits Settlements, 1870–1920." *Past & Present* 236, no. 1 (August 1, 2017): 169–205.

Frühstück, Sabine. *Playing War: Children and the Paradoxes of Modern Militarism in Japan*. Oakland: University of California Press, 2017.

Fuller, Pierre. "'Barren Soil, Fertile Minds': North China Famine and Visions of the 'Callous Chinese' Circa 1920." *International History Review* 33, no. 3 (2011): 453–72.

——. *Famine Relief in Warlord China*. Cambridge, Mass.: Harvard University Asia Center, 2019.

——. "North China Famine Revisited: Unsung Native Relief in the Warlord Era, 1920–1921." *Modern Asian Studies* 47, no. 3 (2013): 820–50.

Fuma Susumu. *Chūgoku zenkai, zendō shi kenkyu* [Research on the history of China's benevolent societies and benevolent halls]. Kyoto: Dōhōsha shuppan, 1997.

Funü Tanhuahui, ed. *Funü Tanhuahui gongzuo baobao* [Women's Symposium work report]. Lushan: Funü tanhuahui, 1939.

Galway, Matthew. *The Emergence of Global Maoism: China's Red Evangelism and the Cambodian Communist Movement, 1949–1979*. Ithaca, N.Y.: Cornell University Press, 2022.

George, Abosede A. *Making Modern Girls: A History of Girlhood, Labor, and Social Development in Colonial Lagos*. Athens: Ohio University Press, 2014.

Gilbert, Helen, and Chris Tiffin, eds. *Burden or Benefit? Imperial Benevolence and Its Legacies*. Bloomington: Indiana University Press, 2008.

Ginzburg, Carlo. "Killing a Chinese Mandarin: The Moral Implications of Distance." *Critical Inquiry* 21, no. 1 (1994): 46–60.

Glick, Clarence Elmer. *Sojourners and Settlers, Chinese Migrants in Hawaii*. Honolulu: University Press of Hawaii, 1980.

Glosser, Susan L. *Chinese Visions of Family and State, 1915–1953*. Berkeley: University of California Press, 2003.

Goldberger, Ben, Paul Moakley, and Kira Pollack, eds. *100 Photographs: The Most Influential Images of All Time*. New York: Time Books, 2015.

Gong, Lina. "Humanitarian Diplomacy as an Instrument for China's Image-Building." *Asian Journal of Comparative Politics* 6, no. 3 (2021): 238–52.

Grant, Richard. *Eurasian Girl*. New York: Universal, 1935.

Greenhalgh, Susan. *Just One Child: Science and Policy in Deng's China*. Berkeley: University of California Press, 2008.

Groves, Derham. *Anna May Wong's Lucky Shoes: 1939 Australia Through the Eyes of an Art Deco Diva*. Ames, Iowa: Culicidae Press, 2011.

Gu, Linmin, ed. *Wangshi huimou: Zhongguo Fulihui shizhi ziliao huicui* [Glancing back on the past: Selected historical records of the China Welfare Institute]. Shanghai: Zhongguo fulihui chubanshe, 2011.

Halttunen, Karen. "Humanitarianism and the Pornography of Pain in Anglo-American Culture." *American Historical Review* 100, no. 2 (1995): 303–34.

Harrison, Henrietta. "'A Penny for the Little Chinese': The French Holy Childhood Association in China, 1843–1951." *American Historical Review* 113, no. 1 (February 1, 2008): 72–92.

Haskell, Thomas L. "Capitalism and the Origins of the Humanitarian Sensibility, Part 1." *American Historical Review* 90, no. 2 (1985): 339–61.

——. "Capitalism and the Origins of the Humanitarian Sensibility, Part 2." *American Historical Review* 90, no. 3 (1985): 547–66.

Hayot, Eric. *The Hypothetical Mandarin: Sympathy, Modernity, and Chinese Pain*. New York: Oxford University Press, 2009.

Hemphill, Elizabeth Anne. *The Least of These: Miki Sawada and Her Children*. New York: Weatherhill, 1980.

Hershatter, Gail. *The Gender of Memory: Rural Women and China's Collective Past*. Berkeley: University of California Press, 2011.

Hevia, James Louis. *English Lessons: The Pedagogy of Imperialism in Nineteenth-Century China*. Durham, N.C.: Duke University Press, 2003.

Hilton, Matthew, et al. "History and Humanitarianism: A Conversation." *Past & Present* 241, no. 1 (November 1, 2018): e1–38.

Ho, Joseph W. *Developing Mission: Photography, Filmmaking, and American Missionaries in Modern China*. Ithaca, N.Y.: Cornell University Press, 2022.

# BIBLIOGRAPHY 301

Hochschild, Adam. *King Leopold's Ghost: A Story of Greed, Terror, and Heroism in Colonial Africa*. Boston: Houghton Mifflin, 1999.

Hochschild, Arlie Russell. *The Managed Heart: Commercialization of Human Feeling*. Berkeley: University of California Press, 1983.

Hollinger, David A. *Protestants Abroad: How Missionaries Tried to Change the World but Changed America*. Princeton, N.J.: Princeton University Press, 2017.

Hsiung, Ping-chen. *A Tender Voyage: Children and Childhood in Late Imperial China*. Stanford, Calif.: Stanford University Press, 2005.

Hsu, Madeline Yuan-yin. *Dreaming of Gold, Dreaming of Home: Transnationalism and Migration Between the United States and South China, 1882–1943*. Stanford, Calif.: Stanford University Press, 2000.

Hu Qing. "Minguo shiqi de ertong zhidao lilun yu shijian yanjiu" [Research on the theory and practice of child guidance during the Republic of China]. MA thesis, Suzhou University, 2020.

Huang Jianyun. *Taishan gujin gailan* [A survey of Taishan from antiquity to the present]. Guangzhou: Guangdong renmin chubanshe, 1992.

Huang Wende. *Feizhengfu zuzhi yu guoji hezuo zai Zhongguo: Huayang Yizhenhui zhi yanjiu* [Nongovernmental organizations and international cooperation in China: Research on the China International Famine Relief Commission]. Taipei: Xiu wei zixun, 2004.

Hunt, Michael H. *The Making of a Special Relationship: The United States and China to 1914*. New York: Columbia University Press, 1985.

Hunter, Jane. *The Gospel of Gentility: American Women Missionaries in Turn-of-the-Century China*. New Haven, Conn.: Yale University Press, 1984.

Iriye, Akira. "A Century of NGOs." *Diplomatic History* 23, no. 3 (1999): 421–35.

Irwin, Julia. *Making the World Safe: The American Red Cross and a Nation's Humanitarian Awakening*. New York: Oxford University Press, 2013.

Isaacs, Harold R. *Scratches on Our Minds: American Views of China and India*. Armonk, N.Y.: M. E. Sharpe, 1980.

Janku, Andrea. "Sowing Happiness: Spiritual Competition in Famine Relief Activities in Late Nineteenth-Century China." *Minsu quyi*, no. 143 (2004): 89–118.

Janss, Edmund W. *A Brief History of Christian Children's Fund, Inc*. Richmond, Va.: Christian Children's Fund, 1967.

——. *Yankee Si! The Story of Dr. J. Calvitt Clarke and His 36,000 Children*. New York: Morrow, 1961.

Jiangmenshi dang'an ju, Jiangmenshi zazhi ban, and Wuyi Daxue Guangdong Qiaoxiang Wenhua Yanjiu Zhongxin, eds. *Qingxi qiaoxiang: Wuyi yinxin dang'an tu'ce* [Maintaining connections with an overseas Chinese village: Archival photographs of silver letters from Wuyi]. Jiangmen: Jiangmenshi dang'an ju, 2010.

Jingye Jiaoyangyuan, ed. *Liulang ertong jiaoyang wenti: Jingye Jiaoyangyuan di yi ci baogao* [The problem of educating street urchins: The first report of the Jingye Reformatory]. Shanghai: Jingye jiaoyangyuan, 1942.

Johansson, Sten, and Ola Nygren. "The Missing Girls of China: A New Demographic Account." *Population and Development Review* 17, no. 1 (1991): 35–51.

Johnson, Kay Ann. *China's Hidden Children: Abandonment, Adoption, and the Human Costs of the One-Child Policy.* Chicago: University of Chicago Press, 2016.

——. "Politics of International and Domestic Adoption in China." *Law & Society Review* 36, no. 2 (2002): 379–96.

——. *Wanting a Daughter, Needing a Son: Abandonment, Adoption, and Orphanage Care in China.* St. Paul, Minn.: Yeong & Yeong, 2004.

Jones, Andrew F. *Developmental Fairy Tales: Evolutionary Thinking and Modern Chinese Culture.* Cambridge, Mass.: Harvard University Press, 2011.

Joyce, Kathryn. *The Child Catchers: Rescue, Trafficking, and the New Gospel of Adoption.* New York: PublicAffairs, 2013.

Kaell, Hillary. *Christian Globalism at Home: Child Sponsorship in the United States.* Princeton, N.J.: Princeton University Press, 2020.

Karthikeyan, Hrishi, and Gabriel J. Chin. "Preserving Racial Identity: Population Patterns and the Application of Anti-Miscegenation Statutes to Asian Americans, 1910–1950." *Asian Law Journal* 9, no. 1 (2002): 1–40.

Kennedy, John James, and Yaojiang Shi. *Lost and Found: The "Missing Girls" in Rural China.* New York: Oxford University Press, 2019.

Kim, Eleana Jean. *Adopted Territory: Transnational Korean Adoptees and the Politics of Belonging.* Durham, N.C.: Duke University Press, 2010.

King, David P. *God's Internationalists: World Vision and the Age of Evangelical Humanitarianism.* Philadelphia: University of Pennsylvania Press, 2019.

King, Michelle Tien. *Between Birth and Death: Female Infanticide in Nineteenth-Century China.* Stanford, Calif.: Stanford University Press, 2014.

Kinney, Anne Behnke, ed. *Chinese Views of Childhood.* Honolulu: University of Hawaii Press, 1995.

Klein, Christina. *Cold War Orientalism: Asia in the Middlebrow Imagination, 1945–1961.* Berkeley: University of California Press, 2003.

Ko, Dorothy. *Cinderella's Sisters: A Revisionist History of Footbinding.* Berkeley: University of California Press, 2005.

Koopman, Colin. *How We Became Our Data: A Genealogy of the Informational Person.* Chicago: University of Chicago Press, 2019.

Koshiro, Yukiko. *Trans-Pacific Racisms and the U.S. Occupation of Japan.* New York: Columbia University Press, 1999.

Kovner, Sarah. *Occupying Power: Sex Workers and Servicemen in Postwar Japan.* Stanford, Calif.: Stanford University Press, 2012.

Lary, Diana. *China's Civil War: A Social History, 1945–1949.* Cambridge: Cambridge University Press, 2015.

Lean, Eugenia. *Public Passions: The Trial of Shi Jianqiao and the Rise of Popular Sympathy in Republican China.* Berkeley: University of California Press, 2007.

Lee, Erika. *At America's Gates: Chinese Immigration During the Exclusion Era, 1882–1943.* Chapel Hill: University of North Carolina Press, 2003.

Lei Jiachun. "Minguo shiqi de Guangzhou Jidujiao cishan huodong yanjiu (1912–1949)" [Research on Christian philanthropic activities in Republican era Guangzhou (1912–1949)]. MA thesis, Guangzhou University, 2009.

Lei Sean Hsiang-lin. "Xiguan cheng siwei: Xin Shenghuo Yundong yu feijiehe fangzhi zhong de lunli, jiating yu shenti" [Habituating the four virtues: Ethics, family, and the body in the anti-tuberculosis campaigns and the New Life Movement]. *Zhongyang yanjiuyuan jindaishi yanjiusuo jikan*, no. 74 (2011): 133–77.

Leung, Beatrice, and William T. Liu. *Chinese Catholic Church in Conflict: 1949-2001.* Boca Raton, Fla.: Universal-Publishers, 2004.

Li Liangming. "Beifa Zhanzheng yu Wuhan gongren yundong" [The Northern Expedition and the workers' movement in Wuhan]. *Huazhong shifan daxue xuebao*, no. 4 (1987): 57–62.

Li, Lillian M. *Fighting Famine in North China: State, Market, and Environmental Decline, 1690s–1990s.* Stanford, Calif.: Stanford University Press, 2007.

Li Xiaowei. "Yi jiu si jiu nian zhi yi jiu wu liu nian guojia zhengquan yu minjian cishan zuzhi de guanxi jiexi" [Analysis of the relationship between state power and nongovernmental charity organizations in 1949–1956]. *Zhonggong dangshi yanjiu*, no. 9 (2012): 66–73.

Liang Qizi [Angela Ki Che Leung]. *Shishan yu jiaohua: Ming Qing shiqi de cishan zuzhi* [Charitable works and moral education: Benevolent institutions during the Ming and Qing dynasties]. Taipei: Lian jing chuban shiye gongsi, 1997.

Lin, Grace. *The Red Thread: An Adoption Fairy Tale.* Park Ridge, Ill.: Albert Whitman, 2007.

Lin Jia-hui. "Zhanshi Ertong Baoyuhui de jianli yu zuzhi yunzuo" [The establishment and organizational operations of the National Association for Refugee Children]. *Shi-Hui*, no. 10 (2006): 269–320.

Lin Jiajin. *Jindai Guangdong qiaohui yanjiu* [Research on remittances in modern Guangdong]. Guangzhou: Zhongshan daxue chubanshe, 1999.

Lipman, Jana K. "'The Face Is the Road Map': Vietnamese Amerasians in U.S. Political and Popular Culture, 1980–1988." *Journal of Asian American Studies* 14, no. 1 (February 2011): 33–68, 166.

Liu Jin. *Wuyi yinxin* [Silver letters from Wuyi]. Guangzhou: Guangdong renmin chubanshe, 2009.

Liu, Lydia. *Translingual Practice: Literature, National Culture, and Translated Modernity—China, 1900-1937.* Stanford, Calif.: Stanford University Press, 1995.

Liu, Monica. *Seeking Western Men: Email-Order Brides Under China's Global Rise.* Stanford, Calif.: Stanford University Press, 2023.

Liubimova, Vera. *Xiao Xuehua* [Little Snowflake]. Trans. Liu Binyan. Beijing: Qingnian chubanshe, 1952.

Lovell, Julia. *Maoism: A Global History.* New York: Knopf, 2019.

Lu Ping. "Wo qinli de Zhongguo Jianshe chuangban shimo" [The story of my experience of the founding of *China Reconstructs*]. *Jinri Zhongguo* 61, no. 2 (February 2012): 39–40.

——. "Zai Song Qingling lingdao xia chuangban Zhongguo Jianshe zazhi" [Founding *China Reconstructs* magazine under the leadership of Song Qingling]. *Bai nian chao*, no. 4 (2012): 53–59.

Lujunbu, ed. *Lujun xingzheng jiyao* [Minutes on army administration]. Vol. 609. Taipei: Wenhai chubanshe, 1981.

Luo, Nili, and David M. Smolin. "Intercountry Adoption and China: Emerging Questions and Developing Chinese Perspectives." *Cumberland Law Review* 35, no. 3 (2004–2005): 597–618.

Lynteris, Christos. *The Spirit of Selflessness in Maoist China: Socialist Medicine and the New Man*. New York: Palgrave Macmillan, 2013.

Mathews, Ellen. "A Study of Emotional Stability in Children by Means of a Questionnaire." *Journal of Delinquency* 8, no. 1 (January 1, 1923): 1–42.

Mao Zedong. *Mao Zedong xuanji* [Selected works of Mao Zedong]. Beijing: Renmin chubanshe, 1960.

Marx, Karl, and Friedrich Engels. *Manifesto of the Communist Party*. Moscow: Progress Publishers, 1977.

May, Elaine Tyler. *Homeward Bound: American Families in the Cold War Era*. New York: Basic Books, 1988.

Maza, Sarah. "The Kids Aren't All Right: Historians and the Problem of Childhood." *American Historical Review* 125, no. 4 (2020): 1261–85.

McCleary, Rachel M. *Global Compassion: Private Voluntary Organizations and U.S. Foreign Policy Since 1939*. New York: Oxford University Press, 2009.

McKeown, Adam. *Chinese Migrant Networks and Cultural Change: Peru, Chicago, Hawaii, 1900–1936*. Chicago: University of Chicago Press, 2001.

——. *Melancholy Order: Asian Migration and the Globalization of Borders*. New York: Columbia University Press, 2008.

Meier, Patricia J., and Xiaole Zhang. "Sold Into Adoption: The Hunan Baby Trafficking Scandal Exposes Vulnerabilities in Chinese Adoptions to the United States Symposium: The Baby Market." *Cumberland Law Review*, no. 1 (2009 2008): 87–130.

Mencken, H. L. "War Words in England." *American Speech* 19, no. 1 (1944): 3–15.

Meyer-Fong, Tobie S. *What Remains: Coming to Terms with Civil War in 19th Century China*. Stanford, Calif.: Stanford University Press, 2013.

Mitter, Rana. *Forgotten Ally: China's World War II, 1937–1945*. Boston: Houghton Mifflin Harcourt, 2013.

——. "Imperialism, Transnationalism, and the Reconstruction of Post-War China: UNRRA in China, 1944–7 1." *Past & Present* 218, no. suppl 8 (2013): 51–69.

——. "Relocation and Dislocation: Civilian, Refugee, and Military Movement as Factors in the Disintegration of Postwar China, 1945–49." *Itinerario* 46, no. 2 (2022): 193–213.

Molumphy, Henry D. *For Common Decency: The History of Foster Parents Plan, 1937–1983*. Warwick, UK: Foster Parents Plan International, 1984.

Moon, Katharine H. S. *Sex Among Allies: Military Prostitution in U.S.-Korea Relations*. New York: Columbia University Press, 1997.

Moore, Aaron William. "Growing Up in Nationalist China: Self-Representation in the Personal Documents of Children and Youth, 1927–1949." *Modern China* 42, no. 1 (2016): 73–110.

Moyn, Samuel. "Theses on Humanitarianism and Human Rights." *Humanity Journal* (blog), September 23, 2016. http://humanityjournal.org/blog/theses-on-humanitarianism-and-human-rights/.

Nathan, Andrew J. *A History of the China International Famine Relief Commission*. Cambridge, Mass.: East Asian Research Center, Harvard University, 1965.

Neubauer, Jack. "Save the Adults: The Little Teacher System and the Politics of Childhood in Modern China." *Journal of the History of Childhood and Youth* 16, no. 2 (2023): 266–86.

Ngai, Mae. *The Chinese Question: The Gold Rushes, Chinese Migration, and Global Politics*. New York: Norton, 2021.

Nolan, Rachel. *Until I Find You: Disappeared Children and Coercive Adoptions in Guatemala*. Cambridge, Mass.: Harvard University Press, 2024.

Niu Jun. *Lengzhan yu xin Zhongguo waijiao de yuanqi, 1949–1955* [The Cold War and the origins of foreign relations of the People's Republic of China]. Beijing: Shehui kexue wenxian chubanshe, 2012.

Oh, Arissa H. *To Save the Children of Korea: The Cold War Origins of International Adoption*. Stanford, Calif.: Stanford University Press, 2015.

O'Sullivan, Kevin. *The NGO Moment: The Globalisation of Compassion from Biafra to Live Aid*. Human Rights in History. Cambridge: Cambridge University Press, 2021.

Ove, Peter. *Change a Life, Change Your Own: Child Sponsorship, the Discourse of Development, and the Production of Ethical Subjects*. Halifax, N.S.: Fernwood, 2018.

Pascoe, Peggy. *What Comes Naturally: Miscegenation Law and the Making of Race in America*. New York: Oxford University Press, 2010.

Peking United International Famine Relief Committee. *The North China Famine of 1920–1921 with Special Reference to the West Chihli Area*. Beijing: Commercial Press Works, 1922.

Peterson, Glen. "Overseas Chinese and Merchant Philanthropy in China: From Culturalism to Nationalism." *Journal of Chinese Overseas* 1, no. 1 (2005): 87–109.

Pfeiff, Alexandra. "Two Adoptions of the Red Cross: The Chinese Red Cross Society and the Red Swastika Society from 1904 to 1949." PhD dissertation, European University Institute, 2018.

Plum, M. Colette. "Unlikely Heirs: War Orphans During the Second Sino-Japanese War, 1937–1945." PhD dissertation, Stanford University, 2006.

Pomeranz, Kenneth. *The Great Divergence: China, Europe, and the Making of the Modern World Economy*. Princeton, N.J.: Princeton University Press, 2000.

Pomfret, John. *The Beautiful Country and the Middle Kingdom: America and China, 1776 to the Present*. New York: Holt, 2016.

Ponte, Iris Chin, Leslie Kim Wang, and Serena Pen-Shian Fan. "Returning to China: The Experience of Adopted Chinese Children and Their Parents." *Adoption Quarterly* 13, no. 2 (May 28, 2010): 100–124.

Porter, Andrew, and Wm Roger Louis, eds. "Trusteeship, Anti-Slavery, and Humanitarianism." In *The Oxford History of the British Empire: Volume III: The Nineteenth Century*. Oxford: Oxford University Press, 1999.

Potter, Sarah. *Everybody Else: Adoption and the Politics of Domestic Diversity in Postwar America*. Athens: University of Georgia Press, 2014.

Powers, Becky Cerling. *Laura's Children: The Hidden Story of a Chinese Orphanage*. Vinton, Tex.: Canaan Home Communications, 2010.

Ransmeier, Johanna S. *Sold People: Traffickers and Family Life in North China*. Cambridge, Mass.: Harvard University Press, 2017.

Reeves, Caroline. "Holding Hostages in China, Holding China Hostage: Sovereignty, Philanthropy, and the 1923 'Lincheng Outrage.'" *Twentieth-Century China* 27, no. 1 (November 2001): 39–69.

—. "The Power of Mercy: The Chinese Red Cross Society, 1900–1937." PhD dissertation, Harvard University, 1998.

—. "Sovereignty and the Chinese Red Cross Society: The Differentiated Practice of International Law in Shandong, 1914–1916." *Journal of the History of International Law* 13, no. 1 (January 2011): 155–77.

Reinhardt, Anne. *Navigating Semi-colonialism: Shipping, Sovereignty, and Nation-Building in China, 1860–1937.* Cambridge, Mass.: Harvard University Asia Center, 2018.

Reinisch, Jessica. "Internationalism in Relief: The Birth (and Death) of UNRRA." *Past & Present* 210, no. suppl 6 (January 1, 2011): 258–89.

Ren Guixiang. *Haiwai Huaqiao yu zuguo Kangri Zhanzheng* [Overseas Chinese and the motherland's War of Resistance Against Japan]. Beijing: Tuanjie chubanshe, 2015.

Rodogno, Davide. "Non-state Actors' Humanitarian Operations in the Aftermath of the First World War." In *The Emergence of Humanitarian Intervention: Ideas and Practice from the Nineteenth Century to the Present*, 185–207. Cambridge: Cambridge University Press, 2015.

Rodriguez, Sarah Mellors. *Reproductive Realities in Modern China: Birth Control and Abortion, 1911–2021.* Cambridge: Cambridge University Press, 2023.

Roebuck, Kristin. "Orphans by Design: 'Mixed-Blood' Children, Child Welfare, and Racial Nationalism in Postwar Japan." *Japanese Studies* 36, no. 2 (May 3, 2016): 191–212.

Rogaski, Ruth. *Hygienic Modernity: Meanings of Health and Disease in Treaty-Port China.* Berkeley: University of California Press, 2004.

Rowe, William T. *China's Last Empire: The Great Qing.* Cambridge, Mass.: Harvard University Press, 2009.

Saada, Emmanuelle. *Empire's Children: Race, Filiation, and Citizenship in the French Colonies.* Chicago: University of Chicago Press, 2012.

Saari, Jon L. *Legacies of Childhood: Growing Up Chinese in a Time of Crisis, 1890–1920.* Cambridge, Mass.: Council on East Asian Studies, Harvard University, 1990.

Sachs, Dana. *The Life We Were Given: Operation Babylift, International Adoption, and the Children of War in Vietnam.* Boston: Beacon Press, 2010.

Salvatici, Silvia. *History of Humanitarianism, 1775–1989: In the Name of Others.* Manchester, UK: Manchester University Press, 2019.

Schencking, J. Charles. *The Great Kantō Earthquake and the Chimera of National Reconstruction in Japan.* New York: Columbia University Press, 2013.

Schneider, Helen M. "Mobilising Women: The Women's Advisory Council, Resistance and Reconstruction During China's War with Japan." *European Journal of East Asian Studies* 11, no. 2 (2012): 213–36.

Selman, Peter. "International Adoptions from the People's Republic of China, 1992–2017." Working paper, New Castle University, 2019.

Sen, Satadru. "The Savage Family: Colonialism and Female Infanticide in Nineteenth-Century India." *Journal of Women's History* 14, no. 3 (2002): 53–79.

Shaffer, Robert. "A Rape in Beijing, December 1946: GIs, Nationalist Protests, and U.S. Foreign Policy." *Pacific Historical Review* 69, no. 1 (2000): 31–64.

Shi, Xia. *At Home in the World: Women and Charity in Late Qing and Early Republican China.* New York: Columbia University Press, 2018.

Shih, Shu-mei. *The Lure of the Modern: Writing Modernism in Semicolonial China, 1917–1937.* Berkeley: University of California Press, 2001.

Shue, Vivienne. "The Quality of Mercy: Confucian Charity and the Mixed Metaphors of Modernity in Tianjin." *Modern China* 32, no. 4 (2006): 411–52.

Simonow, Joanna. "Famine Relief in Colonial South Asia, 1858–1947: Regional and Global Perspectives." In *Routledge Handbook of the History of Colonialism in South Asia*, ed. Harald Fischer-Tiné and Maria Framke, 497–509. New York: Routledge, 2021.

Skinner, Rob, and Alan Lester. "Humanitarianism and Empire: New Research Agendas." *Journal of Imperial and Commonwealth History* 40, no. 5 (December 1, 2012): 729–47.

Smillie, Ian, and Henry Helmich, eds. *Public Attitudes and International Development Co-Operation.* Paris: Organization for Economic Co-Operation and Development, 1988.

Smith, Joanna F. Handlin. *The Art of Doing Good: Charity in Late Ming China.* Berkeley: University of California Press, 2009.

——. "Benevolent Societies: The Reshaping of Charity During the Late Ming and Early Ch'ing." *Journal of Asian Studies* 46, no. 2 (1987): 309–37.

——. "Social Hierarchy and Merchant Philanthropy as Perceived in Several Late-Ming and Early-Qing Texts." *Journal of the Economic and Social History of the Orient* 41, no. 3 (1998): 417–51.

Sontag, Susan. *Regarding the Pain of Others.* New York: Picador, 2003.

Soong Ching-ling. *Song Qingling shuxin ji* [Collected letters of Song Qingling]. Beijing: Renmin chubanshe, 1999.

——. *Song Qingling xuanji* [Selected works of Song Qingling]. Beijing: Renmin chubanshe, 1992.

Stamatov, Peter. "Beyond and Against Capitalism: Abolitionism and the Moral Dimension of Humanitarian Practice." *International Social Science Journal* 65, no. 215/216 (March 2014): 25–35.

——. *The Origins of Global Humanitarianism: Religion, Empires, and Advocacy.* New York: Cambridge University Press, 2013.

Stearns, Peter N. "Challenges in the History of Childhood." *Journal of the History of Childhood and Youth* 1, no. 1 (2008): 35–42.

Stoler, Ann Laura. *Carnal Knowledge and Imperial Power: Race and the Intimate in Colonial Rule.* Berkeley: University of California Press, 2002.

Stuy, Brian. "Domestic Adoption in China's Orphanages." 2006. http://research-china.blogspot .com/2006/01/domestic-adoption-in-chinas-orphanages.html.

Su Hua. "Kangzhan shiqi nantong de yichang xinli wenti" [Abnormal psychological problems of refugee children during the War of Resistance]. *Minguo dang'an*, no. 3 (1995): 121–29.

Sun Yankui. *Kunan de renliu: Kangzhan shiqi de nanmin* [People in misery: Refugees in the War of Resistance]. Guilin: Guangxi shifan daxue chubanshe, 1994.

Sun Yat-sen. *Guofu quanji* [Complete works of Sun Yat-Sen]. Taipei: Jindai Zhongguo chubanshe, 1989.

Teng, Emma. *Eurasian: Mixed Identities in the United States, China, and Hong Kong, 1842–1943.* Berkeley: University of California Press, 2013.

Teng Jiuming, ed. *Zhao Juntao jiaoyu sixiang lunwen ji* [Zhao Juntao's collected essays on education]. Chongqing: Chongqing chubanshe, 2003.

Tillman, Margaret Mih. "Precocious Politics: Preschool Education and Child Protection in China, 1903–1953." PhD dissertation, University of California, Berkeley, 2013.

——. *Raising China's Revolutionaries: Modernizing Childhood for Cosmopolitan Nationalists and Liberated Comrades, 1920s–1950s.* New York: Columbia University Press, 2018.

Tise, Larry E. *A Book About Children: The World of Christian Children's Fund, 1938–1991.* Falls Church, Va.: Hartland, 1993.

Tucker, Nancy Bernkopf. "An Unlikely Peace: American Missionaries and the Chinese Communists, 1948–1950." *Pacific Historical Review* 45, no. 1 (1976): 97–116.

Tyrrell, Ian. *Reforming the World: The Creation of America's Moral Empire.* Princeton, N.J.: Princeton University Press, 2010.

U.S. Congress. *Amerasian Immigration Proposals: Hearing Before the Subcommittee on Immigration and Refugee Policy of the Committee on the Judiciary.* Washington, D.C.: U.S. Government Printing Office, 1982.

U.S. Department of State, ed. *United States Relations with China: With Special Reference to the Period 1944–1949.* Washington, D.C.: U.S. Government Printing Office, 1949.

Van de Ven, Hans. *China at War: Triumph and Tragedy in the Emergence of the New China.* Cambridge, Mass.: Harvard University Press, 2018.

Wales, Nym. *China Builds for Democracy; a Story of Cooperative Industry.* New York: Modern Age Books, 1941.

Waltner, Ann Beth. *Getting an Heir: Adoption and the Construction of Kinship in Late Imperial China.* Honolulu: University of Hawaii Press, 1990.

Wang Chong-hui. *Wang Chonghui xiansheng wenji* [Collected writings of Mr. Wang Chunghui]. Taipei: Zhongyang wenwu zongjingxiao, 1981.

Wang, Dong. *China's Unequal Treaties: Narrating National History.* Lanham, Md: Lexington Books, 2005.

Wang, Guanhua. *In Search of Justice: The 1905–1906 Chinese Anti-American Boycott.* Cambridge, Mass.: Harvard University Asia Center, 2001.

Wang, Leslie K. *Outsourced Children: Orphanage Care and Adoption in Globalizing China.* Stanford, Calif.: Stanford University Press, 2016.

Wang, Leslie K., Debra Jacobs, and Iris Chin Ponte. *From Home to Homeland: What Adoptive Families Need to Know Before Making a Return Trip to China.* St. Paul, Minn.: Yeong & Yeong, 2010.

Wang, Pu. *The Translatability of Revolution: Guo Moruo and Twentieth-Century Chinese Culture.* Cambridge, Mass.: Harvard University Asia Center, 2018.

Wang Wen-ji. "Yufang, shiying yu gaizao: Minguo shiqi de xinli weisheng" [Prevention, adaptation, and transformation: Mental hygiene during the Republican period]. In *Jiankang yu shehui: Huaren weisheng xinshi* [Health and society: A new history of Chinese hygiene], ed. Pingyi Zhu, 237–57. Taipei: Lianjing, 2013.

Wang, Wen-ji, and Hsuan-Ying Huang. "Mental Health." In *The Making of the Human Sciences in China: Historical and Conceptual Foundations*, ed. Howard Chiang, 460–88. Boston: Brill, 2019.

Warnshuis, A. L. "Christian Missions and the Situation in China." *Annals of the American Academy of Political and Social Science* 132 (1927): 80–82.

Watson, James L. "Agnates and Outsiders: Adoption in a Chinese Lineage." *Man* 10, no. 2 (1975): 293–306.

## BIBLIOGRAPHY 309

*Wei kunan ertong er gongzuo: Zhanzai Ertong Yiyanghui Zhongguo Fenhui gongzuo baogao* [Work for the suffering children: Foster Parents' Plan for War Children China Branch work report]. Shanghai: Zhanzai ertong yiyanghui zhongguo fenhui, 1949.

Wen, Jian. "Xin Zhongguo chengli chuqi Zhongguo Renmin Jiuji Zonghui yanjiu" [Research on the People's Relief Administration of China in the early days of New China]. MA thesis, Hebei Normal University, 2012.

Westad, Odd Arne. *Restless Empire: China and the World Since 1750*. New York: Basic Books, 2012.

Williams, Eric Eustace. *Capitalism & Slavery*. London: Deutsch, 1964.

Wolf, Arthur P. *Marriage and Adoption in China, 1854–1945*. Stanford, Calif.: Stanford University Press, 1980.

Wu, Albert Monshan. "The Quest for an 'Indigenous Church': German Missionaries, Chinese Christians, and the Indigenization Debates of the 1920s." *American Historical Review* 122, no. 1 (2017): 85–114.

Wu Minchao. "Cong linshi nanmin dao luodi shenggen: Erzhan qianhou de Xinxilan Huaqiao nüxing" [From temporary refugees to permanent residents: Chinese women in New Zealand around World War II]. *Jindaishi yanjiu*, no. 6 (2018): 89–103.

Wydick, Bruce, Paul Glewwe, and Laine Rutledge. "Does International Child Sponsorship Work? A Six-Country Study of Impacts on Adult Life Outcomes." *Journal of Political Economy* 121, no. 2 (2013): 393–436.

Xiao Gang. *Geng Lishu* [Talitha Gerlach]. Shenyang: Liaoning Renmin Chubanshe, 1993.

Xiao Xiaorong. *Renshi xinli wenti* [Issues in personnel psychology]. Shanghai: Shangwu Yinshuguan, 1944.

Xing, Jun. "The American Social Gospel and the Chinese YMCA." *Journal of American-East Asian Relations* 5, no. 3/4 (1996): 277–304.

Xu Fenghua. *Shenfen, zuzhi yu zhengzhi: Song Qingling he Baomeng—Zhongfuhui Yanjiu (1938–1958)* [Identity, organization, and politics: Song Qingling and the China Defense League—China Welfare Institute]. Shanghai: Shanghai Shudian Chubanshe, 2013.

——. "Zhongguo Jianshe de chuangban yu xin Zhongguo chengli chuqi de duiwai xuanchuan" [The establishment of *China Reconstructs* and foreign publicity in the initial period of the PRC]. *Zhonggong dangshi yanjiu*, no. 5: (2016): 59–67.

*Xuesheng xin chidu* [New students' letter-writing manual]. Hong Kong: Chen Xiang Ji Shuju, n.d.

Yan Juanzhen. "Bu gai hushi de shige fanyijia Zou Lüzhi" [The poetry translator who should not be overlooked: Zou Lüzhi]. *Mudanjiang daxue xuebao* 21, no. 9 (2012): 118–20.

Yang Jianli. "Wanqing shehui zaihuang jiuzhi gongneng de yanbian-yi dingwu 'qihuang' de liang zhong zhenji fangshi weili" [Changes in social disaster relief in the late Qing: Taking two kinds of relief methods during the "incredible famine" of 1877–1878 as examples]. *Qingshi yanjiu*, no. 4 (2000): 59–64.

Yang Ying and Yuan Yao. "Zhongguo waiwen duiwai xuanchuan qikan de lishi kaocha" [Historical investigation of China's foreign-language overseas propaganda periodicals]. *Xianyang shifan xueyuan xuebao* 21, no. 6 (2006): 98–101.

Yip, Hon-ming, and John Fitzgerald, eds. *Chinese Diaspora Charity and the Cantonese Pacific, 1850–1949*. Hong Kong: Hong Kong University Press, 2020.

## 310 BIBLIOGRAPHY

Yu, Renqiu. *To Save China, to Save Ourselves: The Chinese Hand Laundry Alliance of New York.* Philadelphia: Temple University Press, 1992.

Zahra, Tara. *The Lost Children: Reconstructing Europe's Families After World War II.* Cambridge, Mass.: Harvard University Press, 2011.

Zelizer, Viviana A. Rotman. *The Purchase of Intimacy.* Princeton, N.J.: Princeton University Press, 2005.

Zhang Chun. *Kangri Zhanzheng shiqi Zhanshi Ertong Baoyuhui yanjiu* [Research on the National Association for Refugee Children during the War of Resistance Against Japan]. Beijing: Tuanjie chubanshe, 2015.

Zhang Dawei, ed. *Xue di hongqi fei hou—cong Jingye Jiaoyangyuan dao Shanghai Shaoniancun* [A red flag flies above the snowy ground—from the Jingye Foundling to Shanghai Boystown]. Shanghai: Shanghaishi Baoshanqu Fojiao Xiehui, 2001.

Zhang Peiyan. "1947 nian Song Qingling zao e yi feibang" [In 1947 Soong Ching-ling encountered malicious slander]. *Shiji,* no. 6 (2013): 14–17.

Zhanshi Ertong Baoyuhui. *Zhanshi Ertong Baoyuhui liu zhounian jiniankan* [Memorial volume for the sixth anniversary of the National Association for Refugee Children]. Chongqing: Zhanshi ertong baoyuhui, 1944.

Zhishu di qi baoyuyuan yuanshi bianweihui and Zhonggong Sichuan sheng nanchuan shiwei dangshi yanjiushi, eds. *Zhongguo Zhanshi Ertong Baoyuhui Zhishu Di Qi Baoyuyuan shiliao xuanji* [Selected historical materials from the NARC No. 7 Warphanage]. Hubei: Hubeisheng chubanju, 1994.

Zhongguo renmin zhengzhi xieshang huiyi jiangsu sheng xuzhou shi weiyuanhui wenshi weiyuanhui. *Xuzhou wenshi ziliao* [Xuzhou literary and historical materials]. Vol. 27. Xuzhou: Zhengxie Jiangsu sheng xuzhou shi weiyuanhui wenshi wenyuanhui, 2007.

Zhongguo shaonian ertong she. *Peiyang jiaoyu xin de yi dai: di yi ci Quanguo Shaonian Ertong Gongzuo Ganbu Dahui wenxian* [Fostering and educating a new generation: Documents from the first National Conference for Children's Work Cadres]. Beijing: Qingnian Chubanshe, 1950.

Zhou Chuan. *Zhongguo jinxiandai gaodeng jiaoyu renwu cidian* [Biographical dictionary of higher education in modern China]. Fuzhou: Fujian jiaoyu chubanshe, 2018.

Zhou Qiuguang. *Hongshizihui zai Zhongguo (1904–1927)* [The Red Cross in China]. Beijing: Renmin chubanshe, 2008.

Zhu Aiqin. "Meihua Ertong Fulihui zai Huanan diqu de huodong yanjiu: 1945–1952" [Research on the activities of China's Children Fund in the South China region: 1945–1952]. MA thesis, Sun-Yat-sen University, 2005.

Zhu Hu. *Difangxing liudong ji qi chaoyue: wanqing yizhen yu jindai Zhongguo de xinchen daixie* [The fluidity and transcendence of localism: Late-Qing charitable relief and the supersession of the old by the new in modern China]. Beijing: Zhongguo renmin daxue chubanshe, 2006.

Zhu Zhixin. *Zhu Zhixin xiansheng wenji* [Collected writings of Zhu Zhixin]. Taipei: Zhongyang wenwu zongjingxiao, 1985.

Zou, Dongxin. "Socialist Medicine and Maoist Humanitarianism: Chinese Medical Missions to Algeria, 1963–1984." PhD dissertation, Columbia University, 2019.

# INDEX

abolitionist movement, 7
adoption; domestic adoption in China, 212–15, 234–35; end of China's international adoption program, 241–42; international adoption, 4, 14, 28, 218–24, 227–28, 232–36; and child sponsorship, 95–96. *See also* adoption plan
adoption plan, 1; and children's letter-writing, 22–26, 66–74, 121–26, 141–46; and Christianity, 103–7, 111–14; critiques of, 162–65, 182–83, 228; and emotional trauma, 86–89; and foster parents, 146–49; as fundraising strategy, 5–6, 53–66, 127–28; and gift exchange, 74–77; in Hong Kong, 207–9; in Japan, 209–11, 219–20; in Korea, 195–96, 211–12, 219, 223–24; logistical problems, 77–78, 89–91, 116–21; political uses of, 15–16, 20–21, 91–95, 107–11, 128–31, 138–41; in Taiwan, 209–10. *See also* child sponsorship
Amerasian Homecoming Act, 218
American Relief Association (ARA), 9, 165–66
American-Oriental Friendship Association (AOFA), 18, 159, 161–64, 182–83, 195

antimiscegenation laws, 99, 266n10
Arnold, Julean, 44

Bandura, Albert, 238
Barnard, W. E., 55, 89–91, 94
Barnett, Michael, 14, 31
Baughan, Emily, 9
benevolent halls, 33–34
Bethune, Norman, 167, 174–75, 181, 224
*Blessed Children*, 112, 115, 121–24, 169–70, 270n75
Blue, Edna, 133, 137–38, 141, 147, 158
bowl of rice parties, 52, 54
*bo'ai*, 111–14
Buck, Pearl, 105, 223

Cai Tinggan, 44
Canaan Children's Home, 119, 164, 174–76, 180–82, 184–88, 201
Cao Mengjun, 192
capitalism, 4, 7, 39, 250n14
censorship, 22, 24–26, 114, 124–26, 144–46
Central China Famine Relief Fund, 37
Central China Famine Relief Committee, 38–41

312  INDEX

Chateaubriand, François-René, 60
Chen Duxiu, 114
Chen Suk-ying, 57
Chen, W. Y., 185–86
Chen Yuanchi, 224–26
Chiang Kai-shek, 3, 108, 114–15, 168, 218; and
  Chiang Memorial Children's Village, 161,
  181, 185; described in children's letters,
  93, 109
Chiang Memorial Children's Village, 161–64,
  176, 179, 182–90
child psychology, 65, 81–88, 119–20
child sponsorship, 14, 17–19, 23, 211–12,
  228–31, 238. *See also* adoption plan
child trafficking, 4, 235
*Children's Tears*, 201
Children's Theatre. *See* China Welfare Fund
  Children's Theatre
*Children's Voice*, 208–9
China Child Welfare, 17–18
China International Famine Relief
  Commission (CIFRC), 38–39, 45–47
*China Reconstructs*, 198–204, 224
China Welfare Fund (CWF), 132–34, 136, 147,
  158–59; reorganization as China Welfare
  Institute (CWI), 198, 200–4. *See also*
  China Welfare Fund Children's Theatre
China Welfare Fund Children's Theatre,
  150–55, 199, 201–2
China Welfare Institute (CWI). *See* China
  Welfare Fund (CWF)
*China News*, 103–4, 108–10, 170–71
China's Children Fund (CCF), 18, 19, 27,
  96–100, 127–28; administrative practices,
  116–21, 187, 238; and American influence
  in China, 108–11, 114–15, 239; bureaucratic
  structure, 124–26; and Christianity, 103–7,
  111–14; criticisms of, 228–31; fundraising
  statistics, 102, 230–31; global expansion,
  194–96, 207; guidance on children's
  letters, 121–24; in Hong Kong, 207–9; in
  Japan, 209–11; in Korea, 211–12; and legal
  adoption, 212–14, 218–24; relationship

with Communists, 169–76, 193; in Taiwan,
  209–10. *See also* Calvitt Clarke; Canaan
  Children's Home
Chinese Communist revolution, 3, 22, 105,
  128–30; and humanitarian organizations,
  132–38, 164–65, 168–69, 194–95, 205;
  described in children's letters, 128–32,
  139–41
Chinese diaspora, 10, 31; and the adoption
  plan, 53–59; and humanitarian
  fundraising, 48–52, 61; and legal adoption,
  214
Chinese Exclusion, 66, 99, 127, 213
Chinese Industrial Cooperative Movement,
  166
Chinese Liberated Areas Relief Association
  (CLARA), 167–68
Chinese National Relief and Rehabilitation
  Administration (CNRRA), 101
Choy, Catherine Ceniza, 111
Christian Americanism, 108
Chun Yun School, 150
Clarke, Calvitt, 97–99, 103, 106, 112; views
  on children's letters, 116–17, 125; views on
  Communists, 171, 173–74; views on legal
  international adoption, 213, 220–23.
  *See also* China's Children Fund;
  *Eurasian Girl*
Cold War, 3–5; and the adoption plan,
  111, 138, 164–65, 194–96, 207–12; and
  humanitarianism, 8, 14, 28, 131, 229, 239;
  and international adoption, 218
Cold War Orientalism, 111
colonial benevolence. *See* imperial
  benevolence
colonial responsibility. *See* imperial
  benevolence
Comité de Secours aux Réfugiés et Blessés
  Chinois, 57–58
*Communist Manifesto*, 42, 165
Congo Reform Association, 8–9
cooperating organizations, 56–58
COVID-19, 232, 241–42

INDEX 313

*Crimes of Imperialism Against China's Children*, 179–80, 184–85, 188
cultural working corps, 2–3, 156–57

*Da gong bao*, 48, 138
*Daoyuan*, 34
Deng Yingchao, 190, 192
Ding Zan, 82, 85–86
Dong Biwu, 136, 158–59, 168–69, 188, 195
Dougherty, Peggy, 18
*Dying Rooms*, 232–33

Elizabeth Saunders Home, 210, 221
emotion work, 65, 88–89
enemy propaganda, 205–7
epistolary culture, 69–71, 80, 121–24, 142
Epstein, Israel, 199–200
eugenics, 98, 217–18
*Eurasian Girl*, 97–99, 111
extraterritoriality, 10, 35, 99

Fairbank, John, 12
Families with Children from China, 236
Fan Ke, 236
Fassin, Didier, 19
Fieldston, Sara, 14, 111, 219
Foster Parents Plan for War Children China
    Branch. *See* PLAN China Branch
Freud, Anna, 85
Frühstück, Sabine, 20
Fuller, Pierre, 35, 40

*Game of Pawns*, 240–41
Gerlach, Talitha, 199
GIs. *See* soldiers
global intimacy, 5–6; in the adoption plan,
    20–21, 65–66; and gift exchange, 74–77;
    and humanitarian reason, 18–20; and
    institutionalization, 116–21; 124–27; and
    politics, 21–22, 157–58, 240–41; and writing
    practices, 25, 67–74, 79–80, 121–25, 141–46
Great Kantō Earthquake, 16, 61
Guo Moruo, 177–78, 188, 193, 195

handwriting, 24, 72, 75, 120, 144
Hengyang Social Welfare Institute, 235
Hevia, James, 13
Hochschild, Arlie, 88
Holy Childhood Association (l'Oeuvre de la
    Sainte Enfance), 35–39
homeland tours, 236
Hong Kong, 5, 35, 38, 127, 133, 175; and the
    adoption plan, 58–59, 195–96, 207–9; and
    legal international adoption, 231
Hoover, Herbert, 165
Huang Wende, 23
humanitarianism, 1–6; American
    involvement in, 11–13; China's place
    in, 59–62, 237–38; Chinese views
    on, 29–30, 42–48; and Chinese
    Communists, 162–83, 192–93; and
    Chinese diaspora, 49–59; colonial
    humanitarianism, 8–9; globalization of,
    11–12; 15–16; humanitarian reason, 19–20;
    institutionalization of, 117–21, 125–27;
    intimate turn, 17–20, 64–47, 99–100;
    and left-wing causes, 132–34, 146–48,
    165–68; material uses of, 150–56; origins
    of, 7–8; political uses of, 91–95, 107–11,
    129–31, 136–41, 194–96, 207–12; and
    semicolonialism, 35–42
hypo-colony, 28–30, 32, 48, 60–61; hypo-
    colonial humanitarianism, 35–42

imperial benevolence, 4, 8–11, 13–14, 16,
    30–31, 36, 41, 238
India, 8, 13, 36, 203–4, 229
infanticide, 4, 31, 35–37
international adoption. *See* adoption
International Committee of the Red Cross.
    *See* Red Cross
International Labour Organization (ILO), 9
international propaganda, 28, 196–205, 225,
    237; children's letters as, 139–40, 144
International Social Service, 223–24, 231
intimacy. *See* global intimacy
Isaacs, Harold, 12

314 INDEX

Japan, 5; and the adoption plan, 18, 209–11, 238; and imperialism, 4, 10, 12, 29; and legal adoption, 14, 111 218–21, 231; and World War II, 4, 20, 91–95, 101–2. *See also* Great Kantō Earthquake; Red Cross
jeep babies, 215–18
jeep girls, 215–17
Jingye Foundling, 153, 156
Johnson, Kay Ann, 234

Kaell, Hilary, 11
Kang Youwei, 1
Kaung, Z. T., 185
Kim, Eleana, 111
King, Michelle, 33
Klein, Christina, 14, 111
*konketsuji*, 210
Korea, 29; and the adoption plan, 193–96, 211–12, 238; Korean War, 4–5, 131, 143, 156–60, 176–77, 205–7; and legal international adoption, 14, 18, 95, 111, 217–224, 231. *See also* Resist America, Aid Korea
Korean War. *See* Korea

Langdon-Davies, John, 132
Lee, Calvin, 122–23, 172–73
Lee, Kuo-chih, 84–85
Lee, Kuo-ching, 58–59
Li Dequan, 136, 199
Li Hongzhang, 49
Li Lisan, 45
Li Muqun, 186
Liang Qichao, 49
Liao Tsuifeng, 57
Lin Debin, 199, 204
*Little Snowflake*, 151–54
Liu Shaoqi, 45
Longkou Incident, 43–44
Lu Ping, 199, 204

Madame Chiang Kai-shek. *See* Soong Mei-ling
Madame Sun Yat-sen. *See* Soong Ching-ling

Maddry, Charles E., 106–7
mandarin paradox, 60
Mao Zedong, 3, 187, 196, 202, 224; and humanitarian aid, 166–67, 169, 190–91
Marx, Karl, 165
Maza, Sarah, 25
Mencius, 59
mental hygiene, 81–84, 86, 88
Mills, Verent, 102, 116, 211, 220
Ministry of State Security (China), 240–41
missionaries, 4, 66, 98–99; and the adoption plan, 102, 104–7, 117, 209, 212; and imperialism, 111–12, 178; and philanthropy 11–12, 17, 32, 34–37, 40, 164. *See also* Saunders, J. R.; Richards, Laura
monthly donation quotas (*chang yue juan*), 50
Morning Star Orphanage, 112, 213

National Association for Refugee Children (NARC), 18–20, 27, 59–66, 128; and children's mental health, 80–89; and Chinese Communists, 190–92; and Chinese diasporic networks, 53–59; and diplomacy, 91–95, 108, 239; and international adoption, 95–96; and letter-writing, 67–74; logistical problems, 74–78, 89–91, 100, 102, 116, 231
National Child Welfare Association (NCWA), 17–18, 108–9
National Institute of Health Mental Hygiene Laboratory, 82–84, 88
National Relief Commission, 53–54
National Security Education Day, 240
Nationalist government (China), 3, 134, 156, 177–78; and the adoption plan, 5, 18, 92–95, 108, 115, 128; as described in children's letters, 2, 130–31, 139–40, 145; views on humanitarian aid, 30–31, 42–45, 48, 50–51, 61, 101
Near East Relief, 9, 17, 31
New Culture Movement, 122
*New Internationalist*, 229–30

New Zealand, 54–57, 59, 94

New Zealand Council for the Adoption of Chinese Refugee Children, 55–57, 89, 91

Nie Shouguang, 184, 282n85

Nixon, Richard, 224

North China Famine (1876–1879), 33, 37, 49

North China Famine (1920–1921), 30, 34, 38–40

*Ode to Joy* (*Huanle song*), 233

Oei Hui-lan, 57

Oh, Arissa, 108, 111

one-child policy, 4, 234–35, 241

open door policy, 12

Operation Babylift, 231

orphan theology, 107

O'Sullivan, Kevin, 7

PLAN China Branch, 1–2, 20, 27, 129–31, 273n18; closing of, 157–59; and CWF, 132–35; and foster parents, 146–50; guidance on children's letters, 141–46; and international propaganda industry, 196–99, 201–7, 224–25; and people's diplomacy, 138–41, 163–64, 239; and revolutionary humanitarianism, 136–37. *See also* China Welfare Fund; China Welfare Fund Children's Theatre; Shanghai Boystown

paper bullets, 205–6

Peking United International Famine Relief Committee, 12, 38–41

people-to-people diplomacy, 131, 137, 168

People's Liberation Army (PLA), 136, 162, 172, 182, 203; children joining, 156–58, 205; described in children's letters, 130, 139, 141

People's Relief Administration of China (PRAC), 27, 136–37, 158–59, 168, 179–80, 200; Beijing Branch, 181, 187; Chongqing Branch, 162, 182–83, 187–90

people's diplomacy, 128, 136–37, 138–41, 145–46, 148–49, 168; and international propaganda, 202, 204–6

photography, 39, 147, 166, 192; and the adoption plan, 18, 75, 117–18, 143

Pierce, Bob, 211–12

Pu Kong Orphanage, 106–7, 112, 126, 169, 173

*qiaopi*, 79–80, 127

Quo Tai-chi, 51

Raetz, Erwin, 211–12

Rawlinson, Frank, 112

Red Cross, 6, 102, 165; American Red Cross, 12–13, 39, 46–48, 51, 61; Chinese Red Cross, 34; Japanese Red Cross; 43–44

Reeves, Caroline, 43

Ren Deyao, 199, 201

Resist America, Aid Korea, 172, 189

revolutionary humanitarianism, 27, 131, 136–37, 147, 152, 159, 167; and Norman Bethune, 167; and Canaan Children's Home, 174–76

Richards, Laura, 174–76, 181, 184–86

Rockefeller Foundation, 12–13

Russian Famine (1921–1922), 9, 165–66

Saunders, J. R, 106–7, 161–62, 182–83, 188

Save the Children Fund, 9, 17, 31

Sawada Miki, 210, 221

semicolonialism, 10, 13–14, 26, 29, 196, 237

Seoul Choong Hyun Babies' Home, 221–22

*Sex and the City*, 232–33

Shanghai Boystown, 142–43, 153–57, 199, 201

Shen Chong, 114, 218

Shen Dunhe, 44

Shi Jianqiao, 150

Shih, Shu-mei, 13

Shriver, Glenn Duffie, 240–41

Singapore, 38, 49, 51, 98; and the adoption plan, 58, 90

Smith, Adam, 60–61

Smith, Joanna Handlin, 33

soldiers (U.S.), 114, 205–6; and mixed-race children 14, 18, 111, 215–18, 220

# 316 INDEX

Soong Ching-ling (Madame Sun Yat-sen), 132–34, 150; and global humanitarianism, 136–38, 159, 166–68; and international propaganda, 195–99, 204–5

Soong Mei-ling (Madame Chiang Kai-shek) 18, 161; and Chinese diaspora, 53–57, 59; and NARC fundraising, 63, 68, 86–87, 89–94; criticisms by Communists, 190–92; and Soong Ching-ling, 133, 195

South Korea. *See* Korea

Southern Baptists, 106–7, 161

Spanish Civil War, 61, 132, 147, 167

Stamatov, Peter, 7–8, 250n13–14

Stoler, Ann, 66

Sun Yat-sen, 29–30, 42–44, 115

Taiping Civil War, 33

Taiwan, 5, 195–96, 207, 209–10, 217

Tannebaum, Gerald: and *China Reconstructs*, 199, 204–5; marriage to Chen Yuanchi, 224–25; and PLAN China Branch, 133–34, 136, 141, 158

Three Selfs Patriotic Movement, 178, 185

Tianjin Massacre, 36

translation, 24–27, 73–75, 79–81, 90–91, 144–46, 200

unequal treaties, 4, 10, 29, 35, 38, 99

United Council for Civilian Relief in China, 52, 54, 57

United Nations Relief and Rehabilitation Administration (UNRRA), 101, 103, 167–68

Vietnam, 217–18, 229, 231

Wang Chonghui, 43

Wang Feng, 55

Wang, Leslie, 236

warphans, 53–54, 58, 67–69, 190–92

warphanages. *See* warphans

*Weixian de aiqing* (dangerous love), 240

Welcome House, 223

welfare sovereignty, 50

Wong, Anna May, 52

Woodworth Personal Data sheet, 81–83, 119–20

*Work for the Suffering Children*, 139–41, 145, 148

World Red Swastika Society, 34, 159

World Vision, 211–12, 229–31, 238

World War II, 4–5, 18, 20, 27; and the adoption plan, 63, 65–67, 108–19, 238; and Chinese diaspora, 31, 51–53, and child psychology, 80–81, 85; and humanitarian aid, 132–33, 150, 167, 190–92; postwar recovery, 99–102; and U.S.-China relations, 114–15, 215–17

Wu Aizhuang (Madame Feng Wang), 55–56, 59

Wu Chaoshu, 47

Wuhan Nationalist government, 45

Xiao Xiaorong, 81–84, 119

*Xinmin congbao*, 49

Xu Fenghua, 23

Yu Tsai School, 1–3, 20, 129, 139

Zelizer, Viviana, 21

Zhang Chun, 23

Zhang Junci, 179, 187

Zhang Zhidong, 49

Zhang Zong'an, 138, 204–7

Zhao Juntao, 84

Zhao Puchu, 154, 199, 201

Zhou Enlai, 133, 136, 176, 178, 190, 192, 197–99; and Gerald Tannebaum, 133, 136

Zhu Zhixin, 42–43

Zou Lǚzhi, 199, 204